Microsoft®

Internet Explorer 6

Resource Kit

PUBLISHED BY
Microsoft Press
A Division of Microsoft Corporation
One Microsoft Way
Redmond, Washington 98052-6399

Library of Congress Cataloging-in-Publication Data
Microsoft Internet Explorer 6 Resource Kit / Microsoft Corporation.
     p. cm.
   ISBN 0-7356-1401-6
   1. Microsoft Internet Explorer.   2. Internet.   3. World Wide Web.   I. Microsoft
Corporation.

TK5105.883.M53 M5357   2001
025.04--dc21   2001044271

Printed and bound in the United States of America.

1 2 3 4 5 6 7 8 9   QWT   6 5 4 3 2 1

Distributed in Canada by Penguin Books Canada Limited.

A CIP catalogue record for this book is available from the British Library.

Microsoft Press books are available through booksellers and distributors worldwide. For further information about international editions, contact your local Microsoft Corporation office or contact Microsoft Press International directly at fax (425) 706-7329. Visit our Web site at www.microsoft.com/mspress. Send comments to *rkinput@microsoft.com*.

Acquisitions Editor: Juliana Aldous
Project Editor: Maureen Williams Zimmerman

Body Part No. X08-16599

Contributors

Resource Kit Lead:	Karen Deinhard
Production Manager:	Kathleen Liekhus
Writer:	Laura Hemmer
Editor:	Avon Murphy
Production Lead:	Cheri Ahlbeck
Desktop Publishers:	Cheri Ahlbeck Bruce Vanderpool
Indexer:	Rich Carlson Colleen Dunham
Designer:	Jennifer Shetterly
Testers:	Eric Vernon Joe Maza Michael Doran
Technical Contributors:	Brad Aiken, Joseph Beda, Jeff Bisset, Carolyn Cecil, Heather Chong, Adam Chu, Tony Ciccone, Richard Clayton, Michael Collins, LaVonne Copps, Brian Countryman, Tim Daun, Sylvain Dechatre, Gene DeClark, Todd Dooley, Dianna Drake, Ed Elliott, Joe Farro, Pablo Fernicola, Juan Flowers, Kelly Ford, Kirsten Fox, Rob Franco, Craig Gehre, George Gold, Aaron Goldfeder, Peggi Goodwin, Jimmy Grewal, Barton Hanline, Heather Horrocks, Justin Incarnato, Lisa Jahnke, Clint Jorgenson, William Keener, Joan Kelley, Joan Kennedy, Tim Lacy, John Lambert, Denise La Rue, Paul LeBlanc, Dave Massy, Bill Miller, Darren Mitchell, Oscar Morales, Jim Morey, Derek Murman, Ramez Naam, Debbie Newman, Rebecca Norlander, Paula O'Brien, Cem Paya, Stephen Purpura, Rob Relyea, Paula Rodriguez, David Ross, Ryan Roth, Christopher Sager, Katya Sedova, Nithin Shenoy, Lance Silver, Mark Silvey, Sean Sutherland, Michal Tang, Juan Torres, Robert Tucker, Judy Weston, Chris Wilson

Contents

Welcome

The *Microsoft® Internet Explorer 6 Resource Kit* consists of this book and the accompanying programs and tools, including Internet Explorer 6 and Internet Tools and the Microsoft Internet Explorer Administration Kit (IEAK) 6.

This book provides comprehensive information about planning, customizing, installing, and supporting the latest version of Internet Explorer. As a corporate administrator, Internet service provider, Internet content provider, independent software vendor, or Internet developer, you will discover that this book contains useful and compelling solutions for both deploying and customizing Internet Explorer 6 in your organization.

You can use this Resource Kit as a primary source of information about Internet Explorer 6 and its installation. The technical detail, tips, strategies, and tools provided in the Resource Kit make it easy and cost-efficient to customize and deploy Internet Explorer 6, both on the Internet and on your corporate intranet. You can also read this book as a supplement to information provided in the Help systems included with Internet Explorer 6 and the IEAK.

About This Resource Kit

This book describes the ways that you can best customize and use Internet Explorer 6 for your needs. It covers the planning process from deciding which components and features to include to distributing Internet Explorer throughout your organization or to your customers. It describes how you can make the most of browser functionality and showcase your content. It also provides detailed information about installation options and outlines ways to best handle support and maintenance.

Although this technical and planning resource focuses specifically on the latest version of Internet Explorer, its coverage includes much more. It describes customization and deployment features available across platforms (Microsoft® Windows® 64-bit and 32-bit versions) and discusses ways that you can design solutions that combine various tools and integrate with different Microsoft products.

This book contains the following seven parts, each covering a specific subject area:

- **Part 1, Getting Started.** Provides an overview of Internet Explorer 6 features and functionality. It also describes the different platforms on which you can deploy Internet Explorer 6.

- **Part 2, Privacy and Security Features.** Covers important security topics, including users' privacy, security zones, content ratings, digital certificates, and permission-based security for Microsoft virtual machine. It describes how organizations can configure and administer security settings for their users.

- **Part 3, Multimedia, Accessibility, and Other Features.** Provides step-by-step instructions for using new Internet Explorer 6 features, including the Media Bar, Image Toolbar, Automatic Image Resizing, and Print Preview. It describes the Microsoft DHTML platform, which software developers and content authors can use for creating dynamic Web pages and applications. In addition, it provides an overview of accessibility features and functionality.

- **Part 4, Preparation for Deployment.** Describes the new features of the IEAK and provides an overview of customization and administration processes. It describes how to plan and prepare for the deployment of Internet Explorer 6, including how to develop customization and installation strategies, prepare the necessary files and programs, set up servers, and administer a pilot program. In addition, it discusses how to use information (.inf) files to manipulate the download and setup processes.

- **Part 5, Customization and Installation.** Describes how to use the Internet Explorer Customization Wizard and other tools to create a customized browser solution. It outlines the steps required to deploy an Internet Explorer 6 installation, including the process for installing custom browser packages by using System Management Server (SMS). In addition, it provides detailed information about how to use server-based and serverless processes for Internet sign-up.

- **Part 6, Maintenance and Support.** Describes how to change Internet Explorer 6 settings globally after you deploy your custom browser packages by using automatic configuration, automatic proxy, and automatic detection. It describes how to update Internet Explorer programs and settings by using automatic version synchronization, the IEAK Profile Manager, update notification pages, and Group Policy. In addition, it provides an overview of how to implement an ongoing training and support program.

- **Part 7, Appendices.** Provides supplemental material relating to customizing and installing Internet Explorer 6 and Internet Tools, including resource lists, troubleshooting strategies, and a checklist for preparing to use the IEAK. It includes the following reference information: structural definition of .inf files, descriptions of files used in the setup process, country/region and language codes, and batch-mode file syntax and command-line switches. It also describes how to set system policies and restrictions.

This Resource Kit also includes a glossary with definitions for terms commonly used throughout the book.

Resource Kit Tools and Utilities

In addition to the Internet Explorer 6 Web browser, the following tools and utilities accompany this book:

- **Microsoft® Windows NT® 4.0 Service Pack (SP) 6.** Includes the service pack that is required to run Internet Explorer 6.
- **IEAK 6.** Enables administrators to create, distribute, and update customized installations of Internet Explorer 6 using tools included in the kit, such as the Internet Explorer Customization Wizard and the IEAK Profile Manager.
- **Additional Resources page.** Lists product resources and Web sites that are sources of additional information about Internet Explorer 6 and related Microsoft products.

Book Conventions

The following conventions are used in this book.

Convention	Meaning
Bold	Indicates options in the user interface—such as the **Security** tab—that you click when performing procedures. This formatting is also used for keywords, such as the **currentStyle** object, and for commands that must be typed exactly as written, such as **Mkdir** *directory name.*
Italic	Represents a placeholder for a value or string. For example, if a syntax statement contains *filename*, you need to replace *filename* with the name of a file.
ALL UPPERCASE	Indicates an HTML element, such as an ACTION attribute, and registry keys, such as **HKEY_LOCAL_MACHINE**.
MiXed Case	Specifies case sensitivity in API elements, such as the **assertPermission** method.
monospace	Presents example blocks of code: `<FORM NAME="PAGEID"></FORM>`
... (ellipsis)	Stands for elements that can be repeated. For the following command-line switch, 0 refers to the first installation choice, 1 refers to the second choice, 2 refers to the third choice, 3 refers to the fourth choice, and so on: **/M:[0|1|2|3...]**
" " (straight quotation marks)	Specifies quotation marks required by input values or strings in code. For an example, see the monospace convention.

Resource Kit Support Policy

Microsoft does not support the software supplied in the *Microsoft Internet Explorer 6 Resource Kit.* Microsoft does not guarantee the performance of the tools, response times for answering questions, or bug fixes for the tools. However, Microsoft does provide a way for customers who purchase the Resource Kit to report any problems with the software and receive feedback on such issues. To report any issues or problems, send e-mail to rkinput@microsoft.com. This e-mail address is only for issues related to the *Microsoft Internet Explorer 6 Resource Kit.* For issues related to the Internet Explorer 6 product, see the support information included with that product.

Getting Started

Chapter 1: What's New in Microsoft Internet Explorer 6?

This chapter provides an overview of new and enhanced features in Microsoft® Internet Explorer 6, as well as some important features that were introduced in Internet Explorer 5.5. You can learn about new browser features and functions and new browser technologies and platform enhancements. This information can help you evaluate Internet Explorer 6 before you deploy it to your users.

Chapter 2: Working with Different Platforms

This chapter identifies the platforms on which you can install Microsoft Internet Explorer 6 and Internet Tools, and describes the deployment variations among the supported platforms. This information is particularly important if you are deploying Internet Explorer on multiple platforms.

What's New in Microsoft Internet Explorer 6?

This chapter provides an overview of new and enhanced features in Microsoft® Internet Explorer 6, as well as some important features that were introduced in Internet Explorer 5.5. You can learn about new browser features and functions and new browser technologies and platform enhancements. This information can help you evaluate Internet Explorer 6 before you deploy it to your users.

Note Microsoft recommends that Internet Explorer users with earlier versions of the browser upgrade to the latest available version to have the best browsing experience, as well as to incorporate the latest security improvements and enhanced stability provided by the newer version.

In This Chapter

Related Information in the Resource Kit

- For more information about planning your deployment of Internet Explorer, see "Planning the Deployment."

- For more information about rolling out Internet Explorer to your users, see "Deploying Microsoft Internet Explorer 6."

New and Enhanced User Features

Internet Explorer 6 includes many new and enhanced features that can simplify the daily tasks that you perform while helping to maintain the privacy of your personal information on the Web. You have new privacy controls, a new browser appearance, and innovative browser capabilities, including media playback, Image toolbar, and automatic image resizing.

Web Privacy

Internet Explorer 6 supports the Platform for Privacy Preferences (P3P), a standard developed by the World Wide Web Consortium (W3C) that provides a way for users to control how their personal information is used by Web sites that they visit. This standard helps to protect the privacy of users' personal information on the Internet by simplifying the process for deciding whether and under what circumstances personal information is disclosed to Web sites.

When you navigate to Web sites, Internet Explorer determines whether the sites are P3P-compliant. All P3P-compliant Web sites provide a clear definition of their privacy policies. The browser compares your privacy preferences to the privacy policies defined for P3P-compliant Web sites and then determines whether to disclose personal information to the sites. However, P3P does not ensure that P3P-compliant Web sites adhere to their privacy policies, nor does the P3P standard define specific criteria for privacy.

In Internet Explorer, you can use the new **Privacy** tab in the **Internet Options** dialog box to define your privacy preferences for disclosing personal information. You can choose a privacy level, which determines whether Web sites can store and retrieve cookies on your computer and use them to access and track the personal information that you provide.

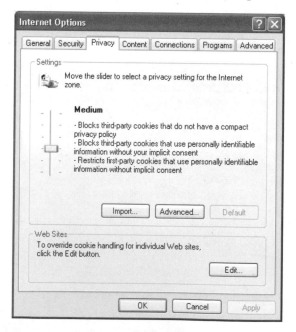

For more information about setting privacy preferences in Internet Explorer, see "Users' Privacy" in this Resource Kit.

New Browser Appearance

When you start Internet Explorer 6, you instantly notice a more attractive browser window with new, stylized buttons in the browser toolbar and more colorful menu background and toolbar areas. If you have installed Microsoft® Windows® XP, you also see visual differences in color and graphics. As an integral part of Windows XP, Internet Explorer adopts the new visual themes for common Windows XP controls. Internet Explorer directly integrates the appearance of Windows XP into all visual aspects of the browser window, including dialog boxes, menus, scroll bars, list boxes, and toolbars.

Media Bar

A new Explorer bar—the Media bar—provides a simple user interface for locating and playing media within the browser window. Expanding on the basic Radio bar functionality in Internet Explorer 5, the Media bar provides simple controls that enable you to perform the following tasks:

- Play music, video, or mixed-media files without opening a separate window.

- Control the audio volume, choose which media files or tracks to play, and stop and restart media files.

- Browse the WindowsMedia.com Web site to locate radio stations, videos, and other media on the Internet.

You can view the Media bar in the Explorer Bar pane or as a separate window (by selecting the Media bar's pop-out player).

For more information about the Media bar, see "Media Bar" in this Resource Kit.

Image Toolbar

The new Image toolbar allows you to quickly and easily save, send by e-mail, and print pictures that you find on Web pages, as well as view all the pictures that you have saved in the My Pictures folder. When you point to pictures on Web pages, the Image toolbar automatically appears in the upper-left corner of the pictures, giving instant access to image functions. If you prefer, you can also turn off the image toolbar for the current browsing session or for all sessions.

To activate the Image toolbar, you must have pictures that are a minimum of 130 x 130 pixels in size, and they cannot be background pictures or use image mapping (indicating some form of Web menu). For smaller pictures, you can still use image functions by right-clicking the pictures and then selecting the functions from the shortcut menu.

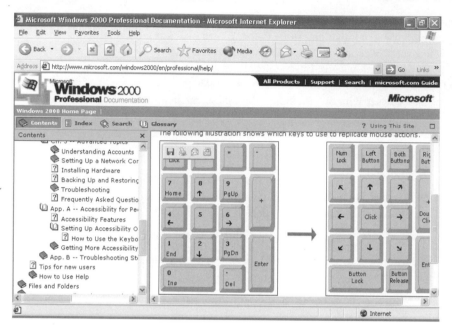

These electronic snapshot-type pictures are intended for your personal use. They are not meant for specialized Web page design, camera-ready artwork, or similar purposes.

For more information about the Image toolbar, see "Image Toolbar and Automatic Image Resizing" in this Resource Kit.

Automatic Image Resizing

You no longer need to scroll horizontally or vertically to view large pictures. If pictures are too large to see in their entirety in the browser window, the new Automatic Image Resizing feature resizes them automatically so they fit within the dimensions of the browser window. An icon appears in the lower-right corner of resized pictures and allows you to expand the pictures back to their original size.

If you navigate to pictures that fit within the browser window but then change the window dimensions, Internet Explorer automatically adjusts the pictures to fit the new window size. To prevent distortion, Internet Explorer adjusts both the picture height and the width, even if only a single dimension needs adjusting for the picture to fit within the browser window.

Automatic Image Resizing is turned on by default. It works only when you navigate directly to pictures. Internet Explorer cannot resize pictures that are embedded within HTML pages.

For more information about Automatic Image Resizing, see "Image Toolbar and Automatic Image Resizing" in this Resource Kit.

Print Preview

Introduced in Internet Explorer 5.5, Print Preview enables you to preview Web pages instantly so that you can see how they will look when you print them. This feature is similar to Print Preview in other Microsoft applications such as Microsoft Word and Microsoft Excel.

With Print Preview, you can:

- Preview each Web page as it will appear in printed form.

- Zoom in and out to view the details of Web pages.

- Move forward or backward between pages and select the specific pages that you want to print.

- Change the page setup features, such as headers and footers.

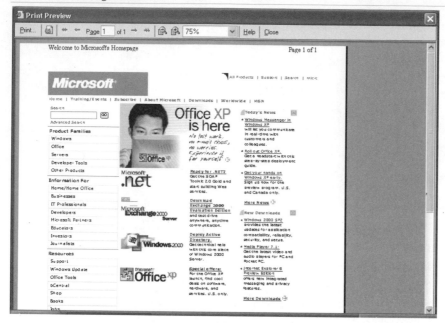

To quickly access the Print Preview feature, you can also add a **Print Preview** button to your Internet Explorer toolbar.

For more information about Print Preview, see "Print Preview" in this Resource Kit.

Improved Performance for Web Pages with Frames

To make Web pages with frames more efficient, Internet Explorer uses the Viewlink technology to host HTML documents for frames. This technology enables a single browser window to host multiple frames rather than a separate instance of the browser opening for each frame, which was necessary with Internet Explorer 5 and earlier versions. This enhancement greatly improves the performance of Web pages that include frames. You experience faster page rendering, reduced memory usage, and faster scrolling.

Outlook Express 6.0

Internet Explorer includes an updated version of its e-mail component, Microsoft® Outlook® Express 6.0. This version includes the following new security features that can help protect your computer and personal information:

- **Warning about harmful e-mail.** To prevent e-mail messages from being sent without your knowledge, Outlook Express warns you when other programs, such as viruses or harmful attachments, attempt to send messages from your computer. This warning appears only if you configure Outlook Express as your default simple MAPI client, and another program attempts to use simple MAPI to programmatically send e-mail messages without presenting a visible user interface on your computer.

- **Blocking of potentially harmful attachments.** You can choose to completely block specific attachments based on their file format. Outlook Express maintains a list of file formats, such as .exe and .zip, that cannot be opened or saved to disk on your computer. This feature is similar to the Microsoft Outlook feature for blocking attachments. If a message contains only attachments with blocked file formats, Outlook Express disables the **Save Attachments** option on the **File** menu.

- **SAFER technology.** If you have installed Windows XP, Outlook Express takes advantage of SAFER technology to run potentially harmful attachments in a *sandbox,* an area in memory outside of which the program cannot make calls. When you attempt to run or save attachments, SAFER technology determines whether the files formats are blocked. If so, Outlook Express displays a warning, and the program running the attachment has only limited access to the computer's hard disk and registry.

Internet Explorer Error Reporting Tool

Internet Explorer 6 takes steps to improve Web browser reliability. When the program stops or closes unexpectedly, the browser displays the new Internet Explorer Error Reporting tool rather than the standard fault dialog box. This tool provides fault collection services. It offers to extract information about the Internet Explorer problem and upload the data to a Microsoft Internet Information Services (IIS) server for analysis. You can view details about the problem and then choose whether to transmit the fault information to Microsoft and restart your computer.

If a known problem occurs, the server might provide a link to a service pack, hot fix, or Knowledge Base article. If Microsoft has not previously found or fixed the problem, the server can transmit the necessary information to a Microsoft problem database for investigation. This information can help identify problems that Microsoft needs to fix with future Internet Explorer service packs.

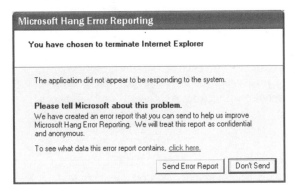

New and Enhanced Web Development Features

Internet Explorer 6 offers a feature-rich platform for building Web-based applications and developing informative content for users. The browser provides enhanced support for standards-based Internet technologies and improves the ease and speed with which developers can take advantage of these technologies. Improvements to the browser programming model, such as enhanced DHTML features, further enrich the Web development platform.

The Microsoft DHTML Platform

The Microsoft DHTML platform enables you to develop more compelling and interactive Web content and Web-based applications and services. With DHTML, you can create interactive Web pages that do not require additional controls or Web server requests to update the pages. After dynamic Web pages are loaded in the browser, you can change any page elements, including the structure, style, or content, and the updates occur on client computers without reloading the pages.

In Internet Explorer 6, you can take advantage of new DHTML features, such as element behaviors, Viewlink technology, and lightweight HTML component support, which provide enhanced creative control and flexibility for building DHTML content. Using the DHTML platform, you can incorporate transparent frames, colored scroll bars, and more.

For more information about DHTML platform features, see "The Microsoft DHTML Platform" in this Resource Kit.

Enhanced CSS1 Support

Internet Explorer provides improved support for Cascading Style Sheets, Level 1 (CSS1). When you build your Web pages and applications, you can take advantage of the following CSS1 features:

- **CSS styles for inline elements.** The cascading style sheets (CSS) styles for borders, padding, and margins are now supported for inline elements, such as SPAN and B, that can wrap across lines of text.

- **Dotted and dashed borders.** You can use the CSS1 **border-style** property to add dotted and dashed border effects to your HTML documents.

- **First-letter and first-line pseudo-elements.** The first-letter and first-line pseudo-elements allow you to lay out articles in the same style used by newspapers and magazines. Using these pseudo-elements, you can apply one or more styles to change the font characteristics for the first letter or the first line of a paragraph.

- **Vertical text layout.** You can now display text vertically on Web pages. This feature is extremely important for authoring in traditional Chinese and Japanese, because these languages require that text be laid out vertically from top to bottom and from right to left on Web pages.

DOM Level 1 Support

Internet Explorer is fully compliant with the W3C Document Object Model (DOM) Level 1, an interface that allows programs and scripts to dynamically access and update document content, structure, and style without operating system or language restrictions. The browser implements all portions of the DOM Level 1 Core functionality that are supported by Microsoft® JScript® in an HTML user agent.

Animation, Timing, and Media Integration

HTML Timed Interactive Multimedia Extensions (HTML+TIME) 2.0, which was first released in Internet Explorer 5.5, adds timing, media, synchronization, and animation support to Web pages. HTML+TIME allows you to define how elements in different parts of Web pages appear, disappear, and respond to events or time values. Using Extensible Markup Language (XML)-based elements and attributes, you can add images, video, animation, and sounds to pages, and then synchronize them with each other and with HTML elements. For example, you can create slide show-style Web presentations with synchronized text, images, audio, video, and streaming media. You can create these presentations so that they are timed, interactive, or a combination of both.

For more information about HTML+TIME support in Internet Explorer 6, see "The Microsoft DHTML Platform" in this Resource Kit.

Additional Resources

These resources contain additional information and tools related to this chapter.

Related Information Outside the Resource Kit

- The Microsoft Windows Technologies Internet Explorer Web site at http://www.microsoft.com/windows/ie/.

- Internet Explorer Help.

- *Microsoft Internet Explorer 6 Software Development Kit (SDK),* which is available on the MSDN® Web site at http://msdn.microsoft.com/.

C H A P T E R   2

Working with Different Platforms

This chapter identifies the platforms on which you can install Microsoft® Internet Explorer 6 and Internet Tools and describes the deployment variations among the supported platforms. This information is particularly important if you are deploying Internet Explorer on multiple platforms.

In This Chapter

Related Information in the Resource Kit

- For more information about planning your browser deployment for different platforms, see "Planning the Deployment."

- For more information about customizing Internet Explorer for different platforms, see "Running the Microsoft Internet Explorer Customization Wizard."

- For more information about installing Internet Explorer on different platforms, see "Deploying Microsoft Internet Explorer 6."

Overview: Platform Support

Internet Explorer 6 provides support for the following platforms:

- Windows 32-bit versions, including the Microsoft Windows® .NET Server family of operating systems, Microsoft® Windows® XP Home Edition, Windows XP Professional, Microsoft® Windows® 2000, Microsoft® Windows® Millennium Edition (Me), Microsoft® Windows® 98 Second Edition (SE), Windows 98, and Microsoft® Windows NT® 4.0

- Windows XP 64-Bit Edition

> **◆ Important** Internet Explorer 6 does not support the Windows 16-bit, UNIX, and Apple Macintosh platforms. If your users are running Microsoft® Windows® 95, they can install Internet Explorer 5.5 or earlier.

Internet Explorer 6 provides a single, standards-based set of technologies for Web authoring, browsing, communication, and collaboration for the Windows 32-bit and 64-bit platforms.

If you plan to customize Internet Explorer 6 for the Windows platforms, you should consider the following issues:

- **Planning the deployment.** To deploy Internet Explorer successfully, you need to determine the platform and browser requirements for all groups that are targeted to migrate to Internet Explorer. For more information about planning your deployment on Windows platforms, see "Planning the Deployment" in this Resource Kit.

- **Conducting a pilot program.** Before you deploy Internet Explorer to your users, you should conduct a pilot program to test the browser on your installation platforms. For more information about conducting a pilot program, see "Setting Up and Administering a Pilot Program" in this Resource Kit.

- **Building custom browser packages.** You can use the Internet Explorer Customization Wizard, which is part of the Internet Explorer 6 Administration Kit (IEAK), to build custom packages of Internet Explorer. For more information about the Internet Explorer Customization Wizard, see "Running the Microsoft Internet Explorer Customization Wizard" in this Resource Kit.

- **Maintaining browser versions.** You can use Windows XP and Windows 2000 Group Policy or the IEAK Profile Manager to administer Internet Explorer on the Windows platforms. These tools enable you to update browser settings and manage different versions of the browser from a single location. For more information about using Group Policy and the IEAK Profile Manager, see "Keeping Programs Updated" in this Resource Kit.

Windows Platform: 32-bit Versions

The 32-bit versions of the Windows platform integrate Internet technology and browser features directly into the operating system. This browser-platform integration means that users who run 32-bit versions of Windows can take advantage of advanced browsing capabilities. Users can browse their hard disk, their local area network (LAN), or the Internet to quickly find the information they need. Using Internet Explorer, they can quickly navigate the Web by using the Search, History, and Favorites bars or get information delivered directly to their computers for offline viewing.

Some Internet Explorer customization features, deployment methods, and maintenance practices are specific to 32-bit versions of Windows.

You should consider the following issues when you deploy Internet Explorer 6 on 32-bit versions of Windows:

- **CD-ROM installation.** If you distribute your custom browser package to users who run 32-bit versions of Windows from a CD-ROM, a splash-screen AutoRun application appears when users insert the disc. This application offers them the choice of installing your custom browser or viewing more information. If the current version of Internet Explorer is already installed, AutoRun detects it. The browser appears in kiosk (full-screen) mode, if you have enabled this feature by using the Internet Explorer Customization Wizard, with the Start.htm file or your own custom start page loaded.

- **Administrative privileges.** For Windows NT 4.0, you must have administrative privileges to install and uninstall Internet Explorer and Internet Tools. Users, therefore, must have administrative privileges the first time they start their computers after installing or uninstalling Internet Explorer and Internet Tools.

- **Setup download folder.** You can find the IE6Setup.exe file in the media type folder created for your language and platform version. For example, the English version of Internet Explorer for 32-bit versions of Windows would reside in the \Download\Win32\En folder of your build directory.

- **Code signing.** If you are distributing Internet Explorer and Internet Tools over the Internet or an intranet, you should sign custom cabinet (.cab) files created by the Internet Explorer Customization Wizard for 32-bit versions of Windows. This is recommended unless you preconfigure the Local intranet zone with the Low security setting. You should also sign any custom components that you distribute with your custom browser packages. Code signing lets users know that they can trust your code before downloading it to their computers. The default settings in Internet Explorer reject unsigned code. If you have a digital certificate, the Internet Explorer Customization Wizard can sign these files automatically.

Options for digital certificates are not available for Windows XP and Windows 2000 in the IEAK Profile Manager, because these operating systems provide advanced certificate-management features. For more information, search for "digital certificates" in Windows XP Help and Support Center or in Windows 2000 Help.

- **Single-disk branding.** When you build custom browser packages by using the Internet Explorer Customization Wizard, you can choose the single-disk branding option for your media type. This option customizes an existing installation of Internet Explorer. It does not install Internet Explorer and Internet Tools.

- **Windows XP and Windows 2000 Administration.** For Windows XP and Windows 2000, you can use Group Policy to customize and manage Internet Explorer settings. Group Policy enables administrators to customize and control settings for users and computers in various groups across an organization. For more information about using Group Policy, see "Keeping Programs Updated" in this Resource Kit.

For more information, consult the Windows XP or Windows 2000 Setup documentation.

Windows Platform: 64-bit Version

A 64-bit version of Internet Explorer and Internet Tools is part of the Windows XP 64-Bit Edition operating system. For this version of Windows, you can customize the browser by using Group Policy. For more information, see the *Microsoft Windows XP Administration Kit*.

Privacy and Security Features

Chapter 3: Users' Privacy

Using the privacy features of Microsoft® Internet Explorer 6, you can create a secure environment that protects users' personal information on the Internet and your intranet. This chapter describes these features and explains how you can configure privacy settings.

Chapter 4: Security Zones

This chapter describes *security zones*, which allow you to effectively manage a secure environment by choosing the level of security for different zones of Internet and intranet content. Read this chapter to learn how to set up security zones within your organization.

Chapter 5: Content Advisor

This chapter describes the Microsoft® Internet Explorer Content Advisor, which allows you to rate the appropriateness of Web content and to control which Web sites your users can visit. This feature can help you create a more secure environment that protects your users from unsuitable content on the Internet.

Chapter 6: Digital Certificates

Microsoft Internet Explorer 6 uses digital certificates to authenticate clients and servers on the Web and to ensure that browser communications are secure. Read this chapter to learn about certificates and about how to configure settings for the certificates that you trust.

Chapter 7: Permission-based Security for Microsoft Virtual Machine

Microsoft Internet Explorer 6 provides comprehensive management and enforcement of Internet and network security. This chapter describes a key feature of security management—permission-based security for Microsoft virtual machine (Microsoft VM). Read this chapter to learn how this security feature can help protect access to information in your organization.

C H A P T E R   3

Users' Privacy

Using the privacy features of Microsoft® Internet Explorer 6, you can create a secure environment that protects users' personal information on the Internet and your intranet. This chapter describes these features and explains how you can configure privacy settings.

In This Chapter

Related Information in the Resource Kit

- For more information about configuring security zones, see "Security Zones."
- For more information about using the Internet Explorer Customization Wizard to preconfigure security settings, see "Running the Microsoft Internet Explorer Customization Wizard."
- For more information about using the Internet Explorer Administration Kit (IEAK) Profile Manager to preconfigure security settings, see "Keeping Programs Updated."

Ensuring Users' Privacy

When you communicate over the Web, you want to know that other people cannot intercept or decipher the information that you send and receive and cannot use your passwords and other private information. You want to ensure that Web sites do not share your personal information without your consent. You also want to ensure that no one can access information on your computer without your knowledge.

Internet Explorer protects your privacy in the following ways:

- It supports a wide range of Internet security and privacy standards that provide secure information transfer and financial transactions over the Internet or your intranet.

- It provides encryption and identification capabilities to help users ensure the privacy of their information on the Web.

Protecting Personal Information

Internet Explorer 6 supports the Platform for Privacy Preferences 1.0 (P3P1.0), which provides a way for users to control how their personal information is used by Web sites that they visit. P3P1.0 helps protect the privacy of users' personal information on the Internet by simplifying the process for deciding whether and under what circumstances personal information is disclosed to Web sites. At the time of this Resource Kit's publication, the *P3P1.0 Specification*, which was developed by the World Wide Web Consortium (W3C), is a candidate recommendation.

In Internet Explorer, users can define their privacy preferences for disclosing personal information. Then when they navigate to Web sites, Internet Explorer determines whether the sites provide P3P privacy information. For sites that provide this information, the browser compares the users' privacy preferences to the site's privacy policy information. Internet Explorer uses HTTP for this exchange of policy information.

A P3P-compliant Web site must provide a clear definition of its privacy policies. The sites must provide the following policy information:

- The organization that is collecting information about users

- The type of information that is being collected

- What the information will be used for

- Whether the information will be shared with other organizations

- Whether users can access the information about them and change how the organization will use that information

- The method for resolving disputes between users and the organization

- How the organization will retain the collected information

- Where the organization publicly maintains detailed information about their privacy policies that users can read

The policies must use the XML-encoded vocabulary defined by P3P and must be stored in a format that can be automatically retrieved and interpreted by browsers that support P3P. However, P3P does not ensure that a P3P-compliant Web site adheres to its privacy policies, nor does P3P define specific criteria for privacy.

The Web site uses policy reference files to identify how its privacy policies are applied throughout the site. A single set of privacy policies can be defined for the entire site, or multiple sets of policies can cover different portions of the site. The browser can easily detect and interpret these different sets of privacy policies. For example, the browser can interpret different sets of policies for a Web site's embedded content, such as frames or pictures.

For more information about setting your privacy preferences, see "Configuring Privacy Options" later in this chapter. For more information about P3P, see the W3C Web site at http://www.w3.org/.

Using Cookie Management Features

P3P supports the browser's cookie management features. A cookie is a small file that an individual Web site stores on your computer. Web sites can use cookies to maintain information and settings, such as your customization preferences.

Web sites might use persistent cookies or session cookies. Persistent cookies include an expiration date that identifies when the browser can delete them. Session cookies do not have an expiration date. When users close the browser, it deletes session cookies.

As part of its privacy policies, a P3P-compliant Web site can provide policy information for its cookies. Internet Explorer includes advanced cookie filtering capabilities that evaluate a Web site's privacy information and determine whether cookies can be stored on a user's computer based on that privacy information and the user's preferences.

When you configure your privacy preferences, you can configure Internet Explorer to handle cookies in the following ways:

- Prevent all cookies from being stored on your computer. This setting might prevent you from viewing certain Web sites.
- Block or restrict *first-party cookies* (cookies that originate in the same domain as the Web site being visited).
- Block or restrict *third-party cookies* (cookies that do not originate in the same domain as the Web site being visited and, therefore, are not covered by that Web site's privacy policy). For example, many Web sites contain advertising from third-party sites that use cookies.
- Allow all cookies to be stored on your computer without notifying you.

Using Profile Assistant

You can use Profile Assistant to securely maintain your computer's privacy and safety when sharing registration and demographic information with Web sites. You can maintain your personal information in a user profile on your computer. A Web site can request information from your profile, but the site cannot access profile information unless you specifically give your consent.

For information about how to write scripts to access Profile Assistant information, see the MSDN Library Web site at http://msdn.microsoft.com/library/.

When a Web site requests information from your user profile, the **Profile Assistant** dialog box opens. You can use the information in this dialog box to verify which Web site is making the request, choose which information (if any) to share, and understand how the Web site intends to use the information.

The following table describes the information displayed in the **Profile Assistant** dialog box.

Option	Description
'Requester name' **has requested information from you**	Displays the name of the requester, which can be an individual or an organization.
Site	Displays the URL of the site requesting information from the user .
Profile information requested	Displays the list of information items requested. Clear the check boxes for any items that you do not want to send to the requester.
Always allow this site to see checked items	Adds this site to a list of sites that you allow to access your user profile without notifying you.
Edit profile	Opens the **My Profile** dialog box so you can edit the profile information that will be sent to this Web site. For example, you might want to send a different fax number.
Privacy	Displays a message that explains whether the information you are sharing will be secure when it is sent over the Internet. It also displays a message describing how the requester intends to use the information.

Web sites can request up to 31 different items of information from your user profile. For more information, see "Configuring Privacy Options" later in this chapter.

Ensuring Secure Communications

Internet Explorer supports the latest Internet security standards for client and server authentication, including Secure Sockets Layer (SSL) and Transport Layer Security (TLS). Internet Explorer uses these protocols to create a secure channel for information exchange over the Web. In addition, Internet Explorer supports Integrated Windows Authentication, which uses cryptographic exchanges between clients and servers to ensure the clients' authentication.

For more information about Internet Explorer support for SSL, TLS, and Integrated Windows Authentication, see "Digital Certificates" in this Resource Kit.

Using Zone-Based Password Security

Internet Explorer prompts you before transmitting your user name or password to sites that are designated as trusted in the security zones settings. You can, however, configure security zones to send information from trusted sites without prompting you. For more information about configuring security zones, see "Security Zones" in this Resource Kit.

Configuring Privacy Options

You can configure Internet Explorer privacy options on the **Privacy**, **Content,** and **Advanced** tabs in the **Internet Options** dialog box. From this dialog box, you can do the following:

- Configure privacy preferences.
- Configure Profile Assistant.
- Configure advanced security options for user privacy.

Configuring Privacy Preferences

On the **Privacy** tab, you can perform the following tasks:

- **Set your privacy level for the Internet zone.** By default, Internet Explorer sets your privacy level to **Medium** for the Internet zone. Internet Explorer automatically accepts all cookies from Web sites in both the Local intranet and Trusted sites zones, and automatically blocks all cookies from Web sites in the Restricted zone. A **Privacy** dialog box appears the first time the browser restricts a cookie at the selected privacy level. The **Privacy** dialog box explains the Privacy icon, which appears in the status bar each time the browser restricts a cookie based on your privacy settings. You can double-click the **Privacy** icon to see a privacy report.

- **Import custom privacy settings.** You can import a custom privacy preferences file. Any privacy settings that are not overridden by the custom privacy preferences file remain unchanged. For example, if your imported file does not define privacy settings for the Internet zone, Internet Explorer retains the existing privacy settings for this zone. If you import custom privacy settings and then you change the default privacy preferences for the Internet security zone, Internet Explorer disables the custom settings for that zone. Also, importing custom privacy settings may remove per-site privacy actions. For information about custom privacy preferences files, see the MSDN Web site at http://msdn.microsoft.com/.

- **Customize your privacy settings for cookie handling.** You can specify settings that override cookie handling for your selected privacy level. The **Advanced Privacy Settings** dialog box enables you to accept, block, or prompt for first-party and third-party cookies. Also, you can choose to always allow session cookies. Even if you choose in this dialog box to block cookies, the Web sites that created the existing cookies on your computer can still read them.

- **Customize your privacy settings for individual Web sites.** You can define cookie management options on a per-site basis. These options override your default privacy preferences for any sites that you add to the **Per Site Privacy Actions** dialog box (unless you choose as your privacy level **Accept All Cookies** or **Block All Cookies**, either of which causes the browser to ignore per-site privacy actions).

▶ **To set your privacy level for the Internet zone**

1. On the **Tools** menu, click **Internet Options**, and then click the **Privacy** tab.

2. Under **Settings**, move the slider to the privacy level you want:

   o **Block All Cookies.** Internet Explorer prevents all Web sites from storing cookies on your computer, and Web sites cannot read existing cookies on your computer. Per-site privacy actions do not override these settings.

   o **High.** Internet Explorer prevents Web sites from storing cookies that do not have a *compact privacy policy*—a condensed computer-readable P3P privacy statement. The browser prevents Web sites from storing cookies that use personally identifiable information without your explicit consent. Per-site privacy actions override these settings.

   o **Medium High.** Internet Explorer prevents Web sites from storing third-party cookies that do not have a compact privacy policy or that use personally identifiable information without your explicit consent. The browser prevents Web sites from storing first-party cookies that use personally identifiable information without your implicit consent. The browser also restricts access to first-party cookies that do not have a compact privacy policy so that they can only be read in the first-party context. Per-site privacy actions override these settings.

   o **Medium (default).** Internet Explorer prevents Web sites from storing third-party cookies that do not have a compact privacy policy or that use personally identifiable information without your implicit consent. The browser allows first-party cookies that use personally identifiable information without your implicit consent but deletes these cookies from your computer when you close the browser. The browser also restricts access to first-party cookies that do not have a compact privacy policy so that they can only be read in the first-party context. Per-site privacy actions override these settings.

o **Low.** Internet Explorer allows Web sites to store cookies on your computer, including third-party cookies that do not have a compact privacy policy or that use personally identifiable information without your implicit consent. When you close the browser, though, it deletes these third-party cookies from your computer. The browser also restricts access to first-party cookies that do not have a compact privacy policy so that they can only be read in the first-party context. Per-site privacy actions override these settings.

o **Accept All Cookies.** Internet Explorer allows all Web sites to store cookies on your computer, and Web sites that create cookies on your computer can read them. Per-site privacy actions do not override these settings.

Notes   If you select a privacy level that does not allow cookies to be saved on your computer, you might not be able to view certain Web sites.

When you change your privacy level, it cannot affect the cookies that Web sites have already stored on your computer, unless you select **Accept All Cookies** or **Block All Cookies**. If you want to ensure that all cookies on your computer meet the selected privacy level, delete all of the existing cookies on your computer. For more information about deleting cookies, see Internet Explorer Help.

► To import custom privacy settings

1. On the **Tools** menu, click **Internet Options**, and then click the **Privacy** tab.
2. Click **Import**.
3. Locate the file that contains the custom privacy settings, and then click **Open**.

   The file must be located on your computer. You can download files that contain custom privacy settings from privacy organizations and other Web sites on the Internet.

► To customize your privacy settings for cookie handling

1. On the **Tools** menu, click **Internet Options**, and then click the **Privacy** tab.
2. Click **Advanced**.

3. Click **Override automatic cookie handling**, and then for first-party and third-party cookies, click **Accept**, **Block**, or **Prompt**.

▶ **To customize your privacy settings for individual Web sites**

1. On the **Tools** menu, click **Internet Options**, and then click the **Privacy** tab.
2. Click **Edit**.

3. In the **Address of Web site** box, type the complete address of the Web site for which you want to specify custom privacy settings.

4. If you want Internet Explorer to always allow cookies from the specified Web site to be saved on your computer, click **Allow**.

   -Or-

   If you want Internet Explorer to never allow cookies from the specified Web site to be saved on your computer, click **Block**.

   The **Managed Web sites** list shows all of the Web sites for which you have specified custom privacy settings. The settings that you choose for the Web sites on this list may override your selected privacy level.

5. If you want to delete custom privacy settings for a specific Web site, highlight the site on the **Managed Web sites** list, and then click **Remove**.

   -Or-

   If you want to delete custom privacy settings for all the Web sites on the **Managed Web sites** list, click **Remove All**.

   When you remove a Web site from the **Managed Web sites** list, your privacy settings for all Web sites without custom privacy settings will apply to that site.

Configuring Profile Assistant

You can use Profile Assistant to store or update your user profile, which contains the information you want to share with Web sites. Other Internet programs, including Microsoft® NetMeeting® and Microsoft® Outlook® Express, also use Profile Assistant.

▶ **To create or update a user profile**

1. On the **Tools** menu, click **Internet Options**, and then click the **Content** tab.
2. Click **My Profile**.
3. If you are creating a new user profile, in the **Address Book - Choose Profile** dialog box, click **Create a new entry** in the Address Book to represent your profile, and then click **OK**.
4. In the appropriate boxes on the **Name**, **Home**, **Business**, **Personal**, and **Other** tabs, type the personal information you want to share.

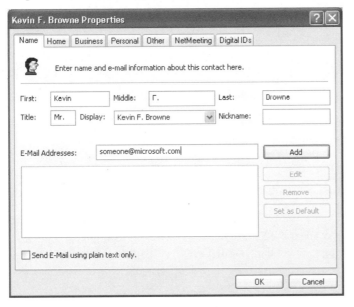

Configuring Advanced Security Options for Users' Privacy

You can configure a variety of security options for users' privacy in Internet Explorer.

▶ **To configure advanced security options for users' privacy**

1. On the **Tools** menu, click **Internet Options**, and then click the **Advanced** tab.
2. In the **Security** area, review the selected options.

3. Depending on your needs, select or clear the Security check boxes. For example, if you want to enable Profile Assistant, select the **Enable Profile Assistant** check box.

C H A P T E R   4

Security Zones

This chapter describes *security zones*, which allow you to effectively manage a secure environment by choosing the level of security for different zones of Internet and intranet content. Read this chapter to learn how to set up security zones within your organization.

In This Chapter

Related Information in the Resource Kit

- For more information about Microsoft® Internet Explorer features that help ensure user privacy, see "Users' Privacy."

- For more information about planning user security before installing Internet Explorer 6 and Internet Tools, see "Planning the Deployment."

Understanding Security Zones

Security zones offer you a convenient and flexible method for managing a secure environment. You can use security zones to enforce your organization's Internet security policies, based on the origin of the Web content. Security zones enable you to:

- Group sets of sites together.
- Assign a security level to each zone.

Grouping Sets of Sites Together

Zone security is a system that enables you to divide online content into categories, or zones. You can assign specific Web sites to each zone, depending on how much you trust the content of each site. The Web content can be anything from an HTML or graphics file to a Microsoft® ActiveX® control, Java applet, or executable file.

 Important You should configure the Local intranet zone to correspond to the particular network and firewall configuration of your organization. The default settings for the Local intranet zone cannot be guaranteed to match your network configuration, and there is no method for automatically detecting your firewall and configuring the zone based on your specific settings. For more information, see "Setting Up Security Zones" later in this chapter.

Internet Explorer includes the following predefined security zones:

- **Local intranet zone.** The Local intranet zone includes all sites inside an organization's firewall (for computers connected to a local network).
- **Trusted sites zone.** The Trusted sites zone can include all Internet sites that you know are trusted. For example, the Trusted sites zone might contain corporate subsidiaries' sites or the site of a trusted business partner.
- **Internet zone.** The Internet zone includes all sites on the Internet that are not in the Trusted sites or Restricted sites zones.
- **Restricted sites zone.** The Restricted sites zone can include all sites that you do not trust.

In addition, the My Computer zone includes everything on the client computer, which is typically the contents of the hard disk and removable media drive. This zone excludes cached Java classes in the Temporary Internet Files folder. You cannot configure the My Computer zone through the security zone settings in Internet Explorer. However, you can configure them by using the Internet Explorer Administration Kit (IEAK).

Assigning a Security Level to Each Zone

A security level assigned to each zone defines the level of browser access to Web content. You can choose to make each zone more or less secure. In this way, security zones can control access to a site based on the zone in which the site is located and the level of trust assigned to that zone. Also, you can choose a custom level of security, which enables you to configure settings for ActiveX controls, downloading and installation, scripting, password authentication, cross-frame security, and Java capabilities. A custom level of security also enables you to assign administrator-approved control, which runs only those ActiveX controls that you have approved for your users.

Zone Architecture

When Internet Explorer opens an HTML page, a dynamic-link library named Urlmon.dll determines the zone from which the page was loaded. To do this, Urlmon.dll performs the following two steps:

1. Determines whether a proxy server retrieved the HTML page. If it did, Urlmon.dll automatically recognizes that the page originated on the Internet. If it did not, Urlmon.dll determines whether the page originated on your company's intranet, based on the proxy server configuration.

2. Checks the registry to see whether the page is from a trusted or a restricted location, and whether the security zone is set appropriately.

Setting Up Security Zones

You can use security zones to easily provide the appropriate level of security for the various types of Web content that users are likely to encounter. For example, because you can fully trust sites on your company's intranet, you probably want users to be able to run all types of active content from this location. To provide this capability, set the Local intranet zone to a low level of security. You might not feel as confident about sites on the Internet, so you can assign a higher level of security to the entire Internet zone. This higher level prevents users from running active content and downloading code to their computers. However, if there are specific sites you trust, you can place individual URLs or entire domains in the Trusted sites zone. For other sites on the Internet that are known to be sources of potentially harmful Web content, you can select the highest restrictions.

You can accept the default security settings for each zone, or you can configure the settings based on the needs of your organization and its users. The options for configuring security zones are the same whether you gain access to them from Internet Explorer 6, the Internet Explorer Customization Wizard, or the IEAK Profile Manager.

◆ **Important** When you upgrade to Internet Explorer 6, Setup maintains the existing security zone settings from previous browser versions, with two exceptions—Java and scripting are disabled in the Restricted sites zone, regardless of your existing settings. Also, because the default settings have changed for some options, your existing settings may move to a custom level of security in Internet Explorer 6.

Configuring Security Zones

You can configure security zones by using the following methods:

- In Internet Explorer, you can use the **Security** tab.

- You can use the Internet Explorer Customization Wizard to create custom browser packages that include security zone settings for your user groups. You can also lock down these settings to prevent users from changing them.

- After the browser is deployed, you can use the IEAK Profile Manager to manage security zone settings through the automatic browser configuration feature of Internet Explorer. You can automatically push the updated security zone settings to each user's desktop computer, enabling you to manage security policy dynamically across all computers on the network.

The options for configuring security zones are the same whether you access them from Internet Explorer 6, the Internet Explorer Customization Wizard, or the IEAK Profile Manager. The following procedure describes how to configure security zone settings in the browser. For more information about using the Internet Explorer Customization Wizard and the IEAK Profile Manager, see "Running the Microsoft Internet Explorer Customization Wizard," and "Keeping Programs Updated" in this Resource Kit.

▶ **To configure security zone settings**

1. On the **Tools** menu, click **Internet Options**, and then click the **Security** tab.

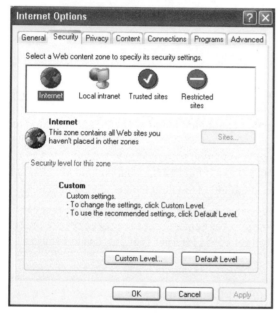

2. Click a security zone to select it and view its current settings.

3. As necessary, change the following settings:

    o   **Security level.** To change the security level for the selected zone to **High**, **Medium**, **Medium-low**, or **Low**, move the slider. The on-screen description for each level can help you decide which level to select.

    o   **Sites.** To add or remove Web sites from the zone, click the **Sites** button, and then click the **Add** or **Remove** button to customize your list of sites for the selected zone.

    o   **Custom level.** For more precise control of your security settings, click the **Custom Level** button, and then select the options you want. At any time, you can click **Default Level** on the **Security** tab to return to the original security level for the selected zone.

The process required for setting up each security zone is described in the following sections.

Setting Up the Internet Zone

The Internet zone consists of all Web sites that are not included in the other zones. By default, the Internet zone is set to the Medium security level. If you are concerned about possible security problems when users browse the Internet, you might want to change the security level to High. If you raise the security level, Internet Explorer prevents some Web pages from performing certain potentially harmful operations. As a result, some pages might not function or be displayed properly. Rather than use the High security level, you might want to choose the Custom level so that you can control each individual security decision for the zone.

Note You cannot add Web sites to the Internet zone.

Setting Up the Local Intranet Zone

To ensure a secure environment, you must set up the Local intranet zone in conjunction with your proxy servers and firewall. All sites in this zone should be inside the firewall, and the proxy servers should be configured so that an external Domain Name System (DNS) name cannot be resolved to this zone. Configuring the Local intranet zone requires that you have a detailed knowledge of your existing networks, proxy servers, and firewalls. For more information, see the MSDN® Web site at http://msdn.microsoft.com/.

By default, the Local intranet zone consists of local domain names in addition to any domains that are specified to bypass the proxy server. You should confirm that these settings are secure for your organization and adjust the settings as necessary. When you set up the zone, you can specify the URL categories in addition to specific sites in the zone.

▶ **To set up sites in the Local intranet zone**

1. On the **Tools** menu, click **Internet Options**, and then click the **Security** tab.
2. Click the **Local intranet** zone.
3. Click **Sites**, and then select the following check boxes that apply:
   - **Include all local (intranet) sites not listed in other zones.** Intranet sites, such as http://local, have names that do not include dots. In contrast, a site name that does contain dots, such as http://www.microsoft.com, is not local. This site would be assigned to the Internet zone. The intranet site name rule applies to File URLs as well as HTTP URLs.
   - **Include all sites that bypass the proxy server.** Typical intranet configurations use a proxy server to gain access to the Internet but have a direct connection to intranet servers. The setting uses this kind of configuration information to distinguish intranet from Internet content. If your proxy server is configured otherwise, you should clear this check box and then use other means to designate the Local intranet zone membership. For systems without a proxy server, this setting has no effect.

o **Include all network paths (UNCs).** Network paths (for example,
   *servername**sharename**file.txt*) are typically used for local network content that should be
   included in the Local intranet zone. If some of your network paths should not be in the Local
   intranet zone, clear this check box and then use other means to designate the Local intranet
   zone membership. In certain Common Internet File System (CIFS) configurations, for
   example, it is possible for a network path to reference Internet content.

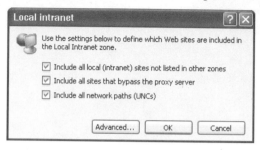

4. Click Advanced.

5. Type the address of the site you want to include in this zone, and then click **Add**.

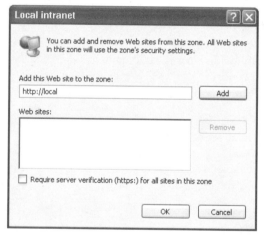

6. To require that server verification be used, select the **Require server verification (https:) for all
    sites in this zone** check box.

The Local intranet zone is intended to be configured by using the Internet Explorer Customization
Wizard or the IEAK Profile Manager, although you can also find Local intranet options on the
Security tab, as described in the previous procedure. After the Local intranet zone is confirmed to be
secure, consider changing the zone's security level to Low so that users can perform a wider range of
operations. You can also adjust individual security settings by using the Custom level of security for
this zone. If parts of your intranet are less secure or otherwise not trustworthy, you can exclude the
sites from this zone by assigning them to the Restricted sites zone.

Setting Up the Trusted and Restricted Sites Zones

You can add trusted and untrusted Web sites to the Trusted sites and Restricted sites security zones. These two zones enable you to assign specific sites that you trust more or less than those in the Internet zone or the Local intranet zone. By default, the Trusted sites zone is assigned the Low security level. This zone is intended for highly trusted sites, such as the sites of trusted business partners.

If you assign a site to the Trusted sites zone, the site will be allowed to perform a wider range of operations. Also, Internet Explorer will prompt you to make fewer security decisions. You should add a site to this zone only if you trust all of its content never to perform any harmful operations on your computer. For the Trusted sites zone, Microsoft strongly recommends that you use the Hypertext Transmission Protocol, Secure (HTTPS) protocol or otherwise ensure that connections to the site are completely secure.

By default, the Restricted sites zone is assigned the High security level. If you assign a site to the Restricted sites zone, it will be allowed to perform only minimal, very safe operations. This zone is for sites that you do not trust. Because of the need to ensure a high level of security for content that is not trusted, pages assigned to this zone might not function or be displayed properly. When you install Internet Explorer 6 or upgrade to this browser version, the Restricted sites zone disables active scripting and Java applets.

A content author can create a frame or IFRAME with the "security=restricted" attribute. This attribute puts the contents of the frame or IFRAME, as well as any *child frames* (initiated by parent frames) that it might contain, in the Restricted sites zone. For example, if the http://a.com/ Web page contains <iframe security=restricted src="http://b.com/"></iframe> and the http://b.com/ Web page contains <iframe src="http://www.microsoft.com/"> </iframe>, both http://b.com/ and http://www.microsoft.com/ will run in the Restricted sites zone. The frame cannot run scripting or ActiveX controls, unless the user changes the default settings for the Restricted sites zone or you used the Internet Explorer Customization Wizard to override the Restricted sites zone settings for the Internet Explorer installation. Also, support for *Meta-refresh* (a mechanism that allows a Web page to redirect to another Web page on a timer without using script) is disabled in the Restricted sites zone.

Working with Domain Name Suffixes

You can address Web content by using either the DNS name or the Internet Protocol (IP) address. You should assign sites that use both types of addresses to the same zone. In some cases, the sites in the Local intranet zone are identifiable either by their local names or by IP addresses in the proxy bypass list. However, if you enter the DNS name but not the IP address for a site in the Trusted sites or Restricted sites zone and the site is accessed by using the IP address, that site might be treated as part of the Internet zone.

If you want to reference a Web server by using a shorter version of its address that does not include the domain, you can use a domain name suffix. For example, you can reference a Web server named sample.microsoft.com as sample. Then you can use either http://sample.microsoft.com or http://sample to view that content.

To set up this capability, you must add the domain name suffix for TCP/IP properties to the domain suffix search order.

▶ **To add the domain name suffix for TCP/IP properties to the domain suffix search order in Microsoft® Windows® XP and Microsoft® Windows® 2000**

1. In Windows XP or Windows 2000, right-click the **My Network Places** icon, and then click **Properties**.
2. Right-click the appropriate network connection, and then click **Properties**.
3. On the **General** tab (for a local area connection) or the **Networking** tab (for all other connections), click **Internet Protocol (TCP/IP)**, and then click **Properties**.
4. Click **Obtain DNS server address automatically** if it is not already selected.
5. Click **Advanced**, and then click the **DNS** tab.
6. Click **Append these DNS suffixes (in order)**, and then click **Add**.

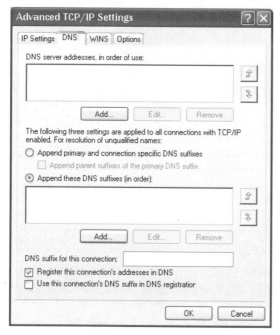

7. Type the domain suffix, and then click **Add**.

▶ **To add the domain name suffix for TCP/IP properties to the domain suffix search order in Microsoft® Windows® 98**

1. In Windows 98, right-click the **Network Neighborhood** desktop icon, and then click **Properties**.
2. On the **Configuration** tab, click **TCP/IP**, and then click **Properties**.

3. Click the **DNS Configuration** tab, and then select **Enable DNS** if it is not already selected.

4. In the **Domain Suffix Search Order** box, add the search order that you want.

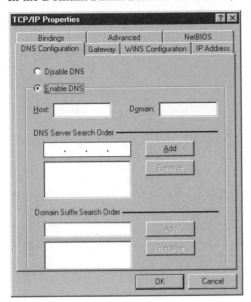

It is important to set up security zones correctly for this capability. By default, the URL without dots (http://sample) is considered to be in the Local intranet zone, and the URL with dots (http://sample.microsoft.com) is considered to be in the Internet zone. Therefore, if you use this capability and no proxy server bypass is available to clearly assign the content to the proper zone, you need to change the zone settings.

Depending on whether the content accessed by the domain name suffix is considered intranet or Internet content, you need to assign the ambiguous site URLs to the appropriate zones. To assign URLs, such as http://sample, to the Internet zone, clear the **Include all local (intranet) sites not listed in other zones** check box for the Local intranet zone, and include the site in the Internet zone.

Selecting Custom Level Settings

The **Custom Level** button on the **Security** tab gives you additional control over zone security. You can enable or disable specific security options depending on the needs of your organization and its users. For more information about how to use Custom level security options, see "Setting Up Security Zones" earlier in this chapter.

The Custom level security options for Internet Explorer are grouped into the following categories:

- ActiveX controls
- Downloads
- Microsoft VM

- Miscellaneous
- Scripting
- User Authentication

📝 **Notes** If you upgrade from Internet Explorer 5.5 or an earlier browser version, Internet Explorer 6 maintains your existing Custom level security settings.

If you have Microsoft virtual machine (VM) installed and you want to configure the Custom level security options for this component, see "Permission-based Security for Microsoft Virtual Machine" in this Resource Kit.

The following table identifies the default value for each Custom level security option at each security level.

Security option	Low	Medium-low	Medium	High
ActiveX controls				
Download signed ActiveX controls	Enable	Prompt	Prompt	Disable
Download unsigned ActiveX controls	Prompt	Disable	Disable	Disable
Initialize and script ActiveX controls not marked as safe	Prompt	Disable	Disable	Disable
Run ActiveX controls and plug-ins	Enable	Enable	Enable	Disable
Script ActiveX controls marked safe for scripting	Enable	Enable	Enable	Disable
Downloads				
File download	Enable	Enable	Enable	Disable
Font download	Enable	Enable	Enable	Prompt
Miscellaneous				
Access data sources across domains	Enable	Prompt	Disable	Disable
Allow META REFRESH	Enable	Enable	Enable	Disable
Display mixed content	Prompt	Prompt	Prompt	Prompt
Don't prompt for client certificate selection when no certificates or only one certificate exists	Enable	Enable	Disable	Disable
Drag and drop or copy and paste files	Enable	Enable	Enable	Prompt
Installation of desktop items	Enable	Prompt	Prompt	Disable
Launching programs and files in an IFRAME	Enable	Prompt	Prompt	Disable

Security option	Low	Medium-low	Medium	High
Navigate sub-frames across different domains	Enable	Enable	Enable	Disable
Software channel permissions	Low safety	Medium safety	Medium safety	High safety
Submit nonencrypted form data	Enable	Enable	Prompt	Prompt
Userdata persistence	Enable	Enable	Enable	Disable
Scripting				
Active scripting	Enable	Enable	Enable	Disable
Allow paste operations via script	Enable	Enable	Enable	Disable
Scripting of Java applets	Enable	Enable	Enable	Disable
User Authentication				
Logon	Automatic logon with current username and password	Automatic logon only in Intranet zone	Automatic logon only in Intranct zone	Prompt for user name and password

These Custom level security options apply to Internet Explorer; other programs might not accept them. These security options are for 64-bit and 32-bit versions of the Microsoft® Windows® operating system. The following sections describe these settings in greater detail.

ActiveX Controls

The following options dictate how Internet Explorer approves, downloads, runs, and scripts ActiveX controls.

☑   **Note** If a user downloads an ActiveX control from a site that is different from the page on which it is used, Internet Explorer applies the more restrictive of the two sites' zone settings. For example, if a user views a Web page within a zone that is set to permit a download, but the code is downloaded from another zone that is set to prompt a user first, Internet Explorer uses the prompt setting.

- **Download signed ActiveX controls.** This option determines whether users can download signed ActiveX controls from a page in the specified zone. This option has the following settings:

   o **Disable**, which prevents all signed controls from downloading.

   o **Enable**, which downloads valid signed controls without user intervention and prompts users to choose whether to download invalid signed controls—that is, controls that have been revoked or have expired.

   o **Prompt**, which prompts users to choose whether to download controls signed by publishers who are not trusted, but still silently downloads code validly signed by trusted publishers.

For more information about trusted publishers, see "Digital Certificates" in this Resource Kit.

- **Download unsigned ActiveX controls.** This option determines whether users can download unsigned ActiveX controls from the zone. This code is potentially harmful, especially when it comes from an untrusted zone. This option has the following settings:
  - o **Disable**, which prevents unsigned controls from running.
  - o **Enable**, which runs unsigned controls without user intervention.
  - o **Prompt**, which prompts users to choose whether to allow the unsigned control to run.
- **Initialize and script ActiveX controls not marked as safe.** ActiveX controls are classified as either trusted or untrusted. This option controls whether a script can interact with untrusted controls in the zone. Untrusted controls are not meant for use on Internet pages, but in some cases they can be used with pages that can be absolutely trusted not to use the controls harmfully. Object safety should be enforced unless you can trust all ActiveX controls and scripts on pages in the zone. This option has the following settings:
  - o **Disable**, which enforces object safety for untrusted data or scripts. ActiveX controls that cannot be trusted are not loaded with parameters or scripted.
  - o **Enable**, which overrides object safety. ActiveX controls are run, loaded with parameters, and scripted without setting object safety for untrusted data or scripts. This setting is not recommended, except for secure and administered zones. This setting causes Internet Explorer to initialize and script both untrusted and trusted controls and ignore the **Script ActiveX controls marked safe for scripting** option.
  - o **Prompt**, which attempts to enforce object safety. However, if ActiveX controls cannot be made safe for untrusted data or scripts, users are given the option of allowing the control to be loaded with parameters or to be scripted.

    For more information about how to make ActiveX controls safe, see the MSDN Web site at http://msdn.microsoft.com/.

- **Run ActiveX controls and plug-ins.** This option determines whether Internet Explorer can run ActiveX controls and plug-ins from pages in the zone. This option has the following settings:
  - o **Administrator approved**, which runs only those controls and plug-ins that you have approved for your users. To select the list of approved controls and plug-ins, use Internet Explorer system policies and restrictions. The Control Management category of policies enables you to manage these controls. For more information about selecting Control Management policies, see the appendix "Setting System Policies and Restrictions" in this Resource Kit.
  - o **Disable**, which prevents controls and plug-ins from running.
  - o **Enable**, which runs controls and plug-ins without user intervention.
  - o **Prompt**, which prompts users to choose whether to allow the controls or plug-ins to run.

- **Script ActiveX controls marked safe for scripting.** This option determines whether an ActiveX control that is marked safe for scripting can interact with a script. This option affects only controls that are loaded with <param> tags. This option has the following settings:
  - o **Disable**, which prevents script interaction.
  - o **Enable**, which allows script interaction without user intervention.
  - o **Prompt**, which prompts users to choose whether to allow script interaction.

    Internet Explorer ignores this option when **Initialize and script ActiveX controls that are not marked safe** is set to **Enable**, because that setting bypasses all object safety. You cannot script unsafe controls while blocking the scripting of the safe ones.

Note In Internet Explorer 5 and earlier versions of the browser, this option was enabled for all security levels. If you upgrade to Internet Explorer 6 and you did not disable this option in your previous browser version, it will remain enabled in Internet Explorer 6.

Downloads

Download options specify how Internet Explorer handles downloads as follows:

- **File download.** This option controls whether file downloads are permitted based on the zone of the Web page that contains the download link, not the zone from which the file originated. This option has the following settings:
  - o **Disable**, which prevents files from being downloaded from the zone.
  - o **Enable**, which allows files to be downloaded from the zone.
- **Font download.** This option determines whether Web pages within the zone can download HTML fonts. This option has the following settings:
  - o **Disable**, which prevents HTML fonts from being downloaded.
  - o **Enable**, which downloads HTML fonts without user intervention.
  - o **Prompt**, which prompts users to choose whether to allow the download of HTML fonts.

Miscellaneous

These options control whether users can access data sources across domains, submit nonencrypted form data, launch applications and files from IFRAME elements, install desktop items, drag and drop files, copy and paste files, and access software channel features from this zone.

- **Access data sources across domains.** This option specifies whether components that connect to data sources should be allowed to connect to a different server to obtain data. This option has the following settings:
  - o **Disable**, which allows database access only in the same domain as the Web page.
  - o **Enable**, which allows database access to any source, including other domains.
  - o **Prompt**, which prompts users before allowing database access to any source in other domains.

- **Allow META REFRESH.** This option specifies whether Web pages can use meta-refreshes to reload pages after a preset delay. This option has the following settings:
  - **Disable**, which prevents Web pages from using meta-refreshes.
  - **Enable**, which allows Web pages to use meta-refreshes.
- **Display mixed content.** This option specifies whether Web pages can display content from both secure and non-secure servers. This option has the following settings:
  - **Disable**, which prevents Web pages from displaying non-secure content.
  - **Enable**, which allows Web pages to display both secure and non-secure content.
  - **Prompt**, which prompts users before allowing Web pages to display both secure and non-secure content.
- **Don't prompt for client certificate selection when no certificates or only one certificate exists.** This option specifies whether users are prompted to select a certificate when no trusted certificate or only one trusted certificate has been installed on the computer. This option has the following settings:
  - **Disable**, which allows users to be prompted for a certificate.
  - **Enable**, which prevents users from being prompted for a certificate.
- **Drag and drop or copy and paste files.** This option controls whether users can drag and drop, or copy and paste, files from Web pages within the zone. This option has the following settings:
  - **Disable**, which prevents users from dragging and dropping files, or copying and pasting files, from the zone.
  - **Enable**, which enables users to drag and drop files, or copy and paste files, from the zone without being prompted.
  - **Prompt**, which prompts users to choose whether they can drag and drop files, or copy and paste files, from the zone.
- **Installation of desktop items.** This option controls whether users can install desktop items from Web pages within the zone. This option has the following settings:
  - **Disable**, which prevents users from installing desktop items from this zone.
  - **Enable**, which enables users to install desktop items from this zone without being prompted.
  - **Prompt**, which prompts users to choose whether they can install desktop items from this zone.
- **Launching programs and files in an IFRAME.** This option controls whether users can launch programs and files from an IFRAME element (containing a directory or folder reference) in Web pages within the zone. This option has the following settings:
  - **Disable**, which prevents programs from running and files from downloading from IFRAME elements on Web pages in the zone.
  - **Enable**, which runs programs and downloads files from IFRAME elements on Web pages in the zone without user intervention.
  - **Prompt**, which prompts users to choose whether to run programs and download files from IFRAME elements on Web pages in the zone.

- **Navigate sub-frames across different domains.** This option controls whether readers of a Web page can navigate the sub-frame of a window with a top-level document that resides in a different domain. This option has the following settings:

    o **Disable**, which allows users to navigate only between Web page sub-frames that reside in the same domain.

    o **Enable**, which allows users to navigate between all Web page sub-frames, regardless of the domain, without being prompted.

    o **Prompt**, which prompts users to choose whether to navigate between Web page sub-frames that reside in different domains.

- **Software channel permissions.** This option controls the permissions given to software distribution channels. This option has the following settings:

    o **High safety**, which prevents users from being notified about software updates by e-mail, software packages from being automatically downloaded to users' computers, and software packages from being automatically installed on users' computers.

    o **Low safety**, which notifies users about software updates by e-mail, allows software packages to be automatically downloaded to users' computers, and allows software packages to be automatically installed on users' computers.

    o **Medium safety**, which notifies users about software updates by e-mail and allows software packages to be automatically downloaded to (but not installed on) users' computers. The software packages must be validly signed; users are not prompted about the download.

- **Submit nonencrypted form data.** This option determines whether HTML pages in the zone can submit forms to or accept forms from servers in the zone. Forms sent with Secure Sockets Layer (SSL) encryption are always allowed; this setting only affects data that is submitted by non-SSL forms. This option has the following settings:

    o **Disable**, which prevents information from forms on HTML pages in the zone from being submitted.

    o **Enable**, which allows information from forms on HTML pages in the zone to be submitted without user intervention.

    o **Prompt**, which prompts users to choose whether to allow information from forms on HTML pages in the zone to be submitted.

- **Userdata persistence.** This option determines whether a Web page can save a small file of personal information associated with the page to the computer. This option has the following settings:

    o **Disable**, which prevents a Web page from saving a small file of personal information to the computer.

    o **Enable**, which allows a Web page to save a small file of personal information to the computer.

Scripting

Scripting options specify how Internet Explorer handles scripts.

- **Active scripting.** This option determines whether Internet Explorer can run script code on Web pages in the zone. This option has the following settings:
  - **Disable**, which prevents scripts from running.
  - **Enable**, which runs scripts without user intervention.
  - **Prompt**, which prompts users about whether to allow the scripts to run.
- **Allow paste operations via script.** This option determines whether a Web page can cut, copy, and paste information from the Clipboard. This option has the following settings:
  - **Disable**, which prevents a Web page from cutting, copying, and pasting information from the Clipboard.
  - **Enable**, which allows a Web page to cut, copy, and paste information from the Clipboard without user intervention.
  - **Prompt**, which prompts users about whether to allow a Web page to cut, copy, or paste information from the Clipboard.
- **Scripting of Java applets.** This option determines whether scripts within the zone can use objects that exist within Java applets. This capability allows a script on a Web page to interact with a Java applet. This option has the following settings:
  - **Disable**, which prevents scripts from accessing applets.
  - **Enable**, which allows scripts to access applets without user intervention.
  - **Prompt**, which prompts users about whether to allow scripts to access applets.

User Authentication

The User Authentication option controls how HTTP user authentication is handled.

- **Logon.** This option has the following settings:
  - **Anonymous logon.** Disables HTTP authentication and uses the guest account only for authentication using the Common Internet File System (CIFS) protocol.
  - **Automatic logon only in Intranet zone.** Prompts users for user IDs and passwords in other zones. After users are prompted, these values can be used silently for the remainder of the session.
  - **Automatic logon with current username and password.** Attempts logon using Windows NT Challenge Response (also known as NTLM authentication), an authentication protocol between the client computer and the application server. If Windows NT Challenge Response is supported by the server, the logon uses the network user name and password for logon. If the server does not support Windows NT Challenge Response, users are prompted to provide their user names and passwords.

    For information about other secure connection options, see "Users' Privacy" in this Resource Kit.
  - **Prompt for user name and password.** Prompts users for user IDs and passwords. After users are prompted, these values can be used silently for the remainder of the session.

C H A P T E R   5

Content Advisor

This chapter describes the Microsoft® Internet Explorer Content Advisor, which allows you to rate the appropriateness of Web content and to control which Web sites your users can visit. This feature can help you create a more secure environment that protects your users from unsuitable content on the Internet.

In This Chapter

Related Information in the Resource Kit

- For more information about configuring security zones, see "Security Zones."
- For more information about using the Internet Explorer Customization Wizard to preconfigure security settings, see "Running the Microsoft Internet Explorer Customization Wizard."
- For more information about using the Internet Explorer Administration Kit (IEAK) Profile Manager to preconfigure security settings, see "Keeping Programs Updated."

Using Content Advisor

Using Content Advisor, you can control the types of content that users access on the Internet. You can adjust the content ratings settings to reflect the appropriate level of content in four areas: language, nudity, sex, and violence. For example, businesses might want to block access to Web sites that offer no business value to their employees, and parents might want to block access to sites that display content inappropriate for their children.

Historically, the motive for filtering sites on the basis of a site's content has been driven by a site's subject matter and the fact that some ideas and images are blatantly offensive to many people. In 1995, the World Wide Web Consortium (W3C) Platform for Internet Content Selection (PICS) began to define an infrastructure that would encourage Web content providers to voluntarily rate their sites. This is done by using a specific set of HTML meta tags that rate the content of Web sites. Software programs can then block access to Web sites based upon the values of those meta tags. Today, the most common content ratings are based on the PICS standard for defining and rating Web content. For more information about PICS, visit the W3C Web site at http://www.w3.org/.

RSACi Rating System

Internet Explorer is installed with a PICS-based content rating system known as the Recreational Software Advisory Council on the Internet (RSACi) system. This built-in PICS support can help you control the types of content that users can access on the Internet. When you enable Content Advisor, Internet Explorer reads the meta tags to determine whether Web sites meet your criteria for suitable content. You can also subscribe to independent ratings bureaus or use third-party ratings to control access to Web content.

RSACi is an open, objective content ratings system for the Internet developed by the Recreational Software Advisory Council (RSAC), which has since been folded into the Internet Content Rating Association (ICRA), an independent, nonprofit organization. The RSACi system provides information about the level of sex, nudity, violence, and offensive (vulgar or hate-motivated) language in software games and Web sites. For more information about ICRA and the RSACi rating system, see the ICRA Web site at http://www.icra.org/. You can also download the ICRA's new content ratings system from this Web site.

The following table shows the five levels of the RSACi rating system and describes the content allowed for each level. Level 0 is the most restrictive, preventing users from accessing Web sites that include offensive language, nudity, sex, and violence. Level 4 is the least restrictive, allowing users to access Web sites that present explicit content.

Level	Language rating	Nudity rating	Sex rating	Violence rating
4	Explicit or crude language	Provocative frontal nudity	Explicit sexual activity	Wanton and gratuitous violence
3	Obscene gestures	Frontal nudity	Non-explicit sexual touching	Killing with blood and gore
2	Moderate expletives	Partial nudity	Clothed sexual touching	Killing
1	Mild expletives	Revealing attire	Passionate kissing	Fighting
0	Inoffensive slang	No nudity	No sexual acts	No violence

You can set content ratings to any level for each of the four content areas. All content ratings are set to Level 0 by default. When Content Advisor is turned on and the PICS rating for a Web site exceeds the rating level you specify, Internet Explorer prevents users from accessing the site. Also, you can configure Internet Explorer to prevent or allow users to access unrated Web content. For more information, see "Configuring Content Advisor Settings" later in this chapter.

Other Rating Systems

Web site publishers can obtain PICS content ratings not only from ICRA but also from a number of other nonprofit and fee-based ratings services. Publishers can voluntarily add PICS ratings to their Web sites. You can also obtain independent PICS ratings from ratings bureaus. Ratings bureaus are typically fee-based and specialize in rating Internet sites. You can specify a ratings bureau other than ICRA that Internet Explorer can use to obtain PICS ratings. Because Internet Explorer must contact the ratings bureau to obtain the ratings, using other ratings bureaus might considerably slow your access to Web pages.

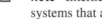 **Note**   Internet Explorer supports only PICS-based ratings systems. You cannot import ratings systems that are based on standards other than PICS.

Supervisor Password

The first time you turn on Content Advisor, you must specify a supervisor password. This password allows administrators or supervisors to turn Content Advisor on or off and to change Content Advisor settings for users. With Internet Explorer 6, you can also add a hint to help you remember your password. Whenever the browser prompts you for your password, it also displays the hint.

In addition, you can configure Internet Explorer so that users can display restricted Web pages by typing the supervisor password. When users attempt to access restricted content, the Content Advisor dialog box prompts them to enter the supervisor password. For more information, see the following section, "Configuring Content Advisor Settings."

Configuring Content Advisor Settings

You can configure Content Advisor settings in several ways:

- In Internet Explorer, you can use the **Content** tab in the **Internet Options** dialog box.
- You can use the Internet Explorer Customization Wizard to create custom browser packages that include preconfigured Content Advisor settings for your user groups. You can also lock down these settings to prevent users from changing them.
- After Internet Explorer has been deployed, you can use the IEAK Profile Manager to update Content Advisor settings through the automatic configuration feature of Internet Explorer. You can automatically push the updated information to each user's desktop computer, enabling you to manage security policy dynamically across all computers on the network.

You can accept the default Content Advisor settings, or you can configure the settings based on the needs of your organization and its users. The options for configuring Content Advisor are the same whether you access them from Internet Explorer 6, the Internet Explorer Customization Wizard, or the IEAK Profile Manager. For more information about using the Internet Explorer Customization Wizard and IEAK Profile Manager, see "Running the Microsoft Internet Explorer Customization Wizard," and "Keeping Programs Updated" in this Resource Kit.

After you have enabled Content Advisor, you can use it to do the following:

- Select content rating levels.
- Configure the list of approved and disapproved Web sites.
- Configure user options for content ratings.
- Change the supervisor password.
- Import new rating systems.
- Specify a different ratings bureau.

▷ **To enable Content Advisor**

1. On the **Tools** menu, click **Internet Options**, and then click the **Content** tab.
2. In the **Content Advisor** area, click Enable.
3. In the **Content Advisor** dialog box, click **OK**.
4. In the **Create Supervisor Password** dialog box, type the password you want to use.

5.   In the **Confirm password** box, type the same password again.

6.   In the **Hint** text box, type a hint to help you remember your password.

▶ **To select content rating levels**

1.   On the **Tools** menu, click **Internet Options**, and then click the **Content** tab.

2.   In the **Content Advisor** area, click Settings.

3.   In the Password box, type your supervisor password, and then click OK.

4.   On the **Ratings** tab, select the **Language**, **Nudity**, **Sex**, or **Violence** ratings category.

5. Drag the slider to the appropriate content level for the selected category.

    The default setting for each category is Level 0, which is the most restrictive setting. For more information about the ratings service, click **More Info**. For more information about ratings levels, see "Using Content Advisor" earlier in this chapter.

▶ **To configure the list of approved and disapproved Web sites**

1. On the **Tools** menu, click **Internet Options**, and then click the **Content** tab.
2. In the **Content Advisor** area, click Settings.
3. In the **Password** box, type your supervisor password, and then click **OK**.
4. Click the **Approved Sites** tab.

5. Type the URL for each Web site that your users can view regardless of its rating level, and then click **Always**.

6. Type the URL for each Web site that your users can never view regardless of its rating level, and then click **Never**.

    Note If you want to delete an approved or disapproved Web site, click the URL in the list, and then click **Remove**.

▷ **To configure user options for content ratings**

1. On the **Tools** menu, click **Internet Options,** and then click the **Content** tab.
2. In the **Content Advisor** area, click **Settings**.
3. In the **Password** box, type your supervisor password, and then click **OK**.
4. Click the **General** tab.
5. In the **User options** area, select the settings you want.

Option	Description
Users can see sites that have no rating	Select this option if you want users to be able to access Web pages that are not rated.
Supervisor can type a password to allow users to view restricted content	Select this option if you want users to be able to view restricted content after you type the supervisor password.

▷ **To change the supervisor password**

1. On the **Tools** menu, click **Internet Options**, and then click the **Content** tab.
2. In the **Content Advisor** area, click **Settings**.
3. In the **Password** box, type your supervisor password, and then click **OK**.
4. Click the **General** tab.
5. Click **Change Password**.

6. In the **Old password** box, type the current password to verify that you are authorized to change Content Advisor settings.
7. In the **New password** box, type the new password.
8. In the **Confirm new password** box, type the new password again.
9. Type a hint to help you remember your new password.

▷ **To import new rating systems**

⬥ **Important**   If necessary, install ratings systems files, following the directions provided by the ratings service. Then proceed with the following steps.

1. On the **Tools** menu, click **Internet Options**, and then click the **Content** tab.
2. In the Content Advisor area, click Settings.
3. In the **Password** box, type your supervisor password, and then click **OK**.
4. Click the **General** tab.

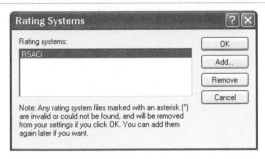

5. Click **Rating Systems**.

6. If the rating system you want to add is displayed on the list, click it, and then click **Add**.

   -Or-

   If the rating system you want to add is not on the list, click **OK**, and then click **Find Rating Systems**.

▶ **To specify a different ratings bureau**

1. On the **Tools** menu, click **Internet Options**, and then click the **Content** tab.

2. In the **Content Advisor** area, click **Settings**.

3. In the **Password** box, type your supervisor password, and then click **OK**.

4. Click the **Advanced** tab.

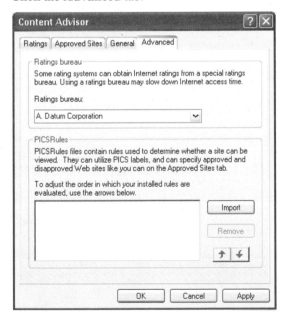

5. In the **Ratings bureau** box, type the name of the ratings bureau (other than RSAC) that Internet Explorer can use to obtain PICS ratings.

6. In the **PICSRules** area, click **Import**, and then type the name of the PICSRules (.prf) file used by the new ratings bureau.

7. Click **Open**.

CHAPTER 6

Digital Certificates

Microsoft® Internet Explorer 6 uses digital certificates to authenticate clients and servers on the Web and to ensure that browser communications are secure. Read this chapter to learn about certificates and about how to configure settings for the certificates that you trust.

In This Chapter

Related Information in the Resource Kit

- For more information about Internet Explorer features that help ensure user privacy, see "Users' Privacy."

- For more information about using the Internet Explorer Customization Wizard to preconfigure security settings, see "Running the Microsoft Internet Explorer Customization Wizard."

Understanding Digital Certificates

To verify the identity of people and organizations on the Web and to ensure content integrity, Internet Explorer uses industry-standard X.509 v3 *digital certificates*. Certificates are electronic credentials that bind the identity of the certificate owner to a pair (public and private) of electronic keys that can be used to encrypt and sign information digitally. These electronic credentials assure that the keys actually belong to the person or organization specified. Messages can be encrypted with either the public or the private key and then decrypted with the other key.

Each certificate contains at least the following information:

- Owner's public key
- Owner's name or alias
- Expiration date of the certificate
- Serial number of the certificate
- Name of the organization that issued the certificate
- Digital signature of the organization that issued the certificate

Certificates can also contain other user-supplied information, including a postal address, an e-mail address, and basic registration information, such as the country or region, postal code, age, and gender of the user.

Certificates form the basis for secure communication and client and server authentication on the Web. You can use certificates to do the following:

- Verify the identity of clients and servers on the Web.
- Encrypt channels to provide secure communication between clients and servers.
- Encrypt messages for secure Internet e-mail communication.
- Verify the sender's identity for Internet e-mail messages.
- Put your digital signature on executable code that users can download from the Web.
- Verify the source and integrity of signed executable code that users can download from the Web.

The following illustration shows the basic process of using public and private keys to encrypt and decrypt a message sent over the Internet.

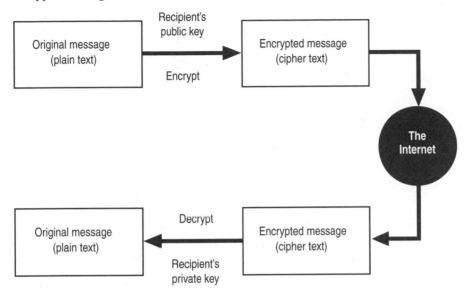

Certificates are authenticated, issued, and managed by a trusted third party called a *certification authority* (CA). The CA must provide a combination of three essential elements:

- Technology, such as security protocols and standards, secure messaging, and cryptography
- Infrastructure, including secure facilities, backup systems, and customer support
- Practices, including a defined model of trust and a legally binding framework for managing subscriber activities and resolving disputes

A commercial CA must provide services that both your organization and your users trust. In addition to obtaining certificates from CAs, you can implement a certificate server, such as Microsoft Certificate Server, and use it to provide certificate services for your Web infrastructure.

Commercial Certification Authorities

Commercial CAs issue certificates that verify the electronic identity of individuals and organizations on the Web. The primary responsibility of a CA is to confirm the identity of the people and organizations seeking certificates. This effort ensures the validity of the identification information contained in the certificate. Many commercial CAs offer certificate services for Microsoft products, in addition to a wide range of other certificate services.

CAs perform the following types of services:

- Issue, renew, and revoke certificates.
- Authenticate the identities of individuals and organizations.
- Verify the registrations of individuals and organizations.
- Publish and maintain a Certificate Revocation List (CRL) of all certificates that the CA has revoked.
- Handle legal and liability issues related to security.

Commercial CAs issue various types of certificates, including the following:

- Personal certificates for digitally signing communications and assuring secure transactions over the Internet and intranet
- Client authentication and server authentication certificates for managing secure transactions between clients and servers
- Software publisher certificates for digitally signing software

CAs can also issue many other types of certificates. Each CA operates within the charter of its Certification Practices Statement (CPS). You can visit the CA's Web site and read the CPS to understand the types of certificates issued by that CA and the operating procedures that the CA follows.

When you choose a CA, you should consider the following issues:

- Is the CA a trusted entity operating a certification practice that can both meet your needs and operate efficiently in your region? Other people should be able to immediately recognize your CA as reputable and trustworthy. If you choose a CA with a questionable reputation, users might reject your certificate. Therefore, you should thoroughly research the commercial CA you plan to use so that you and your users can be assured about the CA's trustworthiness.
- Is the CA familiar with your organization's business interests? Look for a CA from which you can leverage technical, legal, and business expertise.
- Does the CA require detailed information from you to verify your trustworthiness? Most CAs require such information as your identity, your organization's identity, and your official authority to administer the Web server for which you are requesting a certificate. Depending on the level of identification required, a CA might need additional information, such as professional affiliations or financial records, and the endorsement of this information by a notary.
- Does the CA have a system for receiving online certificate requests, such as requests generated by a key manager server? An online system can speed up the processing of your certificate requests.
- Does the CA give you enough flexibility and control over how certificates are issued and authenticated? Some commercial CA services and products might not integrate with your existing security model and directory services.
- Does the cost of the CA service meet your requirements? Substantial costs can be associated with obtaining a server certificate, especially if you need a high level of assurance of identification.

Certificate Servers

Depending on your relationship with your users, you can obtain server certificates from a commercial CA, or you can issue your own server certificates. For services on your intranet, user trust is typically not an issue, and you can easily configure Internet Explorer to trust server certificates issued by your organization. For services on the Internet, however, users might not know enough about your organization to trust certificates issued by your certificate server. Therefore, you might need to obtain server certificates that are issued by a well-known, commercial CA to ensure that users trust your Internet sites.

You can implement a certificate server, such as Microsoft Certificate Server, to manage the issuance, renewal, and revocation of industry-standard certificates. You can use these certificates in conjunction with servers that support Secure Sockets Layer (SSL) or Transport Layer Security (TLS) to build a secure Web infrastructure for the Internet or your intranet. For large organizations with complex Web needs, certificate servers can offer many advantages over commercial CAs, including lower costs and total control over certificate management policies.

Authenticode Technology

Microsoft® Authenticode® 2.0 is client-side software that watches for the downloading of Microsoft® ActiveX® control (.ocx) files, cabinet (.cab) files, Java applets, and executable files in order to provide reliable identity of the code. Authenticode displays certificate information, such as the name included in the digital signature, an indication of whether it is a commercial or personal certificate, and the date when the certificate expires. This information enables users to make a more informed decision before continuing with the download.

The software publisher digitally signs software (including .exe, .dll, .ocx, and .cab files) when it is ready for publication. Software publishers that obtain a code-signing certificate from a CA can use Authenticode signing tools to digitally sign their files for distribution over the Web. Authenticode looks for the signatures (or the lack of signatures) in the files that users attempt to download. For more information about how to digitally sign files by using Authenticode signing tools, see "Preparing for the IEAK" in this Resource Kit and the MSDN® Web site at http://msdn.microsoft.com/.

If a piece of software has been digitally signed, Internet Explorer can verify that the software originated with the named software publisher and that no one has tampered with it. If you enable this feature, Internet Explorer displays a verification certificate if the software meets these criteria. A valid digital signature, though, does not necessarily mean that the software is without problems. It just means that the software originated with a traceable source and that the software has not been modified since it was published. Likewise, an invalid signature does not prove that the software is dangerous, but just alerts the user to potential problems. When a digital signature fails the verification process, Internet Explorer reports the failure, indicates why the signature is invalid, and prompts the user to choose whether to proceed with the download.

You can configure Internet Explorer to handle software in different ways, depending on the status of the digital signature. Software can be unsigned, signed using valid certificates, or signed using invalid certificates. The digital signatures used to sign these certificates can also be valid or invalid.

For each available security zone, users can choose an appropriate set of ActiveX security preferences. These preferences control whether users are prompted or blocked from downloading or running controls for sites that are hosted within the zone. Also, Internet Explorer maintains a list of controls that will never load within the browser and a list of administrator-approved controls.

How you configure Internet Explorer to respond to certificates depends on various factors, such as the level of trust you have in the security zone where the content originated. If you are deploying Internet Explorer in an organization, you might also want to consider the level of trust that you have for the intended user group and the users' level of technical expertise. You might, for example, trust unsigned software from your intranet, but not trust unsigned software from the Internet. In that case, you would configure Internet Explorer to automatically download and run unsigned active content from the intranet without users' intervention and prevent the download of unsigned active content from the Internet. For more information about setting up security zones, see "Security Zones" in this Resource Kit.

Secure Client and Server Communication

Certificates can be used for secure communication and user authentication between clients and servers on the Web. Certificates enable clients to establish a server's identity, because the server presents a server authentication certificate that discloses its source. If you connect securely to a Web site that has a server certificate issued by a trusted authority, you can be confident that the data you securely transmitted is usable only by the person or organization identified by the certificate. Similarly, certificates enable servers to establish a client's identity. When you connect to a Web site, the server can be assured about your identity if it receives your client certificate.

The following sections describe security technologies that ensure secure communication between clients and servers.

Secure Channels

The exchange of certificates between clients and servers is performed by using a secure transmission protocol, such as SSL or TLS. SSL 2.0 supports only server authentication. SSL 3.0 and TLS 1.0 support both client and server authentication. Secure transmission protocols can provide the following four basic security services:

- **Client authentication.** Verifies the identity of the client through the exchange and validation of certificates.
- **Server authentication.** Verifies the identity of the server through the exchange and validation of certificates.
- **Communication privacy.** Encrypts information that is exchanged on a secure channel between clients and servers.
- **Communication integrity.** Ensures the integrity of the contents of messages that are exchanged between clients and servers, by ensuring that messages have not been altered during transmission.

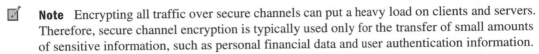

Note Encrypting all traffic over secure channels can put a heavy load on clients and servers. Therefore, secure channel encryption is typically used only for the transfer of small amounts of sensitive information, such as personal financial data and user authentication information.

You can change the set of protocols that are enabled for client and server authentication on the **Advanced** tab in the **Internet Options** dialog box. For more information, see "Using Digital Certificates" later in this chapter.

Server Gated Cryptography

For environments that require the highest-possible level of security, such as online banking, you can implement Server Gated Cryptography (SGC) to provide stronger encryption for communication between clients and servers. SGC enables a 128-bit server with an SGC certificate to communicate securely with all versions of Internet Explorer by using 128-bit SSL encryption. For example, SGC enables financial institutions with Internet servers based on Microsoft® Windows NT® to use 128-bit SSL encryption for secure financial transactions.

Note 128-bit SSL encryption is broadly available both in the United States and internationally. Internet Explorer 6 ships with 128-bit SSL encryption as the default encryption setting.

The key benefits of SGC include the following:

- Banks and financial institutions can securely conduct financial transactions with their retail customers worldwide without those requiring customers to change their standard Web browser or financial software.
- Online banking does not require any special client software. For example, customers can use all standard, off-the-shelf, exportable versions of Internet Explorer to connect to an SGC server and conduct secure transactions by using 128-bit encryption.
- SGC is fully interoperable with Netscape browsers and servers. Therefore, Internet Explorer users can communicate with Netscape servers by using 128-bit encryption.

CryptoAPI 2.0

CryptoAPI 2.0 provides the underlying security services for certificate management, secure channels, and code signing and verification (Authenticode technology). Using CryptoAPI, developers can easily integrate strong cryptography into their applications. Cryptographic Service Provider (CSP) modules interface with CryptoAPI and perform several functions, including key generation and exchange, data encryption and decryption, hashing, creation of digital signatures, and signature verification. CryptoAPI is included as a core component of the latest versions of Microsoft® Windows®. Internet Explorer automatically provides this support for earlier versions of Windows.

Integrated Windows Authentication

Integrated Windows Authentication is a secure authentication method that uses a cryptographic exchange between a client and a server rather than transmitting a user name and a password to determine the client's authentication. This mutual exchange ensures the client's authentication before a secure connection is established.

Integrated Windows Authentication also provides data integrity and privacy services, which ensure that an unsecured party cannot read or modify transmitted data. These services are based on secret key encryption, which is used to encrypt and decrypt the data. This authentication method is particularly useful for transactions between clients and servers on open networks where they are not physically secure.

To enable this authentication method, in the **Internet Options** dialog box, click the **Advanced** tab, and then select the **Enable Integrated Windows Authentication** check box. For more information about enabling advanced security options, see "Using Digital Certificates" later in this chapter.

Server Certificate Revocation

Internet Explorer 6 includes support for server certificate revocation, which verifies that an issuing CA has not revoked a server certificate. This feature checks for CryptoAPI revocation when certificate extensions are present. If the URL for the revocation information is unresponsive, Internet Explorer cancels the connection.

☑   **Note** Microsoft® Outlook® Express also includes certificate revocation, which is controlled through a separate option within the e-mail program.

To enable server certificate revocation, in the **Internet Options** dialog box, click the **Advanced** tab, and then select the **Check for server certificate revocation** check box. For more information about enabling advanced security options, see "Using Digital Certificates" later in this chapter.

Publisher's Certificate Revocation

Internet Explorer 6 includes support for publisher's certificate revocation, which verifies that an issuing CA has not revoked a publisher's certificate. To enable publisher's certificate revocation, in the **Internet Options** dialog box, click the **Advanced** tab, and then select the **Check for publisher's certificate revocation** check box. For more information about enabling advanced security options, see "Using Digital Certificates" later in this chapter.

Using Digital Certificates

You can install certificates and configure certificate settings for Internet Explorer by using the following methods:

- Within the browser, you can use the Internet Explorer Certificate Manager to install certificates. You can also configure advanced security options for certificates on the **Advanced** tab in the **Internet Options** dialog box.

- You can use the Internet Explorer Customization Wizard to create custom packages of Internet Explorer that include preconfigured lists of trusted certificates, publishers, and CAs for your user groups. If you are a corporate administrator, you can also lock down these settings to prevent users from changing them.

- After deploying the browser, you can use the IEAK Profile Manager to manage certificate settings through the automatic browser configuration feature of Internet Explorer. You can automatically push the updated information to each user's desktop computer, enabling you to manage security policy dynamically across all computers on the network.

The options for configuring certificates are the same whether you gain access to them from Internet Explorer 6, the Internet Explorer Customization Wizard, or the IEAK Profile Manager. For more information about using the Internet Explorer Customization Wizard and the IEAK Profile Manager, see "Running the Microsoft Internet Explorer Customization Wizard" and "Keeping Programs Updated" in this Resource Kit.

Note Outlook Express also includes certificates, called *digital IDs,* which can be configured separately within the e-mail program.

Installing and Removing Trusted Certificates

The Internet Explorer Certificate Manager enables you to install and remove trusted certificates for clients and CAs. Many CAs have their root certificates already installed in Internet Explorer. You can select any of these installed certificates as trusted CAs for client authentication, secure e-mail, or other certificate purposes, such as code signing and time stamping. If a CA does not have its root certificate in Internet Explorer, you can import it. Each CA's Web site contains instructions that describe how to obtain the root certificate. You might also want to install client certificates, which are used to authenticate users' computers as clients for secure Web communications.

▶ **To install or remove clients and CAs from the list of trusted certificates**

1. On the **Tools** menu, click **Internet Options**, and then click the **Content** tab.
2. Click Certificates.

3. Click one of the following tabbed categories for the type of certificates you want to install or remove:

    ○ **Personal.** Certificates in the Personal category have an associated private key. Information signed by using personal certificates is identified by the user's private key data. By default, Internet Explorer places all certificates that will identify the user (with a private key) in the Personal category.

    ○ **Other People.** Certificates in the Other People category use public key cryptography to authenticate identity, based on a matching private key that is used to sign the information. By default, this category includes all certificates that are not in the Personal category (the user does not have a private key) and are not from CAs.

    ○ **Intermediate Certification Authorities.** This category contains all certificates for CAs that are not root certificates.

    ○ **Trusted Root Certification Authorities.** This category includes only self-signed certificates in the root store. When a CA's root certificate is listed in this category, you are trusting content from sites, people, and publishers with credentials issued by the CA.

    ○ **Trusted Publishers.** This category contains only certificates from trusted publishers whose content can be downloaded without user intervention, unless downloading active content is disabled in the settings for a specific security zone. Downloading active content is not enabled by default. For each available security zone, users can choose an appropriate set of ActiveX security preferences.

    The following illustration shows the Certificate Manager with the Intermediate Certification Authorities category selected.

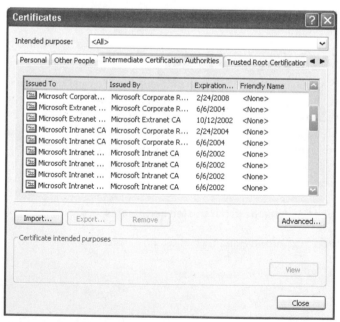

4. In the **Intended Purpose** box, select the filter for the types of certificates that you want to be displayed in the list.

5. Work with particular certificates through one of the following methods:

   o To add other certificates to the list, click **Import**. The Certificate Manager Import Wizard steps you through the process of adding a certificate.

   o To export certificates from the list, click **Export**. The Certificate Manager Export Wizard steps you through the process of exporting a certificate.

   o To specify the default drag-and-drop export file format (when the user drags a certificate from the Certificate Manager and drops it into a folder), click **Advanced**.

   o To delete an existing certificate from the list of trusted certificates, click **Remove**.

   o To display the properties for a selected certificate, including the issuer of the certificate and its valid dates, click **View**.

Adding Trusted Publishers

To designate a trusted publisher for Internet Explorer, use the **Security Warning** dialog box that appears when you attempt to download software from that publisher. Active content that is digitally signed by trusted publishers with a valid certificate will download without user intervention, unless you have disabled the downloading of active content in the settings for a specific security zone. Downloading active content is not enabled by default. For each available security zone, users can choose an appropriate set of ActiveX security preferences.

▶ **To add a trusted publisher**

1. Use Internet Explorer to download signed active content from the publisher.

2. When the **Security Warning** dialog box appears, select the **Always trust content from** *trusted publisher* check box.

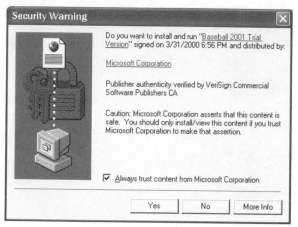

3. To download the software and control and add the publisher to the list of trusted publishers, click **Yes**.

Configuring Advanced Security Options for Certificate and Authentication Features

You can easily configure options for certificate and authentication features that your users might need.

▶ **To configure advanced security options for certificates**

1. On the **Tools** menu, click **Internet Options**, and then click the **Advanced** tab.

2. In the **Security** area, review the selected options.

3. Depending on the needs of your organization and its users, select or clear the appropriate check boxes.

For example, to enable SSL 3.0, select the **Use SSL 3.0** check box.

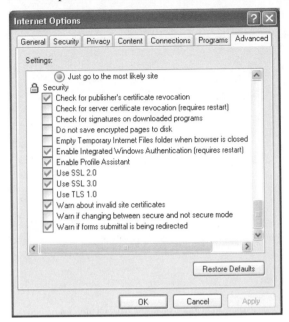

For information about security options for user privacy features, see "Users' Privacy" in this Resource Kit.

Permission-based Security for Microsoft Virtual Machine

Microsoft® Internet Explorer 6 provides comprehensive management and enforcement of Internet and network security. This chapter describes a key feature of security management—permission-based security for Microsoft virtual machine (Microsoft VM). Read this chapter to learn how this security feature can help protect access to information in your organization.

> **Note** Windows Update Setup for Internet Explorer 6 and Internet Tools does not install Microsoft VM. However, if users attempt to run an applet that requires Microsoft VM, the Internet Explorer Install On Demand feature prompts users to download the program. Users can also obtain the latest version of Microsoft VM from the Microsoft Technologies for Java Web site at http://www.microsoft.com/java/ and the Windows Update Web site at http://windowsupdate.microsoft.com/. If you want to include Microsoft VM as part of your custom browser packages, when you run the Internet Explorer Customization Wizard, add Microsoft VM as a custom component.

In This Chapter

Related Information in the Resource Kit

- For more information about Internet Explorer features that help ensure user privacy, see "Users' Privacy."
- For more information about planning user security before you install Internet Explorer 6 and Internet Tools, see "Planning the Deployment."

Overview: Permission-based Security for Microsoft VM

Permission-based security for Microsoft VM (which is Java-compatible) is a Microsoft® Windows® 32-bit security model that provides fine-grained management of the permissions granted to Java applets and libraries. This model uses Java cabinet (.cab) file-signing technology to ensure that an applet can perform actions only for which it specifically requests permissions.

Using permission-based security for Microsoft VM, developers can precisely limit the section of code where permissions have been granted, and administrators can control the permissions granted to Java code, such as access to local files and network connections. Also, when used in conjunction with security zones, permission-based security for Microsoft VM can simplify security decisions, because it enables you to specify sets of Java permissions for each security zone.

Permission-based security for Microsoft VM includes the following elements:

- **Permission-based security model.** This security model provides fine-grained control over the actions that Java classes can perform.
- **Security zones.** You can use security zones to assign security settings to a group of Web sites, such as all sites on a company intranet.
- **Permission signing.** You can use permission signing to associate specific security permissions with a Java package. You can specify the identity of the signer for the package's .cab file and the set of permissions requested by the signed classes.
- **Permission scoping.** This feature enables you to precisely limit the sections of code for which a granted permission is enabled.
- **Package Manager.** Package Manager allows classes to be installed with their associated permissions. Using Package Manager, you can also control the permissions granted to local classes, which are installed on the computer.
- **Trust User Interface.** This interface enables you to greatly simplify or eliminate the decisions that users need to make about the permissions granted to an applet.

The following sections describe these features of permission-based security for Microsoft VM. For more information, see the MSDN® Web site at http://msdn.microsoft.com/ and the *Microsoft Software Development Kit (SDK) for Java,* which you can download from the Microsoft Technologies for Java Web site at http://www.microsoft.com/java/.

Permission-based Security Model

The permission-based security model for Microsoft VM supports a set of permissions, with or without parameters, that can be granted or denied individually. For an applet to obtain access to the set of resources you want, such as a file's input and output, the applet must be signed with the proper permissions.

The following sets of permissions correspond to the standard Java *sandbox*, an area in memory outside of which the program cannot make calls:

- Allow thread access in the context of the current execution.
- Open network connections to the applet host (a remote Web server) so that the applet can communicate with the host and download additional files, as necessary.
- Create a top-level pop-up window with a warning banner that indicates that the window was created from an applet.
- Access reflection application program interfaces (APIs) for classes from the same loader.
- Read base system properties.

Security Zones

Security zones integrate with the permission-based security model to create a configurable, extensible mechanism for providing security for users. Whenever users attempt to open or download content from a Web site, Internet Explorer checks the security settings associated with that site's security zone. For more information about security zones, see "Security Zones" in this Resource Kit.

You can configure three different sets of permissions for each security zone for both signed and unsigned code:

- **Permissions that are granted without user intervention.** These permissions are available to applets from the zone without user intervention. You can specify the permissions separately for signed and unsigned applets.
- **Permissions that are granted with user intervention.** Microsoft VM prompts users about whether to grant these permissions to applets from the zone.
- **Permissions that are denied.** These permissions are considered harmful, and Microsoft VM automatically denies these permissions to applets from the zone.

Only applets that have permissions granted without user intervention run automatically. An applet that has been denied permissions will not run. If an applet uses permissions granted with user intervention, Microsoft VM displays a dialog box showing a list of all the permissions and their associated risks, and prompts the user to choose whether to trust the applet. If the user chooses not to trust the applet, the applet can continue to run with alternate and limited functionality, but Microsoft VM prevents the applet from using the expanded set of permissions.

> **Note** Microsoft VM prompts the user to confirm execution of the applet only if the applet requests more permissions than can be automatically granted for the zone. You can set up the specific permissions that Microsoft VM will automatically grant in each zone.

For more information about setting up permissions for each security zone, see "Setting Up Java Custom Security" later in this chapter.

Permission Signing

Permission signing extends the signed .cab file functionality provided by previous versions of Internet Explorer. Under permission-based security, a signed .cab file can securely specify not only the identity of the signer but also the set of permissions requested for the signed classes.

When the signed .cab file is downloaded, Microsoft VM examines the signature for permission information before it permits any code to run. By signing your applet with Java permission information, you request only the specific permissions that you need. Because your applet can perform only the actions that it specifically requests permission to perform, users can make informed decisions about the risks associated with running your applet.

Microsoft VM uses the permissions requested in the signature, as well as the user's general security preferences, to determine whether to grant the requested access. If Microsoft VM cannot automatically grant the requested access, it displays a dialog box prompting the user to choose whether the applet should be allowed to run. If the user approves, the applet is run with the permissions that it requests. Otherwise, the applet is run in the sandbox. Because the set of permissions are fully defined and understood by Microsoft VM, the requested permission information is displayed, and the user is warned about the risk of each requested access.

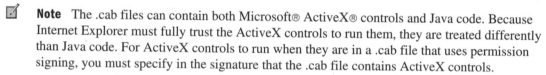

Note The .cab files can contain both Microsoft® ActiveX® controls and Java code. Because Internet Explorer must fully trust the ActiveX controls to run them, they are treated differently than Java code. For ActiveX controls to run when they are in a .cab file that uses permission signing, you must specify in the signature that the .cab file contains ActiveX controls.

You can sign Java code with the default capabilities of the following safety settings:

- **High Safety.** This setting is a restrictive set of capabilities that are the equivalent of "sandboxed" Java code. In addition, High Safety allows the applet to do the following:
  - Allow thread access in the context of the current execution.
  - Open network connections to the applet host (a remote Web server) so that the applet can communicate with the host and download additional files, as necessary.
  - Create a top-level pop-up window with a warning banner that indicates that the window was created from an applet.
  - Access reflection APIs for classes from the same loader.
  - Read base system properties.
- **Medium Safety.** This setting includes the capabilities of High Safety. In addition, Medium Safety allows the applet to do the following:
  - Access *scratch space*, which is the storage area on the client computer that an applet can safely access without needing full access to the client file system.
  - Perform user-directed file input and output.

- **Low Safety.** This setting includes the capabilities of High and Medium Safety. In addition, Low Safety allows the applet to do the following:
    - Perform user-directed and other file input and output.
    - Execute other applications on the client computer.
    - Implement user interface dialog boxes.
    - Provide thread group access in the context of the current execution.
    - Open network connections with computers other than the host.
    - Load libraries on the client computer.
    - Make *native method calls*, which enable Java classes and code to call into Windows DLLs.
    - Determine whether an applet can make native method calls.
    - Create a top-level pop-up window without a warning banner that indicates that the window was created from an applet.
    - Exit the Microsoft VM.
    - Perform registry operations.
    - Perform printing operations.
    - Create a class loader.

If you need closer control of the types of permissions granted to the signed code, you can also use custom permissions. These permissions are defined in an initialization (.ini) file. The .ini file includes a section for each desired permission, which defines its necessary parameters. You can create the .ini file manually, or you can use the Piniedit tool provided with the *Microsoft SDK for Java*.

Permission Scoping

Permission scoping prevents permissions granted to a trusted component from being misused, either inadvertently or intentionally, by a less-trusted component. A trusted class can precisely limit the range of code for which a granted permission is enabled. This is a particularly important feature, because some methods that use enhanced permissions are designed to be safely called by anyone, while other methods are designed to be used internally only by trusted callers and should not expose their permissions to less-trusted callers.

Permission-based security distinguishes between permissions that have been granted to a class and permissions that are actually enabled at a particular time. The granted permissions are determined by the administrative options for a class's zone and the permissions with which the class was signed. The enabled permissions are determined by the permissions granted to other callers on the call stack and by whether any explicit calls have been made to the **assertPermission**, **denyPermission**, or **revertPermission** methods. If there are less-trusted callers on the *call stack* (which identifies the sequence of calls and callers when Java code is run and the different methods contained within the code call into other methods), the enabled permissions can be more restrictive than the granted permissions.

Microsoft VM follows two rules for permission scoping:

- Permissions are never inherited from the caller. If a class has not been directly granted a permission, it can never use that permission, regardless of what permissions its callers have. This means that an untrusted class would never incorrectly be allowed to use the expanded permissions of its caller.

- Even if a class has been granted a permission, its methods must explicitly enable that permission by using the **assertPermission** method whenever a caller on the call stack has not been granted that permission.

  For example, permission P is enabled only if the following statements are true:

  o   P is granted in all of the stack frames from the active frame up to the earliest frame on the stack.

  o   P is granted in all of the stack frames up to a frame that has called **assertPermission** on P.

  o   No intervening frame has called **denyPermission** on P.

Permission-based security for Microsoft VM checks to see whether the code making the call to perform a trusted operation is signed with the proper level of permissions before honoring the **assertPermission** request. A security exception occurs if the caller has not been signed with the permissions for the operation that it is trying to perform.

Package Manager

The Package Manager administers the installation of Java packages and classes and provides a database for storing them. The Package Manager uses permission signing to allow the installation of local class libraries that are not fully trusted. This capability is especially important for *JavaBeans* and class libraries. It is recommended that you allow these components to reside locally and to have some expanded permissions, but not give them unlimited power.

The Package Manager was designed to address the limitations of using the CLASSPATH environment variable. It does so in the following ways:

- **Security.** Packages and classes installed through the Package Manager are not implicitly trusted as system library classes. Any Java package installed through the Package Manager that requires access to certain resources on the user's computer must be signed with the appropriate permissions. The Package Manager, in coordination with the security manager in Microsoft VM, enforces these signed permissions.

- **Versioning.** The Package Manager database stores the version number of every Java package it installs. By tracking version numbers, the Package Manager can upgrade Java packages if a newer version is being installed or downloaded from the network. The Package Manager can also eliminate any downgrading of Java packages.

- **Installing Java packages.** When Java packages are installed through the Package Manager, it is not necessary to update the CLASSPATH environment variable. Therefore, the user does not need to restart the computer.

- **Namespace.** To prevent *namespace collision* (when two different applets have the same name), Java packages can be installed under the global namespace or under an application namespace. Packages installed in the application namespace are visible only to applications running in that namespace. Packages in the global namespace are visible to all Java applications.

- **Load-time performance.** The Package Manager locally stores all of the packages it installs on the user's computer, greatly speeding up class load time performance for Java applets. This improved performance occurs because the classes do not need to be downloaded from the network every time the user visits the Web page containing the applet.

  When the application classes are loaded from the user's computer, they are still restricted to the permissions with which the application was originally signed. The Java package includes specific system permission identifiers that are approved when the package is installed on the user's computer. These permission identifiers determine the maximum permissions that the classes in a specific package can use.

- **Upgrading.** When a user revisits a Web page that contains a newer version of a Java package that was previously installed through the Package Manager, the new version is downloaded and the local classes are automatically upgraded. The Java applet or application must be packaged in a .cab file and signed with the permissions it needs to run.

Trust User Interface

The Trust User Interface defined by permission-based security for Microsoft VM shields users from complicated trust decisions and reduces the number of dialog boxes to which they must respond. The integration of permissions with security zones means that users need to make only a simple "Yes" or "No" choice when deciding whether to trust an application. An administrator has already made the complex decisions about which permissions to allow.

In addition, permission signing allows the security system to predetermine all the permissions required by a class. When a package is installed, the security system can use the signature to determine exactly which system permissions it needs to provide, and a single trust dialog box can reliably present all the permissions required by an application before running any code. Because the default system permissions are well defined and static, their level of risk can be determined and refined over time, ensuring that the level of risk is acceptable.

Setting Up Java Custom Security

You can deploy Internet Explorer with the default settings, or you can configure Java custom settings, which explicitly define the Java permissions for signed and unsigned applets. The options for configuring Java custom settings are the same whether you access them from Internet Explorer 6, the Internet Explorer Customization Wizard, or the IEAK Profile Manager. For more information about using the Internet Explorer Customization Wizard and IEAK Profile Manager, see "Running the Microsoft Internet Explorer Customization Wizard" and "Keeping Programs Updated" in this Resource Kit.

⬥ **Important**   You can configure Java custom settings only if the Microsoft VM is installed on your computer.

Configuring Java Custom Security

You can configure Java custom security by using the following methods:

- In Internet Explorer, you can adjust security settings by using the **Tools** menu.

- You can use the Internet Explorer Customization Wizard to create custom browser packages that include Java custom settings. If you are a corporate administrator, you can also lock down these settings to prevent users from changing them.

- After the browser is deployed, you can use the IEAK Profile Manager to manage Java custom settings through the automatic browser-configuration feature of Internet Explorer. You can automatically push the updated security-zone settings to each user's desktop computer, enabling you to manage security policy dynamically across all computers on the network.

The following procedure describes how to configure Java custom settings in Internet Explorer.

▶ **To configure Java custom settings**

1. On the **Tools** menu, click **Internet Options**.
2. Click the **Security** tab.
3. Click a security zone.
4. Click Custom Level.
5. To control the permissions that are granted to Java applets when they are downloaded and run in the selected zone, in the **Java Permissions** area, select one of the following security levels:

   ○ **Custom**, which controls permissions settings individually.
   ○ **Disable Java**, which prevents any applets from running.
   ○ **High Safety**, which enables applets to run in their sandbox.
   ○ **Low Safety**, which enables applets to perform all operations.
   ○ **Medium Safety**, which enables applets to run in their sandbox. In addition, applets are given other capabilities such as access to scratch space and user-controlled file input and output.

   Note   These options control the maximum permission level silently granted to signed applets that are downloaded from the zone. Also, they control the permissions granted to unsigned applets that are downloaded from the zone and to scripts on pages in the zone that call into applets. If a Java applet is downloaded from a different site than the page on which it is used, the more restrictive of the two sites' zone settings is applied. For example, if a user views a Web page within a zone that is set to allow a download, but the code is downloaded from another zone that is set to prompt a user first, Internet Explorer uses the prompt setting.

6. If you selected **Custom** in Step 5, click **Java Custom Settings**.

7. As necessary, perform the following tasks:

    o   To view Java permissions, click the **View Permissions** tab.

        This tab displays permissions in a hierarchical tree that you can expand and collapse. Permissions are organized into the following categories:

        Permissions Given To Unsigned Content. Unsigned Java applets that request these permissions can run without user prompting.

        Permissions That Signed Content Are Allowed. Signed Java applets that request these permissions can run without user prompting.

        Permissions That Signed Content Are Denied. Signed Java applets are denied these permissions.

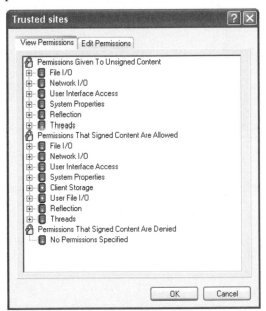

    o   To edit Java permissions, click the **Edit Permissions** tab, and then select the options you want for more precise control of Java permissions.

At any time, you can click the **Reset** button to reset the Java custom settings to the last saved permissions or to the default high, medium, or low security settings.

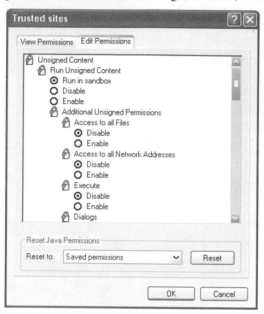

Selecting Java Custom Settings

The **Java Custom Settings** button on the **Security** tab gives you additional control over Java permissions. You can enable or disable specific Java permissions depending on the needs of your organization and its users.

Java custom settings for Internet Explorer are divided into two groups: Unsigned Content and Signed Content. The following tables identify the default value for each option based on the level of security.

Unsigned Content

Java custom option	High security	Medium security	Low security
Run Unsigned Content			
Run Unsigned Content	Run in sandbox	Run in sandbox	Run in sandbox
Additional Unsigned Permissions			
Access to all Files	Disable	Disable	Disable
Access to all Network Addresses	Disable	Disable	Disable
Execute	Disable	Disable	Disable
Dialogs	Disable	Disable	Disable

Java custom option	High security	Medium security	Low security
Additional Unsigned Permissions			
System Information	Disable	Disable	Disable
Printing	Disable	Disable	Disable
Protected Scratch Space	Disable	Disable	Disable
User Selected File Access	Disable	Disable	Disable

Signed Content

Java custom option	High security	Medium security	Low security
Run Signed Content			
Run Unsigned Content	Prompt	Prompt	Prompt
Additional Signed Permissions			
Access to all Files	Prompt	Prompt	Disable
Access to all Network Addresses	Prompt	Prompt	Disable
Execute	Prompt	Prompt	Disable
Printing	Prompt	Prompt	Disable
Protected Scratch Space	Prompt	Enable	Disable
User Selected File Access	Prompt	Enable	Disable

The following sections describe the settings for the **Unsigned Content** and **Signed Content** groups.

Unsigned Content

The **Run Unsigned Content** group determines whether unsigned applets can run in the zone. This group has the following settings:

- **Run in sandbox.** Runs unsigned Java applets for this zone in a Java sandbox that you specify. You can enable or disable individual options in the **Additional Unsigned Permissions** category.
- **Disable.** Disables running unsigned applets for this zone. Internet Explorer disables all options in the **Additional Unsigned Permissions** category.
- **Enable.** Enables running unsigned applets for this zone. Internet Explorer enables all options in the **Additional Unsigned Permissions** category.

The **Additional Unsigned Permissions** options determine whether unsigned applets can have additional permissions, such as access to network addresses and the ability to run other applications. You can choose to disable or enable each of these options for unsigned permissions. If you disable the ability to run unsigned content, Internet Explorer automatically disables all of these options.

For the following unsigned permissions, click **Disable** or **Enable**:

- **Access to all Files.** Determines whether unsigned applets can have read access to all the files on users' systems.
- **Access to all Network Addresses.** Determines whether unsigned applets can have access to network addresses.
- **Execute.** Determines whether unsigned applets can run other applications.
- **Dialogs.** Determines whether unsigned applets can create file dialog boxes.
- **System Information.** Determines whether unsigned applets can read system properties.
- **Printing.** Determines whether unsigned applets can have access to printer resources.
- **Protected Scratch Space.** Determines whether unsigned applets can use storage space on the hard drive.
- **User Selected File Access.** Determines whether unsigned applets can have access to selected files.

> **Note** If you click **Enable**, Internet Explorer prompts users to choose whether unsigned applets can have access to selected files.

Signed Content

The **Run Signed Content** group determines whether users can run signed applets. This group has the following settings:

- **Prompt.** Sets individual options in the **Additional Signed Permissions** category to **Prompt**. You can disable or enable each individual option.
- **Disable.** Disables running signed applets for this zone. Internet Explorer disables all options in the **Additional Signed Permissions** category.
- **Enable.** Enables running unsigned applets for this zone. Internet Explorer enables all options in the **Additional Signed Permissions** category.

The **Additional Signed Permissions** options determine whether signed applets can have additional permissions, such as access to network addresses and the ability to run other applications. You can choose to prompt users about each of these options for signed permissions, or you can prevent or allow the permissions without prompting. If you disable the ability to **Run Signed Content**, Internet Explorer automatically disables all of these options.

For the following signed permissions, click **Prompt**, **Disable**, or **Enable**:

- **Access to all Files.** Determines whether signed applets can have read access to all the files on the users' systems.
- **Access to all Network Addresses.** Determines whether signed applets can have access to network addresses.
- **Execute.** Determines whether signed applets can run other applications.
- **Dialogs.** Determines whether signed applets can create file dialog boxes.
- **System Information.** Determines whether signed applets can read system properties.
- **Printing.** Determines whether signed applets can have access to printer resources.
- **Protected Scratch Space.** Determines whether signed applets can use storage space on the hard disk.
- **User Selected File Access.** Determines whether signed applets can have access to selected files.

PART 3

Multimedia, Accessibility, and Other Features

Chapter 8: Media Bar

This chapter describes the new Media bar, which makes it easy to find and play media files within the Microsoft® Internet Explorer 6 window. You can learn how to use the Media bar to enhance your browsing experience, and use this information to help you respond to users' questions.

Chapter 9: Image Toolbar and Automatic Image Resizing

This chapter describes the Image toolbar and Automatic Image Resizing, two new features of Microsoft Internet Explorer 6 that make it easier to work with Web pictures on the Internet or your intranet. You can learn how to use the Image toolbar and Automatic Image Resizing and then apply this information as you respond to users' questions about these features.

Chapter 10: Print Preview

This chapter describes the new Print Preview feature of Microsoft Internet Explorer 6, which makes it easier to work with Web pages on the Internet or your intranet. You can learn how to use Print Preview and then apply this information when you respond to users' questions about this feature.

Chapter 11: The Microsoft DHTML Platform

This chapter describes the new and enhanced features of Microsoft® Dynamic HTML (DHTML) in Microsoft Internet Explorer 6. As a software developer or content author for the Web, you can use the DHTML platform to develop more compelling and interactive Web content and Web-based applications and services. DHTML enables you to incorporate transparent frames, colored scroll bars, vertical text layout, and more.

Chapter 12: Accessibility Features and Functionality

This chapter describes the different ways that Microsoft Internet Explorer 6 supports enhanced accessibility and explains how you can use the browser to accommodate different accessibility needs. In particular, Internet Explorer has many features that enable users with disabilities to customize the appearance of Web pages to meet their own needs and preferences. If you are a user without disabilities, you might also be interested in this functionality, which enables you to customize colors and fonts to your own tastes and to use time-saving keyboard shortcuts.

C H A P T E R   8

Media Bar

This chapter describes the new Media bar, which makes it easy to find and play media files within the Microsoft® Internet Explorer 6 window. You can learn how to use the Media bar to enhance your browsing experience, and use this information to help you respond to users' questions.

In This Chapter

Related Information in the Resource Kit

- For more information about new Internet Explorer features, see "What's New in Microsoft Internet Explorer 6?"

- For more information about using the Microsoft Internet Explorer Customization Wizard to control access to Internet Explorer features, see "Running the Microsoft Internet Explorer Customization Wizard."

Overview: Playing Media Files

The Media bar enables you to play music, video, and mixed-media files from within the browser. You can use the Media bar to listen to your favorite CD or Internet radio station. From the Media bar, you can also go to the WindowsMedia.com Web site to find more media files.

The Media bar is divided into two sections. The top section provides links to WindowsMedia.com, where you can find and play online media files, including music, radio stations, and movie and entertainment clips. The bottom section is the media player, which allows you to control how media files are played.

Using the Media Bar

The Media bar is simple and easy to use. You will instantly recognize standard media controls for playing, stopping, going forward and backward, and adjusting audio volume. The Media bar includes a **Media Options** menu that enables you to quickly locate media files and set your Media bar preferences. You also have the option to turn off the display of online media content in the Media bar.

Viewing the Media Bar

You can view the Media bar in the vertical Explorer Bar pane on the left side of your browser window.

▷ **To view the Media Bar**

1. On the **View** menu, click **Explorer Bar**, and then click **Media**.

    -Or-

    On the Internet Explorer toolbar, click the **Media** button.

    The Media bar appears in the Explorer Bar pane. A round bullet also appears next to **Media** in the Explorer Bar list.

2. To resize an Explorer Bar pane within the browser window, move the pointer over the edge of the pane until it changes to a double-headed arrow, and then drag the edge to make the pane larger or smaller.

Locating Media Files and Setting Preferences

You can use the **Media Options** menu to locate media files and set your preferences for the Media bar.

▷ **To locate media files and set preferences for the Media bar**

1. In the Media bar, click **Media Options**, and then click one of the following options to locate other media files:

    o **More Media.** View the WindowsMedia.com home page in the browser window, and use the **Music**, **Movies**, **Radio**, and **Entertainment** tabs to locate media files that you want to play.

    o **Radio Guide.** On the WindowsMedia.com guide to radio stations, choose from a list of preset radio stations, or use the station finder to locate the station that you want.

    The following screen shot shows the WindowsMedia.com guide to radio stations.

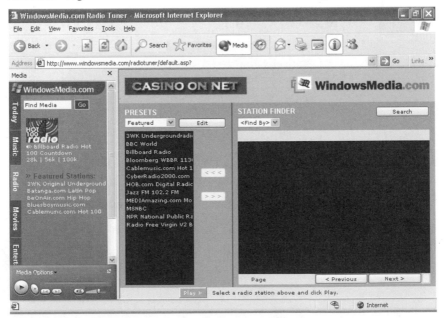

2. To set Media bar preferences, click **Settings**, and then select or clear the following options:

    o **Play web media in the bar.** Automatically play media files in the Media bar rather than your default media player; this option is selected by default.

    o **Ask for preferred types.** When you open a media file from the Web, receive a prompt about whether you want to open the file in the Media bar. If you choose to open the file in the Media bar, in the future all files with this same file format will also be opened in the Media bar.

    If you select **Ask for preferred types**, the following dialog prompt appears when you open a media file from the Web. If you select the **Remember my preference** check box and then click **Yes**, Internet Explorer will open all subsequent files of this same type in the Media bar.

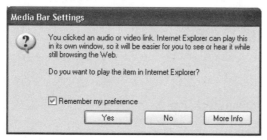

    o **Reset preferred types.** Clear the list of media file types that are automatically opened in the Media bar.

Using Media Bar Controls

You can use the Media bar's simple user interface to play media files from within the browser without opening a separate media player. The following table describes the Media bar controls.

Click this	To do this
Seek bar	View and change the progress of the media file while it is playing. Use the Seek bar to go forward or backward within the media file; the timer identifies your position in the file in minutes and seconds.
Pop-out Player	Use the Media bar in a separate window.
Play/Pause	Play or pause the media file.
Stop	Stop playing the media file.
Previous Track	Go back to the previous audio or video track and play it again.
Next Track	Skip forward to the next audio or video track and play it.
Mute	Turn off the sound.
Volume (slider bar)	Increase or decrease the sound volume from level 1 to level 100.

Turning Off Online Media Content in the Media Bar

If your computer is connected to the Internet, when you view the Media bar, you automatically see online media content. You can turn off the Media bar's display of online media content on the **Advanced** tab in the **Internet Options** dialog box.

▶ **To turn off the display of online media content in the Media bar**

1. On the **Tools** menu, click **Internet Options**, and then click the **Advanced** tab.

2. Select the **Don't display online media content in the media bar** check box.

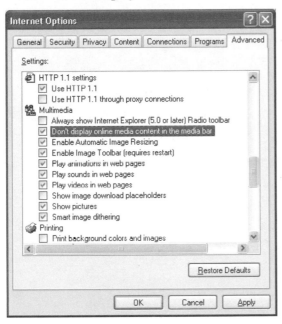

C H A P T E R   9

Image Toolbar and Automatic Image Resizing

This chapter describes the Image toolbar and Automatic Image Resizing, two new features of Microsoft® Internet Explorer 6 that make it easier to work with Web pictures on the Internet or your intranet. You can learn how to use the Image toolbar and Automatic Image Resizing and then apply this information as you respond to users' questions about these features.

In This Chapter

Related Information in the Resource Kit

- For more information about new Internet Explorer features, see "What's New in Microsoft Internet Explorer 6?"
- For more information about using the Internet Explorer Customization Wizard to control access to Internet Explorer features, see "Running the Microsoft Internet Explorer Customization Wizard."

Using the Image Toolbar

The Image toolbar allows you to quickly and easily save, send, and print pictures that you find on Web pages, as well as view all your saved pictures in the My Pictures folder. You can perform these tasks by using one of the following methods:

- Point to a picture to activate the Image toolbar, which appears in the upper-left corner of the picture, and then click the appropriate toolbar button.

- Right-click a picture and then click the appropriate command.

 Note   Not all pictures on Web pages will activate the Image toolbar. A picture must be a minimum of 130 x 130 pixels, and it cannot be a background picture. Also, the picture cannot use image mapping (indicating some form of Web menu). Even if a picture does not activate the Image toolbar, you can still right-click it and use the corresponding commands.

These electronic snapshot-type pictures are intended for your personal use. They are not meant for specialized Web page design, camera-ready artwork, or similar purposes.

Turning On and Off the Image Toolbar

The Image toolbar is turned on by default. When you point to a picture that meets the Image toolbar criteria, the toolbar appears automatically.

You can turn on and off the Image toolbar by using the **Internet Options** dialog box or by using a shortcut menu that appears when you right-click the toolbar. This menu enables you to turn off the Image toolbar for the current session only or for all sessions. Even after you turn off the Image Toolbar, you can still right-click a picture to use the corresponding commands.

▶ **To turn on and off the Image toolbar by using Internet Options**

1. On the **Tools** menu, click **Internet Options**.
2. Click the **Advanced** tab, and then scroll down to the **Multimedia** area.
3. Select or clear the **Enable Image Toolbar (requires restart)** check box.

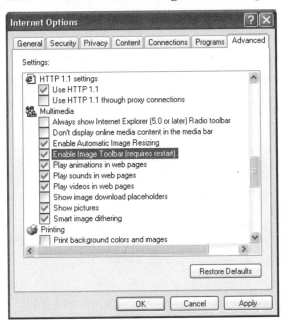

▶ **To turn off the Image toolbar by right-clicking**

1. Point to a picture to activate the Image toolbar.
2. Right-click the Image toolbar, and then click **Disable Image Toolbar**.
3. Depending on whether you want to turn off the Image toolbar for only the current session or for all sessions, click either **This Session** or **Always**.

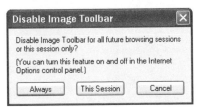

Saving a Picture

If you find a picture on a Web page that you want to keep, you can save the picture on your computer. By default, Internet Explorer saves the picture in the My Pictures folder. If the My Pictures folder does not exist, Internet Explorer creates it automatically within the My Documents folder on your hard disk.

When you save a picture in the My Pictures folder, you can quickly view the picture again by using the Image toolbar or the image shortcut menu.

▷ **To save a picture**

1. Point to the picture that you want to save.

2. On the Image toolbar, click the **Save this image** button.

    -Or-

    Right-click the picture, and then click **Save Picture As**.

3. In the **Save Picture** dialog box, enter values for the following fields:

    o **Save in.** The folder location where you want to store the picture.

       If you save the picture in a location other than the My Pictures folder, this location becomes the default location for all saved pictures during the current browser session. For future sessions, though, the default location returns to the My Pictures folder.

    o **File name.** The name that identifies the picture file.

    o **Save as type.** The extension for the picture file name.

4. Click **Save**.

Sending a Picture in an E-mail Message

If you find a picture on a Web page that you want to send to another person, you can send the picture as an attachment in an e-mail message. Internet Explorer uses the browser's default mail application to send the picture. If you do not have a default mail application, this feature is not available.

▶ **To send a picture in an e-mail message**

1. Point to the picture that you want to send.

2. On the Image toolbar, click the **Send this image in an e-mail** button.

    -Or-

    Right-click the picture, and then click **E-Mail Picture**.

3. In Microsoft® Windows® XP, when you are prompted about whether to resize the picture that you are sending, click either **Make all my pictures smaller** or **Keep the original sizes**, and then click **OK**.

4. Internet Explorer starts the default mail application and opens a new message with the picture included as an attachment. If, for example, Microsoft® Outlook® Express is your default mail application, a new message opens with the picture shown in the **Attach** box. You can then type the e-mail address of the person to whom you want to send the picture, type a message, and then send it.

    The following illustration shows a sample Outlook Express e-mail message with the picture included as an attachment. Note that the picture's name appears as the Subject line of the message.

Printing a Picture

If you find a picture on a Web page that you want to print, you can print it on your local or network printer by using the standard Microsoft® Windows® printing options. The picture prints exactly as it appears on the Web page, so if you enlarge or reduce the size of the picture, the printed picture will also be resized. If you do not have a printer installed, the default **Print** dialog box appears, and you can add a printer for your local computer.

▶ To print a picture

1. Point to the picture that you want to print.
2. On the Image toolbar, click the **Print this image** button.

    -Or-

    Right-click the picture, and then click **Print Picture**.
3. In the **Print** dialog box, select the printing options, and then click **Print**.

Viewing Saved Pictures

If you want to view all of your saved pictures, you can quickly open the My Pictures folder from the Image toolbar or shortcut menu. If the My Pictures folder does not exist, Internet Explorer creates it automatically within the My Documents folder on your hard disk.

▶ To view your saved pictures in the My Pictures folder

1. Point to a picture on a Web page.
2. On the Image toolbar, click the **Open My Pictures folder** button.

    -Or-

    Right-click the picture, and then click **Go to My Pictures**.

Turning Off the Image Toolbar by Using HTML Tags

As a content author, you can turn off image toolbar functions for an individual picture or all pictures on a Web page. This turns off only elements that use the <img> tag; it does not affect other graphics tags, such as <embed> or <object>, or the file type.

If you want to turn off image toolbar functions for individual pictures on a Web page, use the following <img> syntax for the picture:

```
<img border="0" src="filename" galleryimg="no">
<img border="0" src="filename" galleryimg="false">
```

If you want to turn off image toolbar functions for all pictures on a Web page, add the following <meta> syntax to your Web page:

```
<meta http-equiv="imagetoolbar" content="no">
<meta http-equiv="imagetoolbar" content="false">
```

If you turn off Image toolbar functions for all pictures on a Web page, you can enable them for individual pictures by setting the galleryimg attribute to "yes" or "true", using the following <img> syntax:

```
<img border="0" src="filename" galleryimg="yes">
<img border="0" src="filename" galleryimg="true">
```

Note If you use the galleryimg="yes" attribute and you also use image mapping (usemap or ismap), the galleryimg="yes" attribute overrides the mapping attribute, and the menu is turned on.

Using Automatic Image Resizing

If pictures are too large to see in their entirety in the browser window, Automatic Image Resizing resizes them automatically so that they fit within the dimensions of the browser window. An icon appears in the lower-right corner of resized pictures and allows you to expand the pictures back to their original size.

If you navigate to pictures that fit within the browser window but then change the window dimensions, Internet Explorer automatically adjusts the pictures to fit the new window size. To prevent distortion, Internet Explorer adjusts both the picture height and width, even if only a single dimension needs adjusting for the picture to fit within the browser window.

Automatic Image Resizing works only when users navigate directly to pictures. Internet Explorer cannot resize pictures that are embedded within HTML pages.

Turning On and Off Automatic Image Resizing

Automatic Image Resizing is turned on by default. You can turn it on and off by using the **Advanced** tab on the **Internet Options** dialog box.

▶ **To turn on and off Automatic Image Resizing**

1. On the **Tools** menu, click **Internet Options**.
2. Click the **Advanced** tab, and then scroll down to the **Multimedia** area.

3.   Select or clear the **Enable Automatic Image Resizing** check box.

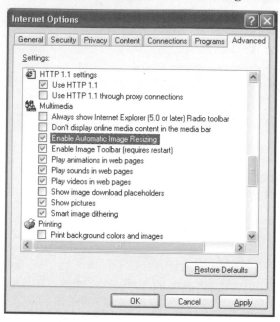

Resizing Pictures

If you view a picture that is too large to see in its entirety in the browser window, Automatic Image Resizing resizes the picture to fit within the browser window. You can then use the Automatic Image Resizing icon that appears in the lower-right corner of the picture to resize it so that it either returns to its original size or fits within the browser window.

▷ To resize a picture

1. To expand a resized picture to its original size, click the **Automatic Image Resizing** icon in the lower-right corner of the resized picture.

2. To resize the image to fit in the browser window, click the **Automatic Image Resizing**
    icon again.

Print Preview

This chapter describes the new Print Preview feature of Microsoft® Internet Explorer 6, which makes it easier to work with Web pages on the Internet or your intranet. You can learn how to use Print Preview and then apply this information when you respond to users' questions about this feature.

In This Chapter

Related Information in the Resource Kit

- For more information about new Internet Explorer features, see "What's New in Microsoft Internet Explorer 6?"
- For more information about using the Internet Explorer Customization Wizard to control access to Internet Explorer features, see "Running the Microsoft Internet Explorer Customization Wizard."

Overview: Previewing Web Pages

Print Preview enables you to instantly preview a Web page so that you can see how the page will look when you print it. This Internet Explorer feature is similar to Print Preview in other Microsoft applications such as Microsoft® Word and Microsoft® Excel.

With Print Preview, you can:

- Preview each Web page as it will appear in printed form.
- Select the specific pages that you want to print.
- Zoom in and out to view Web page details.

Using Print Preview

This section describes how to add a **Print Preview** button to your Internet Explorer toolbar so that you can quickly use this feature. Also, you can learn how to preview a Web page and use Print Preview commands to customize your page preview.

Adding a Print Preview Toolbar Button

You can make it easier to use Print Preview by adding a **Print Preview** button to your Internet Explorer toolbar.

▶ **To add the Print Preview button to the Internet Explorer toolbar**

1. To add an Internet Explorer toolbar button, right-click the toolbar, and then click **Customize**.
2. In the Available toolbar buttons list, click **Print Preview**, and then click **Add**.

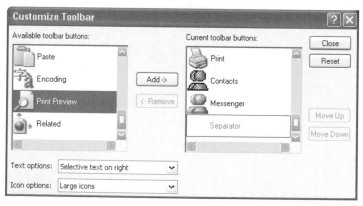

Print Preview moves to the Current toolbar buttons list.

3. Click **Close**.

Previewing a Web Page

You can click **Print Preview** to instantly see how a Web page will look when you print it. Then you can use Print Preview commands to customize your page preview.

▶ **To preview the appearance of a printed Web page**

1. On the **File** menu, click **Print Preview**.

   -Or-

   If you added the **Print Preview** button to your Internet Explorer toolbar, click the button.

2. Choose from the following commands to customize your page preview. When your mouse pointer hovers on the Print Preview toolbar buttons, the command names and shortcut keys appear.

Click this button	To do this	Shortcut key
Print Document	Set printing options and print the page.	ALT+P
Page Setup	Change paper, headers and footers, orientation, and margins for this page.	ALT+U
First Page	Display the first page to be printed.	ALT+HOME
Previous Page	Display the previous page to be printed.	ALT+LEFT ARROW
Preview Page	Type the number of the page you want to display.	ALT+A
Next Page	Display the next page to be printed.	ALT+RIGHT ARROW
Last Page	Display the last page to be printed.	ALT+END
Zoom Out	Decrease the magnification.	ALT+MINUS
Zoom In	Increase the magnification.	ALT+PLUS
Zoom List	Display a list of zoom percentages.	ALT+Z
Print Preview Help	Read Help topics about Print Preview.	ALT+H
Close	Close the Print Preview window.	ALT+C

The Microsoft DHTML Platform

This chapter describes the new and enhanced features of Microsoft® Dynamic HTML (DHTML) in Microsoft® Internet Explorer 6. As a software developer or content author for the Web, you can use the DHTML platform to develop more compelling and interactive Web content and Web-based applications and services. DHTML enables you to incorporate transparent frames, colored scroll bars, vertical text layout, and more.

 Note This chapter provides an overview of the DHTML platform. For more detailed platform information, see the *Microsoft Internet Explorer 6 Software Development Kit (SDK),* which you can locate on the MSDN® Web site at http://msdn.microsoft.com/.

In This Chapter

Related Information in the Resource Kit

- For more information about new software development features, see "What's New in Microsoft Internet Explorer 6?"
- For more information about software development resources for Internet Explorer 6, see the appendix "Microsoft Internet Explorer 6 Resource Directory."

Overview: Microsoft DHTML Technology

Microsoft DHTML increases interactivity by providing the technology to help you build truly dynamic Web content. You are no longer limited to static HTML pages or interactive components that are difficult to build and reuse. Instead, you can take advantage of DHTML features, such as element behaviors and lightweight HTML component support, which provide you with enhanced creative control and flexibility.

DHTML allows you to create interactive Web pages that do not require additional controls or Web server requests to update them. After dynamic Web pages are loaded in the browser, you can change any page elements, including the structure, style, or content, and the updates then occur on client computers without reloading the pages.

DHTML uses standard HTML tags to render and update content on Web pages. With its comprehensive document object model for HTML, DHTML allows you to manipulate any page element at any time. Therefore, everything you see (and many things you cannot see) when you look at a Web page can be manipulated by using DHTML.

To help ensure cross-browser interoperability, DHTML supports open, standards-based technologies. Based on the document object model developed by the World Wide Web Consortium (W3C), the Microsoft implementation of DHTML supports the following W3C specifications:

- HTML 4.0 (working draft)
- CSS1 (recommendation)
- CSS positioning (working draft)
- *Document Object Model Requirements* (preliminary version)

Microsoft DHTML Platform Features

The DHTML platform for building dynamic Web content includes the following key features:

- **Document object model.** DHTML provides a comprehensive document object model for HTML. This model exposes all page elements as objects that you can manipulate by changing their attributes or applying methods to them. DHTML also provides full support for keyboard and mouse events on all page elements.

  Support for this document object model enables the following capabilities:

  o **Dynamic content.** You can add, delete, or modify text or graphics at any time. For example, a Web page can update a page headline without refreshing the page, and the surrounding text then automatically flows around the new headline.

o **Dynamic styles.** Internet Explorer fully supports cascading style sheets (CSS), a style sheet mechanism that allows you to control a document's styles separate from its HTML contents. With DHTML, any CSS attributes on Web pages, including colors and fonts, can change without the downloading of complete new pages from the Web servers. For instance, text can change color or size when a mouse pointer passes over it. You can also apply multimedia filters and transition effects to HTML elements simply by adding the CSS filter attribute. For more information about these effects, see "Enhanced Visual Filters and Transitions" later in this chapter.

o **Absolute positioning.** To create animated effects, you can update the CSS positioning coordinates, which determine the alignment of text and graphics, for existing Web content at any time.

- **Data binding.** You can build user interfaces for data-driven applications that display, manipulate, and update data on client computers without numerous requests to reload the pages from the Web servers.

Benefits of DHTML

The benefits of building Web pages and applications with DHTML technology include the following:

- **Use common scripting languages to develop content.** You can use common scripting languages, such as JavaScript and Microsoft® Visual Basic® Script (VBScript), to make your Web pages interactive. You can also write full-featured Web applications that use DHTML without writing complex applets or controls to add the dynamic behavior to your Web pages.

- **Reuse existing DHTML-based content.** Using scriptlets, you can add DHTML content to your Web pages and applications and then reuse the scriplet components. Reusing the content reduces the total cost of ownership by decreasing the total number of unique components that your organization must maintain and support.

- **Use technology that is supported across browsers.** You can create a single set of Web pages for all browsers that support the document object model for DHTML. You can take advantage of standards-based features, such as CSS, that are implemented in today's popular browsers. These features ensure that most of your users have the same interactive Web experience, regardless of what browsers they are using. Microsoft's DHTML support also advances the standards through such innovations as behaviors that make the process of developing DHTML content more manageable.

- **Author DHTML by using Microsoft and third-party tools.** DHTML supports a wide variety of Microsoft and third-party Web development and authoring tools, including Microsoft® FrontPage® 2000, Microsoft® Visual InterDev®, Bluestone Total-e-Server 7.2, ExperTelligence WebberActive 4.0, SoftQuad HoTMetaL PRO 6.0, and Pictorius iNet Developer 2.0.

Behavior Component Model

DHTML behaviors separate a document's script from its content and style, making DHTML functionality more accessible and easier to use in a document. The enhanced DHTML behavior component model allows you to build components with DHTML behaviors that encapsulate and reuse script. Most importantly, you can build these components without encountering potential behavior name conflicts (when multiple behaviors use the same name) and unforeseen CSS style inheritance (unexpected formatting that occurs when styles from the top-level document affect lower-level document components).

Three key features of this behavior component model for building reusable components are element behaviors, Viewlink, and lightweight HTML component support.

Element Behaviors

Element behaviors, which build on the existing behavior supported in Internet Explorer 5, allow DHTML behaviors to be bound synchronously to *custom elements*. Custom elements are user-defined elements in an HTML document that have explicit name spaces (a collection of names that are used to uniquely qualify elements).

For clarity, behaviors supported in Internet Explorer 5 are referred to as *attached behaviors*, because they bind asynchronously to standard HTML elements either through a CSS declaration of the behavior property or procedurally through the **addBehavior** and **removeBehavior** methods. In contrast, *element behaviors* bind to the element such that they can never be detached, and they are considered an intrinsic part of the element being defined. Attached behaviors overwrite the default behavior of the element to which they are attached, whereas element behaviors are used to define new elements.

Features of Element Behaviors

Element behaviors provide new features that complement the existing capabilities of attached behaviors as well as enhance the functionality of the behavior component model. You can use element behaviors to implement anything from a simple rollover effect to a complex interactive component. Like attached behaviors, element behaviors make it possible to modify the behavior of standard HTML elements by using scripting—HTML component .htc files—or native binary code. Unlike attached behaviors, though, only one element behavior is permitted per element, and only custom elements can use element behaviors.

Element behaviors allow instances of behaviors to occur immediately (replacing object variables with values) when the element is created and when the methods provided by the behavior are reliably present. Because an element behavior is bound synchronously, the custom element is initialized as soon as it has been downloaded and parsed. In addition, the element behavior can be used without any change in the CSS declaration that would result in the behavior being removed unexpectedly. You can achieve this binding of the element behavior to the custom element by declaring the behavior with a special processing instruction that imports the element behavior into a Web page.

After an element behavior has been downloaded and parsed, it exists as a first-class element in the document hierarchy and remains permanently bound to the custom element. Element behaviors differ significantly from attached behaviors in this respect. An attached behavior binds asynchronously to an element and modifies its behavior, and you can attach or remove it programmatically.

When you develop a custom element, you can reuse it in your documents in the same way you would use standard HTML elements, such as DIV, SPAN, and INPUT. The traditional attached behavior mechanism for elements, however, does not allow you to reuse elements, because it employs a secondary attachment mechanism that takes place after the custom element has been created. For example, if you script an element by using the **createElement** method and then attach a behavior by using CSS, any script following **createElement** and referring to a method supplied by the behavior will probably fail, because the behavior will not have been attached at that moment.

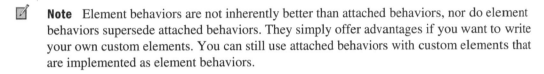 **Note** Element behaviors are not inherently better than attached behaviors, nor do element behaviors supersede attached behaviors. They simply offer advantages if you want to write your own custom elements. You can still use attached behaviors with custom elements that are implemented as element behaviors.

Benefits of Element Behaviors

The benefits of element behaviors include the following:

- **Build element behaviors with simple .htc files.** You can use .htc files to build element behaviors that implement almost any task that is possible with binary DHTML behaviors without restricting the scope or functionality of the task. Implementing element behaviors by using .htc files is also significantly easier, because you can create the behaviors with script rather than with Microsoft® Visual C++® coding. You do not need to learn a programming language in order to write custom browser components with element behaviors.

- **Easily organize content, script, and styles.** Developing compelling interactive Web pages might require several skills, and writers, programmers, and designers can work together to develop a single Web page. Traditional page authoring means working with a single HTML document that contains a mixture of scripting, content, and formatting. Using .htc files makes this development process simpler and easier.

  The .htc files allow you to encapsulate content, script, and styles into discrete containers so that each specialist can concentrate on specific tasks. You can add new and interesting functionality to Web pages while improving the organization of their content, the functionality of the pages, and their style. You can also build a powerful .htc file library with code that is easier to manage and less expensive to maintain than Visual C++ and other types of code.

- **Simplify browser security issues.** When element behaviors are implemented with .htc files, they are automatically downloaded as a part of the Web pages. Because the .htc files do not require any user permission before they are downloaded, the component download is invisible on the client computers. The .htc files must be located in the same domain as the primary document and can be used in any pages within that same domain. Therefore, no access-denied errors occur.

- **Avoid writing additional event-handling functions.** Custom elements are initialized as soon as they have been downloaded and parsed. Therefore, you do not need to add event-handling functions to check the component status—components are automatically parsed before any component scripting executes.

Viewlink

Viewlink is a feature of the DHTML behavior component model that enables you to write fully encapsulated element behaviors—by using either binary DHTML behaviors or scripted HTML components (.htc files)—and then import them as custom elements in Web pages. DHTML content that uses a Viewlink, also known as a document fragment, renders and behaves the same as standard HTML content in the main Web page. You can link together separate document fragments for visual effect, but these document fragments remain isolated from each other within the object model. Script in the primary document (the Web page being displayed by the browser) does not affect the rendering of the behavior unless you add public methods and properties to the component definition to make this possible.

Features of Viewlink

Using document fragments, you can design and build sophisticated Web applications through a highly modular approach. You can encapsulate components such that their functionality, methods, and style sheet properties are completely hidden from the primary document. This eliminates the possibility that the structure of the primary document, which uses the element behavior, will be affected by other document styles that might influence the behavior in unexpected ways.

Element behaviors that use Viewlinks differ from standard element behaviors in several ways. For an element behavior that uses a Viewlink, the custom element in the primary document is referred to as the master element. This distinction is made because each type of element behavior has a different effect on the primary document. The document fragment of an element behavior using a Viewlink does not appear in the primary document, but it is rendered as part of the primary document's content. In contrast, the document fragment of a standard element behavior is appended to the custom element and appears directly in the primary document.

Benefits of Viewlinks

The following list describes some of the many benefits of the Viewlink feature:

- **Reduce the complexity of the primary document.** You can partition the primary document into multiple document fragments by using nested Viewlink components. Encapsulating these document fragments in .htc files reduces the complexity of the primary document. The .htc files can be imported into other .htc files, such that the components are nested. Nesting can be done with standard element behaviors, as well as behaviors that use Viewlinks, and is an efficient method for building content and script in multiple layers.

- **Easily control CSS inheritance.** You can avoid many problems with DHTML behavior development, such as unexpected formatting of the component content. When you define styles in .htc files, they take precedence over styles set in the primary document. Styles in the primary document are not inherited by Viewlink components unless you permit such inheritance by design.

- **Define separate tabbing sequences for Viewlink components.** Tabbing for Viewlink components is encapsulated and independent from the tabbing sequence in the primary document. Elements in document fragments follow their own tabbing sequences, which are defined by the **tabIndex** property. This capability provides an additional measure of control, because you can specify the tabbing within the document fragments as well as whether the master elements of Viewlink components participate in the tabbing sequence of the primary document.

Lightweight HTML Component Support

Internet Explorer provides an additional enhancement to the behavior component model—support for lightweight HTML components. When you implement behaviors as HTML components by using .htc files, the files are built and parsed as separate HTML documents. This capability is extremely useful, because it allows Viewlink components to declaratively define the display of the element behaviors on the Web pages. However, when a large number of element behaviors are assembled in a single Web page, the page might load slowly in the browser window.

To prevent a separate HTML document from being built, you can mark your component as lightweight by specifying the **lightweight** attribute for the PUBLIC:COMPONENT element. The .htc files for these lightweight HTML components contain no HTML content or contain static HTML content that is ignored. Only the <PUBLIC:*> declarations and the script of the component are processed.

Lightweight HTML components are useful when behaviors do not require Viewlinks to render content or when there is no content to render. For example, you might want to use lightweight HTML components when you need to include multiple instances of the same custom element. In this case, using lightweight HTML components eliminates unnecessary parsing and memory usage and reduces the complexity of the primary document structure.

Enhanced Frame and Iframe Support

Internet Explorer uses the Viewlink technology to make frames and iframes (inline floating frames) more efficient. This technology enables a single browser window to host multiple frames, rather than opening a separate instance of the browser for each frame, which was necessary with Internet Explorer 5 and earlier. This enhancement greatly improves the performance of Web pages that include frames, allowing faster rendering, less memory usage, and faster scrolling. As a result, you can build applications that use frames as components and achieve compelling visual effects, such as transparent content and content layering.

The enhanced frame and iframe support includes the following key features:

- **Z-index-positioned elements.** The IFRAME object is now windowless and supports the **z-index** attribute. You can position IFRAME elements, also known as inline floating frames, on Web pages and lay content from the host documents over the iframes by using the **z-index** attribute. By specifying the z-index order for inline floating frames, you can stack one frame on top of another.

  In earlier versions of Internet Explorer, the IFRAME object is windowed and, like all windowed controls, ignores the **z-index** attribute. If you maintain Web pages that were designed for earlier versions of Internet Explorer, you might want to redesign the pages, especially if they contain IFRAME objects that are stacked on top of windowed controls.

- **Transparent content.** You can now overlap IFRAME elements and make the content inside these frames transparent. By declaring the background of the frame's document to be transparent and having the container declare that it allows transparency, the background of the document can show through the transparent container.

Enhanced CSS Support

Internet Explorer provides improved support for Cascading Style Sheets, Level 1 (CSS1). When you build your Web pages and applications, you can take advantage of the following CSS1 features:

- **CSS styles for inline elements.** The CSS styles for borders, padding, and margins are now supported for inline elements, such as SPAN and B, that can wrap across lines of text.

- **Dotted and dashed borders.** You can use the CSS1 **border-style** property to add dotted and dashed border effects to your HTML documents.

- **First-letter and first-line pseudo-elements.** The first-letter and first-line pseudo-elements allow you to lay out articles in the same style used by newspapers and magazines. Using these pseudo-elements, you can apply one or more styles to change the font characteristics for the first letter or the first line of a paragraph. For example, you can use the first-letter pseudo-element to create common typographical effects, such as drop caps, the effect obtained when the first character of a paragraph is rendered in a font larger than the rest.

- **Vertical text layout.** You can now display text vertically on Web pages by setting the CSS1 **writing-mode** attribute to a value of "tb-lr." This feature is extremely important for authoring in traditional Chinese and Japanese, because these languages require that text be laid out vertically from top to bottom and from right to left on Web pages. In previous browser versions, you needed to use images or horizontal layout to render text vertically. However, these techniques are not conducive to optimal publishing of Chinese and Japanese content.

- **Standards-compliant mode.** You can use the **!DOCTYPE** declaration to switch Internet Explorer 6 into standards-compliant mode and specify the Document Type Definition (DTD), such as HTML 4.0 or XML, to which a document theoretically complies. When you turn on this mode, Internet Explorer complies with the CSS1 box model for calculating and rendering the width and height properties of an element.

HTML+TIME 2.0 Multimedia Support

To help you create media-rich interactive content, Internet Explorer provides enhanced multimedia support. HTML+Timed Interactive Multimedia Extensions (TIME) 2.0, which was first released in Internet Explorer 5.5, adds timing, media synchronization, and animation support to Web pages. HTML+TIME allows you to define how elements in different parts of Web pages appear, disappear, and respond to events or time values.

HTML+TIME 2.0 is based on the XHTML+SMIL (Synchronized Multimedia Integration Language) profile in the *SMIL 2.0 Proposed Recommendation*. With HTML+TIME, you can use persistent Extensible Markup Language (XML) elements and attributes to add images, video, animation, and sounds to pages, and then synchronize them with each other and with HTML elements. For example, you can create slide show-style Web presentations with synchronized text, images, audio, video, and streaming media. You can create these presentations so that they are timed, interactive, or a combination of both.

To add timing to an HTML document, you simply add new attributes to your existing HTML elements. The HTML+TIME attributes specify when an element appears on a page, how long it remains displayed, and how the surrounding HTML elements are affected. In addition to the attributes, new XML-based elements make it simple for you to incorporate media into Web pages. For example, you can use the AUDIO or VIDEO element to add media to a page, and then you can add HTML+TIME attributes to specify when the media should start, when it should stop, and how many times it should repeat.

HTML elements can be grouped into hierarchical relationships so that you can easily manipulate multiple HTML elements at the same time. You can specify element grouping by using the PAR, SEQ, or EXCL time container element in a document or by setting the **timecontainer** attribute. This type of time container defines whether HTML elements will appear and disappear sequentially on the page, appear and disappear one at a time in a non-sequential (exclusive) order, or use independent (parallel) timing.

You do not need to know how to program with scripting languages to make your Web pages more dynamic with HTML+TIME. However, if you already know how to use scripting languages, you can use HTML+TIME properties, methods, and events to add even more interactive features to your Web pages.

HTML+TIME 2.0 Features

HTML+TIME 2.0 includes the following features:

- **Animation support.** The animate, set, animateMotion, and animateColor elements allow you to move HTML elements on Web pages along a path or series of points, change an element's color, and change other attributes such as height without using scripts.

- **The EXCL element.** For highly interactive content that includes multiple narratives, advertisements, or instructional material, you can include the EXCL element, which allows users to select from multiple items or media types. For example, users can select from multiple movies or streams to watch; the streams can also include advertisements that pause and restart the main content. The EXCL element automatically disables the inactive media or HTML elements and manages the playback according to users' selections.

- **The switch element.** The switch element allows you to display content based on conditional system test attributes within your Web page. The **systemBitrate** test attribute enables your page to automatically select between high bandwidth and low bandwidth content depending on the user's connection speed. The switch element also works with the **systemCaptions**, **systemLanguage**, and **systemOverdubOrSubtitle** accessibility test attributes.

- **Accessibility support.** New system attributes provide additional accessibility support for the browser. The **systemCaptions** attribute enables you to display text when the user has chosen to display captions. Other new system attributes include **systemLanguage** and **systemOverdubOrSubtitle**, which select content based on the user's system settings. For example, if a Web page includes both French and English language versions and the user's system is set to the French language, the page will display only French text and play only the French multimedia files.

- **t: namespace qualifier.** The **t:** namespace qualifier is no longer needed for attributes (the **t:** prefix is still needed for HTML+TIME elements, however). For example, to specify the start time for a movie clip, now you can use **begin** rather than **t:begin**.

- **The transitionFilter element.** In Internet Explorer 6, you can now use the transitionFilter element to add transitions to your Web page without using script. This element provides very fine control over the progress of the transition and leverages the timing and animation attributes supported by the animate and animateMotion animation elements.

HTML+TIME Timing Model

The timing model for HTML+TIME simplifies the process of authoring timed, interactive content by providing a single set of attributes for adding timing and synchronization to any element. Unlike traditional animation, which uses rigid timelines or event-based relationships to introduce interactive elements, HTML+TIME uses timing attributes to describe static, or determinate, time relationships. These attributes make it easy to place elements in time and to ensure synchronization among media elements.

By using timing attributes, you can author interactive content with beginning and ending times that are synchronized to a specific event. In this case, the time at which the event occurs defines the timing relationship. When the associated event, such as a user's clicking a button, occurs, the element is added into the Web page's running timeline as though it had been defined from the beginning. This running timeline starts as soon as the page loads and continues to progress as long as the browser renders the page. The elements can also have a duration and repeat count just as do other traditional timing elements, even though they begin in response to an event.

Browser Compatibility

HTML+TIME 1.0 features are supported in Internet Explorer 5 and later. You are encouraged to use HTML+TIME 2.0, which is supported in Internet Explorer 5.5 and later, because of the numerous new features and the simplified authoring it offers. If a browser that does not support HTML+TIME encounters a reference to a behavior, the style is ignored, and the element is rendered normally on the Web page. However, if the behavior exposes properties, methods, or events, scripting errors might occur. To address these errors, you should use a version-checking script.

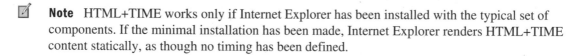

Note HTML+TIME works only if Internet Explorer has been installed with the typical set of components. If the minimal installation has been made, Internet Explorer renders HTML+TIME content statically, as though no timing has been defined.

Enhanced Visual Filters and Transitions

You can take advantage of enhancements to DHTML filters and transitions, which allow you to create multimedia-style effects on Web pages without increasing the requirements for download time and bandwidth on client computers. Visual filters are extensions to CSS properties that change the display of an object's contents. Transitions are time-varying filters that create a transition from one visual state to another.

You can apply visual filters and transitions to standard HTML controls, such as text containers, images, and other windowless objects, and add basic scripting to create visually engaging and interactive documents. You can specify the **filter** property for almost any object, although the object must have layout (a defined height and width) before the filter effect will display. You can also assign multiple filters or transitions to an object by declaring each filter in the **filter** property of the object, and each filter can include a set of optional parameters that define the nature of the effect, such as color or duration. For example, you can use visual filters and transitions to make an object fade in and fade out and to specify parameters to manage the timing of this effect.

Some of the new optimized filters that allow you to create these special effects include the following:

- **Gradient filter.** The gradient filter allows color gradients (including transparency) to be rendered on the client computers at the resolution of their display without the need to author images that contain a pre-determined gradient at a fixed resolution. You can also dynamically change the color values that define the gradient by using the properties exposed by the filter.

- **Matrix filter.** The Matrix filter enables you to transform elements by applying different scales and rotations. At any time, you can increase or decrease the size of objects and rotate them from 0 to 360 degrees.

- **AlphaImageLoader filter.** The AlphaImageLoader filter displays an image within the boundaries of the object and between the object background and content, with options to clip or resize the image. When revealed by a transition, any text that covers an AlphaImageLoader filtered image is initially exposed as transparent. When the transition completes, the text is instantly updated to the applicable color.

Note Because there are behavioral differences between how visual filters and transitions are applied and rendered in Internet Explorer 5.5 and in later versions, it is recommended that you replace filters and transitions developed for earlier versions of the browser.

Browsers that support the **filter** property can do so in different ways without affecting your Web page designs. Browsers that do not support the **filter** property simply ignore the filters.

You cannot apply visual filters and transitions to the following elements:

o   The OBJECT, EMBED, and APPLET elements

o   The SELECT and OPTION form elements

o   The TABLE, TR, THEAD, TBODY, and TFOOT table elements

Other Visual Effects

To make your Web pages more visually appealing, you can add other visual effects, including pop-up windows, colored scroll bars, and zoom capabilities to your HTML content.

Pop-up Windows

Pop-up technology allows you to display HTML content outside the boundaries of the Internet Explorer window. In Internet Explorer versions 4.0 and 5.0, you can create menu and ToolTip effects by positioning DIV elements, but you cannot display them outside the browser window, because they will be clipped. In Internet Explorer 5.5 and later, you are no longer restricted to the browser window.

In your HTML documents, you can include script for the POPUP object, which creates and displays a separate pop-up window. This is particularly useful for displaying menus, ToolTips, dialog boxes, message boxes, and other temporary windows that appear separately from the browser's main window.

Colored Scroll Bars

DHTML documents are no longer restricted to the Windows operating system's standard gray scroll bars. You can now specify the color of scroll bars by using style sheets. This feature is particularly useful when you want to create a user interface with coordinated themes. You can specify scroll bar colors that match the visual theme of your document.

The following <STYLE> syntax identifies the various parts of the scroll bars for which you can choose colors:

```
<STYLE>
    .TA {scrollbar-3dlight-color:<color>;
            scrollbar-arrow-color:<color>;
            scrollbar-base-color:<color>;
            scrollbar-darkshadow-color:<color>;
            scrollbar-face-color:<color>;
            scrollbar-highlight-color:<color>;
            scrollbar-shadow-color:<color>}
</STYLE>
```

Zoom

You can now add to your documents the ability to *zoom*—increase and decrease the magnification—so that users can focus on any part of the application window. Zoom is supported as a CSS property on any element. You can add the **zoom** attribute to your HTML documents and specify a value for the **vMagnification** variable, which sets or retrieves the magnification scale for the object.

Zoom allows you to create a variety of interesting visual effects. For example, you can display a large document on the screen and allow a user to highlight and magnify certain areas, or you can offer thumbnail views of documents.

HTML Editing Support

To support the development of Web pages and applications using DHTML, Internet Explorer includes the Microsoft® MSHTML Editor. This editing environment is built on MSHTML, Internet Explorer's HTML parsing and rendering engine.

MSHTML supports the following important capabilities:

- **Full HTML editing within the browser window.** Internet Explorer provides support for editable regions within an HTML document, allowing you to create documents that can be edited directly in the browser. When you build Web pages, you can use the **contentEditable** attribute to identify the content of an object that can be edited. This means that you can switch any element in a document to edit mode at any time and allow the user to do full WYSIWYG (what you see is what you get) editing of the document's HTML content.

  In earlier versions of Internet Explorer, this editing capability was available only when a document was in design mode. Now, individual elements in a document can be edited while the document is in browse mode. For example, you can develop sophisticated online editing applications, create forms that allow users to enter formatted text, or have a page on a Web site that each user can customize with unique content.

- **The ability to build Window 32-bit applications with full HTML editing.** Applications can now host the Mshtml.dll component of Internet Explorer to provide full HTML text editing and Web authoring features.Host applications can now also extend, modify, or replace the basic functionality of the editing component itself. By writing custom extensions known as *designers*, you can include specialized feature sets and seamlessly integrate them with the editing component's native functionality. For example, you can develop full-featured text editing applications, such as e-mail editors or online word processor, as well as Web authoring applications, such as Web page designers, forms editors, or online greeting card applications.

Text Editing Features

The MSHTML editing environment supports standard text editing features, including font size, text color, indenting, and justification, that were introduced in earlier versions of the browser. In addition, Internet Explorer now supports the following new and enhanced text editing features:

- **Batch undo and redo.** Users can delete and restore an entire sentence rather than one character at a time.

- **Auto-detection undo.** If users do not want an auto-detected link to be active, they can now remove the link by using the BACKSPACE key.

- **Preservation of text formatting during cut, copy, and paste operations.** MSHTML improves the preservation of text formatting during cut, copy, and paste operations. For example, if a user copies a line of text that is formatted in bold red Verdana and then pastes it into a block of text that is formatted in black Times Roman, the pasted text retains its bold red Verdana formatting.

- **Preservation of text formatting for empty lines.** Text formatting that users add to empty lines is now preserved. For example, if a user formats a line as 16-point italic Haettenschweiler, presses ENTER a few times, and then types text in the empty lines, the text is displayed in 16-point italic Haettenschweiler rather than in the document's default font.

- **Tri-state format information.** Host applications can now obtain tri-state formatting information. For example, a host application can determine not only whether a selection is bold but also whether it contains a combination of both bold and non-bold text.

- **Atomic selection.** The new **atomic selection** attribute causes an entire element to be treated as a single unit for purposes of selection and keyboard navigation. You can use this attribute to ensure that an element is kept intact, particularly if users' changes would invalidate the contents. Users can delete or replace the element, but not alter it.

- **Vertical text editing.** This feature is primarily intended for users who are editing in Chinese or Japanese, but vertical text editing is supported for plain ASCII text as well. Characters in Western fonts are rotated to the right so that the text is displayed as though the whole block of text were rotated clockwise.

- **Bidirectional editing.** Bidirectional text support allows the key navigation direction to switch between left-to-right and right-to-left orientation. Bidirectional text is used primarily for Hebrew and Arabic text. Frequently, however, certain words or phrases in English or other Latin-based languages are inserted within Arabic or Hebrew text. The key navigation direction automatically switches to a left-to-right orientation when the Latin character set is encountered, and back to right-to-left when the Hebrew or Arabic character set is detected.

- **Input Method Editor (IME) reconversion.** IME reconversion allows users who are typing in Japanese to convert back and forth between the phonetic spelling of a word (using the standard Western keyboard) and the Japanese character that represents the word. When a user types a phonetic representation of a word, a candidate list is displayed on the screen. The user can select the intended word or phrase from among several different possible representations in the candidate list, and the user's selection then replaces the phonetic representation in the document.

Web Authoring Features

MSHTML supports basic Web authoring features, such as insertion, controls, inline frames, and images, which were introduced in earlier versions of the browser. In addition, Internet Explorer now supports the following new and enhanced Web authoring features:

- **Multiple selection.** Users can select several elements at the same time and drag or resize them simultaneously.

- **Two-dimensional positioning.** Users can position elements anywhere on Web pages by dragging and dropping them.

- **Live resizing.** Users get live WYSIWYG feedback as they resize an element. For example, when a user drags the mouse to resize an image, it is resized in real time rather than when the mouse button is released.

- **Unit preservation.** The units of measurement originally used to specify an element's size and position are now preserved when the element is moved or resized.

- **Unselectable UI elements.** You can create user interface elements that do not cause the current selection to be destroyed when users click the elements. This feature is particularly useful for creating controls that change the formatting of the current selection. It allows you to change several formatting properties, one after another, without having to reselect the text between these changes.

- **Snap-to-grid support.** Host applications can include the new IHTMLEditHost interface to provide snap-to-grid support. If this interface is present, MSHTML allows host applications to control the final placement of elements when they are moved and resized.

- **Acceptance of visibility:hidden and display:none in design mode.** To provide full WYSIWYG editing, host applications can now accept the **visibility:hidden** and **display:none** attributes. By default, these attributes are ignored in edit mode.

- **Overriding of default cursor behavior.** Host applications can override the default cursor behavior in the editor and take full control of the cursor. Applications can also restore the default cursor behavior at any time.

- **Option to generate CSS styles.** For browsers that do not support CSS, MSHTML enables host applications to specify whether to generate CSS styles during editing.

- **Custom extensions.** You can now modify the Internet Explorer editing component itself by building designers. You can add new editing features, augment existing features, and override the default behavior of the editing component. Designers can intercept all events and keyboard accelerators and handle them before and/or after the editing component does. Designers can also define their own custom commands and expose virtually any type of functionality through their own custom interfaces.

Additional Resources

These resources contain additional information and tools related to this chapter.

Related Information Outside the Resource Kit

- The Microsoft Windows Technologies Internet Explorer Web site at http://www.microsoft.com/.
- The MSDN Web site at http://msdn.microsoft.com/.

Accessibility Features and Functionality

This chapter describes the different ways that Microsoft® Internet Explorer 6 supports enhanced accessibility and explains how you can use the browser to accommodate different accessibility needs. In particular, Internet Explorer has many features that enable users with disabilities to customize the appearance of Web pages to meet their own needs and preferences. If you are a user without disabilities, you might also be interested in this functionality, which enables you to customize colors and fonts to your own tastes and to use time-saving keyboard shortcuts.

In This Chapter

Related Information in the Resource Kit

- For more information about planning accessibility features for users with disabilities, see "Planning the Deployment."

- For more information about testing accessibility features before installing Internet Explorer 6 and Internet Tools, see "Setting Up and Administering a Pilot Program."

- For more information about deploying Internet Explorer to your user groups, see "Deploying Microsoft Internet Explorer 6."

Overview: Browser Accessibility

Internet Explorer 6 makes the Web more accessible to computer users with disabilities. If you are blind or have low vision, are deaf or hard-of-hearing, or have physical impairments, seizure disorders, or cognitive or language impairments, you can customize Internet Explorer to meet your needs.

The sections in this chapter cover the following topics:

- Accessibility benefits offered by Internet Explorer

- Upgrade considerations for transitioning from previous versions of Internet Explorer

- Suggested features that can accommodate different types of disabilities

- Keyboard navigation within the Internet Explorer browser, Internet Explorer Help, the Windows Desktop Update (if installed), and Web pages

- Customization of fonts, colors, and styles on Web pages, the Windows Desktop Update (if installed), and Internet Explorer Help

- Advanced Internet accessibility options, such as disabling or enabling sounds, images, and animations; the use of smooth scrolling; and the treatment of links

- Other accessibility resources, including telephone numbers, postal addresses, and Web sites

Accessibility Benefits

Microsoft products are designed to make computers easier to use for everyone, including people with disabilities. In recent years, products have been further enhanced according to feedback from users who have disabilities, organizations representing those users, workers in the rehabilitation field, and software developers who create products for the accessibility market.

If you are a user with disabilities, Internet Explorer 6 offers many features that can enhance your browsing experience. These features enable you to perform the following tasks:

- **Control how Web pages are displayed.** You can customize the colors of background, text, and links based on your preferences. By installing your own style sheets, you can control font styles and sizes for Web pages. You can create style sheets that make headings larger or highlight italicized text with a different color. These Web-page preferences also apply to content within the Microsoft® Windows® Explorer and Internet Explorer Help windows.

- **Work better with screen readers and other accessibility aids.** Internet Explorer 6 uses the HTML 4.0 standard, which enables Web-page designers to specify additional information on Web pages, such as the name of an image or control, for use by screen readers. You can also turn off smooth scrolling and other effects that can confuse screen readers. In addition, the Dynamic HTML Object Model in Internet Explorer enables developers to create other accessibility aids for users with disabilities.

- **Reduce the amount of typing required.** With the AutoComplete feature turned on, Internet Explorer resolves partially typed URLs based on a cached history of sites that you have visited. This feature makes it easier for you to type long or repetitive URLs. Explorer bars for Search, History, and Favorites also make it easier for you to find the items that you need.

- **Perform tasks easily by customizing the desktop layout.** If you have installed Windows Desktop Update, you can further customize your desktop, **Start** menu, and taskbar. You can choose from a range of desktop toolbars, or create your own. By clicking **Favorites** on the **Start** menu, you can quickly access preferred sites. Also, the Address bar enables you to enter URLs directly from the Microsoft Windows desktop, without having to open the browser first.

- **Get better feedback.** Two sound events in Control Panel, Start Navigation and Complete Navigation, signal when a Web page begins loading and when the page finishes loading. These sounds can be helpful if you are blind or have low vision. You can also set the appearance of links to show when they are activated or hovered over with a mouse.

- **Use a mouse with greater ease.** If you have installed Windows Desktop Update, you can choose to single-click rather than double-click the mouse to initiate common computer operations, such as opening folders. Also, you can put the most commonly used commands and shortcuts on desktop toolbars so that you can access them with a single mouse click.

- **Navigate with the keyboard.** Using your keyboard, you can navigate through Web pages, panes, links, toolbars, and other controls. Keyboard shortcuts also make it easy for you to work with Favorites, use the Address bar, and perform editing functions, such as cut and paste.

- **Replace images with textual descriptions.** You might want to turn off the display of pictures in Internet Explorer and read the textual description of the image instead.

- **Turn off animation, pictures, videos, and sounds.** If you are blind or have low vision, you might want to turn off animation, pictures, videos, and sounds to improve computer performance. Sounds can interfere with screen readers that read text aloud. You might also want to disable these functions if you have cognitive disabilities or are sensitive to motion or sound.

- **Use the High Contrast option.** High contrast enables you to choose a simple color scheme and omit images that might make text difficult to read.

Upgrade Considerations

Changes in software architecture might affect the functionality of some accessibility aids that were written for previous versions of Internet Explorer. Test Internet Explorer 6 with your accessibility aids to determine if the behavior differs from previous versions. Also, you can contact vendors to find out how the different accessibility aids function with Internet Explorer 6.

Depending on your specific needs, you might encounter challenges in using the different features of Internet Explorer 6. You can easily customize those features by installing or uninstalling components based on the functionality that works best for you. You can also turn on or off many features, according to your preferences.

The following list provides some general tips to consider when upgrading to Internet Explorer 6:

- If you have installed Windows Desktop Update, it replaces the traditional **Start** menu with a scrolling **Start** menu that supports dragging so that you can rearrange menu items. However, this type of menu limits the number of menu commands that are visible at one time to those commands that fit in a single column. Although long menu lists do not display all of the commands at once, you can navigate to them all by using the keyboard.

  If you need to keep as many options as possible available on the screen at one time and you currently have many commands on your **Start** menu, you might want to remove some commands from the **Start** menu. You might also want to use the desktop toolbar, the Quick Launch toolbar, or the custom toolbar feature to make the commands available from other places on the desktop.

- Internet Explorer 6 uses menus and check boxes that some screen readers might not interpret correctly. If you have installed Windows Desktop Update, Windows Explorer also uses these menus. To determine the level of support, test these features with your accessibility aids. Also, contact the vendors of your accessibility aids to find out about upgrades that might better support Internet Explorer 6.

Suggested Features for Different Types of Disabilities

The following sections suggest features that can benefit users with certain types of disabilities. The list of features for each type of disability is not complete, because the needs and preferences of individuals vary, and some people have a combination of disabilities or varying abilities.

To learn more about these features or to find procedures that explain how to configure a specific setting, see "Using Keyboard Navigation," "Customizing Fonts, Colors, and Styles," and "Configuring Advanced Internet Accessibility Options" later in this chapter.

Features for Users Who Are Blind

If you are blind, you might depend on a screen reader, which provides spoken or Braille descriptions of windows, controls, menus, images, text, and other information that is typically displayed visually on a screen. Internet Explorer 6 provides improved functionality for screen readers and offers a range of other features that might be helpful to you.

You might benefit from the following features:

- Use the keyboard to navigate Internet Explorer, Web pages, and Internet Explorer Help.
- Ignore colors specified on Web pages.
- Ignore font styles and sizes specified on Web pages.
- Format documents by using an individualized style sheet.
- Expand alternate text for images.
- Move the system caret with focus and selection changes. Some accessibility aids use the system caret to determine which area of the screen to read or magnify.
- Disable smooth scrolling.
- Choose not to show pictures, animations, and videos in Web pages.
- Disable smart image dithering.
- Assign a sound to the Start Navigation and Complete Navigation events.

Features for Users Who Have Low Vision

Common forms of low vision are color blindness, difficulty in changing focus, and impaired contrast sensitivity. If you have color blindness, you might have difficulty reading colored text on a colored background. If you have difficulty changing focus or experience eye strain with normal use of a video display, you might have difficulty reading small text, discriminating between different font sizes, or using small on-screen items as targets for the cursor or pointer. If you have impaired contrast sensitivity, you might have difficulty reading black text on a gray background.

You might benefit from the following features:

- Use the keyboard to navigate Internet Explorer, Web pages, and Internet Explorer Help.
- Ignore colors specified on Web pages.
- Ignore font styles and sizes specified on Web pages.
- Format documents by using an individualized sheet.
- Expand alternate text for images.
- Move the system caret with focus and selection changes. Some accessibility aids use the system caret to determine which area of the screen to read or magnify.
- Disable printing of background colors and images.
- Choose text and background colors for Web pages (or create custom colors).
- Choose the visited and unvisited colors for Web links (or create custom colors).
- Display Web pages in the Windows High Contrast color scheme, which offers a simple color palette and omits images that make text difficult to read.
- Assign a sound to the Start Navigation and Complete Navigation events.
- Add the **Size** button to the browser toolbar so font sizes can be changed easily.
- Display large icons.

Features for Users Who Are Deaf or Hard-of-Hearing

Sound cues in programs are not useful when you work in a noisy environment or if you have hearing impairments. If you are deaf, you might use sign language as your primary language and English as your secondary language. As a result, you might have difficulty reading pages that use custom fonts, depart from the standardized use of uppercase and lowercase letters, or use animated text displays.

You might benefit from the following features:

- Select **SoundSentry**, which generates visual warnings when the computer makes a sound.
- Select **ShowSounds**, which displays captions for the speech and sounds that the computer makes.
- Disable sounds in Web pages.

Note If you are deaf, you might also be interested in the features recommended for users with cognitive and language impairments.

Features for Users with Physical Impairments

If you have physical impairments, you might find it difficult to perform certain manual tasks, such as manipulating a mouse or typing two keys at the same time. You might also hit multiple keys or "bounce" fingers off keys, making typing difficult. Therefore, you might want to adapt keyboard and mouse functions to meet your requirements.

You might benefit from the following features:

- Use the keyboard to navigate Internet Explorer, Web pages, and Internet Explorer Help.
- Use Explorer bars.
- Ignore font sizes specified on Web pages.
- Format documents by using an individualized style sheet.
- Add hover colors to links.
- Expand alternate text for images.
- Move the system caret with focus and selection changes. Some accessibility aids use the system caret to determine which area of the screen to read or magnify.
- Use inline AutoComplete.
- Underline links when hovering.
- Add the **Size** button to the browser toolbar so font sizes can be changed easily.
- Display large icons.

Features for Users with Seizure Disorders

If you have a seizure disorder, such as epilepsy, you might be sensitive to screen refresh rates, blinking or flashing images, or specific sounds.

You might benefit from the following features:

- Use the ESC key to turn off animations immediately.
- Disable animation.
- Disable video.
- Turn off sounds.

Note Even if you turn off sounds in Internet Explorer, sounds might still play if you have installed RealAudio or you are playing a movie.

Features for Users with Cognitive and Language Impairments

Cognitive impairments take many forms, including short-term and long-term memory loss, perceptual differences, and developmental disabilities. Common types of language impairment also include dyslexia and illiteracy. If you are learning the language used by your computer software as a second language, you might also be considered to have a form of language impairment.

You might benefit from the following features:

- Use the keyboard to navigate Internet Explorer, Web pages, and Internet Explorer Help.
- Use Explorer bars.
- Ignore colors specified on Web pages.
- Ignore font styles and sizes specified on Web pages.
- Format documents by using an individualized style sheet.
- Choose text and background colors for Web pages (or create custom colors).
- Choose the visited and unvisited colors for Web links (or create custom colors).
- Display Web pages in the Windows High Contrast color scheme, which offers a simple color palette and omits images that make text difficult to read.
- Choose a hover color for links.
- Expand alternate text for images.
- Move the system caret with focus and selection changes. Some accessibility aids use the system caret to determine which area of the screen to read or magnify.
- Choose to open the browser in full-screen mode, which removes all toolbars and scrollbars from the screen. This capability enables you to have more information on the screen at one time or to remove distractions from peripheral controls.
- Choose to display friendly URLs.
- Use inline AutoComplete.
- Choose not to use smooth scrolling.
- Disable images.
- Disable animation.
- Disable video.
- Add the **Size** button to the browser toolbar so font sizes can be changed easily.
- Display large icons.

Using Keyboard Navigation

One of the most important accessibility features is the ability to navigate by using the keyboard. Keyboard shortcuts are useful for people with a wide range of disabilities, as well as anyone who wants to save time by combining key commands with mouse control. This section describes the following keyboard navigation features:

- Internet Explorer shortcut keys
- AutoComplete shortcut keys
- Keyboard navigation of Web pages
- Keyboard navigation of Windows Desktop Update (if it is installed)
- Keyboard navigation of Internet Explorer Help

Internet Explorer Shortcut Keys

Shortcut keys can make it easier for you to move between screen elements, choose commands, and view documents. The following tables describe common tasks and their associated shortcut keys.

Shortcut Keys for Viewing and Exploring Web Pages

To	Press
View Internet Explorer Help	F1
Switch between the regular and full-screen views of the browser window	F11
Move forward through the Address bar, the Explorer bars, and the items, menus, and toolbars on a Web page	TAB
Move backward through the Address bar, the Explorer bars, and the items, menus, and toolbars on a Web page	SHIFT+TAB
Move forward between frames	CTRL+TAB
Move backward between frames	SHIFT+CTRL+TAB
Activate a selected link	ENTER
Display a shortcut menu for the page or link	SHIFT+F10
Go to the previous page	ALT+LEFT ARROW
Go to the next page	ALT+RIGHT ARROW
Scroll toward the beginning of a document	UP ARROW
Scroll toward the end of a document	DOWN ARROW
Scroll toward the beginning of a document in larger increments	PAGE UP or SHIFT+SPACEBAR
Scroll toward the end of a document in larger increments	PAGE DOWN or SPACEBAR
Move to the beginning of a document	HOME
Move to the end of a document	END
Stop downloading a page and stop animation	ESC
Refresh the current page only if the time stamps for the Web version and the locally stored version are different	F5 or CTRL+R

To	Press
Refresh the current page even if the time stamps for the Web version and the locally stored version are the same	CTRL+ F5
In the History or Favorites bar, open multiple folders	CTRL+CLICK
Open the Search Explorer bar	CTRL+E
Find on this page	CTRL+F
Open the History Explorer bar	CTRL+H
Open the Favorites Explorer bar	CTRL+I
Go to a new location	CTRL+O or CTRL+L
Open a new window	CTRL+N
Print the current page or active frame	CTRL+P
Save the current page	CTRL+S
Close the current window	CRTL+W

Shortcut Keys for Using the Address Bar

To	Press
Move the mouse pointer to the Address bar	ALT+D
Display the Address bar history	F4
When in the Address bar, move the cursor left to the next logical break character (. or /)	CTRL+LEFT ARROW
When in the Address bar, move the cursor right to the next logical break character (. or /)	CTRL+RIGHT ARROW
Add **www.** to the beginning and **.com** to the end of the text typed in the Address bar	CTRL+ENTER
Move forward through the list of AutoComplete matches	UP ARROW
Move backward through the list of AutoComplete matches	DOWN ARROW

Shortcut Keys for Working with Favorites

To	Press
Add the current page to the **Favorites** menu	CTRL+D
Open the **Organize Favorites** dialog box	CTRL+B

Shortcut Keys for Editing

To	Press
Select all items on the current Web page	CTRL+A
Copy the selected items to the Clipboard	CTRL+C
Insert the contents of the Clipboard at the selected location	CTRL+V
Remove the selected items and copy them to the Clipboard	CTRL+X

For additional information about using the keyboard with Windows, visit the Microsoft Accessibility Web site at http://www.microsoft.com/enable/.

AutoComplete Shortcut Keys

With the AutoComplete feature turned on, Internet Explorer automatically completes Web page addresses and directory paths as you type them in the Address bar. Internet Explorer resolves this information based on the Web pages or local files that you have visited. AutoComplete also works with the **Run** command on the **Start** menu.

For example, if you type **http://www.micr** and have recently visited http://www.microsoft.com/, AutoComplete suggests http://www.microsoft.com/. You can accept the match, view other potential matches, or override the suggestion by typing over it. AutoComplete also adds prefixes and suffixes to Internet addresses.

You can turn AutoComplete on or off in the **Internet Options** dialog box.

▶ **To turn AutoComplete on or off**

1. On the **Tools** menu, click **Internet Options**, and then click the **Advanced** tab.

2. Select or clear the **Use inline AutoComplete** checkbox, which specifies whether you want Internet Explorer to complete Web addresses automatically as you type them in the Address bar.

    This feature also causes Internet Explorer to complete file names, paths, or folders automatically as you type them in the Address bar or the **Open** box in the **Run** command.

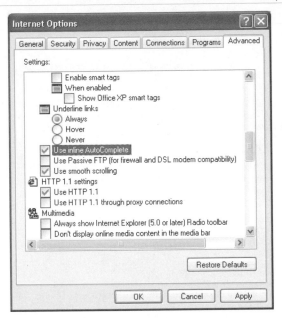

AutoComplete includes the following shortcuts:

- To add to the string that Internet Explorer has automatically completed, press the RIGHT ARROW key, and then type the additional characters.

- To skip to break characters or separator characters in URLs (such as the forward slash [/]), press and hold the CTRL key, and then use the LEFT ARROW or RIGHT ARROW key.

- To search a history file, type the beginning of an address, and then press the UP ARROW or DOWN ARROW key to complete it.

- To add **http://www.** before a partial URL and **.com** after it, press CTRL+ENTER.

Keyboard Navigation of Web Pages

You can move forward and backward through the items in the browser window by using the TAB and SHIFT+TAB keys. A one-pixel-wide border (called the focus box) appears around links, so that you can identify the selected item.

When you press the TAB key, the selection rotates forward through the browser window in the following order:

1. Address bar

   o To display the Address bar, on the **View** menu, point to **Toolbars**, and then click **Address Bar**.

2. Explorer bar

   o If an Explorer bar is open, you see an entry highlighted on the bar.

   o To display an Explorer bar, on the **View** menu, point to **Explorer Bar**, and then click **Search**, **Favorites**, **Media**, **History**, or **Folders**. Or, on the Internet Explorer toolbar, click the **Search**, **Favorites**, **Media**, **History**, or **Folders** icon.

   o To move between the items on the Explorer bar, use the LEFT ARROW, RIGHT ARROW, UP ARROW, and DOWN ARROW keys. To activate a link on the Explorer bar, press ENTER, or to open a shortcut menu for a link, press SHIFT+F10.

3. Links on the page, moving left to right, and then down

   o As a link is highlighted, its URL appears on the message bar.

   o To activate the link, press ENTER, or to open a shortcut menu for the link, press SHIFT+F10.

Note Web-page designers might specify a different order for their links than the standard left-to-right and top-to-bottom order.

To move between the same areas in reverse order, press SHIFT+TAB. Using reverse order, the focus stops on the page as a whole before reaching the links on the page. To quickly skip to the next frame, press CTRL+TAB, or to go to the previous frame, press CTRL+SHIFT+TAB.

Keyboard Navigation of Windows Desktop Update

If you have installed Windows Desktop Update, you can press TAB and SHIFT+TAB to move forward and backward through the desktop elements. A focus box appears around the selected item, so that you can identify it.

When you press the TAB key, the selection rotates forward through the desktop elements in the following order:

1. **Start** button

2. Quick Launch toolbar

   o One of the Quick Launch icons appears selected.

   o To move between the toolbar icons, press the LEFT ARROW, RIGHT ARROW, UP ARROW, and DOWN ARROW keys. After the focus is on an icon, to open the application, press ENTER, or to display the shortcut menu for the toolbar, press SHIFT+F10. (All the toolbars on the desktop share the same shortcut menu.)

   o To bring the focus back to the leftmost icon, continuously press the RIGHT ARROW key.

3. Taskbar

   o A selection does not appear on the taskbar. To display the shortcut menu for the toolbar, press SHIFT+F10. (All the toolbars on the desktop share the same shortcut menu.)

   o To select an application, press the RIGHT ARROW key. To open the selected application, press ENTER, or to display the shortcut menu for that application, press SHIFT+F10.

   o To move between the applications, press the LEFT ARROW, RIGHT ARROW, UP ARROW, and DOWN ARROW keys.

4. Desktop icons

   o An icon on the desktop appears selected.

   o To move between the icons on the desktop, press the LEFT ARROW, RIGHT ARROW, UP ARROW, and DOWN ARROW keys. To open the application or document, press ENTER, or to display the shortcut menu for that icon, press SHIFT+F10.

   o To select or deselect the current icon, press CTRL+SPACEBAR. To display the shortcut menu for the entire desktop when no icon is selected, press SHIFT+F10.

5. Desktop items

   o A desktop item appears selected.

   o To move forward through the links in that item and on to the other items on the desktop, press the TAB key. To activate a link, press ENTER.

6. Desktop Channel bar

   o The topmost button on the Channel bar appears selected.

   o To move between the icons on the Channel bar, press the LEFT ARROW, RIGHT ARROW, UP ARROW, and DOWN ARROW keys. To display a channel by using Internet Explorer, press ENTER.

   Note Internet Explorer 6 does not include the desktop Channel bar; this feature is a part of previous browser versions.

7. **Start** button

To move between the same areas in reverse order, press SHIFT+TAB. If you add other bars, such as the Address bar, Quick Links toolbar, desktop toolbar, or a custom toolbar, you can also navigate to these bars by pressing TAB and SHIFT+TAB. Note that you can reach the Channel bar only by pressing TAB; the Channel bar is skipped when you navigate in reverse order by using SHIFT+TAB.

Keyboard Navigation in Internet Explorer Help

Internet Explorer Help displays Help information as Web pages. This tool offers several significant accessibility advantages, which this section explains in detail. However, if you navigate by using the keyboard, this tool also introduces the following changes:

- When you display a topic in the right pane, it continues to be displayed until you replace it with another selection—that is, when you highlight another topic and then press ENTER. This display can be confusing during navigation, because the topic name currently selected in the left pane might not match the topic shown in the right pane.

- The **Hide** button on the Help toolbar hides the left pane (used for Contents, Index, Search, and Favorites). When the left pane is hidden, you cannot navigate through Help. To return to the **Contents**, **Index**, **Search**, or **Favorites** tab, press ALT+C, ALT+N, ALT+S, or ALT+I, respectively.

The following procedures describe how to navigate through the Internet Explorer Help **Contents**, **Index**, **Search**, and **Favorites** tabs by using the keyboard.

▶ **To navigate through the Help Contents by using the keyboard**

1. To view the **Contents** tab in Internet Explorer Help, press ALT+C.

    The following illustration shows the **Contents** tab for Internet Explorer Help.

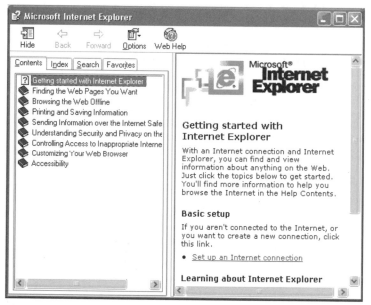

2. To scroll through the list of Contents topics, press the UP ARROW or DOWN ARROW key.
3. To display the expanded list of subtopics for a main topic, highlight the main topic and then press ENTER or the RIGHT ARROW key. An open main topic is represented by an open-book icon. A subtopic is represented by a page icon. To close the main topic, press ENTER or the LEFT ARROW key; the list of subtopics collapses, and a closed book icon appears.
4. To view topic information, highlight the subtopic, and then press ENTER. Internet Explorer Help displays the topic that you selected in the right pane.
5. To shift the keyboard focus to the topic, press F6. Within the topic, you can do the following:
    - To scroll up and down or left and right in the topic pane, press the UP ARROW and DOWN ARROW keys or the LEFT ARROW and RIGHT ARROW keys.
    - To display information about a linked topic, highlight the link, and then press ENTER.
    - To scroll to the beginning or end of the topic, press HOME or END.
    - To display the shortcut menu for the topic, press CTRL+F10.

6. To return to the **Contents** tab, press ALT+C.

7. To exit Help, press ALT+F4.

▶ **To navigate through the Help Index by using the keyboard**

1. To view the **Index** tab in Internet Explorer Help, press ALT+N. Initially, the keyboard focus is in the keyword box, and the box is empty.

    The following illustration shows the **Index** tab for Internet Explorer Help.

2. To scroll through the list of index topics, press the UP ARROW or DOWN ARROW key. As you scroll, each highlighted topic appears in the keyword box.

    You can also type the name of the topic you want to view in the keyword box. As you type, the Index list scrolls to highlight matching topics.

3. To display information about a highlighted topic, press ENTER or ALT+D. Internet Explorer Help displays the topic that you select in the right pane.

4. To move the keyboard focus to the topic, press F6. Within the topic, you can do the following:

    o   To scroll up and down or left and right in the topic pane, press the UP ARROW and DOWN ARROW keys or the LEFT ARROW and RIGHT ARROW keys.

    o   To display information about a linked topic, highlight the link, and then press ENTER.

    o   To scroll to the beginning or end of the topic, press HOME or END.

    o   To display the shortcut menu for the topic, press CTRL+F10.

5. To return to the **Index** tab, press ALT+N.

6. To exit Help, press ALT+F4.

▶ **To navigate through the Help Search by using the keyboard**

1. To view the **Search** tab in Internet Explorer Help, press ALT+S. The keyboard focus moves to the keyword box.

    The following illustration shows the **Search** tab for Internet Explorer Help.

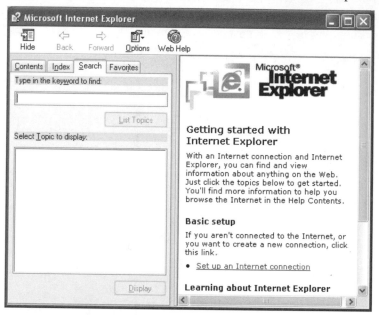

2. Type the keyword you want, and then press ENTER or ALT+L. The **Select Topic to display** list shows topics that contain the keyword you typed.

3. To move the keyboard focus to the first item in the **Select Topic to display** list, press ALT+T and then the DOWN ARROW key.

4. To highlight a topic, press the UP ARROW or DOWN ARROW key.

5. To display information about a highlighted topic, press ENTER or ALT+D. Internet Explorer Help displays the topic that you select in the right pane.

6. To move the keyboard focus to the topic, press F6. Within the topic, you can do the following:

    o   To scroll up and down or left and right in the topic pane, press the UP ARROW and DOWN ARROW keys or the LEFT ARROW and RIGHT ARROW keys.

    o   To display information about a linked topic, highlight the link, and then press ENTER.

    o   To scroll to the beginning or end of the topic, press HOME or END.

    o   To display the shortcut menu for the topic, press CTRL+F10.

7. To return to the **Search** tab, press ALT+S. The keyboard focus returns to the keyword box.

8. To exit Help, press ALT+F4.

▶ **To navigate through the Help Favorites by using the keyboard**

1. To view the **Favorites** tab in Internet Explorer Help, press ALT+I. The keyboard focus moves to the **Topics** list.

    The following illustration shows the **Favorites** tab in Internet Explorer Help.

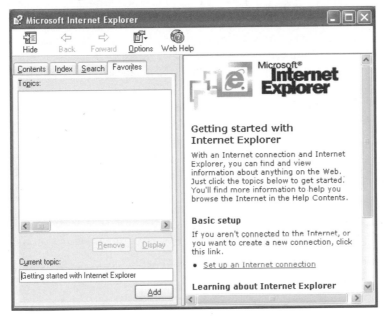

2. To highlight a topic, press the UP ARROW or DOWN ARROW key.

3. To display information about a highlighted topic, press ENTER or ALT+D. Internet Explorer Help displays the topic that you select in the right pane.

4. To move the keyboard focus to the topic, press F6. Within the topic, you can do the following:

    o   To scroll up and down or left and right in the topic pane, press the UP ARROW and DOWN ARROW keys or the LEFT ARROW and RIGHT ARROW keys.

    o   To display information about a linked topic, highlight the link, and then press ENTER.

    o   To scroll to the beginning or end of the topic, press HOME or END.

    o   To display the shortcut menu for the topic, press CTRL+F10.

5. The **Current topic** box displays the last topic that you viewed on the **Content**, **Index**, or **Search** tab. To add this topic to the favorites list so that you can access it quickly in the future, press ALT+A, or press the TAB key until the keyboard focus is on the **Current topic** box, and press ENTER.

6. To delete a highlighted topic from the favorites list, press ALT+R.

7. To return to the **Favorites** tab, press ALT+I.

8. To exit Help, press ALT+F4.

Customizing Fonts, Colors, and Styles

When Web authors and designers create Web pages, they often specify particular fonts, colors, and styles. They might specify the settings for each coded item on the Web page, or they might define the settings in a style sheet. A style sheet provides a template for specifying how different styles should appear throughout a Web site.

Internet Explorer 6 enables you to override any or all of these settings. You can specify your own font and color preferences for all Web pages. You can also use your own style sheet or select the Windows High Contrast option. If you have installed the Windows Desktop Update, these font, color, and style options also affect the Windows desktop and file folders.

Because Internet Explorer Help information is also displayed as Web pages, most of the browser accessibility features are also available for viewing Help topics. You can override and customize formatting and color settings, display text instead of images, disable animation, and even apply your own style sheet to control how Help is presented. When you adjust these options in Internet Explorer and then restart Help, the settings automatically apply to all Help topics.

Overriding Web-Page Formatting

Because of the different methods Web authors and designers can use to format Web pages, some pages might not be affected by customizing the font, color, and style options within the browser. To change the appearance of these pages, you must override the page formatting.

▶ **To override page formatting**

1. On the **Tools** menu, click **Internet Options**.
2. On the **General** tab, click **Accessibility**.
3. Select any of the following options:
   - **Ignore colors specified on Web pages**
   - **Ignore font styles specified on Web pages**
   - **Ignore font sizes specified on Web pages**
   - **Format documents using my style sheet**

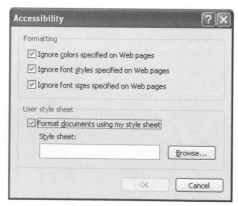

Changing Font Size

When you browse a Web page, you can immediately change the size of the displayed text to a larger or smaller font size.

▶ **To immediately display all text in a larger or smaller font size**

1. On the **View** menu, click **Text Size**, or click the **Size** button on the toolbar.
2. Choose the size you want. A check mark appears next to your choice, and the change takes effect immediately.

    If the **Size** button is not displayed, you can add it to the toolbar.

▶ **To add the Size button to the toolbar**

1. On the **View** menu, click **Toolbars**, and then click **Customize**.
2. In the **Available toolbar buttons** list, select **Size**, and then click **Add**.

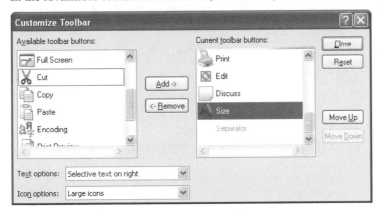

3. Click **Close**.

The changes created by the **Text Size** menu option and **Size** button are active for both current and future sessions.

Creating a High-Visibility Style Sheet

If you have low vision, you might want to create a high-visibility style sheet that adjusts the display of Web pages and Help topics so that you can read them more easily. In particular, this style sheet overrides normal formatting of all displayed pages in the following ways:

*   All items on the Web page appear in high contrast, with a black background and brightly colored text. Body text is white, highlighted text is yellow, and links are brighter versions of their normal blue and purple.
*   All text is displayed in a large, sans serif font. Body text is 24 point, and headings are 32 point.

- All bold, italic, and underlining, which might be difficult to read, are replaced by normal text with a single highlight color.
- The keyboard focus is emphasized by showing the active link in a bright, light green, sometimes called "low-vision green."

These settings affect all pages viewed in Internet Explorer, as well as pages displayed by other programs, such as HTML Help.

Note The style sheet in the following example is just one possible solution for increasing the readability of Web pages. By editing the style sheet, you can change the background color and the size, color, and style of the fonts according to your preferences.

▶ **To create a high-visibility style sheet**

1. Open Microsoft® Notepad.
2. Type the following text into a new file:

```
<STYLE TYPE="text/css">
<!--
BODY, TABLE {
font-size: 24pt;
font-weight: normal;
font-family: sans-serif;
background: black;
color: white;}

B, I, U {color: yellow; font-weight: normal; font-style: normal;}
H1 {font-size: 32pt;}
H2 {font-size: 32pt;}
H3 {font-size: 32pt;}
H4 {font-size: 32pt;}
H5 {font-size: 32pt;}

a:visited {color: #FF00FF}
a:link {color: #00FFFF}
a:active {color: #B1FB17}
-->
</STYLE>
```

3. Save the file with a .css file name extension (for example, Mystyle.css) to the folder of your choice.
4. In Internet Explorer, on the **Tools** menu, click **Internet Options**.

5. On the **General** tab, click **Accessibility**.

6. Click Format documents using my style sheet.

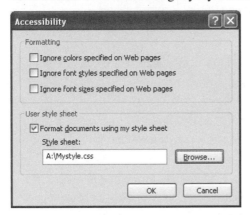

7. Type the path to the style sheet file you just created, or to locate the file, click **Browse**.

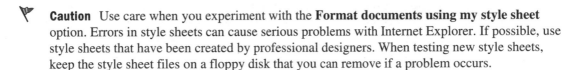

Caution Use care when you experiment with the **Format documents using my style sheet** option. Errors in style sheets can cause serious problems with Internet Explorer. If possible, use style sheets that have been created by professional designers. When testing new style sheets, keep the style sheet files on a floppy disk that you can remove if a problem occurs.

Changing Colors of Text, Backgrounds, and Other Objects

You can select the colors you prefer for text, backgrounds, links, and objects that the mouse pointer hovers over on Web pages.

▶ **To change the color of text, backgrounds, links, and objects that the mouse pointer hovers over**

1. On the **Tools** menu, click **Internet Options**.

2. On the **General** tab, click **Colors**.

3. Clear the **Use Windows colors** check box.

4. Click the **Use hover color** check box. The **Hover** button is enabled with the default color.

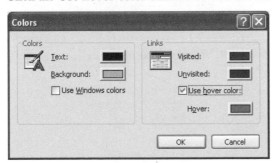

5. Click the **Text**, **Background**, **Visited**, **Unvisited**, or **Hover** button to display the **Color** dialog box, which includes the Basic colors and Custom colors palettes.

6. In the **Color** dialog box, click the color of your choice from the color palettes.

Creating Custom Colors

You can create custom colors for fonts, text background, links, and objects that the mouse pointer hovers over.

▶ **To create custom colors**

1. On the **Tools** menu, click **Internet Options**, and then click the **General** tab.

2. Click the **Colors** button.

3. In the **Colors** dialog box, click the **Text**, **Background**, **Visited**, or **Unvisited** button to display the **Color** dialog box, which includes the Basic colors and Custom colors palettes.

4. In the **Color** dialog box, click **Define Custom Colors**. The dialog box expands to include the Custom colors palette.

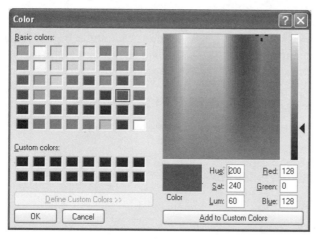

5. Select a custom color by using either of two methods:

    o Either type values for **Hue**, **Sat** (saturation), and **Lum** (luminescence), or type values for **Red**, **Green**, and **Blue**. The sample box changes color to reflect your choices.

    o Click within the color box to select a color, and then move the slider (on the right) up or down to select the luminescence level. The sample box changes color to reflect your choices.

6. Click Add to Custom Colors.

Selecting the Windows High Contrast Color Scheme

Instead of creating your own customized color scheme, you can choose to view Web pages by using the Windows High Contrast color scheme, which offers a simple color palette and omits images that make text difficult to read.

▶ **To view Web pages by using the Windows High Contrast color scheme**

1. On Microsoft® Windows® XP, click **Start**, and then click **Control Panel**.

    -Or-

    On other versions of Windows, click **Start**, point to **Settings**, and then click **Control Panel**.

2. On Windows XP, click Accessibility Options, and then under **or** pick a Control Panel icon, click Accessibility Options.

    -Or-

    On other versions of Windows, click **Accessibility Options**.

3. In the **Accessibility Options** dialog box, click the **Display** tab.

4. Select the **Use High Contrast** check box.

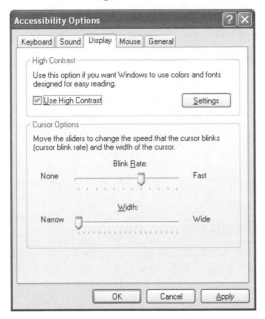

5. To select a specific high-contrast color scheme, click **Settings**.

Selecting a Full-Screen Browser Window

When you browse a Web page, you can choose to immediately change the size of the browser window to full screen.

▶ **To immediately change the size of the browser window to full screen**

- On the **View** menu, click **Full Screen**, click the **Full Screen** button on the toolbar, or click **F11** (shortcut key).

If the **Full Screen** button is not displayed, you can add it to the toolbar.

▶ **To add the Full Screen button to the toolbar**

1. On the **View** menu, click **Toolbars**, and then click **Customize**.
2. In the **Available toolbar buttons** list, select Full Screen, and then click Add.

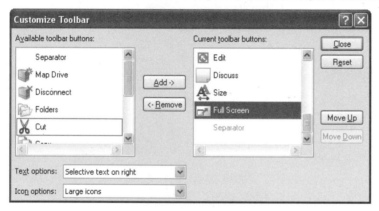

Note The changes created by the **Full Screen** menu option or the **Full Screen** button are active only for the current session.

Changing Button Size and Text Labels on the Toolbar

You might want to change the button size and text labels on the Internet Explorer toolbar. If you have low vision, you might want to view larger buttons on the toolbar rather than the smaller Microsoft® Office-style buttons. You can also choose whether to show text labels for the buttons.

▶ **To change button size and text labels on the toolbar**

1. On the **View** menu, click **Toolbars**, and then click **Customize**.
2. In the **Icon options** list, select the button size that you want to display on the toolbar.

3. In the **Text options** list, select whether to display text labels for the toolbar buttons.

    The following illustration shows the **Customize Toolbar** dialog box with **Show text labels** and **Large icons** selected.

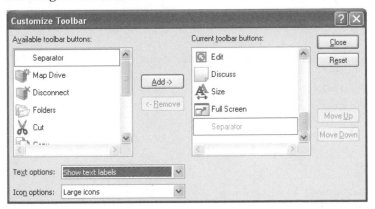

Understanding Font-Size Changes

The following list identifies the factors that affect font size and describes how these factors are applied in Internet Explorer. The factors are listed in the order they are applied when the browser displays a page.

1. The Internet Explorer display defaults (for example, P is size 3 and H1 is size 6).

2. A user-specified style sheet (if one is provided) and whether **Format documents using my style sheet** is selected in the **Accessibility** dialog box.

3. Style-sheet information in the document, unless **Ignore font sizes specified on Web pages** is selected in the **Accessibility** dialog box.

4. FONT tags in the document, unless **Ignore font sizes specified on Web pages** is selected in the **Accessibility** dialog box. Selecting this option does not override relative sizes that are implied by structural tags. For example, a top-level heading (H1) will still be larger than body text, even when **Ignore font sizes specified on Web pages** is turned on.

5. A scaling factor determined by the **Text Size** options accessible from the **View** menu, except in those cases where the font is specified in an absolute size, such as 12 point.

Font sizes can be specified in three ways:

*   As an index value (1–7)
*   As a relative value (+1, +5)
*   Using an absolute size unit, such as point or pixel (for example, 12pt, 32px)

Font sizes that are set by using index or relative values are affected by the **View** menu font options, while fonts set in absolute size units are not.

▶ **To set the font-scaling factor for the current browser session**

*   On the **View** menu, point to **Text Size**, and then click the option you want.

Configuring Advanced Internet Accessibility Options

You can configure many accessibility features on the **Advanced** tab in the **Internet Options** dialog box.

▶ **To configure advanced Internet accessibility options**

1. On the **Tools** menu, click **Internet Options**, and then click the **Advanced** tab.

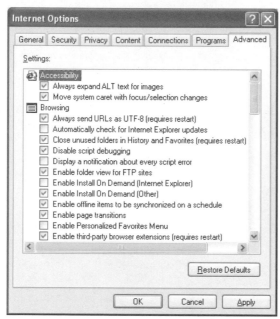

2. Scroll through the checklist, and clear or select the options you want.

For recommendations on selecting options for different types of disabilities, see "Suggested Features for Different Types of Disabilities" earlier in this chapter.

You might want to select the following options, depending on your disabilities:

- **Move system caret with focus/selection changes.** Specifies whether to move the system caret whenever the focus or selection changes. Some accessibility aids, such as screen readers and screen magnifiers, use the system caret to determine which area of the screen to read or magnify.

- **Always expand alt text for images.** Specifies whether to expand the image size to fit all of the alternate text when the **Show Pictures** check box is cleared.

- **Use inline AutoComplete.** Specifies whether to automatically complete Web addresses as you type them in the Address bar. Also, this option specifies whether to automatically complete names of files, paths, or folders as you type them in the Address bar or the **Open** box in the **Run** command. The AutoComplete feature suggests a match based on the Web sites, names of files, paths, or folder that you have visited.

  If you have cognitive disabilities, you might want to turn this option off to avoid distractions. If you have low vision and your accessibility aid reads the suggestions as they appear (making typing difficult), you also might want to turn this option off.

- **Show friendly URLs.** Specifies whether to show the full Internet address (URL) for a page on the status bar.

- **Underline links.** Specifies whether to underline links on Web pages. Older screen readers rely on underlining to recognize links. You can select one of the following settings:

  o **Always**, which underlines all links.

  o **Never**, which does not underline links.

  o **Hover**, which underlines links when the mouse pointer is placed over them.

- **Use smooth scrolling.** Specifies whether to scroll through Web pages, so that information gradually slides up or down the screen when you click on the scroll bar or press navigation keys, such as the DOWN ARROW key. If you have low vision, you might want to turn this option off because it might cause timing problems. If you have cognitive disabilities, you might want to turn this option off because the scrolling motion might be distracting.

- **Play animations in web pages.** Specifies whether animations can play when pages are displayed. Internet Explorer displays alternate text in place of the animations if the text is supplied on the Web page. If you clear this check box, you can still play an individual animation by right-clicking the icon that represents the animation and then clicking **Show Picture**. If you are blind or have seizure disorders, you might want to turn off animations (especially blinking). If you have cognitive disabilities, you might want to turn off animations or selectively download them to prevent distractions.

- **Play sounds in web pages.** Specifies whether to play audio sounds. If you have installed RealAudio or you are playing a movie, sounds might play even if you clear this check box. If you are deaf or hard-of-hearing or you have seizure disorders, you might want to turn off sounds. If you have cognitive disabilities, you might want to turn off sounds or selectively download them to prevent distractions. If you are blind, you might want to turn off sounds or selectively download them so that they do not conflict with the screen reader when it is reading text aloud.

- **Play videos in web pages.** Specifies whether to play video clips. If you clear this check box, you can still play an individual video by right-clicking the icon that represents the video and then clicking **Show Picture**. If you are blind or have seizure disorders, you might want to turn off videos. If you have cognitive disabilities, you might want to turn off videos or selectively download them to prevent distractions.

- **Show pictures.** Specifies whether to include images when pages are displayed. When available, Internet Explorer displays alternate text in place of the image. If you clear this check box, you can still display an individual image by right-clicking the icon that represents the image and then clicking **Show Picture**. If images are turned on or the textual description is cut off by space limitations, you can view the full description by moving the mouse over the image.

  Turning off images allows older screen readers to read the textual description for images aloud. However, newer screen readers can use Microsoft® Active Accessibility® to identify and read descriptions, even when the images are displayed on the screen. Turning off images speeds up browser performance, although it might interfere with the functionality and effectiveness of some Web sites.

- **Print background colors and images.** Specifies whether to print background colors and images when users print Web pages. If you have low vision or you want to speed up print time, you might want to turn this option off. If you are preparing text to be scanned—for example, to provide the text to a text reader—you might also want to turn this option off.

Accessibility Resources

The Microsoft Accessibility Web site at http://www.microsoft.com/enable/ contains information about Microsoft products and accessibility. This site also discusses how to design accessible Web pages that take advantage of new features in Internet Explorer 6 and offers information about tools and utilities that make Internet Explorer even more accessible.

The following sections describe additional resources that are available for people with disabilities.

Microsoft Services for People Who Are Deaf or Hard-of-Hearing

If you are deaf or hard-of-hearing, complete access to Microsoft product and customer services is available through a text telephone (TTY/TDD) service.

You can contact the Microsoft Sales Information Center on a text telephone by dialing (800) 892-5234 between 6:30 A.M. and 5:30 P.M. Pacific time.

For technical assistance in the United States, you can contact Microsoft Product Support Services on a text telephone at (425) 635-4948 between 6:00 A.M. and 6:00 P.M. Pacific time, Monday through Friday, excluding holidays. In Canada, dial (905) 568-9641 between 8:00 A.M. and 8:00 P.M. Eastern time, Monday through Friday, excluding holidays. Microsoft support services are subject to the prices, terms, and conditions in place at the time the service is used.

Microsoft Documentation in Other Formats

In addition to the standard forms of documentation, many Microsoft products are available in other formats to make them more accessible. Many Internet Explorer documents are also available as online Help or online user's guides, or from the Microsoft Web site. You can also download many Microsoft Press® books from the Microsoft Accessibility Web site at http://www.microsoft.com/enable/.

If you have difficulty reading or handling printed documentation, you can obtain many Microsoft publications from Recording for the Blind & Dyslexic, Inc. Recording for the Blind & Dyslexic distributes these documents to registered, eligible members of their distribution service, either on audiocassettes or on floppy disks. The Recording for the Blind & Dyslexic collection contains more than 80,000 titles, including Microsoft product documentation and books from Microsoft Press. For information about the availability of Microsoft product documentation and books from Recording for the Blind & Dyslexic, Inc., contact:

Recording for the Blind & Dyslexic, Inc.
20 Roszel Road
Princeton, NJ 08540

Telephone: (609) 452-0606
Fax: (609) 987-8116

Microsoft Products and Services for People with Disabilities

Microsoft provides a catalog of accessibility aids that you can use with Windows XP, Microsoft® Windows® 2000, Microsoft® Windows® Millennium Edition, Microsoft® Windows® 98, Microsoft® Windows NT® 4.0, and Microsoft® Windows® 95. You can obtain this catalog from the Microsoft Accessibility Web site at http://www.microsoft.com/enablc/ or by phone at the Microsoft Sales Information Center.

For more information about this catalog, contact:

Microsoft Sales Information Center
One Microsoft Way
Redmond, WA 98052-6393

Voice telephone: (800) 426-9400
Text telephone: (800) 892-5234

Computer Products for People with Disabilities

The Trace R&D Center at the University of Wisconsin-Madison publishes a database containing information about more than 18,000 products and other topics for people with disabilities. The database is available on the Trace Center Web site at http://www.trace.wisc.edu/. The database is also available on a compact disc, titled the *Co-Net CD*, which is issued twice a year. The Trace R&D Center also publishes a book, *Trace Resourcebook,* which provides descriptions and photographs of approximately 2,000 products.

To obtain these directories, contact:

Trace R&D Center
University of Wisconsin
S-151 Waisman Center
1500 Highland Avenue
Madison, WI 53705-2280

Fax: (608) 262-8848

Information and Referrals for People with Disabilities

Computers and accessibility devices can help people with disabilities overcome a variety of barriers. For general information and recommendations about how computers can help you with your specific needs, consult a trained evaluator. For information about locating programs or services in your area that might be able to help you, contact:

National Information System
University of South Carolina
Columbia, SC 29208

Voice/text telephone: (803) 777-1782
Fax: (803) 777-9557

Preparation for Deployment

Chapter 13: What's New in the IEAK?

This chapter provides an overview of new and enhanced administrative features in the Microsoft® Internet Explorer Administration Kit (IEAK), as well as some important features that were introduced in the IEAK 5.5. You can learn about new customization and setup options and use this information to help you evaluate the IEAK before you begin building your custom browser packages.

Chapter 14: Understanding Customization and Administration

You can customize Microsoft® Internet Explorer 6 in many ways to accommodate the different preferences and needs of your organization and its users. To help you get started, this chapter describes the Internet Explorer Administration Kit (IEAK) and how you can use it to customize and administer Internet Explorer installations.

Specifically, this chapter focuses on the ways that the following Resource Kit audiences can use the IEAK:

- Corporate administrators
- Internet service providers (ISPs)
- Internet content providers (ICPs)
- Independent software vendors (ISVs) and Internet developers

Chapter 15: Planning the Deployment

To install Microsoft® Internet Explorer 6 and Internet Tools successfully, you must first plan your deployment processes and strategies. By understanding how to plan and automate your browser installation, you can reduce the cost of migration and ensure a smooth transition to Internet Explorer. This chapter describes how to plan your deployment.

Chapter 16: Preparing for the IEAK

Before you run the Microsoft® Internet Explorer Customization Wizard to customize Microsoft Internet Explorer 6, you should take some time to gather the custom files and information that you will need and to set up your computers. You must also accept the license agreement. This advance preparation will help you use the Customization Wizard more effectively.

Chapter 17: Working with .inf Files

In addition to using the Microsoft Internet Explorer Administration Kit (IEAK) 6, batch files, command-line switches, and third-party applications to customize setup, you can create customized setup solutions by using setup information (.inf) files. The .inf files allow you to use the built-in Windows setup engine to automate setup tasks such as creating files and folders and providing uninstall functionality for the software components that you install as part of your custom browser packages. This chapter describes .inf files and discusses the ways you can use these text files to customize your installations of components.

Chapter 18: Setting Up Servers

As you customize Microsoft Internet Explorer 6 and prepare for your browser rollout, you should also prepare any servers that you will need to support the deployment. This chapter describes how to configure your servers to support browser features, set up automatic search and roaming user capabilities, and prepare for Internet sign-up using the Internet Connection Wizard.

Chapter 19: Setting Up and Administering a Pilot Program

Before you deploy Microsoft Internet Explorer 6 to your users, set up and administer a pilot program. Begin by testing the installation of Internet Explorer 6 and Internet Tools in a lab, and then conduct the pilot program to refine your deployment configurations and strategies using a limited number of pilot participants. This process will help you validate your deployment plan and ensure your readiness for full-scale deployment. This chapter describes how to set up a computer lab to test your deployment process and outlines the steps for conducting a successful pilot program.

CHAPTER 13

What's New in the IEAK?

This chapter provides an overview of new and enhanced administrative features in the Microsoft® Internet Explorer Administration Kit (IEAK), as well as some important features that were introduced in the IEAK 5.5. You can learn about new customization and setup options and use this information to help you evaluate the IEAK before you begin building your custom browser packages.

In This Chapter

Related Information in the Resource Kit

- For more information about planning your deployment of Internet Explorer, see "Planning the Deployment."

- For more information about rolling out Internet Explorer to your users, see "Deploying Microsoft Internet Explorer 6."

Overview: New and Enhanced Administrative Features

Using the Internet Explorer Administration Kit (IEAK), you can easily customize, deploy, and manage your installations of Internet Explorer 6 and Internet Tools. The IEAK includes the Internet Explorer Customization Wizard and the IEAK Profile Manager, which enable you to build and maintain custom browser packages that are tailored to meet the needs of your users. You can easily specify user setup options and control most browser and component features.

Building on the IEAK 5.5, the IEAK 6 provides a faster and easier customization experience. With its integrated license agreement, you no longer need to sign up for a specialized license key code to run the IEAK. You can also take advantage of many new and enhanced options to customize the browser for your users.

Customizing Privacy Settings

When you run the Internet Explorer Customization Wizard, you can customize the privacy settings for your users. You can define privacy preferences that determine whether Internet Explorer will check Web sites for an established privacy policy and whether Internet Explorer will disclose users' personal information to those Web sites. The privacy preferences also determine whether Internet Explorer will allow these Web sites to store cookies on users' computers.

For more information about privacy settings in Internet Explorer, see "Users' Privacy" in this Resource Kit. For more information about using the Customization Wizard to customize privacy settings, see "Running the Microsoft Internet Explorer Customization Wizard" in this Resource Kit.

Customizing the Internet Explorer Toolbar

When you run the Internet Explorer Customization Wizard, you can personalize the look and feel of the Internet Explorer toolbar, giving you additional flexibility and design opportunities. You can change the toolbar background and the icons for the standard toolbar buttons, such as **Search** and **History**. Also, you can customize the appearance and number of additional toolbar buttons.

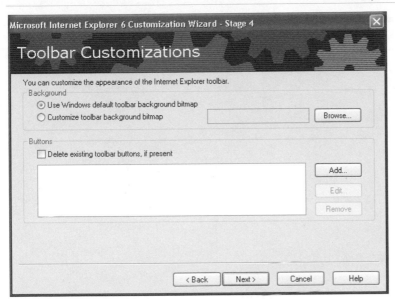

For more information about using the Customization Wizard to customize the Internet Explorer toolbar, see "Running the Microsoft Internet Explorer Customization Wizard" in this Resource Kit.

Working with Resultant Set of Policy Features

The IEAK includes a new Resultant Set of Policy (RSoP) snap-in to help you plan browser policies before you deploy your custom browser packages. You can use this snap-in to review policy information that is set up for computers and users. When you add the snap-in, the RSoP Wizard allows you to choose either logging mode to access the policy information for an existing computer and user, or planning mode to generate policy information based on the Microsoft® Active Directory™.

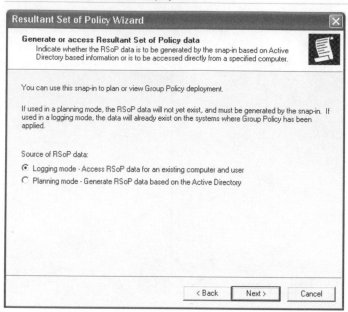

You can review this policy information, including software settings, window settings, and administrative templates, and plan the policies and restrictions that you want to configure for your users. Then you can use the Internet Explorer Customization Wizard or the Internet Explorer Profile Manager to set your policies. After deploying the policies to your users, you can use RSoP to review the policies.

Note RSoP is supported only on the Microsoft® Windows® XP and Microsoft® Windows® 2000 operating systems.

For more information about policies and restrictions for Internet Explorer 6, see the appendix "Setting System Policies and Restrictions" in this Resource Kit.

Using New Policies and Restrictions

The IEAK 6 includes new system policies and restrictions that allow you to preconfigure settings for Internet Explorer 6 features. You can use either the Internet Explorer Customization Wizard or the IEAK Profile Manager to set the following policies and restrictions:

- **Privacy.** You can prevent users from viewing the **Privacy** tab on the **Internet Options** dialog box.
- **Multimedia.** You can specify settings to enable the image toolbar, automatic image resizing, and automatic playback of media files on the Media bar.
- **Fault collection.** If you do not want to send Internet Explorer fault information to Microsoft, you can turn off Internet Explorer Error Reporting tool.

For more information about the system policies and restrictions, see the appendix "Setting System Policies and Restrictions" in this Resource Kit.

Using Additional Features Introduced in the IEAK 5.5

The IEAK 6 includes the following customization features that were first introduced in the IEAK 5.5:

- **Custom components.** You can choose when to install custom components: before or after Internet Explorer is installed, after the computer restarts, or only if the Internet Explorer installation is completed successfully. This feature is particularly useful with utilities that prepare computers for a browser installation. For example, registry-cleaning utilities can be run before installing Internet Explorer so that browser-created registry keys are affected.

- **Administrative privileges.** You can customize your package to retain administrator privileges after the computer restarts. This feature is necessary for users who do not have administrator privileges on the Microsoft® Windows NT® and Windows 2000 operating systems. After the computer restarts and a user logs on, the Windows Installer component completes the registration of the Internet Explorer system files. You can then distribute this package to users manually or as part of an automated deployment method such as Systems Management Server (SMS). In either case, users are not required to have administrator privileges the next time they log on to the computer.

- **Outlook Express links and icons.** You can include Microsoft® Outlook® Express in your package and configure the installation so that no links to the Outlook Express program appear on your users' desktop, **Start** menu, or Quick Launch bar. Similarly, you can remove links to channels or the Internet Connection Wizard from your users' Quick Launch bar.

- **Packages for Windows 32-bit versions.** The IEAK enables you to build custom browser packages for only Microsoft® Windows® 32-bit versions. To customize the browser for the 64-Bit Edition, use Group Policy instead. For more information about Group Policy, see "Keeping Programs Updated" in this Resource Kit.

Additional Resources

These resources contain additional information and tools related to this chapter.

Related Information Outside the Resource Kit

- The Microsoft Windows Technologies Internet Explorer Web site at http://www.microsoft.com/windows/ie/.
- Internet Explorer Help.

CHAPTER 14

Understanding Customization and Administration

You can customize Microsoft® Internet Explorer 6 in many ways to accommodate the different preferences and needs of your organization and its users. To help you get started, this chapter describes the Internet Explorer Administration Kit (IEAK) and how you can use it to customize and administer Internet Explorer installations.

Specifically, this chapter focuses on the ways that the following Resource Kit audiences can use the IEAK:

- Corporate administrators
- Internet service providers (ISPs)
- Internet content providers (ICPs)
- Independent software vendors (ISVs) and Internet developers

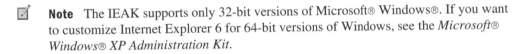 **Note** The IEAK supports only 32-bit versions of Microsoft® Windows®. If you want to customize Internet Explorer 6 for 64-bit versions of Windows, see the *Microsoft® Windows® XP Administration Kit.*

In This Chapter

Related Information in the Resource Kit

- For more information about preparing for your Internet Explorer deployment, see "Planning the Deployment."
- For more information about preparing custom graphics files and obtaining digital signatures, see "Preparing for the IEAK."
- For more information about creating custom browser packages, see "Running the Microsoft Internet Explorer Customization Wizard."

Overview: Microsoft Internet Explorer Administration Kit

IEAK programs and tools make it easy for you to create and deploy custom browser packages and to manage the browser after the installation. The *Microsoft Internet Explorer 6 Resource Kit* CD-ROM contains the following IEAK programs and tools:

- **Internet Explorer Customization Wizard.** The Internet Explorer Customization Wizard divides the browser customization into five stages. Step-by-step screens for each stage guide you through the process of creating custom browser packages. When these packages are installed on users' desktops, the users receive customized versions of Internet Explorer with the settings and options that you selected.

- **IEAK Profile Manager.** After you deploy Internet Explorer, you can use the IEAK Profile Manager to change browser settings and restrictions automatically.

- **IEAK Toolkit.** The IEAK Toolkit contains helpful tools, programs, and sample files, such as the animated bitmap tools and sample signup and add-on files, which you can use to extend the IEAK functionality for your organization. The toolkit also includes the IExpress Wizard; you can use this to control setup options and to integrate command-line switches, which control how your custom browser packages are installed. The Toolkit contents are located in the Toolkit folder in the IEAK program folder.

- **IEAK Help.** The IEAK Help includes many conceptual and procedural topics that you can view by using the **Index**, **Contents**, and **Search** tabs. You can also print topics from the IEAK Help.

As you read this chapter, you can identify ways that you might want to customize and administer your Internet Explorer installations by using the IEAK programs and tools. Before you begin using the IEAK, though, you should spend some time planning the Internet Explorer deployment so that you will be prepared to choose the settings and options that are appropriate for your organization and its users.

The following list identifies some of the preparation tasks that you might want to complete:

- Assess your users' needs.

- Analyze your organization's needs.

- Develop a deployment plan and set up a deployment lab where you can test a pilot installation.

- Gather the URLs and other information that you will need, and create any custom graphics.

- Obtain a digital certificate to sign the custom cabinet (.cab) files that you create with the IEAK and any custom programs that you include (if your users will download your custom browser packages over the Internet). These .cab files are used to organize and compress installation files that are copied to your users' computers.

- Register to use the IEAK on the Microsoft Windows Technologies Internet Explorer Administration Kit Web site at http://www.microsoft.com/windows/ieak/. This Web site also includes useful deployment and customer assistance information.

For more information about preparing for deployment, including developing a deployment plan and setting up a pilot program, see the chapters in the part "Preparation for Deployment." For more information about getting ready to run the IEAK, including the files and data that you need to collect and the steps that are necessary to prepare your deployment servers, see the chapters in the part "Customization and Installation."

Corporate Administrators

As a corporate administrator, you can save time by centrally administering Internet Explorer installations. When you run the Internet Explorer Customization Wizard to create custom browser packages, you can determine how Internet Explorer is installed, how the browsing software and Internet Explorer components are customized, and what browser and messaging options are available to your users.

If the needs of your organization change after Internet Explorer is installed, you can use the IEAK Profile Manager to update browser settings. Then you can use the automatic configuration feature in Internet Explorer to deploy the updated settings to your users' desktops without leaving your office.

You can also set policies and restrictions for the browser, including security, messaging, and desktop settings. These policies and restrictions can help you manage your organization's resources and bandwidth. Does your accounting department have different needs than your marketing department? You can create different profiles that contain settings and restrictions tailored to each department.

Customizing Windows Update Setup for Internet Explorer 6 and Internet Tools

When you run the Internet Explorer Customization Wizard, you can customize Windows Update Setup for Internet Explorer 6 and Internet Tools in several ways. You can extend the Minimal, Typical, and Full options that are available for default installations by creating up to 10 additional setup options. These additional options can be helpful if your employees have different usage needs and varying disk-space limitations. Also, you can alter the appearance of the Setup program by adding your own graphics and including custom descriptions for your additional setup options.

To make the installation easier, you can configure Internet Explorer so that the browser can be installed with few or no setup choices. This type of setup, which is sometimes referred to as a *silent install*, is often used for setting up Internet Explorer after business hours when employees are not at their desks. You can further control this type of installation by using command-line switches or batch files. Because you are making setup choices for your users, you can create only one silent install setup option.

If you suppress all user feedback, including error messages and status information, you should make sure your setup plan includes error handling. If you suppress restarting after installation, you must create a custom program or script to handle restarting and to ensure that Internet Explorer is set up correctly.

When you install Internet Explorer, you might also find it convenient to include your own components, such as virus-checking programs or scripts. You can install up to 16 additional components in a custom browser package.

For more information about customizing Windows Update Setup for Internet Explorer and Internet Tools, see "Running the Microsoft Internet Explorer Customization Wizard" in this Resource Kit.

Customizing the Browser, the Desktop, and Other Features

You can customize the appearance and behavior of the browsing software, the user's desktop, and the Internet Explorer messaging component. These customizations can help you create a standard corporate desktop that is easier to manage.

To customize the browser, you can add your organization's name or other wording to the title bar. For example, the phrase "Microsoft Internet Explorer Provided by Woodgrove Bank" could appear on your title bar. You can also customize the static and animated logos that appear in the upper-right corner of the browser window.

You can preset the following Web pages and links:

- Corporate support page
- Users' home page
- Users' search page
- Links on the Links bar
- Links on the Favorites bar
- Add-on Components page (for optional components)

The following illustration provides an example of how you might customize a user's Favorites list with helpful links.

If your organization has standardized on the Microsoft® Active Desktop® feature that was included with Internet Explorer 4.0, you can reinstall the desktop component with Internet Explorer 6. Even if only some of your users' computers are running Internet Explorer 4.0, you can include the desktop component with Internet Explorer 6 so that all users have the same desktop. If your users are running Microsoft® Windows® 2000, Microsoft® Windows® Millennium Edition, or Microsoft® Windows® 98, they already have this desktop.

You can customize the Internet Explorer messaging component, Microsoft® Outlook® Express. You can preset server information for Outlook Express. You can add a signature to all e-mail and newsgroup messages, such as a disclaimer that the sender's views do not represent your organization's policies.

In addition, you can customize remote dialing for your users, including the dialing settings they need, the icon they click, and the dialog box they see when they dial in to your services. Providing a preconfigured dialer, called the Connection Manager, can help reduce the amount of support that your help desk must provide for remote access services.

For more information about customizing the browser, the desktop, and the messaging component, see "Running the Microsoft Internet Explorer Customization Wizard" in this Resource Kit.

Maintaining Internet Explorer

If you need to update browser settings after Internet Explorer is installed, you can use the automatic configuration feature to change these settings globally at any time. First, you must use the IEAK Profile Manager to create an installation (.ins) file and associated .cab files that contain the browser configuration information, and post these files to your server. When you run the Internet Explorer Customization Wizard to create your custom browser packages, you can point your users' browsers to this .ins file and specify how often the browser should check for updated configuration information. Then you can post a new .ins file at any time to automatically update the browser on your users' computers.

When you run the Internet Explorer Customization Wizard, you can also import connection settings, such as proxy servers. After the browser is installed, you can use the IEAK Profile Manager to customize and maintain these connection settings. If your organization uses an automated program, such as a script in a proxy automatic configuration (.pac) file, a Microsoft® JScript® (.js) file, or a JavaScript (.jvs) file to control proxy settings, you can also incorporate it into your custom browser package.

For more information about using automatic configuration and the IEAK Profile Manager, see "Using Automatic Configuration, Automatic Proxy, and Automatic Detection" and "Keeping Programs Updated" in this Resource Kit.

Setting System Policies and Restrictions

When users customize their programs, they sometimes create challenges for corporate administrators. Although some changes simply reflect user preferences, other changes might make it difficult for corporate administrators to manage resources, control security, or maintain consistent functionality.

When you run the Internet Explorer Customization Wizard to create your custom browser packages, you can select browser settings and, if necessary, disable browser features that do not fit your organization's needs. If you are familiar with system policies, you can also import your existing administration (.adm) files. Then after the browser is installed, you can use the IEAK Profile Manager to update and maintain these settings.

Both the Internet Explorer Customization Wizard and the IEAK Profile Manager have graphical interfaces that enable you to easily set and clear options. You can even "lock down" settings, preventing users from changing them. As you prepare to create your custom browser packages, you should also consider whether you want to control options on a per-computer or per-user basis. If you have roaming users whose needs differ from other users', you might not want to lock down settings on a per-computer basis.

For more information about system policies, see the appendix "Setting System Policies and Restrictions" in this Resource Kit.

Customization Examples for Corporate Administrators

To accommodate the varying needs of your organization and its users, you might want to consider the following customization options:

- Include fewer components in the custom browser packages that you create for employees in the field who might have limited disk space on their laptop computers.

- Include support for different character sets for employees who communicate with overseas departments, so that they can correctly view Web pages in different languages.

- Create a CD-ROM setup for users in a remote country, so that they do not need to connect to the local area network (LAN) or wide area network (WAN) to download your custom browser packages.

- Increase the level of security for employees who will download your custom browser packages from the Internet by creating specific versions with enhanced security options or by using automatic configuration to modify their security settings.

Internet Service Providers

As an ISP, you can customize Internet Explorer and make it easy for customers to sign up for your services. Using the IEAK, you can customize the appearance of the browser and the Setup program, tailor Internet Explorer packages to meet various customer needs, and develop and incorporate sign-up solutions.

Customizing the Browser and Other Features by ISPs

You can customize the appearance of the browser software by adding your organization's name or other wording to the title bar. For example, the phrase "Microsoft Internet Explorer Provided by A. Datum Corporation" could appear on your title bar. You can also customize the static and animated logos that appear in the upper-right corner of the browser window.

You can preset the following Web pages and links:

- Customer support page
- Users' home page
- Users' search page
- Links in the Links bar
- Links in the Favorites bar
- Add-on Components page (for optional components)
- Sign-up and billing pages

The following illustration provides an example of how you can customize the title bar, Links bar, and logo.

You can also customize the Internet Explorer messaging component, Outlook Express. You can preset server information for Outlook Express. You can add a signature to all e-mail and newsgroup messages, such as a link that advertises your ISP services.

For more information about customizing the browser and the messaging component, see "Running the Microsoft Internet Explorer Customization Wizard" in this Resource Kit.

Tailoring Internet Explorer to Different Customer Needs

If you have customers who live in different parts of the world or who have different configurations, you can use the IEAK to create different Internet Explorer packages that address their needs. Depending on your customers, you might want to customize your packages in the following ways:

- Create custom browser packages for different language versions of Internet Explorer and include the necessary components with each package. For example, if you distribute Internet Explorer in different countries, you can add the appropriate language packs, font packs, and versions of Internet Explorer components. You can also include different sets of sign-up pages that use the appropriate languages.

- Include up to 16 custom components in your custom browser package. For example, you can add a custom component that you have created, such as an address book utility, for your customers to install when they set up Internet Explorer.

- Create up to 10 setup options for your customers to accommodate different hard disk limitations and needs for advanced components. You can also design packages for different distribution media, such as a Web server or a CD-ROM.

- Customize remote dialing for your customers by including the dialing settings they need, the icon they click, and the dialog box they see when they dial in to your services. These customization options can give your Internet service a "branded" look so that customers have a consistent experience with your services.

- Create a logon script that configures logon settings so that customers with specialized logon requirements do not need to manually enter complicated settings each time they connect. You can also manage pauses between dialing sequences for your customers.

For more information about creating custom browser packages that are tailored to different customer needs, see "Running the Microsoft Internet Explorer Customization Wizard" and "Time-saving Strategies That Address Diverse User Needs" in this Resource Kit.

Developing and Incorporating Sign-up Solutions

In addition to customizing Internet Explorer for your customers, you might also need to sign up customers and bill them for your services. The IEAK comes with sample sign-up pages and scripts that you can customize to create a complete sign-up solution.

You can use the IEAK to design both server-based and serverless solutions. You can use a sign-up server to provide a new customer with a fully active account, or if a customer already has an account with your service or another service, you can update the user's settings through single-disk branding. This setup option allows you to customize Internet Explorer features without actually installing the browser.

If you plan to set up a sign-up server solution, you need to use kiosk-mode sign-up for Internet Explorer 4.01 SP1 users. If you anticipate that some customers' computers will have Internet Explorer 6 but other users will have earlier versions of the browser, you can create a customer browser package that includes both single-disk branding and kiosk-mode sign-up.

You can also use a server-based solution to customize Internet Explorer for different sets of customers without having to create a separate browser package for each group. In this case, all of the compact discs that you send out are the same, but they are branded differently when the customer signs up.

For more information about Internet and kiosk-mode sign-up, see "Implementing the Sign-up Process" in this Resource Kit.

Customization Examples for ISPs

To accommodate different customer preferences, you might want to consider the following customization options:

- Create an Internet Explorer package that includes several installation choices. In this way, you can accommodate customers who want to use a different e-mail program from Outlook Express, as well as experienced users who want to use more advanced components.

- Customize and control connection settings. For example, you can have a program run either before or after your customers connect to the Internet. You can also add your organization's logo to the dialog box that appears when customers dial in to the Internet.

- Customize Outlook Express. You can preconfigure Outlook Express servers and customize the appearance of this program. In this way, your customers can get connected and start using their software more quickly and with less technical support from your organization.

Internet Content Providers

As an ICP, you can choose customization options for Internet Explorer that help showcase your content in a number of ways. The IEAK enables you to customize the appearance of the browser and the Setup program.

Customizing the Browser by ICPs

To customize the browser, you can add your organization's name or other wording to the title bar. For example, the phrase "Microsoft Internet Explorer Provided by Proseware, Inc." could appear on your title bar. You can also customize the static and animated logos that appear in the upper-right corner of the browser window.

You can preset the following Web pages and links:

- Customer support page
- Users' home page
- Users' search page
- Links in the Links bar
- Links in the Favorites bar
- Add-on Components page (for optional components)

You can customize the appearance of the browser software so that your organization's content is more prominent when the user browses the Internet. For example, you might want to customize the user's home page with content and links related to your business. By continually updating the content on your Web sites, you can keep your customers interested in and informed about your products or services.

For more information about customizing the browser, see "Running the Microsoft Internet Explorer Customization Wizard" in this Resource Kit.

Customization Examples for ICPs

To showcase your organization's information and services on the Internet, you might want to consider the following customization options:

- Add links to your organization's Web sites. For example, if your organization is a radio station, you could add links to Web pages that highlight playlists and composers' biographies.

- Update the browser with your organization's logo and appropriate graphics. You can add your organization's name to the title bar and your organization's logo seen in Windows Update Setup for Internet Explorer and Internet Tools. In addition, you can replace the browser logo with your organization's logo or other graphics.

- Track information about your customized browser by using a user *agent string*, which is a string of characters that a Web browser sends when it visits an Internet site. The custom string that you append to the user agent string enables Web sites to compile statistics about how many of your customers are using your browser to view those sites.

Independent Software Vendors and Internet Developers

As an ISV or Internet developer, you can easily distribute your custom program with the browser. IEAK programs and tools enable you to create custom browser packages that include your own components and to control how your users install the packages.

Customizing the Browser by ISVs and Internet Developers

Using the IEAK, you can include Internet Explorer technologies, such as the WebBrowser control, with your custom program and easily create Internet Explorer distribution media. You can also specify home and search pages and add Web sites to the Favorites list when you create your custom browser packages.

You can redistribute Internet Explorer. By using setup scripts or command-line switches, you can reduce or eliminate the user interaction required to install Internet Explorer and Internet Tools. This helps ensure smooth installation when users set up your custom program with Internet Explorer.

For more information about customizing the browser, see "Running the Microsoft Internet Explorer Customization Wizard" in this Resource Kit. For more information about setup scripts and command-line switches, see the appendix "Batch-Mode File Syntax and Command-Line Switches" in this Resource Kit.

Customization Examples for ISVs and Internet Developers

To distribute your program with Internet Explorer, you might want to consider the following customization options:

- Create a custom program that uses, or "hosts," the WebBrowser control but does not display the Setup interface during installation.

- Use a batch file and command-line switches to install Internet Explorer in redistribution mode. This mode installs the underlying program files without overwriting the Internet Explorer icon if Internet Explorer already exists on the user's computer. You can also suppress Setup prompts, so that your custom program provides setup feedback to the user.

- Customize the Web browser with links to your organization's Web sites or to sources of related technologies. Then you can use the IEAK to create a CD-ROM package that includes your custom program.

Planning the Deployment

To install Microsoft® Internet Explorer 6 and Internet Tools successfully, you must first plan your deployment processes and strategies. By understanding how to plan and automate your browser installation, you can reduce the cost of migration and ensure a smooth transition to Internet Explorer. This chapter describes how to plan your deployment.

In This Chapter

Related Information in the Resource Kit

- For more information about testing the deployment process before installation, see "Setting Up and Administering a Pilot Program."

- For more information about setting up your servers to work with Internet Explorer and the components and options you select, see "Setting Up Servers."

- For more information about building custom browser packages for installation, see "Running the Microsoft Internet Explorer Customization Wizard."

- For more information about deploying the browser to your users, see "Deploying Microsoft Internet Explorer 6."

Evaluating Internet Explorer 6

The first steps in planning the deployment process are to evaluate the new and enhanced features and functions of Internet Explorer 6 and to understand how these features and functions can help you reduce the total cost of ownership.

Understanding New Features and Functions

To evaluate Internet Explorer 6, review the contents of this Resource Kit, which is a technical supplement to other browser product documentation. Obtain a copy for each team member who will assist with Internet Explorer planning and installation so that members can read and use the book during the deployment process. In particular, review "What's New in Microsoft Internet Explorer 6?" which provides an overview of Internet Explorer 6. This chapter can help you evaluate new features and functions so that you can better prepare for deploying Internet Explorer in your organization and training and supporting your users.

Reducing the Total Cost of Ownership

Microsoft has implemented in Internet Explorer features and functions that can help you reduce the total cost of ownership while maximizing the return on your technology investment. Internet Explorer delivers both economic and business benefits without affecting browser scalability and flexibility. Your organization can quickly recover the time spent on Internet Explorer deployment and continue to realize cost savings by taking advantage of the following features and functions:

- **Integrated, multiple-platform capabilities.** By integrating browser, desktop, network, messaging, and productivity applications, Microsoft offers a single desktop solution for users. The Microsoft® Internet Explorer Active Desktop® enables users to browse the Internet, intranet, local network, or hard disk, and provides a standard method for accessing content, applications, and resources. Internet Explorer further enhances desktop integration by providing a common browser across multiple versions of the Microsoft® Windows® platform, including Windows 64-bit and Windows 32-bit versions.

- **Internet Explorer Administration Kit.** You can use the Microsoft® Internet Explorer Administration Kit (IEAK) to centrally customize, deploy, and manage Internet Explorer on your users' desktops from one central location. The IEAK includes the Internet Explorer Customization Wizard, which enables you to create custom browser packages that you can distribute to your users, and the IEAK Profile Manager, which enables you to manage Internet Explorer settings after the browser is installed. These comprehensive tools work with your existing infrastructure without additional browser or server expenses.

  For more information about using the Internet Explorer Customization Wizard, see "Running the Microsoft Internet Explorer Customization Wizard" in this Resource Kit. For more information about using the IEAK Profile Manager, see "Keeping Programs Updated" in this Resource Kit.

- **System policies and restrictions.** Using the Internet Explorer Customization Wizard or the IEAK Profile Manager, you can set system policies and restrictions to control user and computer access to Internet Explorer features and functions. System policies and restrictions enable you to customize the Internet Explorer work environment by deploying a standard configuration that best meets the requirements of your users. You can limit functionality to reduce browser complexity, or provide access to more advanced browser functions, as needed.

  These tools provide a simple, flexible method for customizing and administering user and computer settings. The system policies and restrictions you set are stored in a policy file, which overwrites default settings for **HKEY_CURRENT_USER** (user-specific policies) and **HKEY_LOCAL_MACHINE** (computer-specific policies) registry keys when users log on to the network. You can allow users to change these predefined settings, or you can choose to lock down all system policies and restrictions, preventing users from making any changes. For more information about system policies and restrictions, see the appendix "Setting System Policies and Restrictions" in this Resource Kit.

- **Privacy and Security.** You can preconfigure Internet Explorer privacy and security settings to protect your work environment and your users' privacy. These settings enable you to control the types of information and software that users can access, download, or run on the Internet or local intranet. You can define privacy preferences that determine whether Internet Explorer will check Web sites for an established privacy policy and whether Internet Explorer will allow these Web sites to store cookies on users' computers.

  You can set security zones to differentiate between trusted and untrusted content on the Internet and the intranet, so you provide rich browser functionality within the safety of the local firewall while restricting entry of untrusted content from outside this environment. You can also manage content ratings, which control users' access to undesirable content. For more information about privacy and security in Internet Explorer 6, see the chapters in the part "Privacy and Security Features" in this Resource Kit.

- **Application development.** Using Internet Explorer as a platform, you can develop your own custom Web-based applications that take advantage of state-of-the-art Web technologies based on Internet standards. Microsoft simplifies the development process by using familiar languages, such as HTML, Dynamic HTML (DHTML), and Microsoft® Visual Basic® Script (VBScript). For more information about DHTML support, see "The Microsoft DHTML Platform" in this Resource Kit. For more information about developing Web applications using Internet Explorer, see the MSDN® Web site at http://msdn.microsoft.com/.

- **Usability features.** Users can benefit from the many usability features in Internet Explorer, which enable them to quickly and easily access important Web sites and desktop information. These features, including the Search page, History bar, Media bar, and Favorites, can help users complete tasks more efficiently and increase productivity. For more information about usability features in Internet Explorer 6, see "What's New in Microsoft Internet Explorer 6?" in this Resource Kit.

Assembling Project Teams

After you have a general understanding of the features and functions of Internet Explorer, assemble the people needed to plan and carry out the Internet Explorer deployment. Typically, a project manager oversees the deployment of Internet Explorer. That project manager assembles the necessary teams of system administrators and other information technology (IT) professionals to help plan, test, implement, and support the deployment.

> **Note** The size and number of teams will vary depending on the needs of your organization. For small organizations, the deployment might involve only a few people who perform the roles of all the teams. Also, your organization might use external resources to supplement your internal teams.

Your organization might assemble the following project teams:

- Planning teams that help determine the deployment requirements, develop deployment strategies, and write the deployment plan.

- Installation teams that set up the test lab and use it to test the deployment strategies.

- Training teams that develop the training plan and training documentation, promote Internet Explorer, and train the users during the pilot program and Internet Explorer deployment.

- Support teams that develop the support plan and assist users during and after the pilot program and Internet Explorer deployment.

When you set up your deployment planning teams, consider including representatives from other groups involved in the deployment process. For example, you might want to include people from standards committees and finance groups.

Determining Time and Resource Requirements

Next, determine your project goals, including the number of computers on which to install Internet Explorer and Internet Tools and the anticipated time required for completion. Also, identify all the tools that you will need to complete the process within the stated time frame. If necessary, propose a formal budget for the companywide implementation, including the cost of staff and additional resources, and present it to management for approval. Be sure to document all time and resource requirements in your deployment plan. For more information, see "Developing a Deployment Plan" later in this chapter.

After obtaining approval (if necessary), purchase any additional equipment or software that you need to facilitate the installation. If you need additional staff, you might want to hire skilled Microsoft Certified Professionals to train your users, a solution that can prove cost-effective for many organizations.

Assessing System Requirements

The project teams should study the technical documentation for Internet Explorer and identify the system requirements for deployment. Teams can review the following sources of technical information:

- This Resource Kit
- The Microsoft Windows Technologies Internet Explorer Web site at http://www.microsoft.com/windows/ie/
- Internet Explorer Help that is included with the product
- The Internet Explorer Customization Wizard Help, which is included with the Microsoft Internet Explorer Administration Kit (IEAK)

The following sections describe the system requirements for installing and running Internet Explorer and Internet Tools, and the Internet Explorer Customization Wizard.

Requirements for Internet Explorer 6

Windows Update Setup for Internet Explorer 6 and Internet Tools offers four installation options: minimal, typical, full, and custom. The following table provides a list of components included with each of these options. If you select a custom installation, you can install only the Web browser—the minimal custom installation—or you can install the Web browser with as many other components as you like. In addition, you can use the Internet Explorer Customization Wizard to build custom browser packages that include up to 16 additional custom components.

Internet Explorer 6 Components

This option	Includes these components
Minimal installation	Microsoft Internet Explorer 6 Web browser (all other components can be installed using Install on Demand)
Typical installation	Microsoft Internet Explorer 6 Web browser, Microsoft® Outlook® Express 6, Microsoft® Windows Media™ Player, and other multimedia enhancements
Full installation	Microsoft Internet Explorer 6 Web browser, Microsoft Outlook Express 6, Microsoft Windows Media Player, and other enhancements
Custom installation	Microsoft Internet Explorer 6 Web browser and any of the following components: **Microsoft Internet Explorer 6:** Microsoft Internet Explorer Help, Microsoft Internet Explorer core fonts, Dynamic HTML data binding, Microsoft Internet Explorer browsing enhancements **Communication component:** Microsoft Outlook Express 6 **Multimedia components:** Microsoft Windows Media Player, Microsoft Windows Media Player codecs, Microsoft® DirectAnimation®, Vector Graphics Rendering, AOL Art Image Format support **Web authoring components:** Microsoft Visual Basic scripting support, additional Web fonts **Multi-language support:** Language auto-selection, Arabic text display support, Chinese (simplified) text display support, Chinese (simplified) text input support, Chinese (traditional) text display support, Chinese (traditional) text input support, Hebrew text support, Japanese text display support, Japanese text input support, Korean text display support, Korean text input support, Pan-European text display support, Thai text support, Vietnamese text support

Disk space requirements depend on the components that you install. The following table lists the minimum hardware system requirements to deploy Internet Explorer 6 on Windows 32-bit versions. For information about requirements for other systems, including the Windows 64-bit version, see the Microsoft Windows Technologies Internet Explorer Web site at http://www.microsoft.com/windows/ie/.

Requirements for Windows 32-Bit Operating Systems

Operating system	Processor	Minimum memory (RAM)	Size of full installation
Microsoft® Windows® XP	486/66 (Intel Pentium recommended)	(automatically installed)	(automatically installed)
Microsoft® Windows® 2000	486/66 (Intel Pentium recommended)	32 MB	12 MB
Microsoft® Windows® Millennium Edition	486/66 (Intel Pentium recommended)	32 MB	8.7 MB
Microsoft® Windows® 98 Second Edition (SE)	486/66 (Intel Pentium recommended)	16 MB	12.4 MB
Windows 98	486/66 (Intel Pentium recommended)	16 MB	11.5 MB
Microsoft® Windows NT® 4.0 Service Pack 6a and later	486/66 (Intel Pentium recommended)	32 MB	12.7 MB

Requirements for the Internet Explorer Customization Wizard

The following table lists the system requirements that must be met to install and run the Internet Explorer Customization Wizard, which is part of the IEAK. To run the Customization Wizard and build your custom browser packages, you must install the IEAK.

Requirements for the Customization Wizard

Item	Requirements
Processor	486/66
Operating system	Windows 32-bit versions
Minimum memory (RAM)	Same as the requirements for installing Internet Explorer 6 and Internet Tools
Disk space	80 MB to install the IEAK and download all components Add an additional 100 MB for each media type
Connection	A modem and Internet connection to run the wizard the first time if Internet Explorer and Internet Tools is installed from a Web download site (not from a CD-ROM)

Note Windows Desktop Update is included with Internet Explorer 4.0, but not with Internet Explorer 6. To install Windows Desktop Update with Internet Explorer 6, you must select this feature when you build your custom browser packages by using the Internet Explorer Customization Wizard.

Before you run the Internet Explorer Customization Wizard, you must install Internet Explorer and Internet Tools. If you attempt to run the wizard without installing Internet Explorer and Internet Tools, you receive a message requesting that you install the browser first.

The disk space required to build custom browser packages varies considerably, depending on the number of components you plan to include. For example, a minimal installation, which includes only the Web browser, requires approximately 8 MB of free disk space. A typical installation, which includes the Web browser, Outlook Express, Media Player, and other multimedia enhancements, requires 36 MB of free disk space. Also, you will need additional disk space for any custom components that you include with your browser installation.

The disk space required to install custom browser packages varies according to the distribution method you use. If you plan to distribute Internet Explorer on CD-ROMs or other removable media, the custom browser packages include the distribution files for these media. For example, CD-ROM packages require about twice as much disk space.

Assessing Bandwidth Usage

Bandwidth usage and its impact on network traffic and server load can be a major concern for corporations that are implementing browser software. Microsoft designed Internet Explorer as a "bandwidth-smart" application with built-in mechanisms for caching and compressing data, as well as tools that optimize information dynamically. System policies that limit bandwidth and restrict access to bandwidth-intensive features, such as audiovisual components, can provide you with additional control of bandwidth usage.

Internet Explorer achieves optimal bandwidth use by focusing on the most efficient methods for minimizing network traffic while maximizing performance. Primarily, Internet Explorer does this by using the following two methods:

- Optimizing data through caching, compression, and other methods
- Using system policies and restrictions to control bandwidth

In addition, organizations that distribute Internet Explorer from Web download sites should consider the impact of this distribution media on bandwidth usage and server load. For more information about potential bandwidth issues, review "Assessing Network Performance and Bandwidth Issues" later in this chapter.

Optimizing Data Through Caching, Compression, and Other Methods

Internet Explorer uses the following methods to minimize the amount of data transmitted over the network and maximize the performance for users:

- **Caching content.** Internet Explorer optimizes bandwidth by caching Web content. The first time you connect to a Web page, Internet Explorer downloads the page and its supporting content to a cache stored in the Temporary Internet Files folder on your hard disk. By default, Internet Explorer uses the cached content instead of downloading new content when you return to browse a cached page. Using cached content provides faster performance for browsing Web sites because the same content is downloaded only once.

- **Providing data compression with the HTTP 1.1 protocol.** For faster, more efficient downloading of Web content, Internet Explorer supports the HTTP 1.1 protocol. This protocol compresses packets of data transferred with the HTTP protocol, which can boost performance as much as 50 to 100 percent over compressed data using HTTP 1.0. Web communications using HTTP 1.1 require fewer delays and consume less bandwidth, and Web content downloads faster to the browser. By default, HTTP 1.1 communications are enabled in Internet Explorer to optimize performance when the browser interacts with servers that support HTTP 1.1.

- **Supporting bandwidth-smart tools to develop Web content.** Internet Explorer supports the Portable Network Graphics (PNG) specification, DHTML, and the Microsoft® DirectX® multimedia extensions, which enable developers to design faster, more bandwidth-efficient graphics and interactive and animated Web content. For more information about these tools, see the MSDN Web site at http://msdn.microsoft.com/.

Using System Policies and Restrictions to Control Bandwidth

You can use Internet Explorer system policies and restrictions to control access to bandwidth-intensive features and to enforce a limit on bandwidth usage. For example, you can control the following capabilities:

- **Access to multimedia capabilities.** By default, Internet Explorer shows or plays a wide range of standard multimedia content, including graphics, video, and audio. Internet Explorer also uses image-dithering technology to smooth images, so they appear less jagged. However, multimedia content and dithering can use a significant amount of network bandwidth, causing Web pages to download and be displayed slowly.

  Using system policies and restrictions, you can limit access to multimedia functions, such as Web pictures, animation, videos, and sound, which allows Web pages with multimedia content to download faster and use less bandwidth. You can also turn off image dithering to speed up image display time. Be aware, however, that when you disable multimedia features, the pages will not appear as intended and some relevant content might not be available.

- **Access to offline features.** If you have many users who download Web content for offline browsing, you might be concerned about the server load. To address this concern, with the system policies and restrictions Internet Explorer provides, you can disable or limit access to offline functions. For example, you can reduce bandwidth usage by increasing the minimum number of minutes between scheduled updates of offline content and reducing the size of subscriptions that can be updated for offline viewing.

For more information about using Internet Explorer system policies and restrictions, see the appendix "Setting System Policies and Restrictions" in this Resource Kit.

Identifying Client and Server Configurations

Because your current system environments dictate your deployment plan, gather information about the existing client and server configurations for all groups that will migrate to Internet Explorer 6. Interview the appropriate group managers, system administrators, and users for these groups. Be sure that you survey a representative sample so that you can compile an accurate inventory of hardware and software used on client and server computers.

Specifically, consider the following configuration elements:

- **Minimum hardware requirements.** Your organization might need to upgrade computers to meet minimum hardware requirements for Internet Explorer, so review the hardware configurations currently in use by all groups.

- **Laptops and desktop computers.** Laptop and desktop computers have different configurations, including disk space and access to the network. Therefore, select installation options that work for each type of computer.

- **Network access.** Users without network access need to install Internet Explorer and Internet Tools locally from a CD-ROM or other removable media. Users with network access can install Internet Explorer and Internet Tools from a network.

- **Server load.** Many users installing the browser from a Web download site can impact server load. Microsoft Certified Professionals can provide information about server load patterns and how to distribute the server load by using multiple download sites.

For more detailed information about working with a large number of computers on a network, you can use system management programs, such as Microsoft® Systems Management Server (SMS), to conduct the inventory. This tool can produce a report describing the computers' hardware and settings. In addition, you can use SMS to query the inventory database and quickly get information about equipment that might need to be upgraded.

After you identify the existing hardware and software for client and server computers, use that configuration information to determine the preferred deployment strategies for your custom browser packages. As part of this process, evaluate any possible migration issues, including the need for hardware and software upgrades to support migration.

Identifying Migration and Compatibility Issues

Whether your users currently run Internet Explorer or a different browser, planning how you want to migrate these users is critical. Determine in advance whether you need to convert existing files and custom programs. It is important to identify and solve migration issues, such as compatibility problems, before you attempt to migrate from your current browser software to Internet Explorer 6.

To identify migration issues, test the migration process using the actual user configurations. Testing enables you to identify solutions, such as the best method for upgrading existing, noncompatible systems. For more information about testing the migration process, see "Setting Up and Administering a Pilot Program" in this Resource Kit. After you identify your migration solutions, document them in your deployment plan.

The following sections discuss some of the general migration issues that you should consider. For more information about migration issues:

- See the Internet Explorer 6 Release Notes, included with the browser software.
- Visit the Microsoft Internet Explorer Support Center on the Web at http://www.microsoft.com/windows/ie/support/.
- Contact the manufacturer of the existing software or hardware.

Upgrading from Earlier Versions of Internet Explorer

Setup installs over existing versions of Internet Explorer and imports proxy settings, favorites, and cookies from the previous version. However, you must reinstall any add-ons that you want to keep. For more information about installing Internet Explorer and Internet Tools, see "Deploying Microsoft Internet Explorer 6" in this Resource Kit.

Migrating from Netscape Navigator

Setup imports proxy settings, bookmarks (called favorites in Internet Explorer), and cookies from Netscape Navigator. If you want helper applications to run when Internet Explorer calls them, add the applications' Multipurpose Internet Mail Extensions (MIME) types and file extensions to the list of Windows file-type extensions. Also, specify the program that opens files with each of those extensions.

Using Previously Existing Browser Add-ins

You can use most existing helper applications with Internet Explorer 6 by including them as custom components when you build your custom browser packages. For more information about building custom browser packages, see "Running the Microsoft Internet Explorer Customization Wizard" in this Resource Kit.

Note Some earlier add-ins might not be compatible with Internet Explorer 6. Contact the manufacturers of these add-ins for patches or updates.

Using Previously Existing Internet E-Mail and News Programs

Using the Internet Explorer Customization Wizard, you can preconfigure Internet Explorer 6 to work with your previously existing e-mail and news applications. If the e-mail application is already installed, users can select the application from within the browser.

▷ **To select a previously installed e-mail application**

1. On the **Tools** menu, click **Internet Options**, and then click the **Programs** tab.
2. In the **E-mail** box, click the application that you want to use.

If you want to introduce another e-mail or news application in conjunction with Internet Explorer, include each application as a custom component when you build your custom browser packages. For more information about building custom browser packages, see "Running the Microsoft Internet Explorer Customization Wizard" in this Resource Kit.

You can also specify Outlook Express as your Internet e-mail and news program when you build custom browser packages. If you select a standard installation, Outlook Express is automatically included. If you select a custom installation, you can choose Outlook Express from the list of available components. Outlook Express can import folders from existing e-mail packages — such as Netscape Mail, Eudora Light, and Eudora Pro — into Outlook Express.

Addressing Compatibility Issues

Some previously existing software might not be compatible with Internet Explorer 6. You can often correct such compatibility problems by obtaining upgrades or patches from the software manufacturers or by migrating to other, compatible applications.

In addition, Web pages that were developed for other Web browsers and for proprietary HTML or scripting extensions might not function the same way in Internet Explorer 6. Test your Web pages to identify any compatibility problems with Internet Explorer 6. You might need to redesign any Web pages that do not function properly. For more information about third-party compatibility issues, see the Internet Explorer 6 Release Notes included with the Internet Explorer software.

Managing Multiple Browsers

Internet Explorer 6 can coexist on the same computer with Netscape Navigator. Setup looks for an installed browser that you have specified as the current default browser. It then adopts the user-configurable settings — including proxy settings, dial-up connections, and favorites — from the current default browser. Setup might also adopt additional settings if the corresponding optional components are installed.

For example, Setup configures the following Outlook Express settings:

*   Simple Mail Transfer Protocol (SMTP) server information
*   Post Office Protocol 3 (POP3) server name and user name

- Identity information (user's name, e-mail address, reply address, organization, and signature information)

- Personal address book

- Internet telephone program and Web-based telephone book

- Send and post settings, which include the 8-bit characters in message headers and compliance with Multipurpose Internet Mail Extensions (MIME), if different from the Netscape default settings

- Settings for **Check new message every x minutes** if different from the Netscape Navigator default

Specifying Custom Package Configurations

Using the Internet Explorer Customization Wizard, you can select which components of Internet Explorer and Internet Tools to install. This capability means that you can tailor client installations to include the best set of features for your users, while reducing the amount of disk space needed. The Customization Wizard also enables you to specify a wide variety of configuration options. For example, you can specify security and proxy settings and the media and setup options used to distribute the custom browser package to your users.

For more information about determining whether any additional user requirements might affect your configuration choices, see "Considering User Needs," later in this chapter. For more information about documenting your components and options in a deployment plan, see "Developing a Deployment Plan" later in this chapter.

Using Additional Deployment Tools

When you use the Microsoft Internet Explorer Customization Wizard to build your custom browser, you might also want to use additional tools as part of the deployment process. Consider the following applications and how you can use them to support your rollout of Internet Explorer:

- **Microsoft Systems Management Server.** SMS can help you automate a large-scale deployment of Internet Explorer by distributing and installing the browser on your users' computers. This automated installation requires no intervention from you or your users. You can create a deployment package that contains all the Internet Explorer installation files, and a package definition (.sms) file that defines how Internet Explorer is installed on users' computers. Then you can create a job to distribute your package to users' computers. For more information about incorporating SMS into your deployment process, see "Using SMS to Install Microsoft Internet Explorer 6" in this Resource Kit.

- **Microsoft Internet Information Server.** Microsoft® Internet Information Server (IIS) can help you deploy Internet Explorer and other business applications, host and manage Web sites, and publish and share information securely across a company intranet or the Internet. You can use IIS during the deployment process to perform the following tasks:

  o Manage the Web sites where you distribute and maintain your custom browser packages and other related files and programs.

  o Generate dynamic Web pages by using Active Server Pages (.asp) files.

  o Customize Web site content, including error messages and expiration dates for the content.

  o Capture user information in log files, so that you can collect and analyze valuable customer and usage data.

  For more information about using IIS to deploy Internet Explorer, see "Setting Up Servers" in this Resource Kit, and the Microsoft® BackOffice® Server Web site at http://www.microsoft.com/backofficeserver/.

Considering User Needs

When you are deciding which configuration options to install on your users' computers, consider the following user needs:

- Browser security and privacy requirements that your users might have
- Language versions of the browser that you will need to install for users
- Accessibility features needed to accommodate users with disabilities
- Training and support that your users will need during and after the installation

Providing User Security and Privacy in the Corporate Environment

> **Note** This section describes security and privacy options of Internet Explorer that are particularly important for administrators who need to protect the information, network, and users within their corporate environment. These options, however, might also be valuable for many other organizations and users.

Because Web browsers enable users to actively exchange important information and programs through the Internet and the intranet, consider the security requirements needed to protect your users' privacy and the contents of their exchanges. You need to make educated choices about the types of browser security and privacy that you want to implement for your users.

Internet Explorer supports a wide range of Internet protocols for secure information transfers and financial transactions over the Internet or the intranet. Internet Explorer also provides a variety of features to help users ensure the privacy of their information and the safety of their work environment. Users can set their own security and privacy options from within the browser, or you can preconfigure these options as part of your custom browser packages. When you preconfigure these settings, you have the option of locking them down, thus preventing users from changing them. For more information about preconfiguring security options, see "Running the Microsoft Internet Explorer Customization Wizard" in this Resource Kit.

You can implement the following options, depending on your users' security and privacy needs:

- **Privacy preferences.** You can define privacy preferences for disclosing personal information to Web sites. These privacy settings are based on the *Platform for Privacy Preferences 1.0 (P3P1.0) Specification*, which provides a way for you to control how your personal information is used by Web sites that you visit. When you navigate to Web sites, Internet Explorer determines whether to disclose your personal information based on your privacy preferences and the site's privacy policy information. Your privacy preferences also determine whether Web sites can store cookies on your computer.

- **Security zones.** Internet Explorer security zones enable you to divide the Internet and intranet into four groups of trusted and untrusted areas and to designate the particular safe and unsafe areas that specific Web content belongs to. This Web content can be any item, from an HTML or graphics file to a Microsoft® ActiveX® control, a Java applet, or an executable program.

  After establishing zones of trust, you can set browser security levels for each zone. Then you can control settings for ActiveX controls, downloading and installation, scripting, cookie management, password authentication, cross-frame security, and Microsoft® virtual machine (VM) capabilities based on the zone to which a site belongs.

- **Digital certificates.** To verify the identity of individuals and organizations on the Web and to ensure content integrity, Internet Explorer uses industry-standard digital certificates and Microsoft® Authenticode® 2.0 technology. Together with security zones, certificates enable you to control user access to online content based on the type, source, and location of the content. For example, you can use security zones in conjunction with certificates to give users full access to Web content on your organization's intranet but limit access to content from restricted Internet sites.

- **Content ratings.** The Internet Explorer Content Advisor enables you to control the types of content that users can access on the Internet. You can adjust the content rating settings to reflect the appropriate content in four areas: language, nudity, sex, and violence. You can also control access by specifying individual Web sites as approved or disapproved for user viewing.

- **Permission-based security for Microsoft virtual machine.** Internet Explorer provides permission-based security for Microsoft VM with comprehensive management of the permissions granted to Java applets and libraries. Enhanced administrative options include fine-grained control over the capabilities granted to Java code, such as access to scratch space, local files, and network connections. These options enable you to give an application some additional capabilities without offering it unlimited access to every system capability.

For more information about Internet Explorer security, see the chapters in the part "Privacy and Security Features" in this Resource Kit.

Addressing Language Needs

You might need to deploy Internet Explorer in more than one language, depending on the diversity of your user community. To do so, create and distribute a separate custom browser package for each language version you want to deploy. When you create additional packages for different language versions, you do not need to reenter your setup and browser settings. For more information about selecting the language for your custom browser package, see "Running the Microsoft Internet Explorer Customization Wizard" in this Resource Kit.

Internet Explorer also includes several Input Method Editors (IMEs), which you can deploy with your custom browser packages. IMEs enable users to input Chinese, Japanese, and Korean text into Web forms and e-mail messages using any Windows 32-bit language version. Then users can start any language version of Internet Explorer, Outlook Express, or Outlook and write in Chinese, Japanese, or Korean without the need for a special keyboard or a different language browser. For example, a business based in New York could use its English version of the browser to send messages in Korean to an overseas affiliate, or a student attending classes in Paris could write home in Japanese.

Implementing Accessibility Features

You might need to address the needs of users who are affected by the following disabilities:

- Blindness
- Low vision
- Deafness
- Physical impairments that limit their ability to perform manual tasks, such as using a mouse
- Cognitive or language impairments
- Seizure disorders

Internet Explorer provides many features that benefit users who have disabilities, such as screen readers, customizable layout, and other accessibility aids. For more information about using accessibility features, see "Accessibility Features and Functionality" in this Resource Kit.

Providing User Training and Support

You might need to customize your user training and support to meet the different learning needs, backgrounds, and skill levels of your users. Consider the following groups, which might be part of your user community:

- **Novice users.** Novice users have little or no experience using browser programs and browsing the Internet or the intranet. They require full training and support, starting with the most basic Internet Explorer features and functions. Also, these users might become overwhelmed by new information, so tailor your training and support to their special needs.
- **Intermediate users.** These users already have some experience using Internet Explorer or another browser, either at home or at work. Typically, they require training and support for new browser features and job-specific functions that enhance their existing knowledge.
- **Advanced users.** Advanced users have an expert knowledge of browser software and advanced features and functions. These users might include people who develop their own Web pages and Web applications. Training and support for these users should concentrate on adding new information to their existing knowledge.

After assessing your user groups, you might decide not to implement formal training and support, depending on the components and features of Internet Explorer and Internet Tools that you install. Instead, you can point your users to the built-in browser support. Help files included with Internet Explorer provide users with a comprehensive set of topics, which they can access from within the browser. Also, Microsoft offers complete support services through the **Online Support** option on the browser **Help** menu.

If you decide to offer formal training and support for your users, acquire the following resources:

- **Training and support methods.** Determine the training and support methods users need to master Internet Explorer, and structure those methods to meet their learning needs and anticipated use of the browser. If you plan to implement custom browser packages, tailor your training and support to the features and functions that you will install.

  You might choose to offer a variety of learning methods—including online or in-person demonstrations, training and support Web pages, computer-based training (CBT), instructor-led training classes, self-paced learning materials, or desk-side support—depending on the needs of your users. Also, the types of training and support that you offer can depend on the amount of time that users can dedicate to those activities and the available resources and facilities.

  If your organization does not have an in-house training and support staff, you might want to use outside vendors to develop and conduct your user training and support. A vendor must be able to meet your schedule and budget, and tailor training and support based on the needs of your organization and users.

- **Learning facilities, materials, and aids.** Decide what learning space, materials, and additional aids you need to train and support your users. These items can include videos, books, quick-reference cards, handouts, practice exercises and files, and multimedia presentations. You might choose to develop some materials internally or purchase them from an outside vendor, depending on the unique needs of your users, the type of installations, and the resources available. Also, to help your users learn more quickly, make these learning materials relevant by including information pertinent to your organization, such as job-specific policies and procedures and company software and templates.

- **Training and support schedule.** Decide how many users you need to train and support and the timeline for completing training and support tasks. Then schedule your first training sessions right before Internet Explorer deployment so that users can retain their knowledge by putting it to use immediately. Also, make sure that support services are in place before deployment.

- **Budget for training and support expenses.** Prepare a complete budget for training and support expenses. These expenses might include developing or purchasing learning materials and aids, renting external classroom facilities, and hiring an outside vendor for training and support.

After you have decided on the best training and support strategies for your organization, document this information in formal training and support plans. For more information, see "Developing User Training and Support Plans" later in this chapter. Also, plan for ongoing training and support for your users. For more information, see "Implementing an Ongoing Training and Support Program" in this Resource Kit.

Determining Installation Media and Methods

After you run the Internet Explorer Customization Wizard to build custom browser packages, you can use several methods to distribute them to your users. You can automate installations of Internet Explorer and Internet Tools with preselected components and browser settings so that no user action is required, or you can allow users to choose from up to 10 different installation options.

You can distribute Internet Explorer from:

- FTP or Web download sites on the Internet or the intranet
- Flat network shares (all files in one directory)
- CD-ROMs
- Single-disk branding (customize existing installations of Internet Explorer)

The following sections discuss some of the factors to consider when you choose your distribution media and methods. For more information about selecting your media for distribution, see "Running the Microsoft Internet Explorer Customization Wizard" in this Resource Kit.

Reaching Your Users

Identify the media that will work best for your users. For example, you might need to distribute your custom browser packages to the following types of users:

- **Stand-alone users.** For stand-alone users who are not connected to the local area network (LAN), you can distribute custom browser packages from the Internet or on CD-ROMs or other removable media.
- **Remote-access users.** If your users access the Internet or intranet through remote-access modems, it can be time-consuming for them to download the custom browser package over their modems. Instead of using the Internet or the intranet, you can distribute the custom browser package to these users on CD-ROMs or other removable media.
- **Local network users.** For corporate users who connect to your network, you can distribute custom browser packages from download sites on your intranet.

Assessing the Size and Geographical Distribution of Your User Groups

The size and geographical distribution of your user groups will influence your distribution strategy. For example, consider these options:

- For a large number of users, you might want to produce and distribute custom browser packages on CD-ROMs at a volume discount.
- For a smaller number of users, it might be more economical to distribute custom browser packages over the intranet or the Internet.
- If your users are located worldwide, you might decide to distribute multiple-language versions of custom browser packages over the Internet.

Assessing Resources Available to Your Organization

The resources available to your organization will influence your distribution strategy. For example, if your organization does not have a wide area network (WAN), you might decide to distribute custom browser packages to your worldwide user community over the Internet.

Assessing Network Performance and Bandwidth Issues

When determining your distribution method, consider your network capacity as well as the performance expectations of your users. If your users access the custom browser packages on the intranet, your distribution methods will affect network performance and the available bandwidth. Installing Internet Explorer and Internet Tools over the network places different demands on network bandwidth, both in response time and connection time. Choose distribution methods that help optimize network performance and bandwidth.

For example, if you distribute custom browser packages over the Internet to users on your intranet, it can cause excessive loads on firewalls and proxy servers. Distributing custom browser packages from only one download server on a large WAN can overload the server and cause traffic problems across the interconnecting routers and bridges of subnets and LANs. You can usually achieve the best network performance by distributing custom browser packages from download servers that are located in multiple domains or subnets of your intranet.

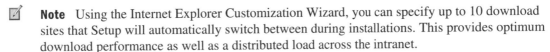 **Note** Using the Internet Explorer Customization Wizard, you can specify up to 10 download sites that Setup will automatically switch between during installations. This provides optimum download performance as well as a distributed load across the intranet.

To help alleviate performance and bandwidth impact, you might also want to consider distributing a smaller browser package with only a limited number of browser components. For example, users can install a browser-only version, which includes the majority of the components used on the Web, and then install additional components as needed using Install on Demand.

Assessing Network Security Issues

The distribution methods available to you depend on the security configuration of your intranet as well as the level of Internet access that you allow your users to have. You can distribute custom browser packages from the Internet to users on the intranet if you configure firewalls and proxy servers to allow users to download the Internet Explorer components. Internet Explorer components are authenticated when users download them from the Internet. However, distributing custom browser packages over your intranet still provides maximum security and does not require additional configurations for firewalls and proxy servers.

If your organization does not provide the required level of Internet access to users, you do not have the option of distributing custom browser packages over the Internet. However, you still must provide Internet access to the administrators who will run the Internet Explorer Customization Wizard and build the custom browser packages. The Internet Explorer Customization Wizard must access the Internet to download the most current components of Internet Explorer from the Microsoft download site.

Developing a Deployment Plan

To ensure a successful Internet Explorer deployment, develop a written plan. The following four-step process can help you complete your deployment plan:

1. **Get organization-wide input.** Collect information from your project teams, staff, and user groups. You might want to conduct surveys or interviews to determine the full scope of your organization's deployment requirements.

2. **Identify and document key topics.** Include sections in your deployment plan for the following topics:

   o Deployment goals

   o Critical success factors

   o Deployment tasks, resources, and tools

   o Task and resource dependencies

   o Budget for resources needed to meet deployment goals

   o Task responsibilities and timelines for completion

   o Significant risks and contingency plans

   As you read through the planning sections in this chapter, you can develop your deployment strategies and collect the information needed to write your plan. For example, as you read the "Identifying Client and Server Configurations" section, identify and document the number of computers for installation, the software and hardware configurations, the best types of installations for these existing configurations, the time and cost for additional hardware upgrades, and any network access requirements for deployment.

3. **Test the plan.** After you write the plan, test it thoroughly. Verify all deployment strategies and identify any potential issues. Then update the plan based on your test results. For more information about testing your deployment plan in the lab, see "Setting Up and Administering a Pilot Program" in this Resource Kit.

4. **Review and accept the plan.** Finalize the deployment plan before you deploy Internet Explorer. All project teams should review and accept the contents of the plan before deployment begins.

Developing User Training and Support Plans

After you assess your users' training and support needs, prepare the training and support plans. The training and support teams should collaborate with the planning team to develop and review the plans. The purpose of these plans is to define the training and support objectives, tasks, resources, and methods that you will use. Finalize the training and support plans before you deploy Internet Explorer to your users.

You can follow the same four-step process used to develop your deployment plan. For more information, see the previous section, "Developing a Deployment Plan." In addition, consider the following items as you write your training and support plans:

- **Roles and responsibilities.** If you plan to use an outside vendor for training and support services, differentiate between tasks completed by internal staff members and tasks performed by a representative from the outside vendor. Make sure that you clearly assign responsibility for each task and identify any additional costs. For example, identify the people responsible for developing the curriculum and courseware, training the trainers and support staff, setting up equipment and classroom facilities, scheduling student training, and delivering training and user support.

- **Migration costs.** Carefully consider the costs for migration training and support. You might need to commit a percentage of your budget to preparing your users for Internet Explorer deployment, customizing training and support options to match their specific needs, and helping them learn how to use the new browser software. This investment is necessary to ensure that your users master browser skills quickly and to minimize additional migration support costs.

- **Ongoing training and support demands.** Anticipate increasing resource demands for ongoing support and training as users begin working with Internet Explorer. Determine a process for ensuring that users successfully complete training objectives. Also, decide how you want to track and resolve support issues, and relay information about frequently asked questions to your users. For more information about ongoing training and support methods, see "Implementing an Ongoing Training and Support Program" in this Resource Kit.

Preparing for the IEAK

Before you run the Microsoft® Internet Explorer Customization Wizard to customize Microsoft® Internet Explorer 6, you should take some time to gather the custom files and information that you will need and to set up your computers. You must also accept the license agreement. This advance preparation will help you use the Customization Wizard more effectively.

In This Chapter

Related Information in the Resource Kit

- For more information about customizing Internet Explorer, see "Understanding Customization and Administration."
- For more information about using the Microsoft® Internet Explorer Administration Kit (IEAK), see "Running the Microsoft Internet Explorer Customization Wizard."
- For a checklist of specific information you need to gather before running the Internet Explorer Customization Wizard, see the appendix "Checklist for Preparing to Use the IEAK."

Overview: Preparing to Customize Microsoft Internet Explorer

You can make a wide variety of changes to Internet Explorer. You can modify the setup program, preset Internet options, and make visual changes. As a corporate administrator, you can control, or "lock down," many important settings to prevent users from changing them. As an Internet service provider (ISP), you can provide sign-up solutions for your customers.

Evaluate the needs of your organization and then determine the preparation steps that you need to take. Depending on your role—corporate administrator, ISP, or Internet content provider (ICP)—and the options that you want to customize, you will need to complete only a subset of the preparation tasks described in this chapter.

Gathering Custom Files and Information

This section describes the key files and information that you need to collect before you run the Customization Wizard. Use this section in conjunction with the appendix "Checklist for Preparing to Use the IEAK," which identifies all the files and information necessary to build custom browser packages.

Step 1: Using Settings from an Existing Custom Browser Package

If you want to create a custom browser package that contains similar settings to a package that you have already built, you can import the settings from the existing package's Internet settings (.ins) file. Then you can use these settings as a starting point for the new package. Before you run the Customization Wizard, locate the .ins file that you want to use. You will specify this .ins file on the **Advanced Options** dialog box, which you can access from the **File Locations** page in Stage 1 of the wizard.

Step 2: Customizing Windows Update Setup for Internet Explorer 6 and Internet Tools

When you run the Customization Wizard, you can customize the appearance and functionality of Windows Update Setup for Internet Explorer 6 and Internet Tools to meet the needs of your organization. Adding custom titles and graphics changes its appearance, while specifying different installation and browser options changes its functionality.

You can include custom components or installation scripts when you install Internet Explorer. You can suppress prompts to users so that Setup can integrate smoothly with your custom setup program. You can also determine how much control users have over the setup process.

The following sections describe how Setup works and identifies the information and files that you need to collect before you run the Customization Wizard.

How Windows Update Setup for Internet Explorer 6 and Internet Tools Works

When users click Windows Update Setup for Internet Explorer and Internet Tools (IE6Setup.exe), it causes the .cab files for Internet Explorer and its components to begin downloading from the sites specified in the file IE6Sites.dat. Setup is designed to minimize the download time and to recover by itself if it is interrupted (for example, if an Internet connection is broken). This can eliminate the need to run Setup multiple times, reducing user frustration.

Setup is based on a Microsoft® ActiveX® engine, which runs on the client computer. The process begins with a small setup package. This self-extracting file can be downloaded to the computer by using an existing browser, or it can be copied directly onto a computer with no existing browser. Because of its small file size, it downloads quickly.

This small package also allows Setup to collect information about the host computer before the download process begins. Setup uses this information to intelligently manage the download of Internet Explorer .cab files and make the installation as efficient and problem-free as possible.

When you run Setup, it creates log files. The file Active Setup Log.txt is a log of the entire setup process from the moment IE6Setup.exe is executed until the download of the last .cab file is completed. When IE6Setup.exe starts, it creates Active Setup Log.txt in the C:\<Operating System> folder. If an Active Setup Log.txt from a previous session exists, Setup renames that file to Active Setup Log.bak.

The log begins with the date and time that users start Setup and ends with the date and time that it successfully downloads the last .cab file. As users run Setup, Setup continually writes logging entries to this file. It is the most informative log file for determining what caused a download failure and when the failure occurred. Most entries logged in this file are also written to the registry.

For more information about Active Setup Log.txt, as well as other log files created during the setup process, see the appendix "Troubleshooting" in this Resource Kit.

Preparing Custom Components

You can add up to 16 custom components that Setup will install as part of your custom browser package. A custom component can be an application that adds Internet functionality or an installation script that runs immediately after Internet Explorer is installed. For example, you might want to add a registry-checking program or a version of a Microsoft component that is different from the version installed with Internet Explorer 6. As an ISP, you might want to install custom components or installation scripts that are part of your Internet services.

Collect and prepare these custom components. When you run the Customization Wizard, you will add each custom component to your custom browser package on the **Add Custom Components** page in Stage 2 by specifying the following information:

- The location of each cabinet (.cab) or executable (.exe) file name
- If you specify a .cab file, the command to run it
- Any command-line switch that you want to run with the command

- The install conditions for the custom component—whether you want to install it before or after Internet Explorer, after the computer restarts, or only if Internet Explorer installs successfully

- An uninstall script, if you want users to be able to uninstall the component by clicking **Add or Remove Programs** (Microsoft® Windows® XP) or **Add/Remove Programs** (other versions of Microsoft® Windows®) in Control Panel

When you prepare your custom components, you can use the IExpress Wizard to package the component files. You can find the IExpress wizard (IExpress.exe) in the \Program Files\IEAK6\Tools folder in your IEAK installation directory. The IExpress Wizard can create self-extracting .cab files that automatically run the setup program contained inside. This wizard condenses and packages any file type, including .doc, .inf, and .txt files. It also allows installations that require specifications for registry settings.

The IExpress Wizard creates an .sed file that contains the information and instructions about the setup package. The wizard can help you carry out specialized installations of your customized browser package, such as determining whether the computer will need to be restarted after installation. Certain choices you make in the wizard correspond to batch mode setup switches. In addition, the IExpress Wizard automatically removes setup files after the installation.

▶ **To build a self-extracting executable file by using the IExpress Wizard**

1. To start the wizard, in the \Program Files\IEAK6\Tools folder, double-click IExpress.exe.
2. Follow the steps in the wizard to package your custom component files.

Customizing the Appearance of the Setup Wizard

You can customize the appearance and functionality of the Setup Wizard, which steps users through the installation process. You might want to customize the wizard so that its appearance is unique to your organization. Or you might want to install Internet Explorer without the icons or browser interface (for example, you might want to host Internet Explorer as part of a custom program).

To customize the appearance and functionality of the Setup Wizard, prepare the following information and files:

- The Setup Wizard title bar text.

- The 162 x 312 pixel bitmap that appears vertically on both the left side of the wizard's first page and the path to that bitmap.

- The 496 x 56 pixel bitmap that appears horizontally on both the top of the remaining wizard pages and the path to that bitmap. This banner bitmap should be light, similar to a watermark, to allow text in the user interface to be readable.

- The title for any custom components that you plan to install.

Selecting the Type of Installation

As a corporate administrator, you can select from three different types of installations that allow you to control whether Setup prompts users for information and provides the installation progress and error messages. You will select the installation type on the **User Experience** page in Stage 3 of the Customization Wizard. The type of installation that you select also directly affects other customization options that you will use in the wizard.

Choose one of the following installation types:

- **Interactive installation.** Provides an interactive installation in which your users make installation decisions and can see the installation progress and error messages.
- **Hands-free installation.** Suppress prompts that users receive during the setup process to make the installation hands-free. Users can still view the installation progress and error messages. This option can be useful if you want to specify setup options for your users and install your custom browser package after normal business hours.
- **Completely silent installation.** Suppress all user prompts, the installation progress, and error messages. This installation option is not interactive; users do not have control over the installation process. Select this option when you want to control all setup options and suppress feedback to users or for installations deployed when users are not present. If the installation does not finish successfully, users do not see an error message.

During a hands-free installation or a completely silent installation, the setup program performs the following activities:

- Answers prompts that enable Setup to continue.
- Accepts the license agreement.
- Specifies that Internet Explorer will be installed, not just downloaded.
- Carries out the type of installation that you specify (such as Standard or Custom).
- Installs Internet Explorer in the location you specify, unless Internet Explorer is already installed. In that case, the new version of the browser is installed in the same location as the previous version.
- Connects to the first specified download site.

> **Note** When you select a completely silent installation, you can specify only one setup option (such as Typical or Full) and one download site.

Creating Installation Options

When you run the Customization Wizard, you can create up to ten installation options, which Setup presents to users when they install your custom browser package. Determine which installation combinations you want to create based on the needs of your organization and its users. You can use the default installation options—Minimal, Typical, and Full—or you can create your own custom installation options that include any combination of standard and custom components that you choose.

You will create these installation options on the **Installation Options** page in Stage 3 of the Customization Wizard. The wizard will prompt you to provide a name and description for each custom installation option that you create. This text appears in the Setup Wizard that users will see.

ISPs can create different installation options for different sets of customers. Corporate administrators can create installation options for different divisions or offices in different regions. For example, an international division might need multiple-language support that the domestic division does not use.

> **Note** If you are an ISP and your customers will use the Internet Connection Wizard (ICW) to sign up for your services, include the Dynamic HTML Data Binding component among your installation options.

Identifying Component Download Sites

You can specify up to ten sites that users can download your package from. Decide which Web or FTP sites on your Internet or intranet servers you want to use. You will add this information on the **Component Download Sites** page in Stage 3 of the Customization Wizard.

Including a Custom Add-on Components Page

You can specify and host a custom add-on component page, rather than the Microsoft Windows Update Web site, from which users can download components. By default, this page appears when users click **Windows Update** on the Internet Explorer **Tools** menu, or when they click **Add/Remove Programs** in Control Panel. If you choose to customize this page, you can specify its URL on the **Component Download** page in Stage 3 of the Customization Wizard.

The IEAK Toolkit contains a sample Add-on Components Web page, Addon.htm, which you can customize. This page is located in the \Program Files\IEAK6\Toolkit\Addons\HTML folder in your IEAK installation directory. This page also links to the files Head.htm, Main.htm, and Info.htm.

The \Program Files\IEAK6\Toolkit\Addons\HTML folder contains the following four sample files:

- **Addon.htm.** Frameset that references the following two files:
  - **Head.htm.** Header frame for title
  - **Main.htm.** Main frame that includes the installation scripting and a link to Info.htm
- **Info.htm.** Information about all the available components

▶ **To use the sample files**

1. Copy all four sample files to your download location or to the location you specify.
2. Edit the files in a text editor or an HTML editor.
3. For the scripting to work properly, set up your files as follows:
   - The IEcif.cab file should be on a Web server. In Main.htm, the L_cab_Address= entry in the <script LANGUAGE="VBScript"> section should point to the same folder location.
   - The table in Main.htm should contain only the components you have downloaded from Microsoft and want to provide.

▶ **To add new components**

1. Make sure you have downloaded the components during Automatic Version Synchronization (AVS).
2. Look up the correct name of the component in IESetup.cif.
3. Add a check box with that name to Addon.htm.

Step 3: Creating a Custom Autorun Screen

If you are creating CD-ROM packages, you can include a custom Autorun screen, which appears when users insert the compact disc into the CD-ROM drive. The screen provides installation instructions and other helpful information. You will specify information for your custom Autorun screen on the **CD Autorun Customizations** page in Stage 3 of the Customization Wizard.

If you want to include an Autorun screen, prepare the following items:

- A 256-color, 540 x 357-pixel background bitmap. The dimensions of the bitmap are important, because the dialog box resizes to the bitmap dimensions. If the bitmap is not wide enough, text in the dialog box might appear clipped.
- A custom button bitmap, if you do not want to use the standard beveled buttons or the 3D bitmap buttons.
- The title bar text and the text color.

When you customize the Autorun screen, you can provide a text file that gives users additional or late-breaking information; this file is sometimes called a readme file. In addition, you can specify a Web page that appears in kiosk (full-screen) mode after users install the browser. If you plan to add an informational file or specify a Web page for kiosk mode, you will need to prepare the files and know their paths before you run the Customization Wizard. You will specify this information on the **More CD Options** page in Stage 3 of the Customization Wizard.

Step 4: Customizing the Connection Manager

As a corporate administrator or ISP, you can use the Microsoft Connection Manager Administration Kit (CMAK) to customize the appearance and functionality of the Connection Manager, a tool that enables users to dial up to the Internet or an intranet. If you want to customize the Connection Manager, create a custom profile by using the CMAK, which is available as part of Microsoft® Windows® 2000 Server and the *Microsoft® Windows® 2000 Resource Kit*. You will import this profile on the **Connection Manager Customization** page in Stage 3 of the Customization Wizard.

Step 5: Obtaining Digital Signatures

If you are deploying your custom browser packages over the Internet, you must ensure that the package files are digitally signed. Digital signatures show where programs come from and verify that they have not been altered. You must obtain a digital certificate from a certification authority (CA) if you do not already have one.

If you have a digital certificate from a CA, the Customization Wizard can use it to automatically sign your package files, including any custom components that you add to the package. You will enter your digital certificate information on the **Digital Signatures** page in Stage 4 of the Customization Wizard.

In addition, if you are an ISP and plan to use a root certificate, you can specify the certificate URL on the **Add a Root Certificate** page in Stage 3 of the Customization Wizard. If you specify a root certificate, all certificates lower in the hierarchy inherit the same level of trust, and users are not continually prompted with security messages. For more information about digitally signing your package files, see "Digital Certificates" in this Resource Kit.

Importing Digital Certificates

To prepare certificates for the Customization Wizard, you can import them onto your computer by using the Certificate Manager Import Wizard. If you have received a file with a software publishing certificate (.spc) extension, you can start the Certificate Manager Import Wizard by double-clicking the .spc file in Windows Explorer or My Computer. You can also open the Certificate Manager from Internet Explorer.

▶ **To import digital certificates onto your computer**

1. Click the **Tools** menu, click **Internet Options**, click the **Content** tab, and then click **Certificates**.
2. Click **Import** to start the Certificate Import Wizard, and then follow the steps in the wizard.

Specify the company name, descriptive text, a URL that users can click for more information, the .spc file name, and the private key (.pvk) file name.

Signing Files Manually

Although the Customization Wizard provides an automated method of signing files, you can sign files manually as well if you have a digital certificate. If you plan to use the manual method, you must sign all the package files, including any custom files or components that you will distribute as part of your custom browser packages.

Make sure that you sign the following files:

*   Branding.cab
*   Desktop.cab
*   IEcif.cab
*   IE6Setup.exe
*   Any cabinet (.cab) files that are created by using the IEAK Profile Manager

By default, the .cab files created by the IEAK Profile Manager will be preceded by the root name of the corresponding .ins file. For example, if your .ins file is named Finance.ins, the corresponding default file name for the Configuration .cab file is Finance_Config.cab.

Step 6: Customizing the Browser Appearance

You can customize the browser's appearance by including a custom toolbar background, toolbar buttons, and static and animated logos.

Customizing the Toolbar Background

You can include a custom toolbar background, similar to a watermark, that appears behind the browser toolbar. The background bitmap has no specific dimensions or resolutions. It should be the size of the toolbar and be light enough to show black text. You will specify this bitmap on the **Toolbar Customizations** page in Stage 4 of the Customization Wizard.

Creating Custom Toolbar Buttons

You can specify a custom toolbar button that appears in the browser toolbar. This toolbar button can start a custom program or script, including opening a custom Explorer bar. You will specify the information for your custom toolbar buttons on the **Toolbar Customizations** page in Stage 4 of the Customization Wizard.

If you want to include a custom toolbar button, prepare the following items:

- For each custom browser toolbar icon, two ico files. The first .ico file contains the active images (color) in the appropriate sizes and color depths. The second .ico file contains the default images (grayscale) in the appropriate sizes and color depths.

  It is recommended that you use a graphics program to draw your icons and a development environment, such as Microsoft® Visual C++® Development Studio, to create the .ico files.

- The script or custom program that you want to run when you start the browser.

To create a custom browser toolbar icon, you will need to provide each image in two sizes for two toolbar states (grayscale for the default state and color for the active state, when the user's mouse is pointing to it), and in two color depths. The following summary describes the image icons that you need:

- One 20 x 20-pixel color image (256-color Windows halftone palette)
- One 20 x 20-pixel gray image (256-color Windows halftone palette)
- One 20 x 20-pixel color image (16-color Windows palette)
- One 20 x 20-pixel gray image (16-color Windows palette)
- One 16 x 16-pixel color image (16-color Windows palette)
- One 16 x 16-pixel gray image (16-color Windows palette)

For example, if you used the image of a house as the icon, the images would look similar to this:

▶ **To draw images for your icons**

1. After drawing your images in a graphics program, place the 16-color and 256-color images in separate files.

   For example, your two icon files might contain the following 16-color and 256-color graphics:

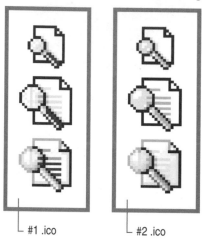

2. Index each file to the appropriate palette, either the Windows 16-color palette or the Windows halftone palette.

3. Save each file as a .bmp file.

Keep the following points in mind as you design toolbar icons:

- Make sure the visual transitions between your default and active images are smooth. An easy way to test this is to create separate layers for the default and active images in a photo imaging program so that you can view the images on top of each other.

- When you design 16-color icons, use the Windows 16-color palette. For both the default and active states, a black border should appear around the icon, except where the readability of the image might be affected, such as for an arrow or an "X." The images should have little shading and should appear flat.

- When you design 256-color icons, use the Windows halftone palette. For both the default and active states, the icons should have icon-style borders with gray or color top and left borders, and black bottom and right borders. They can have more shade and visual depth than 16-color images, with a light source from the upper left and shading where appropriate.

Including Static and Animated Bitmaps

You can customize the Internet Explorer logo in the browser window. This logo in the upper-right corner of the browser appears in two states: animated when the browser is in use and static when no action is taking place. You can replace the logo bitmap with your own animated or static bitmaps. You will specify the information for your bitmaps on the **Custom Logo and Animated Bitmaps** page in Stage 4 of the Customization Wizard.

If you want to include static and animated bitmaps, prepare the following items:

- Two 256-color static bitmaps—one should be 22 x 22 pixels and the other 38 x 38 pixels. Save the files in the custom bitmap folder (\CIE\Bitmaps). When the browser is not active, the first frame of the animated logo will be used as the static logo.

- Two 256-color animated bitmaps—one should be 22 x 22 pixels and the other 38 x 38 pixels. The bitmaps must contain a vertical stack of animation cell images. Cells 1 through 4 are lead-in cells, which are played when Internet Explorer begins to browse; cells 5 through X, where X is the total number of cells, loop until the browse operation is complete. Save the files in the custom bitmap folder (\CIE\Bitmaps). When the browser is not active, the first frame of the animated logo will be used as the static logo.

The IEAK includes two separate tools to help you create customized animated bitmaps for your browser:

- The Animated Bitmap Creator takes a series of sequentially numbered bitmaps and stacks them into one bitmap, using the correct format for animation.

- The Animated Bitmap Previewer allows you to preview the animation of the bitmap. This tool can also be used to display any correctly formatted bitmap.

> **Note** Do not distribute these tools as supported Microsoft products. You can find both tools in the \Program Files\IEAK6\Toolkit\Tools\Animate folder in your IEAK installation directory.

▶ To use the Animated Bitmap Creator (Makebmp.exe)

- To run this tool, type the following at the command line:

  makebmp *basename numfiles outputname*

  Where:

  o **makebmp** is the executable file.

  o *basename* is the root file name (without numbers or the .bmp extension).

  o *numfiles* is the number of bitmaps to sequentially add.

  o *outputname* is the output file name (you must include the .bmp extension).

Example:

To combine the files Bitmap0.bmp through Bitmap19.bmp, you would type the following command line:

makebmp bitmap 20 final.bmp

Number these files sequentially beginning with 0. For example, if you are using 25 files, they would be numbered IEbmp0.bmp IEbmp1.bmp IEbmp2.bmp ... IEbmp24.bmp. When typing *basename* at the command line, you would use IEbmp.

▷ **To use Animated Bitmap Previewer (Animbmp.exe)**

1. Start the previewer from either a command line or Windows Explorer.
2. Preview an animated bitmap by dragging the file into the box, or by clicking the **File** menu and then clicking **Open**. The lead-in frames are shown only once, and then the bitmap loops continuously.

Step 7: Customizing Search, Home, and Support Pages

You can customize the following browser pages:

*   **Home page.** The home page, sometimes known as a start page, appears when users click the **Home** button.
*   **Search bar.** The Search bar appears in the Explorer bar on the left side of the screen and enables users to see the search query and search results at the same time.
*   **Online support page.** In Internet Explorer, support information is available by clicking **Help** and then clicking **Online Support**.

You do not have to create these pages before you run the Customization Wizard, but you will need to make sure they are in place when you deploy Internet Explorer. You will specify the URLs for your custom search, home, and support pages on the **Important URLs** page in Stage 4 of the Customization Wizard.

Step 8: Customizing Links and Favorites

You can customize the links to Web pages that appear in users' Links bar, across the top of the browser, and in the Favorites list, which appears in the left part of the browser when users click the **Favorites** button. You will specify the information for your bitmaps on the **Favorites and Links** page in Stage 4 of the Customization Wizard.

If you want to include custom links and favorites, prepare the following items:

*   Up to 200 URLs. You can import them directly from your computer when you build your custom browser package.
*   If you want graphics for the Favorites list, custom 16 x 16-pixel icons.

Step 9: Creating a Custom Welcome Page

You can customize the welcome page that appears when users start the browser. This HTML welcome page can be different from the home page, which is the page that appears when users start the browser (after the first time) or click the **Home** button. You might want to create a welcome page that greets your users, introduces them to your Internet services, or provides additional links for more information. You will specify the URL for your custom welcome page on the **Welcome Page** page in Stage 4 of the Customization Wizard.

Step 10: Choosing Your Internet Sign-up Method

As an ISP, you can specify whether your customers will sign up for Internet services when they install Internet Explorer. You can use a server-based sign-up process and post your sign-up files on an Internet server. You can have customers use the ICW, or they can use the browser in kiosk mode as the sign-up interface for your server-based solution. You can also use a serverless, or local, solution that you include in your custom browser package. You will specify information about your sign-up process, including the method you want to use, the working directory for your sign-up files, and your sign-up server information, on a series of sign-up pages in Stage 4 of the Customization Wizard.

For a server-based sign-up process, prepare the following files:

- Sign-up files, including Signup.isp, Signup.htm, and Icwsign.htm, that will point to your sign-up server. Signup.isp contains the signup server connection information and is called by Signup.htm and Icwsign.htm. You can use the Filewiz.exe tool, which is located in the \Program Files \IEAK6\Toolkit\Isp\Wizard folder in your IEAK installation directory, to create customized Signup.isp files. To use this tool, you must have Microsoft® Visual Basic® 4 or later installed.

- Settings files that you want to include in your custom browser package. The Customization Wizard can generate .ins files to post to your server (for a server-based sign-up process) or to include in your custom browser package (for a serverless, or local, sign-up process). If you want the Customization Wizard to generate these files for you, you will need to know the settings that you plan to specify, such as area code, gateway, and connection settings.

- If you want to customize the appearance of the ICW, two bitmaps. The first bitmap is a 49 x 49-pixel banner that appears in the upper-right corner of the ICW. The second bitmap is a 164 x 458-pixel watermark image that appears on the left side of the ICW.

Before you deploy Internet Explorer, you must post the sign-up and settings files on your sign-up servers. For more information about these files and about setting up sign-up servers, see "Setting Up Servers" in this Resource Kit. For more information about the sign-up process, see "Implementing the Sign-up Process" in this Resource Kit.

Step 11: Customizing Microsoft Outlook Express

As a corporate administrator or ISP, you can customize many settings for Microsoft® Outlook® Express. Some key settings include account and server information and advanced settings, such as service information for obtaining additional accounts and for determining whether Outlook Express is the default e-mail program. You will specify these Outlook Express settings on a series of Outlook Express-related pages in Stage 5 of the Customization Wizard.

To customize Outlook Express, collect the following information:

- **Incoming mail server.** A Post Office Protocol (POP3) or Internet Message Access Protocol (IMAP) server. POP3 is used by most Internet subscribers for e-mail. An example is pop01.microsoft.com. IMAP is used mainly by corporate users who want to read their e-mail from a remote location. POP3 servers allow access to a single inbox, but IMAP servers provide access to multiple server-side folders.

- **Outgoing mail server.** A Simple Mail Transfer Protocol (SMTP) server. An example is smtp.microsoft.com.

- **Internet news server.** A Network News Transfer Protocol (NNTP) server that is used to distribute network news messages to NNTP servers and to NNTP clients (news readers) on the Internet. An example server name is nntp.microsoft.com.

- **HTML welcome message.** A custom message that appears in users' inboxes when they first install Outlook Express. You need to specify the location of the .htm message, the sender (your name or your group's name) address, and the recipient's name (the group of users you will send the message to).

- **Subscribed newsgroups.** The list of newsgroups that users will automatically be subscribed to. You should collect these names before you run the Customization Wizard.

- **Service for additional accounts.** The menu item that users can access to get an additional mail account. You will need to know the service name and service URL of the account provider. This entry is added to the **New Account From** menu in Outlook Express. When the user selects this service name from the menu, the Web page is opened. An account number, which can be specified in the .ins file, and a unique identifier for each user will be sent to the ISP when the user opens the Web page.

- **Compose settings.** The default signature that you can add to each e-mail or news message. Often, this is a disclaimer that shows that messages submitted by employees over the Internet do not represent official company policies. The maximum size of the signature is 1 KB.

Step 12: Customizing Address Book Directory Services

Corporate administrators and ISPs can provide custom directory or "address book" services using the Lightweight Directory Access Protocol (LDAP). You can include your own LDAP server and Web site, and you can customize the bitmap that appears when users access directory services. You will specify this information on the **Address Book Directory Service** page in Stage 5 of the Customization Wizard.

To customize LDAP settings, prepare the following items:

- The service name, server name, service Web site URL, search base, search timeout (30 seconds to 5 minutes), and maximum number of matches to return (1 to 9999).

- If you plan to customize the service bitmap, a 134 x 38-pixel, 16-color bitmap that identifies a custom directory service where users look up reference information, such as addresses or phone numbers.

Setting Up Your Computers

The next stage in preparing for running the Customization Wizard is to ensure that your build computer and your users' computers meet the appropriate system requirements. You should also prepare any settings on your build computer that you plan to import into your custom browser package.

Preparing Your Build Computer

You must build your custom browser packages and run the Customization Wizard from a computer that is running a Windows 32-bit operating system. Before you start the Customization Wizard, check the amount of disk space available in the computer's Program Files folder and on the destination drive (where you build your custom browser package). The destination drive can be, but is not required to be, on the same computer.

For each media type that you build, you will need to have additional space on your build computer. For more information about system requirements for the IEAK and Internet Explorer, see "Planning the Deployment" in this Resource Kit.

Understanding IEAK Build Locations

You can build a custom browser package on the computer where you are running the Customization Wizard and then move the files to servers where users will download them. Or, you can build on a network server on your local area network (LAN) or on a Web server, such as Microsoft® Internet Information Services (IIS).

When you build custom browser packages, folders for each media type are created in your build folder. For flat (network) and download (Web) packages, you can build at the location where files will be available for downloading. For CD-ROM packages, you can drag the appropriate folder from Windows Explorer to a CD-recording program.

If you are building directly on a Web or network server, you should have the necessary folder structure in place before building your custom browser packages. For more information about deploying your custom browser packages, see "Deploying Microsoft Internet Explorer 6" in this Resource Kit.

Importing Your Settings

If your computer already contains settings or options you want to use, you can save time by importing them directly from your computer. For some customizations, such as your Favorites list and channels, you can import items from your computer as a starting point and then further customize them while you are using the Customization Wizard.

It is a good idea to prepare your computer before you run the Customization Wizard. However, if last-minute adjustments are necessary, you can switch away from the wizard by pressing ALT+TAB, change the settings on your computer, and then switch back to the wizard to import your settings.

Here are the items you can import from your computer:

- **Links and favorites.** You can import the URLs and titles for your Links bar and Favorites list as well as custom graphics that you have used for items in your Favorites list. To see your current Favorites list, click the **Favorites** button in your browser. To see your current links, point to **Toolbars** on the **View** menu in the browser, and then click **Links**.

- **Connection settings (corporate administrators only).** You can import your current connection settings in Internet Explorer, such as proxy server information. To see these settings, click the **Tools** menu, click **Internet Options**, and then click the **Connections** tab. To see network and proxy settings, click **LAN Settings**.

- **Certification authorities (corporate administrators only).** You can import your certification authorities and then use the Certificate Manager to further customize settings, if necessary. To see the current settings in Internet Explorer, click the **Tools** menu, and then click **Internet Options**. Click the **Content** tab, and then click **Certificates**.

- **Authenticode security (corporate administrators only).** Authenticode settings designate software publishers and credentials agencies as trustworthy,. To see your current Authenticode settings in Internet Explorer, click the **Tools** menu, click **Internet Options**, click the **Content** tab, and then click **Publishers**.

- **Security Zones and Privacy (corporate administrators only).** Your security zones and privacy preferences allow you to manage Internet and intranet security and users' privacy. To see your current security zone settings in Internet Explorer, click the **Tools** menu, click **Internet Options**, and then click the **Security** tab. To see your current privacy preferences in Internet Explorer, click the **Tools** menu, click **Internet Options**, and then click the **Privacy** tab.

- **Content ratings (corporate administrators only).** Content ratings provide a way to control the type of content that your users can access on the Internet. To see your current content settings in Internet Explorer, click the **Tools** menu, click **Internet Options**, click the **Content** tab, and then click **Settings**. If you have not yet enabled Content Advisor, click **Enable**, and then set the options you want.

- **Policies and restrictions.** Your policies and restrictions control user and computer access to Internet Explorer 6 features and functions. These policies and restrictions allow you to predefine Internet Explorer options and customize the Internet Explorer environment for different groups of users.

Note If you import settings from your computer and then change them within the Customization Wizard, the settings on your computer will also be updated.

Working with .inf Files

In addition to using the Microsoft® Internet Explorer Administration Kit (IEAK) 6, batch files, command-line switches, and third-party applications to customize setup, you can create customized setup solutions by using setup information (.inf) files. The .inf files allow you to use the built-in Microsoft® Windows® setup engine to automate setup tasks such as creating files and folders and providing uninstall functionality for the software components that you install as part of your custom browser packages. This chapter describes .inf files and discusses the ways you can use these text files to customize your installations of components.

In This Chapter

Related Information in the Resource Kit

- For more information about testing the deployment process before the final rollout of Microsoft Internet Explorer 6, see "Setting Up and Administering a Pilot Program."

- For more information about building custom browser packages, see "Running the Microsoft Internet Explorer Customization Wizard."

- For more information about rolling out Internet Explorer to your users, see "Deploying Microsoft Internet Explorer 6."

- For more information about .inf files, see the appendix "Structural Definition of .inf Files."

Overview: Customizing Installations by Using .inf Files

You can use .inf files to create customized setup instructions, including registry entries and destination directories, for the software components that you want to install as part of your custom browser packages. When users install Internet Explorer, Windows Update Setup for Internet Explorer 6 and Internet Tools follows these instructions to install and register the components and any required files. For each component, you need to ship only the .inf file, which contains your customized setup instructions, and the component's program files.

The .inf files specify the program files required for components to run on 32-bit versions of Windows. By using the setup engine built into Windows, .inf files can take advantage of the setup engine's small size, as well as functions of the Windows operating system such as copying files, adding registry entries, and creating shortcuts. The .inf files can also provide limited platform independence and specify limited software dependencies.

To get started, you can use the guidelines in this chapter to edit one of your existing .inf files or the sample .inf file, which is located in the \IEAK6\Toolkit\Inf folder of your installation directory. These guidelines walk you through the process of customizing the setup instructions for software components. To review a sample .inf file and learn more about .inf file sections, see the appendix "Structural Definition of .inf Files" in this Resource Kit.

After you edit the .inf file for a component, you can use the IExpress Wizard, which is part of the IEAK, to package the .inf file and the component's program files into a self-extracting cabinet (.cab) file. When you run the Internet Explorer Customization Wizard, you can use the Add Custom Components page to add this .cab file to your custom browser packages. For more information about the IExpress Wizard, see "Preparing for the IEAK" in this Resource Kit. For more information about the Add Custom Components screen, see "Running the Microsoft Internet Explorer Customization Wizard" in this Resource Kit.

Manipulating Program Files and Folders by Using .inf Files

You can use .inf files to manipulate the program files and folders for the components that you want to install. You can create folders and links in folders, manage long file names, set attributes for files and folders, and copy files to the Program Files folder.

Creating Folders and Links in Folders

After Setup installs a component, it creates a folder in the Program Files folder or creates links in a folder. Setup looks in the Setup.ini file for a **[progman.groups]** section and then parses it to create the folders or the links in those folders.

Setup.ini uses the following syntax to create the folders and links:

```
[progman.groups]
folder_1=Folder_1_Name
folder_2=Folder_2_Name
:
folder_n=Folder_n_Name
[folder_1]
link-name, .exe-name, icon-file-name, icon-index, profile
```

These folders are relative to the **Start** menu. If you specify NULL as the .exe-name and the name already exists in the group, Setup deletes it. If you specify NULL as the profile, Setup always adds the link to the folder. Also, if a folder or link has a space in its description, you must use double quotation marks.

If you want to install a component that requires a folder or links in the Program Files folder, you must also add to your .inf file an **[UpdateInis]** section that creates the proper entries for the folders and links in the Setup.ini file. An **UpdateInis** entry in the **[Install]** section of the .inf file initiates the **[UpdateInis]** section. For complete information about the **[UpdateInis]** section and the **UpdateInis** entry in the **[Install]** section of the .inf file, see the appendix "Structural Definition of .inf Files" in this Resource Kit.

> **Note** Microsoft® Windows® 2000 does not support the **[UpdateInis]** section for creating links. Instead, Windows 2000 uses a new method, **ProfileItems**, which also supports ToolTip pop-up text. Therefore, you must write a separate .inf file for Windows 2000. For more information, see your Windows 2000 documentation.

The following example shows a Games entry that appears in the **Optional Components** dialog box during setup. If the user selects this option, Setup creates in the Program Files folder a Games folder with links to Solitaire, Minesweeper, Hearts, and FreeCell.

```
[Optional Components]
games

[games]
OptionDesc= %GAMES_DESC%
CopyFiles= wingames.files
UpdateInis= wingames.links

[wingames.files]
cards.dll
freecell.exe
freecell.hlp
mshearts.exe
mshearts.hlp
sol.exe
sol.hlp
winmine.exe
winmine.hlp
```

```
[wingames.links]
setup.ini, progman.groups,, "gamesfolder=%GAMES_DESC%" ;creates folder
setup.ini, gamesfolder,, """Solitaire Game""",SOL.EXE,,," ;creates link
setup.ini, gamesfolder,, "Minesweeper,WINMINE.EXE,,," ;creates link
setup.ini, gamesfolder,, """Hearts Card Game""",MSHEARTS.EXE,,,";
creates link
setup.ini, gamesfolder,, "FreeCell,FREECELL.EXE,,," ;creates link
```

Managing Long File Names

To support backwards compatibility, the setup engine in Windows 32-bit versions of the browser is a 16-bit dynamic-link library (.dll) file. Because of this 16-bit limitation, the setup engine can copy only files that have short (8.3) file names.

To manage files with long names, before the setup engine closes, it runs a Windows 32-bit program that renames these short file names to their long file names. During an uninstall, the same program can delete the long file names. This program gets its instructions from predefined paths in the registry. You can specify the registry settings for these rename and delete operations by including this information in the **[AddReg]** section of your .inf file.

The following registry key specifies the rename operations:

```
HKEY_LOCAL_MACHINE\Software\Microsoft\Windows\CurrentVersion\RenameFile
s
```

The following registry key specifies the delete operations:

```
HKEY_LOCAL_MACHINE\Software\Microsoft\Windows\CurrentVersion\DeleteFile
s
```

You must add each group of rename and delete operations as separate entries under each registry key. Each group of operations can rename or delete only files in a single folder. For each rename or delete operation, you must include a minimum of two entries in each subkey: the folder path for the files that you want to rename or delete, and the actual rename or delete operation. The first element in each group of operations is the folder entry. After the program processes these rename and delete operations, it removes the entries from the registry.

Rename Operations

Each rename operation in the folder entry uses the following format:

```
"old_short_name"="new_long_name,[attrib_flag]"
```

You can use the optional *attrib_flag* to set file attributes during the rename operation. This flag can accept the following values:

```
READONLY              1
HIDDEN                2
SYSTEM                3
```

To set multiple attributes for a file or folder, you must add the values. For example, to set the **READONLY** and **HIDDEN** attributes, you would set the *attrib_flag* to a value of 3.

The following example shows an **[AddReg]** entry that sets the **SYSTEM** and **HIDDEN** attributes for the \Windows\System32\Sample folder:

```
HKLM,Software\Microsoft\Windows\CurrentVersion\RenameFiles\Sys,,,%11%
HKLM,Software\Microsoft\Windows\CurrentVersion\RenameFiles\Sys,SAMPLE,,
"SAMPLE,5"
```

As shown in the previous example, you must use all capital letters to maintain a short file name.

The following example shows an **[AddReg]** entry that renames Oldname.txt to New_Long_Name.txt in the C:\Samples folder and then renames Myreadme.txt to My_App_Readme.txt in the Windows folder.

```
[MyAppShort2Long]
HKLM,Software\Microsoft\Windows\CurrentVersion\RenameFiles\Samples,,,
C:\Samples
HKLM,Software\Microsoft\Windows\CurrentVersion\RenameFiles\
Samples,Oldname.txt,,"New_Long_Name.txt"
HKLM,Software\Microsoft\Windows\CurrentVersion\RenameFiles\Win,,,%25%
HKLM,Software\Microsoft\Windows\CurrentVersion\RenameFiles\Win,Myreadme.txt
,,"My_App_Readme.txt"
```

 Note Before renaming any files, the Windows 32-bit program deletes the destination file. Therefore, if you repeat a rename operation, it could result in a loss of the file. For example, if Windows_Screen_Picture.bmp already exists from an earlier rename operation and you attempt to rename Picture.bmp to Windows_Screen_Picture.bmp, the originally existing file might get deleted before the rename operation occurs. If the existing destination file name is a folder, though, this rule does not apply.

Delete Operations

Each delete operation in the folder entry uses the following format:

```
"arbitrary_key_name"="long_name_to_delete"
```

The following example shows an **[AddReg]** entry that deletes New_Long_Name.txt from the C:\Samples folder and then deletes My_App_Readme.txt from the Windows folder.

```
[MyAppDelLong]
HKLM,Software\Microsoft\Windows\CurrentVersion\DeleteFiles\Samples,,,
C:\Samples
HKLM,Software\Microsoft\Windows\CurrentVersion\DeleteFiles\
Samples,oldname.txt,,"New_Long_Name.txt"
HKLM,Software\Microsoft\Windows\CurrentVersion\DeleteFiles\Win,,,%25%
HKLM,Software\Microsoft\Windows\CurrentVersion\DeleteFiles\
Win,myreadme.txt,,"My_App_Readme.txt"
```

Setting Attributes for Files and Folders

To set the attributes for a file or folder, you must use the same convention that you use to create long file names with the optional *attrib_flag* parameter. For more information, see "Managing Long File Names" earlier in this chapter.

Copying Files to the Program Files Folder

Because copying Windows files is a 16-bit operation, you must use only short file names. Therefore, to access the Program Files folder, you must use the 8.3 equivalent, "24,PROGRA~1", in the **[DestinationDirs]** section of your .inf file. Similarly, you must use the short file name equivalent to access any folders with long file names in the Program Files folder.

The following example copies three files to the \Program Files\Accessories folder and creates links to one of the files:

```
[WordPadInstall]
CopyFiles = WordPadCopyFiles
UpdateInis = WordPadInis

[DestinationDirs]
WordPadCopyFiles = 24,%PROGRAMF%\%ACCESSOR%

[WordPadCopyFiles]
mswd6_32.wpc
wordpad.exe
write32.wpc

[WordPadInis]
setup.ini, progman.groups,, "group4=%APPS_DESC%"
;creates Accessories folder (if not already there)
setup.ini, group4,, """%WORDPAD_LINK%""",
"""%24%\%PROGRAMF%\%ACCESSOR%\WORDPAD.EXE"""
;creates link in Accessories folder

[Strings]
APPS_DESC = "Accessories"
WORDPAD_LINK = "WordPad"
; Folder names - note that the short versions must match the truncated
; 8-character names for the long versions, or there will be problems.
PROGRAMF = "Progra~1" ; first 6 chars of Program_Files, + "~1"
ACCESSOR = "Access~1" ; first 6 chars of Accessories, + "~1"
```

Extending Setup

You can use .inf files to extend Setup in the following ways:

- Execute Windows .inf files from the command line by using the **Run** command.
- Install optional Windows components by using 32-bit program code rather than by using the **Add/Remove Programs** dialog box in Control Panel.
- Create file icons on the Windows desktop that the user can right-click to run .inf files.

Running .inf Files from the Command Line

If you want to start the setup program for a component from the command line, you can use the **Run** command (Rundll.exe or Rundll32.exe) to carry out the **[Install]** section in the component's .inf file.

The following command-line syntax executes the **[Install]** section:

```
RunDll setupx.dll,InstallHinfSection section reboot-mode inf-name
```

The *section* parameter specifies the **[Install]** section in the .inf file. The *reboot-mode* parameter identifies how the computer should restart after the installation is complete.

The following table describes the five reboot modes that you can specify from the command line.

Reboot Mode	Value	Description
define HOW_NEVER _REBOOT 0	0 or 128	The computer does not restart automatically, and the user must decide whether to restart the computer without prompting from Setup.
define HOW_ALWAYS _SILENT_REBOOT 1	1 or 129	Setup always restarts the computer automatically without prompting the user.
define HOW_ALWAYS _PROMPT_REBOOT 2	2 or 130	Setup always prompts the user about whether to restart the computer without attempting to determine whether the computer requires restarting.
define HOW_SILENT _REBOOT 3	3 or 131	If necessary, Setup restarts the computer without any user interaction.
define HOW_PROMPT _REBOOT 4	4 or 132	If the computer requires restarting, Setup prompts the user with a dialog box.

 Important If *inf-name* specifies an .inf file that you provide rather than an .inf file that was shipped with a Windows 32-bit product, use the values 128 through 132. Also, if you specify an .inf file that you provide, all of the program files must exist in the same folder location on the installation disk as that .inf file.

The only recommended values for *reboot-mode* are 4 (for a Windows 32-bit .inf file) and 132 (for an .inf file that you provide). Using any of the other *reboot-mode* values might cause the computer to restart unnecessarily or cause the computer not to restart when it should.

This **Run** command assumes that the computer has the disk space required to install the files. It is recommended that you make your installation program check for available disk space before installing the component.

Your installation program must not include any code that executes after the call to **Rundll** or **Rundll32**, because after Setupx.dll takes control, the additional code might cause the user's computer to restart. If your installation process requires other code to run after the call to **Rundll** or **Rundll32**, include a **RunOnce** entry in your .inf file. You should not use a **RunOnce** entry to run the installation program. For more information about **RunOnce**, see "Using RunOnce Technology" later in this chapter.

The following example shows the command line that installs the Games optional component. If Setup needs to restart the computer after the installation, it prompts the user with a dialog box.

```
RunDll setupx.dll,InstallHinfSection games 4 applets.inf
```

In this example, *reboot-mode* for the Games optional component uses a value of 4 because Applets.inf is a Windows 32-bit .inf file. If you want to install a component with your own .inf file, set *reboot-mode* to 132.

Installing Optional Components by Using 32-bit Programs

After you install Windows on a computer, you might want to add one or more of the Windows optional components (for example, Games). This type of installation, which occurs after Setup initially installs Windows, is called *maintenance-mode setup*. Typically, you start maintenance-mode setup from Windows by clicking **Add/Remove Programs** in Control Panel. However, as a vendor or a supplier of an optional software component, you can also install the optional component by using a call to the **CreateProcess** function in a Windows 32-bit program.

To install an optional component from a Windows 32-bit program, you can use a combination of the following methods:

- Registry keys
- The **CreateProcess** function

Checking the Registry

Before starting the installation operation, you must determine whether the optional component is already installed on the computer by either checking the registry or looking for the component's program files. Windows uses the following registry path to maintain information about all the currently installed optional components:

```
HKEY_LOCAL_MACHINE\SOFTWARE\Microsoft\Windows\CurrentVersion\SETUP\
OptionalComponents
```

Values under **OptionalComponents** point to subkeys, and each subkey contains information about the optional components installed on the computer as well as information needed to install a new optional component. For example, to check whether the Games optional component is installed, look for the following entry under **OptionalComponents**:

```
"Games"="Games"
```

Then open the **Games** subkey under **OptionalComponents**. The following example shows that the Games optional component is not installed on this computer, because the **Installed** entry is set to 0:

```
HKEY_LOCAL_MACHINE\SOFTWARE\Microsoft\Windows\CurrentVersion\SETUP\
OptionalComponents\Games
"INF"="applets.inf"
"Section"="games"
"Installed"="0"
```

Calling the CreateProcess Function

You can install an optional component, such as Games, by using the **INF** and **Section** values in the **Games** subkey (shown in the previous example) in a call to the **CreateProcess** function. This function then uses Rundll.exe to run Setupx.dll, which is the same event that occurs when the **Add/Remove Programs** dialog box in Control Panel installs a component. The command-line string specified in the *lpCommandLine* parameter for **CreateProcess** uses the following syntax:

```
RunDll setupx.dll,InstallHinfSection section reboot-mode inf-name
```

The *section* parameter specifies the **[Install]** section in your .inf file. The *reboot-mode* parameter identifies how the computer should restart after the installation is complete. For a description of reboot-mode values, see "Extending Setup" earlier in this chapter.

This command assumes that the computer has the disk space required to install the files. It is recommended that your installation program check for available disk space before installing the component. The program should determine whether sufficient disk space exists for system swap files.

Your installation program must not include any code that executes after the call to **CreateProcess**, because after Setupx.dll takes control, the additional code might cause the user's computer to restart. If your installation process requires other code to run after the call to **CreateProcess**, include a **RunOnce** entry in your .inf file. You should not use a **RunOnce** entry to run the installation program. For more information about **RunOnce**, see "Using RunOnce Technology" later in this chapter.

The following example shows the command-line string used by **CreateProcess** to install the Games optional component. If Setup needs to restart the computer after the installation, it prompts the user with a dialog box.

```
RunDll setupx.dll,InstallHinfSection games 4 applets.inf
```

Using File Icons to Run .inf Files

You can use the **[DefaultInstall]** special installation section in your .inf file to install optional components. If you include the **[DefaultInstall]** section in your .inf file, a user running a 32-bit version of Windows can right-click a file icon to run the **[DefaultInstall]** section of your .inf file. After the user right-clicks the file icon, a shortcut menu displays a set of installation options. The user can select from these options to run the **[DefaultInstall]** section.

The **[DefaultInstall]** section in the .inf file provides a convenient method for installing optional components. It is particularly useful when you develop your installation program, because it provides a method for installing the optional components before you write the installation program. For complete information about the **[DefaultInstall]** section, see the appendix "Structural Definition of .inf Files" in this Resource Kit.

The following example shows typical entries in a **[DefaultInstall]** section:

```
[DefaultInstall]
CopyFiles=QCD.copy.prog, QCD.copy.hlp, QCD.copy.win, QCD.copy.sys,
QCD.copy.inf
UpdateInis=QCD.Links
AddReg=QCD.reg, QCD.run
Uninstall=FlexiCD_remove
```

Providing Uninstall Functionality in .inf Files

You can provide uninstall functionality to remove program files, registry entries, and shortcuts by adding the [DelFiles] and [DelReg] sections to your .inf file. DelFiles and DelReg entries in the *[OtherInstall]* section of the .inf file initiate the [DelFiles] and [DelReg] sections. For complete information about the [DelFiles] and [DelReg] sections and the DelFiles and DelReg entries in the *[OtherInstall]* section of the .inf file, see the appendix "Structural Definition of .inf Files" in this Resource Kit.

You can also include in the [AddReg] section of your .inf file registry information that adds your component to the list of programs that the user can uninstall from the Add/Remove Programs dialog box in Control Panel.

To add your component to the Add/Remove Programs dialog box, include the following [AddReg] entries in your .inf file:

```
HKLM,SOFTWARE\Microsoft\Windows\CurrentVersion\Uninstall\
app-name,"DisplayName",,"display description"
```

```
HKLM,SOFTWARE\Microsoft\Windows\CurrentVersion\Uninstall\
app-name,"UninstallString",,"command-line"
```

The "display description" appears in the list box in the Add/Remove Programs dialog box. The "command-line" executes when the user selects the component from the list box in the Add/Remove Programs dialog box. To execute a section in an .inf file, you can use the InstallHinfSection entry-point function in Setupx.dll.

> **Note**   When Setup installs the component, your installation code must copy the .inf file to the \Windows\Inf folder. Setup searches this default folder location when your installation code calls the InstallHinfSection entry-point function.
>
> Your code for uninstalling the component should remove the subkey that you created under the Uninstall registry key so that your component will no longer appear in the Add/Remove Programs list box after the user uninstalls it.

The following example shows [AddReg] entries that add "My Test Application" to the list box in the Add/Remove Programs dialog box and execute the [Remove_TestApp] installation section in Test.inf:

```
HKLM,SOFTWARE\Microsoft\Windows\CurrentVersion\Uninstall\Test,
"DisplayName",,"My Test Application"
```

```
HKLM,SOFTWARE\Microsoft\Windows\CurrentVersion\Uninstall\Test,
"UninstallString",,"RunDll setupx.dll,InstallHinfSection Remove_TestApp
4 test.inf"
```

Using RunOnce Technology

You can run any program after an .inf file has run by adding entries to the **RunOnce** registry key. This registry key allows you to start programs one time in Windows and specify whether the programs install *silently* (without prompts to your users) or as part of a list of programs or actions that users see.

You can add entries to the **RunOnce** registry key by including them in the **[AddReg]** section of your .inf file. If the .inf file specifies that the computer must restart, the **RunOnce** entries execute after the computer restarts. Setup then deletes the reference to the program so that it does not run again.

The following registry key specifies that programs run silently:

```
HKEY_LOCAL_MACHINE\Software\Microsoft\Windows\CurrentVersion\RunOnce
```

The following registry key specifies that programs run as part of a list of programs or actions that the user sees:

```
HKEY_LOCAL_MACHINE\Software\Microsoft\Windows\CurrentVersion\RunOnce\Se
tup
```

The **RunOnce** entries use the following format:

```
"description-string"="command-line"
```

The *"description-string"* provides the name of the program, which appears in the list of programs or actions that the user sees. The *"command-line"* starts the program.

The following example shows an **[AddReg]** entry that starts Myapp.exe (located in the Windows folder) and installs the program silently. A second **[AddReg]** entry then starts Test.exe (located in the System32 folder) and displays the following message to the user: "Windows Setup is now setting up the following items."

```
HKLM,Software\Microsoft\Windows\CurrentVersion\RunOnce,"SilentApp",,"%25%\
myapp.exe"
HKLM,Software\Microsoft\Windows\CurrentVersion\RunOnce\Setup,"Test
Utility",,"%11%\test.exe"
```

Limitations of .inf Files

The following limitations apply to .inf files:

- You cannot delete a directory.
- The **RenFiles** entry only renames a file in its existing location. You cannot use this entry to move a file to a different location.
- The **CopyFiles** entry only copies files from the source disk to the destination directory. You cannot use this entry to copy a file to another location on your hard disk.

C H A P T E R   1 8

Setting Up Servers

As you customize Microsoft® Internet Explorer 6 and prepare for your browser rollout, you should also prepare any servers that you will need to support the deployment. This chapter describes how to configure your servers to support browser features, set up automatic search and roaming user capabilities, and prepare for Internet sign-up using the Internet Connection Wizard.

In This Chapter

Related Information in the Resource Kit

- For more information about testing the deployment process before the final rollout, see "Setting Up and Administering a Pilot Program."

- For more information about preparing to use the Internet Explorer Administration Kit (IEAK), see "Preparing for the IEAK."

- For more information about building custom browser packages, see "Running the Microsoft Internet Explorer Customization Wizard."

- For more information about rolling out Internet Explorer to your users, see "Deploying Microsoft Internet Explorer 6."

Overview: Preparing Servers for Your Microsoft Internet Explorer Deployment

You might need to set up your servers as part of your Internet Explorer deployment. When you set up the servers, you should consider your users' needs in terms of deployment, browser use, and software updates. As an Internet service provider (ISP), you should also decide how users will sign up for your services. If you distribute files over the Internet or an intranet, consult your Web server documentation for specific information about how to set up your servers.

This chapter describes the server setup tasks that you need to complete, depending on the features that you plan to deploy with your custom browser packages. In addition, consider the following general deployment issues that can impact how quickly and easily users can install your packages:

- **Digital certificates.** You must digitally sign the files included with your custom browser packages. Otherwise, certain security levels might prevent users from downloading these files from your servers or prompt users with warning messages. For general information about digital certificates, see "Digital Certificates" in this Resource Kit. For information about preparing digital certificates before you run the Internet Explorer Customization Wizard, see "Preparing for the IEAK" in this Resource Kit.

- **Bandwidth and server load.** You might need to set up your servers in different locations or stagger the Internet Explorer rollouts to avoid an overwhelming demand on a specific server. For example, you might schedule installation for different divisions or regions a few days or weeks apart, depending on the size of your organization and the resources available.

  You can also use the Internet Explorer Customization Wizard to specify up to 10 sites from which users can download and install your custom browser packages. Then if one server is not available, Windows Update Setup for Internet Explorer 6 and Internet Tools attempts to download files from the next site in the list. However, if you plan to install Internet Explorer silently with no user interaction, you can choose only one site. For more information about deploying the browser to your users, see "Deploying Microsoft Internet Explorer 6" in this Resource Kit.

- **Important URLs.** As a corporate administrator, you can help offset some of the server load associated with Internet usage by specifying and setting up on your local intranet key user pages, such as the home, support, and search pages. When you run the Customization Wizard, you can preconfigure these pages for your custom browser packages in Stage 4 on the **Important URLs** page. If your users do not have Internet access, you must set up these pages on your intranet. For more information about the **Important URLs** page, see "Running the Microsoft Internet Explorer Customization Wizard" in this Resource Kit.

- **Software updates.** If your deployment plan includes software updates, you might want to schedule them during off-hours or stagger updates among groups of users to minimize the server load. For more information about software updates, see "Keeping Programs Updated" in this Resource Kit.

Configuring Servers for Automatic Configuration

and Automatic Proxy

When you run the Internet Explorer Customization Wizard, you can set up automatic configuration and automatic proxy and deploy these features as part of your custom browser packages. After you deploy Internet Explorer, you can use these features to update browser settings globally on users' computers.

If you plan to use automatic configuration and automatic proxy, you must configure your intranet servers for these features. You must install Web server software, such as Microsoft® Internet Information Services (IIS), and copy your automatic configuration and automatic proxy files to the server location that you specify when you run the Customization Wizard.

The number of servers required for automatic configuration and automatic proxy can vary according to the size and demands of your organization. For large organizations, you might need to configure your servers for each domain. For example, you might specify the following automatic configuration and automatic proxy URLs for user groups in domain 1:

```
http://domain1_server/autoconfig/<usergroup>.ins
http://domain1_server/autoconfig/proxy1.pac
```

Based on these URLs, you would install a Web server at http://domain1_server/ and then copy the <usergroup>.ins file, the associated <usergroup>.cab files, and the proxy1.pac file to the server at http://domain1_server/autoconfig/. When users in domain 1 start Internet Explorer, it reads the appropriate automatic configuration files and the automatic proxy file located at http://domain1_server/autoconfig/.

For more information about setting up automatic configuration and automatic proxy, see "Using Automatic Configuration, Automatic Proxy, and Automatic Detection" in this Resource Kit.

Configuring Servers for Automatic Detection

(Corporate Administrators)

As a corporate administrator, when you run the Internet Explorer Customization Wizard, you can set up automatic detection of browser settings and deploy this feature as part of your custom browser packages. Enabling automatic detection can help reduce administrative costs and potentially reduce help desk calls about browser settings.

Both Dynamic Host Configuration Protocol (DHCP) servers and Domain Name System (DNS) servers support automatic detection. With the appropriate settings, DHCP servers that support the DHCPINFORM message and DNS servers can automatically detect and configure Internet Explorer settings the first time users start the browser, even if you do not customize the browser first. For example, if a user downloads a non-customized browser from the Internet rather than installing a customized version from the corporate servers, automatic detection can automatically configure and customize the user's browser.

If you plan to use automatic detection, you must configure your DHCP and DNS servers for these features. Using DHCP servers with automatic detection works best for local area network (LAN)–based clients, while DNS servers enable automatic detection on computers with both LAN-based and dial-up connections. Although DNS servers can handle network and dial-up connections, DHCP servers provide faster access to LAN users and greater flexibility for specifying configuration files.

For more information about setting up automatic detection of browser settings, see "Using Automatic Configuration, Automatic Proxy, and Automatic Detection" in this Resource Kit.

Setting Up Automatic Detection on DHCP Servers

DHCP servers enable you to centrally specify global and subnet-specific TCP/IP parameters and to define parameters for clients by using reserved addresses. When client computers move between subnets, DHCP servers automatically reconfigure the client computers for TCP/IP when the computers restart on the new subnets.

To set up automatic detection of browser settings on DHCP servers, you must create a new option type with the code number 252. Also, your DHCP servers must support the DHCPINFORM message.

Note Depending on the types of DHCP servers available, the option names might vary slightly.

▶ **To add a new DHCP option type in Microsoft® Windows® 2000 Server**

1. Open the DHCP Manager.
2. Right-click the DHCP server, and then select **Set Predefined Options**.
3. In the **Option Class** list, click the class for which you want to add a new option type, and then click **Add**.

4. In the **Name** box, type a new option name.

5. In the **Data type** list, click **String**.

6. In the **Code** box, type the code number **252** to associate with this option type.

7. In the **Description** box, type a description, and then click **OK**.

8. For the default **Value** of the string, type the URL that points to your configuration file. This file can be a .pac, .jvs, .js, or .ins configuration file.

   Examples:

   http://www.microsoft.com/webproxy.pac
   http://marketing/config.ins
   http://###.#.###.#/account.pac

▶ **To add a new DHCP option type in Microsoft® Windows NT® 4.0 Server**

1. Open the DHCP Manager, and select a DHCP server.

2. On the **DHCP Options** menu, click **Defaults**.

3. In the **Option Class** list, click the class for which you want to add a new option type, and then click **New**.

4. In the **Name** box, type a new option name.

5. In the **Data Type** list, click **String**.

6. For the default value of the string, type the URL that points to your configuration file. This file can be a .pac, .jvs, .js, or .ins configuration file.

   Examples:

   http://www.microsoft.com/webproxy.pac
   http://marketing/config.ins
   http://###.#.###.#/account.pac

7. In the **Identifier** box, type the code number **252** to associate with this option type.

8. In the **Comment** box, type a description, and then click **OK**.

Setting Up Automatic Detection on DNS Servers

DNS servers support a set of TCP/IP network protocols and services that allow users to search for other computers by using hierarchical user-friendly names, often known as *host names*, instead of numeric IP addresses.

To set up automatic detection of browser settings on your DNS servers, you must configure one of the following record types in the DNS database file:

- **Host record.** Internet Explorer uses a host record to statically associate host (computer) names to IP addresses within a zone. A host record contains entries for all hosts that require static mappings, such as workstations, name servers, and mail servers.

  Host records use the following syntax:

  `<host name> IN A <ip address of host>`

  The following table shows some examples of host records.

Host name	IN	A	Host IP address
corserv	IN	A	192.55.200.143
nameserver2	IN	A	192.55.200.2
mailserver1	IN	A	192.55.200.51

- **CNAME record.** *Canonical name* (CNAME) records, sometimes called "aliases," allow you to use more than one name to point to a single host. Using CNAME records makes it easy to do such things as host both an FTP server and a Web server on the same computer.

▶ **To configure a DNS database file for automatic detection of browser settings**

1. In the DNS database file, type a host record named **wpad** that points to the IP address of the Web server containing the .pac, .jvs, .js, or .ins automatic configuration file.

    -Or-

    In the DNS database file, type a CNAME record named **wpad** that points to the name (the resolved name, not the IP address) of the server containing the .pac, .jvs, .js, or .ins automatic configuration file.

    After you add the record and the database file propagates to the DNS server, the DNS name wpad.*domain*.com resolves to the same computer name as the server that contains the automatic configuration file. Internet Explorer constructs a default URL template based on the host name wpad. For example:

    http://wpad.*domain*.com/wpad.dat

2. On the Web server, wpad, set up a file or redirection point named wpad.dat that delivers the contents of your automatic configuration file.

Working with Proxy Servers

Proxy servers act as intermediaries between computers and the Internet. Organizations typically use proxy servers when they set up corporate intranets and users connect to local area networks. Proxy servers can also work with firewalls to provide a security barrier between an organization's internal network and the Internet. Corporate administrators can use proxy servers to balance proxy loads and block undesirable sites. Proxy servers can also help reduce network traffic by caching content that browsers request frequently.

The following sections describe three setup tasks for organizations that use proxy servers:

- Configuring proxy server settings
- Configuring proxy bypass lists
- Configuring FTP sites for CERN-compliant proxy servers

Configuring Proxy Server Settings (Corporate Administrators and ISPs)

As a corporate administrator or ISP, when you run the Internet Explorer Customization Wizard, you can configure proxy server settings for your custom browser packages on the **Proxy Settings** page in Stage 4. You can specify the addresses and port numbers of the proxy servers that your users can connect to when they browse the Internet or intranet. The **Proxy Settings** page in the Customization Wizard corresponds to the **Proxy Settings** page in the IEAK Profile Manager as well as to the **Proxy Settings** dialog box in the browser, which users can access by clicking **LAN Settings** on the **Connections** tab in the **Internet Options** dialog box.

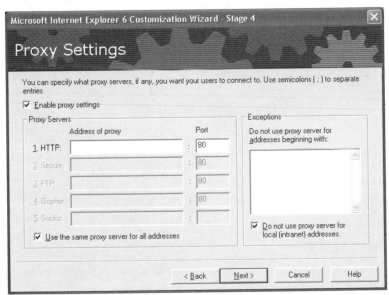

If you plan to preconfigure the proxy server settings as part of your custom browser packages, identify the proxy server addresses and port numbers for each protocol setting: **HTTP**, **Secure** (HTTPS requests based on the Secure Sockets Layer [SSL] technology), **FTP**, **Gopher**, and **Socks**.

Use the following syntax for your proxy server settings:

```
http://<address>:<port>
```

Here, *<address>* identifies the Web address of the proxy server, and *<port>* identifies the port number assigned to the proxy server. For example, if the address of your proxy server is proxy.example.microsoft.com and its port number is 80, use the following proxy server information:

```
http://proxy.example.microsoft.com:80
```

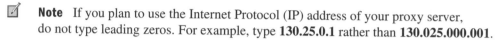 **Note**   If you plan to use the Internet Protocol (IP) address of your proxy server, do not type leading zeros. For example, type **130.25.0.1** rather than **130.025.000.001**.

Internet Explorer assumes that proxy locations that do not begin with a protocol (such as http:// or ftp://) use the CERN-type HTTP protocol. For example, when the user types **proxy**, Internet Explorer treats this entry the same as if the user had typed **http://proxy**. For FTP gateways, such as the Trusted Information Systems (TIS) FTP gateway, type the proxy address with ftp:// in front of the proxy name.

The operating system stores the proxy server settings in the following registry location:

```
HKEY_CURRENT_USER\SOFTWARE\MICROSOFT\WINDOWS\CURRENTVERSION\
Internet Settings\
"ProxyEnable"="01 00 00 00"
"ProxyServer"="data"
"ProxyOverride"="local"
```

For more information about configuring proxy server settings when you run the Customization Wizard, see "Running the Microsoft Internet Explorer Customization Wizard" in this Resource Kit. Corporate administrators can also preconfigure and manage proxy settings by using an automatic proxy configuration file in .js, .jvs, or .pac format. For more information about automatic proxy configuration, see "Configuring Servers for Automatic Configuration and Automatic Proxy" earlier in this chapter.

Configuring Proxy Bypass Lists

Some network requests, such as those for local (intranet) addresses, need to bypass the proxy server. When you run the Internet Explorer Customization Wizard, you can use the proxy bypass list in the **Exceptions** area of the **Proxy Settings** page to specify addresses that Internet Explorer can access directly without going through the proxy server. Users can also update the proxy bypass list on the corresponding **Proxy Settings** dialog box in the browser.

Generally, the addresses listed on the proxy bypass list do not contain periods (for example, http://contoso). In the **Exceptions** area of the **Proxy Settings** page, you can also choose to automatically bypass the proxy server and directly resolve all addresses without a period.

If you plan to configure the proxy bypass list as part of your custom browser packages, identify the addresses that you want to include. The following list provides guidelines and requirements for your proxy bypass entries:

- Entries are case-insensitive; use a semicolon (;) to separate multiple entries.

- Entries can begin with a protocol type: http://, https://, ftp://, or gopher://.

- If you use a protocol type, the entry applies only to requests for that protocol.

- If you do not use a protocol type, Internet Explorer bypasses any requests that use the address.

- If you specify a port number, Internet Explorer processes the request only when it uses the specified port number.

To bypass more complex addresses, you can set up exceptions for specific addresses or wildcards. You can use the wildcard character * in place of characters in your proxy bypass list entries. The following list provides examples that show how to use wildcards:

- To bypass proxy servers, type a wildcard at the beginning of an Internet address, IP address, or domain name with a common ending. For example, to bypass any addresses ending in ".example.microsoft.com" (such as some.example.microsoft.com and www.example.microsoft.com), type ***.example.microsoft.com** as the proxy bypass entry.

- To bypass proxy servers, type a wildcard in the middle of an Internet address, IP address, or domain name with a common beginning and ending. For example, the entry **www.*.com** causes Internet Explorer to bypass any addresses that starts with "www" and ends with "com."

- To bypass proxy servers, type a wildcard at the ending of an Internet address, IP address, or domain name with a common beginning. For example, to bypass any addresses that begin with "www.microsoft." (such as www.microsoft.com, www.microsoft.org, and www.microsoftcorporation.com), type **www.microsoft.*** as the proxy bypass entry.

- To bypass addresses with similar patterns, use multiple wildcards. For example, to bypass addresses such as 123.144.66.12, 123.133.66.15, and 123.187.66.13, type **123.1*.66.*** as the proxy bypass entry.

- To bypass the proxy server for a local domain, use ***.domain.com**. This entry will not use the proxy server for any computer name ending in .domain.com. You can use this wildcard for any part of the name.

Although wildcards are powerful, use them carefully. For example, the entry **www.*.com** causes Internet Explorer to bypass the proxy server for most Web sites.

Configuring FTP Sites for CERN-compliant Proxy Servers

Users can access FTP sites through CERN-compliant proxy servers. To access an FTP site, users type the URL for the FTP site they want to connect to, as in the following example:

ftp://ftp.microsoft.com

If the site requires a user name and a password, users also need to include that information in the address:

ftp://*username*:*password*@ftp.microsoft.com

If your system uses a CERN-compliant proxy server, users can only download files from and view files at FTP sites. To enable them to perform other services, such as uploading files, you need to provide a different proxy server solution.

Working with Automatic Search

When you prepare your intranet servers for your Internet Explorer deployment, you might want to customize the browser's automatic search feature. Automatic search enables users to search for frequently used pages by typing a conversational word into the Address bar. They do not need to remember the URLs for the pages, so they can find key information more easily. For example, when users type the word *invoice* into the Address bar, you might enable a Web page about invoices to appear, even if the URL of the page does not contain this term.

Internet Explorer already uses this feature for searching the Internet. For example, typing certain well-known, recognizable words, such as *Microsoft* or *MSN,* into the Address bar causes the Web sites associated with those words to appear. When the automatic search feature cannot distinctly associate a term with a Web site—for example, several apparent matches exist—Internet Explorer displays a Web page showing the top search results.

The Web site that appears does not necessarily contain the exact search word in its URL. If a Web site with the same domain as the search word is not the best match (for example, if the search word is the same as the URL without "www." and ".com"), Internet Explorer tells users that it is redirecting their search to the site with the best match for that word.

The following sections describe how corporate administrators can customize automatic search and provide an example of an .asp AutoSearch script. If you are an ICP or ISP and you want more information about customizing the automatic search feature, send an e-mail message to autosrch@microsoft.com.

Configuring the Automatic Search URL

You can configure the Automatic Search URL, which redirects users to Web pages based on the automatic search script that you create. The URL contains two parameters denoted by a percent sign (%). The value %1 represents what users type in the Address bar. The value %2 represents the type of search option that users choose. You can use the following values for %2:

- 3 = Display the results and go to the most likely site.
- 2 = Just go to the most likely site.
- 1 = Just display the results in the main window.
- 0 = Do not search from the Address bar.

▶ To set up Automatic Search

1. Create an automatic search script, and post it to your intranet server. To review a sample script, see the section "Reviewing a Sample .asp AutoSearch Script" later in this chapter.

   You can use a script file, such as an Active Server Pages (.asp) file, that conditionally checks for search terms. You must host the script at the following location:

   http://ieautosearch/response.asp?MT=%1&srch=%2.

   If you do not use IIS, you must remap this URL to the address of your script location.

2. When you run the Internet Explorer Customization Wizard, go to the **Policies and Restrictions** page in Stage 5.

   -Or-

   When you run the IEAK Profile Manager, click **Policies and Restrictions**.

3. Click Internet Settings, and then click Advanced settings.

4. Under **Searching**, in the Search Provider Keyword box, type intranet.

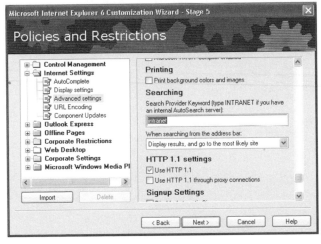

5. If you want to redirect users to another site rather than return search results, in the **When searching from the address bar** box, select **Just go to the most likely site**.

☑ **Note** If you do not want to customize automatic search and your organization does not have Internet access, you might want to disable this feature. To do this, in the **When searching from the address bar** box, select **Never search from the Address bar**.

Reviewing a Sample .asp AutoSearch Script

The following sample script shows how you can redirect search queries on an intranet to the appropriate Web page.

```
<%@ Language=VBScript %>
<%
' search holds the words typed in the Address bar by the user, without
' the "go" or ' "find" or any delimiters like "+" for spaces.
' If the user types "Apple pie," search = "Apple pie."
' If the user types "find Apple pie," search = "Apple pie."
search = Request.QueryString("MT")
search = UCase(search)
searchOption = Request.QueryString("srch")


' This is a simple if/then/else script to redirect the browser
' to the site of your choice based on what the user typed.
' Example: expense report is an intranet page about
' filling out an expense report
if (search = "NEW HIRE") then
Response.Redirect("http://admin/hr/newhireforms.htm")
elseif (search = "LIBRARY CATALOG") then
Response.Redirect("http://library/catalog")
elseif (search = "EXPENSE REPORT") then
Response.Redirect("http://expense")
elseif (search = "LUNCH MENU") then
Response.Redirect("http://cafe/menu/")
else
' If there is not a match, use the
' default IE autosearch server
Response.Redirect("http://auto.search.msn.com/response.asp?MT="
+ search + "&srch=" + searchOption +
"&prov=&utf8")
end if
%>
```

Working with Roaming User Profiles

(Corporate Administrators)

As a corporate administrator, you can set up roaming user profiles, which allow multiple users to access and use a single installation of Internet Explorer on a computer while retaining unique individual settings for each user. This feature also allows browser settings to follow users to other computers.

By storing each roaming user's copy of User.dat on a central server, Microsoft® Windows® can download the user's settings to any computer on which the user logs on. Users can then see the same environment no matter what computers they use. Maintaining roaming user profiles on a central server also allows you to maintain control over individual user settings.

If you plan to implement roaming user profiles on your corporate network, decide how you want to configure the profiles for your network configuration and user needs. Also, consider the following issues that affect roaming user profiles:

- **Per-user settings.** You can control content and settings saved on a per-user basis. This control helps you conserve disk space and avoid excessive network traffic. Even if a server might have unlimited disk space to store content, it is not always practical for content in a profile to pass back and forth between the server and the client. Therefore, you might want to control content and settings on a per-user basis to minimize the amount of data stored in profiles.

- **Folders and files.** You can set up roaming user profiles so that folders and files roam with the users from one computer to another. Keep in mind that although you can allow any files to roam, not all files should. When Windows copies large numbers of files to and from the users' logon server, both performance and security issues arise. For example, users might not want or expect Windows to copy sensitive documents to any workstation on which they log on and to remain there even after they log off.

- **Links to programs.** Links usually contain hard-coded paths (such as a shortcut to C:\Program Files\Internet Explorer\IExplore.exe) that might not roam well. If you want the contents of a folder that contains shortcuts to roam, create shortcuts that do not contain absolute paths.

For more information about issues that affect roaming user profiles, see your Windows documentation.

Creating Roaming User Profiles

Because the operating system controls roaming user profiles, they are bound by the different ways of handling profiles among the different operating systems. On Windows, the process of creating a new roaming user profile includes the following basic steps:

1. **Enable user profiles.** Before you can create a user profile, enable profiles on your operating system.

2. **Create a profile directory.** Determine where you want to store the user profiles. If you have not prepared a location, create a directory on the server and establish a network share.

3. **Create new user accounts.** Create the necessary user accounts (if they do not already exist), and specify the User Profile path where you plan to store the profiles. When you add accounts, you can also choose the level of access for the new users.

4. **Assign profiles.** Specify whether each user will use a specific user profile or the default user profile from the workstation.

On Microsoft® Windows® XP and Microsoft® Windows® 2000 operating systems, you can set up and administer roaming user profiles by using Group Policy and the Internet Explorer Maintenance (IEM) Group Policy snap-in extension. For more information about Group Policy and the IEM Group Policy snap-in extension, see Windows XP or Windows 2000 Help. You can also review Group Policy information in the Windows XP or Windows 2000 Resource Kits. For more information about setting up and administering roaming user profiles on other Windows operating systems, see the appropriate Windows documentation.

Using Caching Options

The Internet Explorer Customization Wizard includes a system policy for caching temporary Internet files. You can locate the **Delete saved pages when browser closed** check box under **Advanced settings** on the **Policies and Restrictions** page in Stage 5. The IEAK Profile Manager and the Internet Explorer browser also include corresponding options for caching temporary Internet files.

This system policy determines whether Internet Explorer deletes all cached Internet files when users close the browser. This option does not delete cookie information, which the operating system copies when the profile is saved.

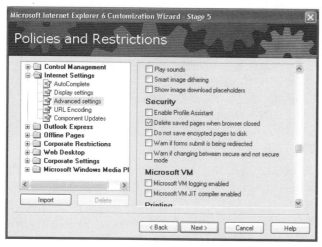

If you plan to use roaming user profiles, decide whether you want to enable this system policy. If you do not enable it, when the user logs off, Internet Explorer copies all temporary Internet files to the user's profile folder. Then Internet Explorer copies the temporary Internet files back to the local computer the next time the user logs on. This copy process can be time-consuming and can use a large amount of server space.

Preparing Servers for Internet Sign-up (ISPs)

As an ISP, you can implement an Internet sign-up server (HTTP server) to automate the task of adding new customers to your customer database. The Internet sign-up server collects information from each new customer, adds the information to the customer database, and then passes a configuration packet back to the customer's desktop computer. The configuration packet contains information that configures the customer's Internet browser for subsequent connections to your Internet services.

To add a new customer to the customer database, the Internet sign-up server performs the following activities:

- Causes the client computer to establish an HTTP connection with the sign-up server.
- Collects sign-up information from the customer.
- Handles the customer's acceptance or refusal of the Internet services.

When you run the Internet Explorer Customization Wizard to create your custom browser packages, you can choose from four options for Internet sign-up:

- Server-based sign-up by using the Internet Connection Wizard (ICW)
- Server-based sign-up by using the browser in Kiosk mode
- Serverless sign-up
- No sign-up

Server-based sign-up is the preferred option, because you can change settings more easily on the server than on the client. Of the two server-based options, the ICW-mode sign-up is recommended, because it uses a standard wizard interface that you can customize to fit your needs.

> **Note** If you plan to use single-disk branding and you anticipate that some of your users might have Internet Explorer 4.01 Service Pack 1 installed, do not use ICW-mode sign-up; instead, use Kiosk-mode sign-up. If you think some customers might have a later version of Internet Explorer, you can create a custom browser package that contains both sign-up solutions.

The following sections describe how to prepare the files necessary to create an ICW-mode sign-up process. Although these sections describe a tested, comprehensive sign-up solution, you can customize the sign-up process further to meet the needs of your organization. For general information about Internet sign-up, see "Implementing the Sign-up Process" in this Resource Kit.

Using the Sample ICW-mode Sign-up Files

The IEAK6\Toolkit folder in your IEAK installation directory contains customizable solutions for both server-based and serverless Internet sign-up. The IEAK6\Toolkit\Isp\Server\ICW\Signup subfolder includes sample files in both .asp and Perl format that allow you to build an ICW-mode sign-up process for Web servers with minimal effort. If you use the sample files, you need to integrate the sign-up server with only your registration and billing systems. In the Microsoft® Windows® 98 Referral Server Program, the sign-up server code is similar for both IEAK sign-up and Referral Server registrations.

If you prefer to create your own Internet sign-up files rather than use the sample files provided with the IEAK, you might still want to review the sample files before creating your own. The files can give you a general idea about how the sign-up process works and the types of information that you will need to provide.

▶   **To review the sample ICW sign-up files on your server**

1. In your server's wwwroot folder, create a subfolder named Signup.
2. Copy the files from the IEAK6\Toolkit\Isp\Server\ICW folder in your IEAK installation directory to the Signup subfolder that you created in Step 1.
3. In the files, change all the references to point to your sign-up server.
4. In the HTML code on the sign-up server pages, change all the references from the sample company name to your organization's name.
5. Modify the last sign-up server page to reflect your .ins settings.

Creating the .isp File

When you implement the sign-up process with your custom browser packages, the Internet sign-up (.isp) file, Signup.isp, provides dial-up information for your Internet services. For the server-based sign-up method, this sign-up file also contains a link to the URL of the server script that generates your .ins configuration file.

📝   **Note** If your sign-up solution includes multiple Internet sign-up (.isp) files for different customer needs, you must include the Dynamic HTML Data Binding component with your custom browser packages.

The IEAK includes a tool, the ISP File Wizard, that you can use to generate your .isp file automatically.

▶ **To install and start the ISP File Wizard**

1. In the IEAK6\Toolkit\ISP\Wizard folder in your IEAK installation directory, double-click **Filewiz.exe**, and then complete the steps to install the ISP File Wizard.

2. Click the **Start** menu, point to **Programs** (in Windows XP, point to **All Programs**), and then click **ISP File Wizard**.

3. Follow the instructions in the wizard to create an .isp file with your custom settings.

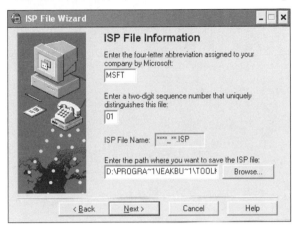

☑ **Note**   You can prevent a default area code from being set by setting a flag in the .isp file. The syntax for this flag is:

```
Dial_As_Is=Yes
```

You might want to set this flag if, for example, some users might call from an area code that is different from the default. If users do not know that the default area code differs from their current area code, they could unexpectedly incur long-distance charges.

Creating the ICW-mode Sign-up Pages

This section describes each of the sample pages included in the ICW sign-up process. When you customize these pages for your own sign-up process, make sure that you follow the coding and accessibility requirements described in "Coding Requirements for ICW-mode Sign-up" and "Accessibility Requirements for ICW-mode Sign-up" later in this chapter.

Initial Sign-up Page (Icwsign.htm)

After users install Internet Explorer 6 and Internet Tools and restart their computers, the Initial Sign-up page (Icwsign.htm) appears as the first sign-up page. When you run the Internet Explorer Customization Wizard, you can specify this page as part of your custom browser package so that your Internet Explorer build automatically includes this page. You do not host this page on your sign-up server.

On the Icwsign.htm page, users see your welcome information. This first page prompts them to either click **Next** to begin the sign-up process (if they need only one ISP file for sign-up), or select their city and state for dial-up connections. Based on the city and state, the ICW can select the appropriate sign-up server ISP file to use. When users click **Next**, the ICW dials and connects them to the ISP sign-up server.

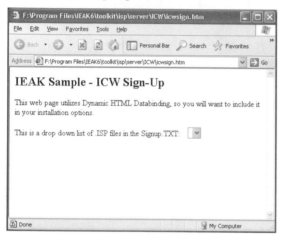

Name and Address Page

When users first connect to your sign-up server, they can type their contact information, including name, address, and telephone number, on the Name and Address page. This page appears in a frame, which measures 444 pixels wide by 273 pixels high, within the wizard window. If the HTML page exceeds these dimensions, scroll bars do not appear.

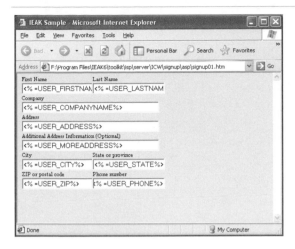

Billing Options Page

On the Billing Options page, you can present the service billing options that users can choose from. Users can select an option by clicking an HTML option button, or they can accept your pre-selected default option.

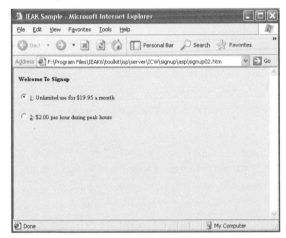

This page presents the options using an HTML form in a floating frame, which measures 444 pixels wide by 273 pixels high, within the wizard window. If the HTML page exceeds these dimensions, scroll bars do not appear. If users need to make multiple selections, you can also include HTML check boxes in the frame.

Method of Payment Page

On the Method of Payment page, users can specify how they want to pay for the Internet service. You can control which payment methods appear in the Payment Method list. The ICW collects the payment information in the form that appears in the frame below the selection, which changes depending on the payment method that users select in the list.

You can offer the following types of payment methods:

- Credit card (you can specify the type of card, such as Visa or American Express)
- Debit card
- Invoice
- Phone bill charges

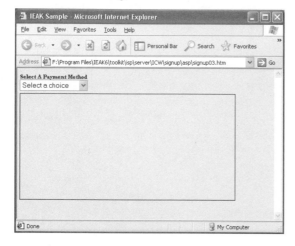

ISP Account Login/E-mail Page

On the ISP Account Login/E-mail page, users can select their account login and/or e-mail ID and password. This page appears in a floating frame, which measures 444 pixels wide by 273 pixels high, within the wizard window. If the HTML page exceeds these dimensions, scroll bars do not appear.

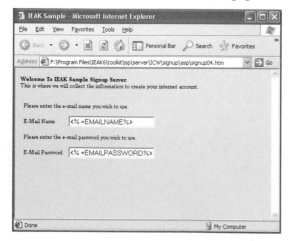

ISP POP Selection Page

On the ISP POP selection page, users can select local phone numbers to use for Internet access. This page appears in a floating frame, which measures 444 pixels wide by 273 pixels high, within the wizard. If the HTML page exceeds these dimensions, scroll bars do not appear.

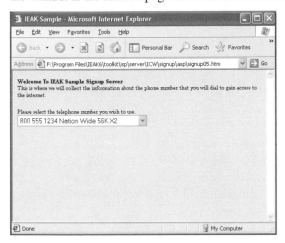

This page should not prompt users to type an area code or phone number a second time. Your sign-up server should populate any area code or phone number fields in the frame using the information already collected from the Name and Address page.

ISP Terms and Conditions Page

On the ISP Terms and Conditions page, users can read and accept your legal agreement for Internet services. This page should begin with the agreement title and instructions that explain how users can find a copy of the agreement on your Web site if they want to view it again or print it.

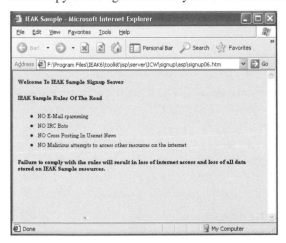

To ensure that users accept the agreement, you can add an **I accept the agreement** check box and then dim the **Next** button until users select the check box. To allow users to save the ISP Terms and Conditions page for later viewing, you can also add a **Save Copy** button to this page. The ICW prompts users to type a file name and location where they want to save the file. Then the ICW saves the actual terms and conditions file from your sign-up server to the selected location.

This page appears in a floating frame, which measures 426 pixels wide, within the wizard window. This width does not include an additional 2-pixel border and a vertical scroll bar. If the HTML page exceeds the width dimension, a horizontal scroll bar does not appear.

 Note The accessibility requirements do not apply to this page, because it does not allow HTML form elements.

Finish Page

When users click **Next** on the Finish page, the ICW processes the .ins file and configures the computer for the new Internet account. After completing this process, the ICW displays the final page, which informs users about the Internet connection and tells them how to begin browsing the Internet. No ISP-configurable interface appears on the final page.

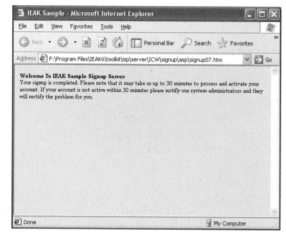

You can also add a **Begin browsing immediately** check box, which allows users to begin browsing immediately. You can use the StartURL value in the .ins file to specify the page that the browser displays when it first opens.

 Note After users finish the ICW-mode sign-up process, your sign-up server must return information about how to configure their computers for Internet access. The .ins file, which the ICW downloads to users' computers at the end of the sign-up process, contains this information.

Error Pages

You might also want to create error pages. Then, if users submit any invalid data to the sign-up server during the sign-up process, the server can display an HTML page with a friendly error message. For example, if a user requests an e-mail name that the server has already assigned to another user, the server can display a friendly error message that prompts the user to choose an alternate password.

The error pages should contain text that identifies the invalid data and provides the FORM elements required for users to type new data. These pages appear in floating frames, which measure 444 pixels wide by 273 pixels high, within the wizard window. If the HTML pages exceed these dimensions, scroll bars do not appear.

Using ICW Automatic Reconfiguration

If users have already set up their Internet accounts, the ICW automatic reconfiguration feature allows them to automatically reconfigure their account settings for the Internet service. For example, when a user buys a new computer, this feature can configure the computer for the same Internet account that the person used on a previous computer or on a computer at work. ICW automatic reconfiguration also helps users whose Internet settings become corrupted.

When users download your custom browser package, they can navigate to the automatic reconfiguration server by clicking a link on the Initial Sign-up page (Icwsign.htm). After users connect to your server, you can use two methods to restore the users' settings:

- Prompt users for their existing user name, password, and POP server. Using this information, automatic reconfiguration can recreate the .ins file and then send it to the users' computers to reconfigure their accounts.

- Store .ins files in the same location as the rest of the users' account information. When users connect to the automatic reconfiguration server, they can obtain the .ins files by providing only their user name and password. The server looks up a user's account and delivers a copy of the original .ins file.

> **Note** If you think that users might abuse the automatic reconfiguration feature, you might want to re-collect each user's credit card number and check it against the registration database.

The following sections describe how to prepare the files necessary to create an ICW automatic reconfiguration process. Although these sections describe a tested, comprehensive solution, you can customize this process further to meet the needs of your organization.

Using the Sample ICW Automatic Reconfiguration Files

The IEAK6\Toolkit\Isp\Server\ICW\Reconfig folder includes sample files in both .asp and Perl formats that allow you to build an ICW automatic reconfiguration process for Web servers with minimal effort. If you use the sample files, you need to integrate the sign-up server with only your registration and billing systems.

If you prefer to create your own ICW automatic reconfiguration files rather than use the sample files provided with the IEAK, you might still want to review the sample files before creating your own. The files can give you a general idea about how the ICW automatic reconfiguration process works and the types of information that you will need to provide.

▶ **To review the sample sign-up pages for ICW automatic reconfiguration**

1. In your server's wwwroot folder, create a folder named Autocfg.
2. Copy the files from the IEAK6\Toolkit\Isp\Server\ICW\Reconfig folder in your IEAK installation directory to the Autocfg subfolder that you created in Step 1.
3. In the files, change all the references to point to your sign-up server.
4. In the HTML code of the sign-up server pages, change all the references from Acme ISP to your organization's name.
5. Modify the last sign-up server page to reflect your .ins settings.

Creating the ICW Automatic Reconfiguration Pages

This section describes each of the sample pages included in the ICW automatic reconfiguration process. When you customize these pages for your own ICW automatic reconfiguration process, make sure that you follow the coding and accessibility requirements described in "Coding Requirements for ICW-mode Sign-up" and "Accessibility Requirements for ICW-mode Sign-up" later in this chapter.

ISP Account Login/E-mail Page

As the first page on the automatic reconfiguration server, the ISP Account Login/E-mail page prompts users for their account login and/or e-mail ID and password. This page is similar in design to the ISP Account Login/E-mail page for traditional ICW-mode sign-up. For more information about the ISP Account Login/E-mail page for traditional ICW-mode sign-up, see "Creating the ICW-mode Sign-up Pages" earlier in this chapter.

ISP POP Selection Page

On the ISP POP Selection page, users can select local phone numbers to use for Internet access. After users provide this information, the automatic reconfiguration server can recreate their .ins files. This page is similar in design to the ISP POP Selection page for traditional ICW-mode sign-up. For more information about the ISP POP Selection page for traditional ICW-mode sign-up, see "Creating the ICW-mode Sign-up Pages" earlier in this chapter.

Finish Page

When users click **Next** on the Finish page, ICW automatic reconfiguration processes their .ins files and reconfigures their computers for the Internet accounts. After completing this process, the ICW displays the final page, which informs users about the Internet connection and tells them how to begin browsing the Internet. This page is similar in design to the final page for traditional ICW-mode sign-up. For more information about the final page for traditional ICW sign-up, see "Creating the ICW-mode Sign-up Pages" earlier in this chapter.

You can also decide whether you want to display the **Save Information** check box and text on the final page. If users select this check box, the ICW sign-up server saves this page's HTML code to their desktops as an HTML file. Users can refer to this file to remember passwords or service information.

By default, the final page does not show the **Save Information** check box. To turn on this check box, add the following form type to the HTML code for this page:

```
<FORM NAME=PAGEFLAG ACTION=1></FORM>
```

Coding Requirements for ICW-mode Sign-up

You must design the HTML pages that will interact with the customer during the sign-up process according to the coding requirements for ICW-mode sign-up. The ICW-mode sign-up mechanism makes the Internet sign-up server look and act like a standard Windows wizard. Although the ICW uses the power and flexibility of HTML, however, it does not use the same formatting.

Each page of the ICW-mode sign-up process must include the following design elements and adhere to the following design conventions:

- **Colors and fonts attributes.** All HTML pages in the ICW, except the Icwsign.htm page, must use the Windows system colors and fonts. If you use a style sheet, do not specify any font style or color attributes in it. The parent wizard sets these attributes.

- **HTML formatting.** Unless otherwise specified, the HTML pages cannot contain any special HTML formatting, such as tables with visible borders, images, or anchors. These pages allow only plain text and FORM elements (where required). You can use tables with invisible borders for layout.

  If you use a TABLE element in your error pages, the element must include a STYLE attribute. For example:

  ```
  <TABLE style="font: 8pt 'ms sans serif' buttontext"> </TABLE>
  ```

- **Text and FORM elements.** The HTML pages accept only text and FORM elements. Do not use images, links, or scroll bars in your design.

  FORM elements within the HTML pages must use the **NAME** attribute. The ICW is case-sensitive; capitalize all letters in the **NAME** attribute and its value.

  The HTML pages must include four FORM elements that specify different page properties:

  - **The unique PAGEID for the page.** Specify "PAGEID" (case-sensitive) as the **NAME** attribute for this FORM element. Also, specify a unique ID as the **ACTION** attribute of this FORM element, as shown in the following example:

    ```
    <FORM NAME="PAGEID" ACTION="page4"></FORM>
    ```

    The unique ID cannot match the PAGEID of any other page in the ISP section of the wizard.

  - **The characteristics of the page.** Specify "PAGETYPE" (case-sensitive) as the **NAME** attribute for this FORM element. Also, specify an empty string as the **ACTION** attribute for the FORM element, as shown in the following example:

    ```
    <FORM NAME="PAGETYPE" ACTION=""></FORM>
    ```

  - **The Back button function.** Specify "BACK" (case-sensitive) as the **NAME** attribute for this FORM element. Also, specify the absolute URL for the previous page as the **ACTION** attribute of this FORM element. To retain the data previously collected in the sign-up process, append it to the URL for the **Back** button page, as shown in the following example:

    ```
    <FORM NAME="BACK"ACTION="http://myserver/page2.asp"?
    firstname=bob&lastname=smith&address=..."></FORM>
    ```

    In this example, the data for the first and last names is appended to the URL in name/value pairs. Note, however, that no data is posted to this page.

  - **The Next button function.** Specify "NEXT" (case-sensitive) as the **NAME** attribute for this FORM element. No restrictions apply to the token names for the INPUT elements within the FORM element. Also, specify the absolute URL where the form information should be posted as the **ACTION** attribute for the FORM element, as shown in the following example:

    ```
    <FORM NAME="NEXT" ACTION="http://myserver/page2.asp"></FORM>
    ```

    For the data collected to be passed to the next page in the sign-up process, you must add hidden FORM fields on each of your sign-up server pages that contain the data elements collected on this and all previous pages. The URL that you reference must contain code that collects the data from the previous page and displays the next page of the sign-up process.

Accessibility Requirements for ICW-mode Sign-up

To ensure that users can access the elements on your HTML pages by using only the keyboard, all FORM elements must meet the following requirements:

- **ACCESSKEY attribute.** Associate an access key (hot key) with every FORM element by using the Internet Explorer **ACCESSKEY** attribute in the INPUT element and highlighting the access-key character with an Underline tag. Do not use the letters *b*, *f*, *g*, *n*, and *o* as access keys, because these letters are reserved for the ICW. For more information about the **ACCESSKEY** attribute, see the MSDN® Web site at http://msdn.microsoft.com/.

- **ICW tab-key order.** Include all FORM elements on the page in the ICW tab-key order by assigning a unique ID in the INPUT element.

- **LABEL attribute.** Associate a label with every FORM element by using the Internet Explorer **LABEL** attribute.

The following example shows a radio button FORM element that meets these accessibility requirements:

```
<input ID="option2"
type="radio"
name="billing"
value="hour"
accesskey="h"
checked>

<label for="option2">
5 <u>H</u>ours per month for $10.
</label>
```

Sign-up Server Considerations for IIS

If you use the Internet Information Services (IIS) as your sign-up server, you must configure the server to provide a DHCP IP address to the client when the client connects to the server. Because the sign-up process is relatively short, the expiration time for the IP address might be brief, possibly only a few minutes.

The sign-up process assumes that users will establish point-to-point dial-up connections, so you do not need to assign specific IP addresses for the DHCP server. However, you must determine whether the DHCP IP addresses will be valid Internet addresses or arbitrary addresses.

You must register the Multipurpose Internet Mail Extensions (MIME) type, "application/x-Internet-signup," for the .ins file with the sign-up server so that the client can process the .ins file automatically. When the client requests the .ins file, the sign-up server responds with this MIME type, which starts the associated installation application on the client side.

C H A P T E R   1 9

Setting Up and Administering a Pilot Program

Before you deploy Microsoft® Internet Explorer 6 to your users, set up and administer a pilot program. Begin by testing the installation of Internet Explorer 6 and Internet Tools in a lab, and then conduct the pilot program to refine your deployment configurations and strategies using a limited number of pilot participants. This process will help you validate your deployment plan and ensure your readiness for full-scale deployment. This chapter describes how to set up a computer lab to test your deployment process and outlines the steps for conducting a successful pilot program.

◆ **Important** Although the processes described in this chapter assume deployment within a corporate business setting, Internet service providers and Internet content providers can follow similar procedures when they administer a pilot program.

In This Chapter

Related Information in the Resource Kit

- For more information about developing deployment, training, and support plans, which you will test during the pilot installation, see "Planning the Deployment."

- For more information about building custom browser packages for the pilot installation, see "Running the Microsoft Internet Explorer Customization Wizard."

- For more information about rolling out Internet Explorer to your users following the pilot program, see "Deploying Microsoft Internet Explorer 6."

Overview: Testing Deployment Processes and Methods

Typically, a period of lab testing precedes a pilot program. Lab testing enables you to experiment with deployment processes and methods by building and installing custom browser packages on lab computers. For the lab testing, develop a separate plan and checklist, because this testing encompasses only a subset of actual deployment tasks. Your users do not need to participate in lab testing, so you do not need to provide user training and support.

When you are comfortable with the installation process in the lab, plan and conduct a pilot program. This program uses a small group of pilot users to simulate the activities that will occur during the actual deployment. Complete the tasks for deploying Internet Explorer, which are identified in your deployment, training, and support plans. Also, finalize your deployment plan based on the results of your pilot program. For more information about planning your deployment, including choosing browser configurations, selecting training and support staff, and developing formal, written plans, see "Planning the Deployment" in this Resource Kit.

 Important This chapter assumes that your organization has an optimum budget, time frame, staffing, and resources for testing and pilot program tasks. Smaller companies might need to implement a scaled-down version, with fewer computers and participants. For example, if your organization does not have a designated, on-site support team to address users' questions and issues during the pilot program, you might need to rely on other knowledgeable staff members or Microsoft Product Support Services for browser support services.

Preparing the Test Plan and Checklist

First, prepare a test plan and checklist. When you test the deployment process in the computer lab, use the checklist as a guide. Mark the completed tasks on the checklist, and note any problems with the process.

Include each of the following sets of tasks on your checklist:

Prepare custom browser packages for deployment.

- Install and run the Microsoft® Internet Explorer Customization Wizard.
- Build custom browser packages containing the distribution files.
- Configure automatic browser configuration and automatic detection process files.
- Configure download sites, and install the distribution files.
- Copy distribution files to your distribution media, if necessary.

Deploy custom browser packages to lab computers.

- Run Windows Update Setup for Internet Explorer 6 and Internet Tools to install the custom browser package on each lab computer.
- Install Internet Explorer and Internet Tools using each available user option.

Test browser software after you install the custom browser packages.

- Run the sign-up server process, if applicable.
- Run Internet Explorer to test all features.
- Run any custom components that you included as part of your custom browser packages to make sure they work properly.
- Run other desktop and business applications to make sure they work properly.

Restore lab computers to their original state.

- Uninstall Internet Explorer.
- Uninstall any custom components that you included as part of your custom browser packages.
- Verify that you removed Internet Explorer and all components.
- Run other desktop and business applications to make sure they work properly.

Testing the Deployment Process in the Lab

To help ensure a smooth deployment of Internet Explorer, configure your lab computers to represent your typical user groups. If your user groups are large or have very different computing environments or requirements, you might need to prepare multiple labs and conduct tests at several different sites.

To test the deployment process in the lab, complete the following tasks:

- Prepare the lab.
- Conduct the lab testing.
- Test the uninstall process.

Preparing the Lab

Set aside physical space for each computer lab. Acquire a mix of computers that accurately reflects the hardware and software environments of your users' computers. Also, set up lab computers to represent existing browser configurations so that you can accurately test the migration process.

Before you install Internet Explorer and Internet Tools, complete the following tasks to ensure that your lab computers are functioning properly:

- Select a production computer that meets the system requirements for the Internet Explorer Customization Wizard. For more information about system requirements for the wizard, see "Planning the Deployment" in this Resource Kit.
- Verify that each lab computer has enough disk space, memory, and processing speed to run Internet Explorer. For more information about hardware requirements for Internet Explorer, see "Planning the Deployment" in this Resource Kit.
- Test basic operating system functions, including starting each computer and connecting to the server.

- Run virus detection, disk scanning, and defragmentation programs on each computer to prevent problems that might occur during testing. Although the computers might appear to be operating properly, software upgrades often uncover or create hardware or software problems because of the way they read and write data to the hard disk. Checking the computers before you install Internet Explorer and Internet Tools helps you to focus on issues related to deployment.

- Make sure you have the appropriate network connection hardware. If your users dial in from remote locations using portable computers, or you need to use additional servers or mainframe computers for business data, equip the lab computers with an analog phone line and appropriate network access. You might need power supplies and surge protectors, depending on the number of computers you use for testing. Also, research and eliminate any potential problems related to overheating or frequency distortion from the lab location.

- When the system hardware is ready, verify that the existing network is fully operational.

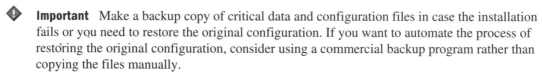 **Important** Make a backup copy of critical data and configuration files in case the installation fails or you need to restore the original configuration. If you want to automate the process of restoring the original configuration, consider using a commercial backup program rather than copying the files manually.

Make sure that you document the lab setup completely. Maintain a record of any changes you make so that you can duplicate the setup process during the pilot program.

Conducting the Lab Testing

To conduct the lab testing, perform all the tasks identified on the checklist. Install Internet Explorer and Internet Tools on the lab computers in the same way that you plan to install Internet Explorer and Internet Tools on your users' computers. In some cases, this might mean setting up the network installation location on the server and then installing Internet Explorer and Internet Tools on the lab computers from the server.

Automating your installation is an important step in reducing the cost of migration. You can choose to run the installation process from start to finish without user intervention. Also, you can install Internet Explorer and Internet Tools from the server so that you do not need to configure individual computers. Complete any automation work in the lab before you conduct the pilot program. For more information about automating the installation process, see "Preparing for the IEAK" in this Resource Kit.

When you run the Internet Explorer Customization Wizard, you can predefine a number of options for your users. Before you run your pilot program, make sure that you test the selected Internet Explorer configuration and any changes you make. Depending on how the test installation proceeds, you might want to modify the configuration by adding or removing components or features. If you want to consider several different configurations, you can evaluate them side by side in the lab. For more information about using the Internet Explorer Customization Wizard to predefine user options, see "Running the Microsoft Internet Explorer Customization Wizard" in this Resource Kit.

After you install Internet Explorer and Internet Tools on the lab computers, verify that the software runs correctly and that you can perform basic browser tasks, such as navigating to a Web page or adding a Web page to the Favorites list. After you determine that the basic configuration works as expected, test any optional features and any additional components that you installed as part of your custom browser packages.

During the testing process, maintain a record of all issues and problems. These records will help you design solutions to correct the problems you encounter. Then verify each solution using the same testing process in the lab.

Testing the Uninstall Process

After you have successfully completed the installation process on the lab computers, uninstall the browser and restore the computers to their original state. You can remove Internet Explorer by using the **Add/Remove Programs** dialog box in Windows Control Panel. You also have the option to restore the previous version of Internet Explorer that was installed on the computer.

Using the corporate administrator version of the Internet Explorer Customization Wizard, you can choose not to install the files needed to uninstall the browser. This reduces the amount of hard disk space required for the installation, but users will not be able to uninstall the browser from Control Panel. Also if you are using system management programs, such as Microsoft Systems Management Server (SMS), to install Internet Explorer and Internet Tools, you cannot uninstall the browser using Control Panel.

 Important Because of the large number of changes made to the system by Setup, a manual uninstall would be a time-consuming process requiring many steps. Attempting a manual uninstall is not recommended.

For information about troubleshooting the uninstall process, see the appendix "Troubleshooting" in this Resource Kit.

Planning the Pilot Program

After you test the deployment process in the lab, plan your pilot program. This program provides a scaled-down version of the final deployment. The goal of the pilot program is to further test and refine deployment strategies and configurations in everyday use among a limited group of users.

Project teams assigned to the pilot program can help you determine the best methods for installing your custom browser package configurations. Even though you are only testing the installation process, the pilot program sets a precedent for the final deployment; therefore, it is important that all participants be completely prepared. For more information about assembling project teams and selecting your custom browser package configurations, see "Planning the Deployment" in this Resource Kit.

To plan the pilot program, complete the following tasks:

- Identify resources and tasks.
- Select appropriate pilot groups.
- Create a database to document your progress.

Identifying Resources and Tasks

First, identify the resources and tasks you need to conduct the pilot program. Because the pilot program is your rehearsal for the final deployment, the tasks and resources should be similar to those identified in your deployment plan.

Selecting Appropriate Pilot Groups

Next, identify your pilot groups, and prepare them for the pilot program. Select groups that represent the diversity of your computer users. If your organization includes large user groups or groups with very different computing environments or requirements, you might need to select several pilot groups. Make sure that the people have enough time in their schedules and are willing to participate in the pilot program. Consider asking for volunteers—you should not ask people to participate who might be too busy with other projects and deadlines.

Creating a Database to Document Your Progress

Before the actual pilot installation begins, create a central database in which you can document your progress and any areas that might require further action. You can use the database to track open items and issues and to measure your actual progress against the original objectives documented in your deployment plan.

Conducting the Pilot Program

The pilot program helps you identify problems that might impede or delay deployment and also helps you determine the resources you will need. A successful pilot program can help your final deployment of Internet Explorer run more smoothly.

To conduct the pilot program, complete the following tasks:

- Prepare the training and support teams.
- Prepare the pilot groups.
- Implement the pilot installation.

Preparing the Training and Support Teams

Before the pilot installation begins, the training and support teams must become skilled users of Internet Explorer and Internet Tools and any custom components that you plan to install with your custom browser packages. First, give the team members access to the browser software so that they can explore the functions and features on their own. Then decide how you want to train the teams.

Some team members might already be proficient with earlier versions of Internet Explorer or third-party browser software, while others might not be skilled in this area. Consider self-paced and instructor-led training options based on the skill levels of your team members and the types of information you want to present. A classroom that allows hands-on practice is recommended when you instruct teams about more complex browser functions. If an external company will instruct your training and support teams, inform their representative about any company-specific or job-specific policies or applications for Internet Explorer.

After training, encourage team members to work with Internet Explorer every day. Continue to provide follow-up information and practice exercises so that team members become confident in their knowledge and ability before you start the pilot program.

Preparing Pilot Groups

Inform the pilot groups about the pilot program. Explain the benefits of migrating to Internet Explorer 6, and describe the overall plan and process that each group will follow. Then pilot groups can anticipate and plan for the browser installation.

Announce the pilot program well in advance of the start date, and follow up your announcement with several reminders. Conduct meetings with the pilot group managers and with all pilot group participants to set their expectations and to answer any questions. Provide a deployment presentation that explains how pilot groups will install Internet Explorer and Internet Tools. Describe any installation options that participants can select, and explain how they can get support for any questions or issues. Also, recommend that participants make a backup copy of important files on their computers.

Conduct Internet Explorer training. Training and support for the pilot program should simulate—on a smaller scale—the user training for the final deployment. Also, encourage participants to visit the Microsoft Windows Technologies Internet Explorer Web site at http://www.microsoft.com/windows/ie/ for more information. If you implement a training Web page on the Internet or intranet, use a memo or e-mail message to broadcast the URL and a description of the training page. Be sure to explain how participants can benefit from visiting your training page.

Implementing the Pilot Installation

Perform the pilot installation in the same way that you expect to install Internet Explorer and Internet Tools during the final deployment. As you conduct the pilot installation, you might need to revise the pilot schedule because certain tasks can take more or less time than expected, or you might need to add or remove some tasks. Use the revised pilot schedule for projecting the final deployment timetable, and then update the deployment plan with the new schedule information.

To implement the pilot installation, perform the following tasks:

- Deploy custom browser packages to pilot groups.
- Test Internet Explorer performance and capabilities.
- Monitor and support pilot groups.

Deploying Custom Browser Packages to Pilot Groups

Use the appropriate distribution methods to deploy the custom browser package that you created and tested in the lab. For example, you can send an e-mail message to pilot groups that directs them to the download site where they can follow instructions to download the custom browser package. If you are using compact discs, you can distribute them to the users and provide e-mail instructions about how to install the custom browser package from these media.

Testing Internet Explorer Performance and Capabilities

In addition to the project team members responsible for conducting the pilot installation, you might want to assign additional team members to measure, observe, and test the installation. By tracking the time per installation, handling problems that arise, and identifying areas for improvement or automation, these individuals can help ensure the success of both the pilot and the final installations.

After the pilot installation, these team members can test system capabilities, such as remote administration, to make sure that all functions are operating correctly. They should monitor the pilot computers for performance, stability, and functionality and highlight any inconsistencies with the lab configuration. Also, they should document ways to improve the installation, training, and support processes.

Monitoring and Supporting Pilot Groups

Dedicate the support team to the pilot program for the first few weeks. Support team members could be part of your existing help desk, staff members whom you have trained as subject matter experts, or representatives from an external vendor whom you have hired to provide support services to browser users. Assigned team members should carry pagers or be available by phone to assist pilot group participants at all times. Team members should also monitor the progress of the pilot program.

Track the volume of support calls during the pilot program to gauge the effect of deploying Internet Explorer on your support team. Make sure to document all trouble calls and problems, as well as the resources required to support pilot groups. Then use your experience during the pilot program to plan the support resources for the final deployment. You might want to plan for additional staffing or use this information to revise the final deployment schedule.

Finalizing the Deployment Plan

The results of the pilot installation provide the basis for developing a final plan for deploying Internet Explorer to your user groups. To finalize your deployment plan, you need to:

- Incorporate feedback from pilot program participants.
- Determine the time and resource requirements for final deployment.
- Update company policies and standards regarding Internet Explorer use.

Incorporating Feedback from Pilot Program Participants

Survey the pilot groups to measure their satisfaction and proficiency with the new installation and to evaluate the level of training and support provided. Test their proficiency by having them perform a few common tasks or use several of the new Internet Explorer 6 features.

Obtain feedback from all pilot program participants, including pilot groups and training and support team members, and document the lessons learned during the pilot program. Based on this initial feedback, record changes that will increase the satisfaction level and the effectiveness of the installation process.

Continue to monitor the pilot installation for a week or more to ensure that everything runs smoothly. Track open items and issues using the central database that you created for the pilot installation. Then incorporate the feedback into your deployment, training, and support plans. If the pilot program did not run smoothly or if feedback was negative, conduct additional pilot installations until the process works well.

Determining the Time and Resource Requirements for Final Deployment

Using the actual time and resource requirements determined during the pilot program, project teams can estimate the time and resources required for the final deployment. If you need additional resources, identify and acquire them at this time.

Updating Company Policies and Standards

Before beginning the final deployment, update all company policies regarding the use of browser software and Internet and intranet access by user groups. In addition, update the corporate standards lists for software usage, and ensure that all computers are compliant.

Customization and Installation

Chapter 20: Running the Microsoft Internet Explorer Customization Wizard

This chapter will help you understand how to use the Microsoft® Internet Explorer Customization Wizard to create custom browser packages that you can distribute to your users. The Customization Wizard, which comes with the Microsoft® Internet Explorer Administration Kit (IEAK), allows you to customize the appearance and functionality of the browser, its components, and Windows Update Setup for Microsoft® Internet Explorer 6 and Internet Tools. You can also preset browsing options and, if you are a corporate administrator, set system policies and restrictions.

Chapter 21: Customizing New Browser Features

This chapter describes how to customize the new Microsoft® Internet Explorer 6 features—privacy preferences, Media bar, Image toolbar, Automatic Image Resizing, Print Preview, and the Internet Explorer Error Reporting tool—by using the Microsoft Internet Explorer Customization Wizard, as well as other tools and methods. You can install these customized features on users' computers as part of your custom browser packages.

Chapter 22: Time-saving Strategies That Address Diverse User Needs

If your users have diverse needs—for example, your marketing department requires different Microsoft Internet Explorer 6 settings than your finance department—you can use the strategies described in this chapter. These strategies can help you save time by suggesting ways to customize Internet Explorer efficiently for multiple user groups.

Chapter 23: Deploying Microsoft Internet Explorer 6

After extensive research, planning, testing, and analysis, the final step in the deployment process is rolling out the installation of Microsoft Internet Explorer 6 and Internet Tools to your users. This chapter describes the steps to follow when you are ready to deploy Internet Explorer.

Chapter 24: Using SMS to Install Microsoft Internet Explorer 6

This chapter describes the steps required to deploy Microsoft Internet Explorer 6 and Internet Tools by using Microsoft® Systems Management Server (SMS). This systems management software can help you automate a large-scale deployment by automatically distributing and installing your custom browser packages on users' computers. This automated installation requires no intervention from you or your users.

Chapter 25: Implementing the Sign-up Process

Internet service providers (ISPs) can use the Microsoft Internet Explorer Customization Wizard to create custom browser packages that specify how new users sign up with their service and connect to the Internet. You can select a server-based or a serverless sign-up process, or disable the sign-up feature altogether. This chapter describes how to implement a sign-up process, with or without a server, for your custom browser installation.

Running the Microsoft Internet Explorer Customization Wizard

This chapter will help you understand how to use the Microsoft® Internet Explorer Customization Wizard to create custom browser packages that you can distribute to your users. The Customization Wizard, which comes with the Microsoft® Internet Explorer Administration Kit (IEAK), allows you to customize the appearance and functionality of the browser, its components, and Windows Update Setup for Microsoft® Internet Explorer 6 and Internet Tools. You can also preset browsing options and, if you are a corporate administrator, set system policies and restrictions.

> **Important** Before you run the Customization Wizard, verify that you have completed all preparation tasks, including accepting the license agreement. You must prepare the necessary information and files that you will need when you run the wizard. For more information about these preparation tasks, see "Preparing for the IEAK" in this Resource Kit.

In This Chapter

Related Information in the Resource Kit

- For more information about testing the deployment process before the final rollout, see "Setting Up and Administering a Pilot Program."
- For more information about preparing to run the Internet Explorer Customization Wizard, see "Preparing for the IEAK."
- For more information about rolling out Internet Explorer to your users, see "Deploying Microsoft Internet Explorer 6."
- For a list of preparation steps for running the Customization Wizard, see the appendix "Checklist for Preparing to Use the IEAK."

Overview: How the Customization Wizard Works

As a corporate administrator, Internet service provider (ISP), Internet content provider (ICP), independent software vendor (ISV), or Internet developer, you can use the Internet Explorer Customization Wizard to build custom browser packages. These packages contain customized versions of Internet Explorer 6 that you can distribute to your users. You can create packages in multiple languages and distribute them on various types of media. The Customization Wizard also enables you to customize existing installations of Internet Explorer.

When you run the Customization Wizard, you can create a custom browser package from scratch. Or, if you have already built a package with similar settings, you can build a new package more quickly by importing those settings from the existing package's Internet settings (.ins) file when you run the Customization Wizard. Either way, when you click **Finish** on the final page, the Customization Wizard builds a custom browser package for you.

Each custom browser package includes the following files:

- Program files that you have downloaded
- The setup file (IE6Setup.exe, which is based on IESetup.inf)
- The branding cabinet file (Branding.cab, which consists of custom files, including .ins files, information (.inf) files, and any custom files that you have specified)
- The component information cabinet file (IEcif.cab), which includes components and component settings)

After you build a custom browser package, you can copy these package files to your distribution media. For more information about preparing distribution media for deployment, see "Deploying Microsoft Internet Explorer 6" in this Resource Kit.

Running the Customization Wizard

When you install the IEAK, it prompts you to choose the version that you want to install based on your role—either Corporate, ISP, or ICP. The role that you choose determines the version of the Internet Explorer Customization Wizard that is installed with the IEAK. Depending on your role, you must also accept the appropriate license agreement.

After you install the IEAK, you can run the Customization Wizard from the **Start** menu.

▶ **To run the Internet Explorer Customization Wizard**

1. On the **Start** menu, point to **All Programs** (Microsoft® Windows® XP) or **Programs** (other versions of Microsoft® Windows®), point to **Microsoft IEAK 6,** and then click **Internet Explorer Customization Wizard**.

2. Follow the steps in the wizard.

The Customization Wizard provides step-by-step pages that prompt you for the necessary information and files to customize Internet Explorer. The wizard displays specific pages based on the version of the IEAK (Corporate, ISP, or ICP) that you installed. If you need to return to a page before you finish the wizard, click **Back** until the page appears. After you have completed all of the pages, the Customization Wizard builds your custom browser package.

Because the wizard provides a wide range of customization options, some of the wizard pages might not apply to your situation. In Stage 1 on the **Feature Selection** page, you can select or clear feature check boxes, depending on the options you want to customize. In that way, you do not need to view or supply answers on pages that do not apply to your situation. This helps you proceed through the wizard more quickly.

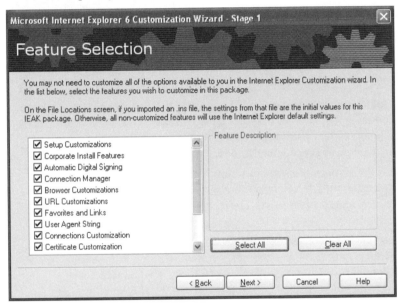

> **Note** On the **Feature Selection** page, if you inadvertently select options that you do not need and a wizard screen appears that does not apply to your situation, simply click **Next** to proceed to the next page.

Stages of the Customization Wizard

The Customization Wizard is organized into the following five stages:

- Stage 1—Gathering Information
- Stage 2—Specifying Setup Parameters
- Stage 3—Customizing Setup
- Stage 4—Customizing the Browser
- Stage 5—Customizing Components

The following sections provide a brief description of each of the pages that appear in the five wizard stages. To obtain additional information about the options on a specific wizard page, click **Help** on that page.

Stage 1: Gathering Information

This stage allows the wizard to gather basic information, such as the language and media type, for the custom browser package that you want to build. The following paragraphs describe each of the wizard pages in Stage 1.

File Locations

This wizard page contains two parts:

- The destination folder
- Advanced options

Destination Folder

Accept the default destination folder, or choose your own. If you build the custom browser package on the computer where you are running the Internet Explorer Customization Wizard, you can copy the package files from this computer to your distribution media. When you build a custom browser package, subfolders for each media type are created in this destination folder.

For flat (network) and download (Web) packages, you can build your custom browser packages at the location where users will download the files. For example, you can build the packages on a network server located on your local area network (LAN) or on a Web server, such as Microsoft® Internet Information Services (IIS).

If your build computer is also set up as a Web server, you can create the package in a folder from which your users can download the files. For example, if you use IIS, the Web server structure on your local hard disk might be: C:\Inetpub\Wwwroot\Build1. If you build your custom browser package in that folder and add a Web page that links to the IE6Setup.exe file in the \Download*platform**language* folder, users can download and install the setup program from your Web server.

Advanced Options

To see more options on the **File Locations** page, click **Advanced Options**. In the **Advanced Options** dialog box, you can specify the following settings:

- **Check for latest components via Automatic Version Synchronization.** Select this check box to indicate that the Customization Wizard should check on the Internet for the latest versions of components when you create your custom browser package. If you have downloaded the IEAK from the Internet, you must run the Customization Wizard with Automatic Version Synchronization (AVS) at least once, so that the wizard can check for updated versions of components. For more information about AVS, see "Keeping Programs Updated" in this Resource Kit.

- **Path of .INS file to import settings from.** If the settings for your new custom browser package are similar to the settings for an existing package, you can save time by importing settings from the existing package's .ins file. Then you can use these settings as a starting point for the new package. To use an existing .ins file, enter the full path to the file. After importing the settings, you can use the Customization Wizard to refine them to fit your needs.

- **Component Download folder.** Use this box to specify the location for the components and setup files for your custom browser package. If you change this location, the AVS feature will not be able to determine whether you have the latest components available. You should change this folder only if you plan to retain the files that you downloaded the last time you ran the wizard, and you want to download a new set of components.

Language Selection

Specify a target language so that the wizard can build your custom browser package in a localized subfolder for the appropriate language and media type. You must run the Customization Wizard for each language version that you plan to deploy. To retain settings across packages for multiple language versions, specify the same destination folder for all versions. The wizard saves each language version in a different subfolder within the destination folder.

Media Selection

Select the distribution methods you plan to use—Download (for Internet or intranet download), CD-ROM, Flat (for network download), or Single-disk branding. You will need additional disk space for each type of media that you select.

You can use single-disk branding to customize the browser on computers that are running Internet Explorer 5.01 Service Pack 2 or later. Single-disk branding enables you to customize Internet Explorer features, including Internet sign-up services, without reinstalling Internet Explorer. This option, however, does not enable you to package and install custom components. It creates a Setup.exe file in the \BrndOnly folder of your build folder, which you can distribute on any media or on a server.

Important Some features branded for Internet Explorer 6 do not apply to earlier versions of the browser.

Feature Selection

On this page, select the features that you want to customize, or clear the features that you do not want to see. The wizard shows only the pages for the features you select.

Stage 2: Specifying Setup Parameters

This stage allows you to customize Windows Update Setup for Internet Explorer and Internet Tools. Setup is a small, Web-based setup package that enables users to install the latest Internet Explorer components directly from a Web site. When Setup downloads Internet Explorer 6, it breaks the program up into several small segments. This makes it possible, in the event of a failure or a dropped connection, to restart an installation from where it was interrupted, rather than having to start over.

The following paragraphs describe each of the wizard pages in Stage 2.

Automatic Version Synchronization

Download or update the setup files for Internet Explorer and other components that the wizard will use to build your custom browser package. At a minimum, you must download Internet Explorer to proceed to the next wizard page. You should also download any component that you plan to install or make available to users through the Install on Demand feature.

Add Custom Components

Specify information about the optional custom components that you want to include as part of your custom browser package. You can add up to 16 custom components. This option can be helpful if you have custom programs or scripts that you want to distribute with Internet Explorer. On this wizard page, you can choose when you want each custom component to be installed—either before or after Internet Explorer or after the computer restarts. You can also decide whether you want the component to be installed only if Internet Explorer is installed successfully.

Stage 3: Customizing Setup

This stage allows you to customize setup program features, such as the installation options that you want to offer to your users and the components that are available through the Install on Demand feature. The following paragraphs describe each of the wizard pages in Stage 3.

CD-ROM Autorun Customizations

If you are creating a custom browser package for CD-ROM distribution, use this wizard page to customize the CD-ROM Autorun screen. The Autorun screen is a graphical interface that appears when users insert the CD-ROM for 32-bit versions of Internet Explorer. You can customize the Autorun title bar text, background, colors, and buttons.

More CD Options

If you are creating a custom browser package for CD-ROM distribution, you can also provide a text file (such as a readme file) that appears as a link from the CD-ROM Autorun screen. Users can click this link to get more information about the CD-ROM contents. On this wizard page, you can also specify an HTML page that opens in kiosk mode, without the toolbar showing.

 Note To customize the CD-ROM Autorun screen, you must select CD-ROM as one of your distribution media in Stage 1 of the Customization Wizard. If you do not see the **CD-ROM Autorun Customizations** and **More CD Options** pages, and you want to set CD-ROM Autorun options, click **Back** until you see the **Media Selection** page. Then select the **CD-ROM** option, and click **Next** until you see these pages.

Customize Setup

Use the options on this wizard page to customize how the setup program appears to your users. You can change the title bar and the graphics that appear when users run the Setup Wizard. If you provide a group of customized components, you can also assign a name to them.

User Experience (Corporate Version Only)

Depending on how you plan to install your custom browser package, decide how much interaction should occur between the setup program and the users. You can choose one of the following installation types:

- An interactive installation, in which users make installation decisions

- A hands-free installation, in which users do not make installation decisions and receive prompts only if errors occur.

- A completely silent installation, in which users do not make decisions and do not receive prompts.

If you choose a completely silent installation, you control all setup options and suppress feedback to users. You can specify only one installation option and one download site. If installation does not finish successfully, users will not see an error message.

On this wizard page, you also specify whether you want to customize your package to retain administrator-level access after the computer restarts. This setting is necessary for installations on computers running Microsoft® Windows NT® 4.0, Microsoft® Windows® 2000, and Windows XP. The security model in these operating systems can prevent users who do not have administrator-level access from installing software on their computers. This setting is also necessary if you plan to distribute your custom browser package by using Microsoft® Systems Management Server (SMS). For more information about how to install Internet Explorer using SMS, see "Using SMS to Install Microsoft Internet Explorer 6" in this Resource Kit.

Installation Options

Specify up to 10 unique installation options, and determine which components are included with each option. Creating multiple installation options can be helpful if your users have different needs. For example, as an ISP, you might want to create different setup options for customers who subscribe to specific sets of services. As a corporate administrator, you might want to specify multiple setup options for different divisions of your company.

Component Download Sites

If you selected **Download** as one of your distribution media, specify up to 10 download sites, using an HTTP or FTP server, from which your users can download the custom browser package. You must place all the Microsoft components and custom components at each URL you specify.

Component Download

Decide whether you want users to download additional components from the Microsoft Windows Update Web site, or to use a custom add-on component page to install components from the original media or download servers. The add-on component page appears when users click the **Tools** menu and then click **Windows Update**, or when they click **Add or Remove Programs** (Windows XP) or **Add/Remove Programs** (other versions of Windows) in Control Panel. As a corporate administrator, you can also remove the **Windows Update** option from the **Tools** menu.

Installation Directory (Corporate Version Only)

Decide whether you want to specify a specific installation directory for your users or allow them to choose their own. You can specify a subfolder in the Program Files folder or enter a custom folder path. If Internet Explorer is already installed on users' computers, by default the new version is installed over the existing version. The customized browser, in this case, is not installed in any custom location you specify.

Corporate Install Options (Corporate Version Only)

Decide to what extent users can customize the setup program. You can specify the following settings:

- **Whether users can run a custom installation to add or remove specific components.** To prevent users from adding or removing specific components, you can select the **Prohibit users from selecting the Custom Installation option** check box.

- **Whether the uninstall information is saved.** Setup automatically saves uninstall information. To save disk space, you can disable this feature by selecting the **Disable saving uninstall information** check box. However, users will not then be able to remove Internet Explorer 6 by clicking **Add/Remove Programs** in Control Panel.

- **Whether users can select the Internet Explorer compatibility mode.** With this mode installed, users can test Internet Explorer 4 Web page features on the same computer as Internet Explorer 5 and later. This mode is designed for testing purposes—for example, when a Web author needs to view Web content in both versions of the browser. It is not recommended for a corporate rollout configuration. To prevent users from selecting this option during Setup, select the **Prohibit users from installing Internet Explorer Compatibility Mode** check box.

- **Whether you want to include Windows Desktop Update as part of your custom browser package.** Windows Desktop Update makes the desktop and folders look and work more like Web features. If your users are running Microsoft® Windows® 98, they already have these desktop features installed. To include Windows Desktop Update on computers that are running only Microsoft Windows NT 4.0 Service Pack 6a, select the **Integrate the Windows Desktop Update into the package** check box.

- **Whether Internet Explorer is set as the default browser.** You can determine whether or not Internet Explorer is the default browser, and whether or not users can make this choice. The default browser runs when users open .htm, .html, and other associated file types. This option also determines whether Microsoft® Windows Media Player™ is the default program for playing multimedia files.

Note If you selected a completely silent installation on the **User Experience** page, corporate install options are not be available.

Advanced Installation Options

Customize the setup program further by having it detect whether components already exist on users' computers and by fine-tuning which components users can add if they customize the setup process.

If you want the setup program to detect whether the same version of a component is already installed on users' computers, select the **Optimize for Web download** check box. If a version of the same component is already installed and it will work with Internet Explorer 6, the setup program does not download it. This feature can save download time.

If your users can customize their installations but you do not want them to customize specific components, clear the check boxes for the components that you do not want the users to customize. Use this feature when you want to ensure that a component is installed with your custom browser package. **Force Install** appears in the right column beside the components that the setup program will install automatically with the browser.

Components on Media

This wizard page lists the components that were downloaded to your computer but are not included as part of an installation option. If users attempt to use a feature that requires these components, the components can be made available for installation through the Install on Demand feature.

With Install on Demand, the component becomes part of your custom browser package, but is not installed with Internet Explorer unless you include it with an installation option. You might not want to include a component in every custom browser package, because all users might not need the component or have hard-disk space for it. However, you may want to ensure that users can easily install that component if the need arises.

Install on Demand prompts users to install the appropriate component if they visit a Web page that uses it. For example, a user might be prompted to install the Dynamic HTML Data Binding component when visiting a Web page that contains a form using that feature. When the user accepts the prompt, the component is installed.

If you are a corporate administrator, and you do not want Install on Demand to be used, you can disable it on the **Policies and Restrictions** page in Stage 5 of the Customization Wizard.

Connection Manager Customization (Corporate and ISP Versions Only)

Use the Connection Manager Administration Kit (CMAK) to customize and manage how your users connect to the Internet. With the CMAK, you can change the appearance and settings of the Connection Manager dialer. If you want to include a custom profile created with CMAK as part of your custom browser package, specify the profile on this wizard page. The CMAK is available as part of Microsoft Windows 2000 Server and the *Microsoft® Windows 2000 Resource Kit.*

Digital Signatures

If you have a digital certificate from a certification authority or from Microsoft® Certificate Server, the Customization Wizard can automatically sign your package files, including the files for any custom components that are part of your custom browser package. On this wizard page, specify information for your digital certificate.

Certificates are electronic credentials that bind the identity of the certificate owner to a pair (public and private) of electronic keys that can be used to encrypt and sign information digitally. These electronic credentials assure that the keys actually belong to the person or organization specified.

Stage 4: Customizing the Browser

In this stage, you can customize the appearance and functionality of the browser. As an ISP, you can also specify settings for Internet sign-up. The following paragraphs describe each of the wizard pages in Stage 4.

Browser Title

Customize the text that appears in the title bar of the Internet Explorer Web browser and Microsoft® Outlook® Express, if you include Outlook Express in your custom browser package. Type the text that you want to appear after the phrase "Microsoft Internet Explorer Provided by" or "Outlook Express Provided by."

Toolbar Customizations

Customize the toolbar background and buttons in the browser. You can use the Windows default toolbar background or specify a custom bitmap. For toolbar buttons, you can specify the script or program that the buttons launch as well as their appearance.

Custom Logo and Animated Bitmaps

Determine whether you want to customize the Internet Explorer logo in the browser window. This 16-color or 256-color logo in the upper-right corner of the browser appears in two states: animated when the browser is in use and static when no action is taking place. You can replace the logo bitmap with your own animated or static bitmap.

If you use an animated bitmap, the first frame will appear static when no action is taking place in the browser, and the remaining frames will appear animated when the browser is in use. To use your own animated logo, you must provide two animated bitmaps; one should be 22 x 22 pixels and the other 38 x 38 pixels.

If you use a static bitmap, it will appear static whether or not any action is taking place in the browser. To use your own static logo, you must provide two static bitmaps; one should be 22 x 22 pixels and the other 38 x 38 pixels.

Important URLs

Determine whether you want to specify URLs for the following items:

- **Home page.** The home page, sometimes known as a start page, appears when users click the **Home** button. Internet Explorer can show a default home page, or you can specify a URL for your own page.

- **Search bar.** The Search bar appears in the Explorer bar on the left side of the screen. This bar enables users to see the search query and search results at the same time. The Search bar comes with the Search Assistant and multiple search engines. You can overwrite this page if you want.

- **Online support page.** In Internet Explorer, support information is available by clicking **Help** and then clicking **Online Support**. You can develop your own support page and make it available to your users.

Favorites and Links

Customize the Favorites folder and Links bar by adding your own favorites and links. For example, you might want to add favorites and links related to your organization or services. You can add favorites and links to the default folders or add new folders. You can specify the order of favorites and move specific favorites to the top of the folder so they are easier to find. Also, you can import a folder containing the favorites and links that you want to install on your users' computers.

As a corporate administrator, you can delete users' existing favorites and links. It is recommended that you use this setting with caution, however, because it removes the links and favorites that the users have set up for their own use.

Welcome Page

Determine whether to customize the welcome page, which Internet Explorer displays when the browser is first started. You can display the default Internet Explorer welcome page, or you can specify your own custom welcome page. The welcome page can be different from the home page, which is the page that opens when users start the browser (after the first time) or click the **Home** button.

User Agent String

Append a custom string to the user-agent string for Internet Explorer. This string helps identify the browser type when compiling site statistics. This feature is particularly useful for companies that are tracking statistics, such as how many times Web content is accessed and by which types of Web browsers.

You do not need to customize the user-agent string, unless you want to track the usage of your custom browser and you gather browser statistics from other Internet sites. Your customized string will appear in any statistics that include the user-agent string. Because other companies that track statistics will see your customized string, avoid using a string that you do not want others to see.

Connection Settings (Corporate and ISP Versions Only)

Preset the connection settings for your users by importing the connection settings from your computer. If the settings displayed are not the settings you want to use, you can change them. Changing these settings from within the wizard also changes them on your build computer. As a corporate administrator, you can also clear the existing dial-up settings on your users' computers.

Automatic Configuration (Corporate Version Only)

Determine whether you want to automatically detect configuration settings and enable automatic configuration. This feature is helpful if you want to control the settings on your users' computers from one central location. If you enable automatic configuration, you must assign URLs to the files that will automatically configure the customized browsers. You can also specify the interval in minutes for automatic configuration. If you enter zero or do not enter a value, automatic configuration occurs only when users restart their computers.

Automatic configuration settings are maintained in .ins files, which you can update by using the IEAK Profile Manager. You can also specify script files in Microsoft® JScript® (.js), JavaScript (.jvs), or proxy automatic configuration (.pac) format that enable you to configure and maintain advanced proxy settings. Network servers using Domain Name System (DNS) and Dynamic Host Configuration Protocol (DHCP) can automatically detect and configure a browser's proxy settings using proxy configuration keys. For more information about these automatic configuration files, see "Using Automatic Configuration, Automatic Proxy, and Automatic Detection" in this Resource Kit.

Proxy Settings (Corporate and ISP Version Only)

Specify which proxy servers that your users connect to. A proxy server acts as an intermediary between users' computers and the Internet, and it helps you maintain administrative control and caching services. If your organization uses proxy servers, specify the address and port numbers for the proxy server protocols. You can also use the same address and port number for all protocols.

For certain addresses, such as those on your corporate intranet, you might not want to use a proxy server. In this case, type these addresses in the exceptions list. You can also choose to bypass proxy servers for all addresses on your intranet. For more information about setting up your proxy servers for Internet Explorer 6, see "Setting Up Servers" in this Resource Kit.

Add a Root Certificate (ISP Version Only)

The customization option on this wizard page does not work properly. If you add any root certificate information, it will not be applied.

Sign-up Method (ISP Version Only)

If you are an ISP, specify how users can sign up for your service and connect to the Internet. You can create server solutions that exchange information with the pages of the Internet Connection Wizard or with the browser in kiosk mode. You can also select a serverless sign-up method. This method does not require a sign-up server; it works locally on users' computers instead. The server-based solutions provide a more dynamic way to interact with users and update information, but serverless sign-up enables you to sign up users for Internet services without a sign-up server. For more information about Internet sign-up, see "Implementing the Sign-up Process" in this Resource Kit.

Sign-up Files (ISP Version Only)

If you are an ISP, specify the sign-up files that you want to include as part of your custom browser package. These sign-up files configure users' computers to connect to your servers. The Customization Wizard checks for copies of the Internet sign-up files and prompts you to copy them to the build folder.

Sign-up Server Information (ISP Version Only)

Specify sign-up server information to configure your users' dial-up connections, so that they can make a connection to your Internet server. This information includes such items as the name of your sign-up server, the area code and telephone number for the connection, and the URL for the first page of the sign-up process. After you specify the information for your sign-up server, you can click **Advanced Options** to configure additional dialing and gateway settings. For example, you can select settings to use a static DNS address for your server, negotiate TCP/IP, encrypt passwords, and use software compression.

Internet Connection Wizard (ISP Version Only)

If you plan to use the Internet Connection Wizard (ICW) as the tool that customers use to sign up for Internet services, customize the title bar text and images that appear on the wizard pages. This feature is not available for the serverless sign-up method. For more information about using the ICW for Internet sign-up, see "Setting Up Servers," in this Resource Kit.

 Note You must include the Dynamic HTML Data Binding component with your custom browser package to ensure that the ICW can interact with your server. Data binding allows the wizard pages to display the list of .isp files in Signup.txt. You can specify that this option does not appear as a custom installation choice, so that users cannot choose whether to install it. To do this, on the **Advanced Installation Options** page, clear the **Dynamic HTML Data Binding** check box; **Force Install** will appear in the right-hand column.

Security (Corporate Version Only)

Decide whether you want to use the default settings for certification authorities and Authenticode security or import the settings from your local computer. If you choose to import your existing settings, you can use the Customization Wizard to refine these settings to fit your needs. Changing these settings from within the wizard also changes them on your build computer.

You can use certification authorities to control the sites where users can download certain content, such as Microsoft® ActiveX® controls. Microsoft® Authenticode® security information identifies where programs come from and verifies that the programs have not been altered. It can be used to designate software publishers and credentials agencies as trustworthy. For more information about these security management features, see "Digital Certificates" in this Resource Kit.

Security and Privacy Settings (Corporate Version Only)

Decide whether you want to use the default settings for the following security features, or import the existing settings from your local computer:

- **Security zones.** You can set security zones to differentiate between trusted and untrusted content on the Internet and your intranet.

- **Privacy settings.** You can define privacy preferences that determine whether Internet Explorer will check Web sites for an established privacy policy and whether Internet Explorer will allow these Web sites to store cookies on users' computers.

- **Content ratings.** You can restrict users' access to content that might be considered offensive. You can adjust the settings to reflect what you think is appropriate content in four areas: language, nudity, sex, and violence.

If you choose to import your existing settings, you can use the Customization Wizard to refine these settings to fit your needs. Changing these settings from within the wizard also changes them on your build computer. In Stage 5 on the Policies and Restrictions page, you can also specify whether users will be able to change these settings. For more information about these security features, see "Users' Privacy," "Security Zones," and "Content Advisor" in this Resource Kit.

Stage 5: Customizing Components

In this stage, you can customize Outlook Express and Windows Address Book settings, if these components are included with your custom browser package. You can also specify policies and restrictions for your users' computers. The following paragraphs describe each of the wizard pages in Stage 5.

Programs

Decide whether you want to use the default program settings or import the settings from your local computer. Program settings determine the programs that Windows automatically uses for Internet services, such as e-mail and HTML editing. If you choose to import your existing settings, you can use the Customization Wizard to refine these settings to fit your needs.

Outlook Express Accounts (Corporate and ISP Versions Only)

Specify your e-mail and news servers and indicate whether you will require users to log on using Secure Password Authentication (SPA) to access each server. For the incoming mail server, specify a Post Office Protocol 3 (POP3) server, used by most Internet subscribers for e-mail, or an Internet Message Access Protocol (IMAP) server, used mainly by corporate users who want to read their e-mail from a remote location. For the outgoing mail server, specify the SMTP server for outgoing e-mail. In some cases, the SMTP server might have the same name as your POP3 server. For the news server, specify the Network News Transfer Protocol (NNTP) address for this Internet server.

On this wizard page, you can also control account settings for your users. When users set up their accounts, such as e-mail and news, those accounts will be configured using the restrictions you specify. For example, you can choose the option to disable access to accounts, which prevents users from adding, deleting, or changing their account information.

Outlook Express IMAP Settings (Corporate and ISP Versions Only)

Create default IMAP settings for your users. These settings are preconfigured for users when they create their IMAP accounts. You can specify the root folder path, which is the mailbox that contains all of the users' folders on the IMAP server. For Cyrus servers, all users' folders must be contained in the Inbox folder. Some IMAP servers, such as Microsoft® Exchange Server, do not require a root folder path.

To specify that folders for the users' sent messages and in-progress messages should be created on the IMAP server, select **Store special folders on IMAP server**. You can also specify the path for the Sent Items folder and the Draft folder. These paths will be used by all users who create IMAP accounts.

You can also specify whether Outlook Express checks subscribed folders for new messages. This occurs when users start Outlook Express and also at the send/receive interval specified in Outlook Express.

Outlook Express Custom Content (Corporate and ISP Versions Only)

Specify information for a custom welcome message that is delivered to new Outlook Express users. The welcome message is contained in an HTML file. You can create the text for the message and specify the sender and reply-to names and addresses. The Customization Wizard does not provide a way to add an image to the welcome message. However, if you edit the welcome message outside of the IEAK, you can add a link to an image from the Web.

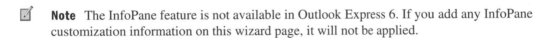 **Note** The InfoPane feature is not available in Outlook Express 6. If you add any InfoPane customization information on this wizard page, it will not be applied.

Outlook Express Custom Settings (Corporate and ISP Versions Only)

Specify the following settings for Outlook Express that will apply to all of your users:

- **Whether you want to make Outlook Express the default program for mail and for news.** The default e-mail client is also used by many programs when a user sends documents by e-mail. Note that this setting replaces any current default e-mail client that the user has specified.

- **The newsgroups that you want users to be subscribed to automatically.** For example, your ISP or organization might have several newsgroups that provide assistance and information beneficial to your users.

- **The service information that allows users to obtain additional e-mail accounts after the installation.** Outlook Express will include a menu item that users can click to get an additional e-mail account from your ISP.

- **Whether you want to delete all Outlook Express links.** No links to the Outlook Express program appear on users' desktops or the Windows **Start** menu.

Outlook Express View Settings (Corporate and ISP Versions Only)

Determine which elements of Outlook Express are displayed and how they are displayed. You can specify which of the following elements of the Outlook Express interface are included in the default view for new users:

- Folder bar
- Outlook Bar
- Folder list
- Status bar
- Contacts
- Tip of the day

You can choose whether you want users to see the Outlook Express toolbar and whether you want to include text on it. The toolbar appears at the top of the Outlook Express window. It contains buttons that correspond to common commands and can be configured by the user.

You can also choose whether you want users to see the preview pane in the default view for e-mail and news messages. The preview pane can either be a horizontal pane located below the list of messages or a vertical pane located beside and to the right of the list of messages. The preview pane includes a preview pane header area that can be used to display message header information, including the From, To, Cc, and Subject lines of the message.

Outlook Express Compose Settings (Corporate Version Only)

Use this setting to include a default signature, such as a corporate disclaimer, that will appear in Outlook Express newsgroup or e-mail messages. A disclaimer is often used to show that messages submitted by employees over the Internet do not represent official company policies. The maximum size of the signature is one KB. You can append signatures only to newsgroup messages, only to e-mail messages, or to both types of messages.

You can choose whether to use HTML to compose both e-mail messages and news postings. By default, e-mail messages are composed in HTML, and news postings are composed in plain text. You might want to change these settings if, for example, you are in an environment where bandwidth is limited or many users have simple e-mail programs that cannot understand HTML.

Address Book Directory Service (Corporate and ISP Versions Only)

Specify additional Internet directory service options and customize your Lightweight Directory Access Protocol (LDAP) servers for the Windows Address Book. Internet directory services are powerful search tools that help your users find people and businesses around the world. The Windows Address Book supports LDAP for accessing directory services, and it comes with built-in access to several popular directory services.

Targeting Policies and Restrictions (Corporate Version Only)

Depending on which operating systems your users are running, determine whether you want to display all the policies and restrictions on the **Policies and Restrictions** page, or whether you want to display only the policies and restrictions for users that do not have administrative privileges. If your users are running Microsoft® Windows® Millennium Edition or Windows 98, you can configure all the policies and restrictions through the Customization Wizard.

If your users are running Windows XP, Windows 2000, or Windows NT 4.0, you must configure most of these settings through Group Policy rather than through the policies and restrictions in the Customization Wizard. In this case, you can display only the policies for users who do not have administrative privileges, and then you can use Group Policy to configure the remaining settings.

Policies and Restrictions

Use policies and restrictions to specify settings for your users' computers, including options that control desktop features, Internet components, the operating system, and security. Corporate administrators, ISPs, and ICPs/developers can specify default settings for their users. In addition, corporate administrators can customize and "lock down" numerous settings, ranging from whether users can delete printers to whether they can add items to their desktops.

The policies and restrictions displayed in the wizard are maintained in administration (.adm) files that come with the IEAK. If you are familiar with .adm files, you can use also import the policies and restrictions that you have set up in your own .adm files. For more information about policies and restrictions, see the appendix "Setting System Policies and Restrictions" in this Resource Kit.

C H A P T E R   2 1

Customizing New Browser Features

This chapter describes how to customize the new Microsoft® Internet Explorer 6 features—privacy preferences, Media bar, Image toolbar, Automatic Image Resizing, Print Preview, and the Internet Explorer Error Reporting tool—by using the Microsoft® Internet Explorer Customization Wizard, as well as other tools and methods. You can install these customized features on users' computers as part of your custom browser packages.

In This Chapter

Related Information in the Resource Kit

- For more information about new Internet Explorer features, see "What's New in Microsoft Internet Explorer 6?"

- For more information about using the Internet Explorer Customization Wizard to control access to Internet Explorer features, see "Running the Microsoft Internet Explorer Customization Wizard."

Customizing Privacy Preferences

You can use the new **Privacy** tab in the **Internet Options** dialog box to define the privacy preferences for disclosing your personal information to Web sites. You can choose a privacy level, which determines whether Web sites can store and retrieve cookies on your computer and use them to access and track the personal information that you provide. You can also import custom privacy settings, customize your privacy settings for cookie handling, and customize your privacy settings for individual Web sites. For more information about using the **Privacy** tab to define your privacy preferences, see "Users' Privacy" in this Resource Kit.

When you run the Internet Explorer Customization Wizard, you can define custom privacy settings. On your local computer, you can configure the privacy settings that you want to install on users' computers and then import these settings into your custom browser packages. You can also prevent users from changing these settings by turning off access to the **Privacy** tab in the **Internet Options** dialog box.

▶ **To define custom privacy settings**

1. In Stage 1 on the **Feature Selection** page, select the **Security Zones and Content Ratings** and **Policies and Restrictions** check boxes.

2. In Stage 4 on the **Security and Privacy Settings** page, click **Import the current security zones and privacy settings**. If you want to change any privacy settings, click **Modify Settings**.

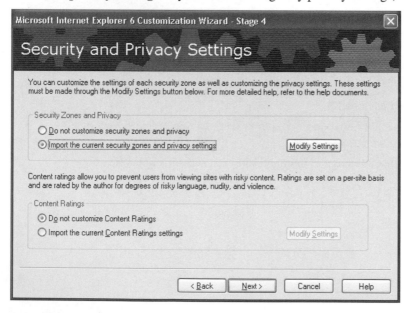

3. If you want to turn off access to the **Privacy** tab, in Stage 5 on the **Policies and Restrictions** page, in the left pane under **Corporate Restrictions** (available only with the Corporate version of the Customization Wizard), click **Internet Property Pages**, and then in the right pane, select the **Disable viewing the Privacy Page** check box.

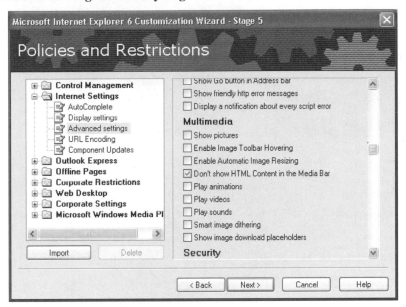

Customizing the Media Bar

The new Media bar provides simple controls that enable you to locate and play music, video, or mixed-media files within the browser window. You can browse the WindowsMedia.com Web site to locate radio stations, videos, and other media on the Internet. For more information about this feature, see "Media Bar" in this Resource Kit.

When you run the Internet Explorer Customization Wizard to customize the browser for your users, you can customize the Media bar. Policy settings on the **Policies and Restrictions** page allow you to turn on or off HTML content in the Media bar, to disable the automatic playing of media files in the Media bar, and to turn on or off the Media bar itself.

▶ **To customize the Media bar**

1. In Stage 1 on the **Feature Selection** page, select the **Policies and Restrictions** check box.

2. In Stage 5 on the **Policies and Restrictions** page, select or clear the following options:

    o   In the left pane under **Internet Settings**, click **Advanced settings**, and then in the right pane under **Multimedia**, select or clear the **Don't show HTML Content in the Media Bar** check box.

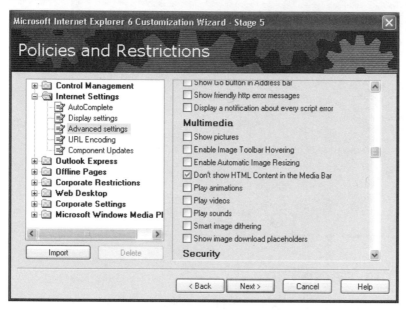

    o   In the left pane under **Corporate Restrictions** (available only with the Corporate version of the Customization Wizard), click **Explorer Bars**, and then in the right pane, select or clear the Media bar check boxes.

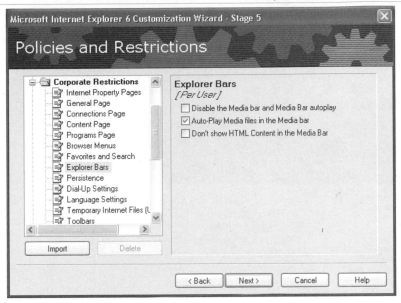

Customizing the Image Toolbar

The new Image toolbar allows you to quickly and easily save, send in e-mail, and print pictures that you find on Web pages, as well as view all the pictures that you have saved in the My Pictures folder. When you point to pictures on Web pages, the Image toolbar automatically appears in the upper-left corner of the pictures, giving instant access to image functions. For more information about this feature, see "Image Toolbar and Automatic Image Resizing" in this Resource Kit.

You can turn on or off the Image toolbar on the **Policies and Restrictions** page in Stage 5 of the Customization Wizard. This option is set per user, so turning on or off the Image toolbar for one user on a shared computer does not affect other users who log in to the shared computer by using different logon IDs.

▷ **To turn on or off the Image toolbar**

1. In Stage 1 on the **Feature Selection** page, select the **Policies and Restrictions** check box.

2. In Stage 5 on the **Policies and Restrictions** page, in the left pane under **Internet Settings**, click **Advanced settings**, and then in the right pane under **Multimedia**, select or clear the **Enable Image Toolbar Hovering** check box.

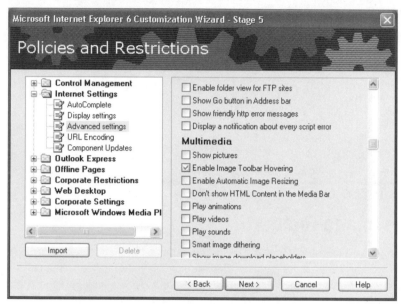

The following registry keys control the Image toolbar functionality:

- **HKEY_CURRENT_USER\Software\Policies\Microsoft\Internet Explorer\Main**

  When the DWORD is set to a value of 1, the Image toolbar is completely turned off via system policies. Users cannot change this setting.

- **HKEY_CURRENT_USER\Software\Microsoft\Internet Explorer\Main\ Enable_Image_Toolbar_Hovering**

  Depending on whether the Image toolbar is turned on or off, this registry key is set to a value of "yes" or "no."

- **HKEY_LOCAL_MACHINE\SOFTWARE\Microsoft\Internet Explorer\ AdvancedOptions\MULTIMEDIA\MYPICS**

The following table identifies the registry key values that control the Image toolbar functions.

Name	Type	Data
(Default)	REG_SZ	(value not set)
CheckedValue	REG_SZ	Yes
DefaultValue	REG_SZ	Yes
HelpID	REG_SZ	iexplore.hlp#50043
HkeyRoot	REG_DWORD	0x80000001 (2147483649)
PlugUIText	REG_SZ	@inetcplc.dll, -4865
RegPath	REG_SZ	SOFTWARE\Microsoft\Internet Explorer\Main
Text	REG_SZ	Enable Image Toolbar Hovering
Type	REG_SZ	Check box
UncheckedValue	REG_SZ	No
ValueName	REG_SZ	Enable_MyPics_Hoverbar

Customizing Automatic Image Resizing

If pictures are too large to see in their entirety in the browser window, the new Automatic Image Resizing feature resizes them automatically so they fit within the dimensions of the browser window. An icon appears in the lower right corner of resized pictures and allows you to change the pictures back to their original size. For more information about this feature, see "Image Toolbar and Automatic Image Resizing" in this Resource Kit.

When you run the Internet Explorer Customization Wizard to customize the browser for your users, you can turn on or off this feature.

▶ **To turn on or off automatic image resizing**

1. In Stage 1 on the **Feature Selection** page, select the **Policies and Restrictions** check box.

2. In Stage 5 on the **Policies and Restrictions** page, in the left pane under **Internet Settings**, click **Advanced settings**, and then in the right pane under **Multimedia**, select or clear the **Enable Automatic Image Resizing** check box.

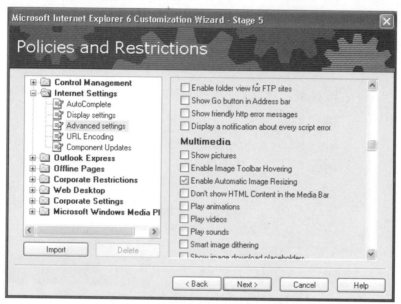

The following registry key controls the automatic image resizing functionality:

HKEY_LOCAL MACHINE\SOFTWARE\Microsoft\Internet Explorer\ AdvancedOptions\MULTIMEDIA\AUTOIMAGERESIZE

Customizing Print Preview

Print Preview enables you to preview Web pages instantly so that you can see how they will look when you print them. In the browser, you can access Print Preview from the **File** menu or from the **Print Preview** button, which you can add to the Internet Explorer toolbar. For more information about this feature, see "Print Preview" in this Resource Kit.

The **Print Preview** menu item is available by default, and no specific options exist in the Internet Explorer Customization Wizard to directly disable this feature on users' computers. However, on the **Policies and Restrictions** page in Stage 5 of the Customization Wizard, you can disable browser printing options. This action also disables Print Preview.

▶ **To disable browser printing options**

1. In Stage 1 on the **Feature Selection** page, select the **Policies and Restrictions** check box.

2. In Stage 5 on the **Policies and Restrictions** page, select one or more of the following options:

   o To disable printing from the browser, in the left pane under **Corporate Restrictions** (available only with the Corporate version of the Customization Wizard), click **Browser Menus**, and then in the right pane under **File Menu**, select the **Disable printing from the browser** check box.

   o To turn off the **Print** button, in the left pane under **Corporate Restrictions** (available only with the Corporate version of the Customization Wizard), click **Toolbars**, and then in the right pane under **Print button**, click **Turn button off**.

   o To disable changes to Printers and Control Panel Settings, in the left pane under **Web Desktop**, click **Start Menu**, and then in the right pane, select the **Disable changes to Printers and Control Panel Settings** check box.

   o To disable the **File** menu in the browser window, where the **Print** and **Print Preview** menu items appear, in the left pane under **Web Desktop**, click **Shell**, and then in the right pane, click the **Disable File menu in browser Window** check box.

Customizing the Internet Explorer Error Reporting Tool

The new Internet Explorer Error Reporting tool replaces the standard fault dialog box that appears when the browser stops or closes unexpectedly. This tool provides fault collection services, allowing Internet Explorer to extract information about the problem and upload the data to a Microsoft® Internet Information Services (IIS) server for analysis. You can view details about the problem and then choose whether to transmit the fault information to Microsoft and restart your computer.

If your organization is concerned about sending the fault information directly to Microsoft, you can disable the Internet Explorer Error Reporting tool on users' computers by using one of the following methods:

- In Microsoft® Windows XP and Microsoft® Windows 2000, use Group Policy to disable this tool. For more information about using Group Policy, see "Keeping Programs Updated" in this Resource Kit.

- In other versions of Windows, use an .inf file to provide customized setup instructions for the Internet Explorer installation, and add the following registry entry with a value of 0 in the **[AddReg]** section of your .inf file:

  HKEY_LOCAL_MACHINE\Software\Microsoft\Internet Explorer\ Main\IEWatsonEnabled

  For more information about including registry entries as part of the customized setup instructions in your .inf file, see "Working with .inf Files" and the appendix "Structural Definition of .inf Files" in this Resource Kit.

Time-saving Strategies That Address Diverse User Needs

If your users have diverse needs—for example, your marketing department requires different Microsoft® Internet Explorer 6 settings than your finance department—you can use the strategies described in this chapter. These strategies can help you save time by suggesting ways to customize Internet Explorer efficiently for multiple user groups.

In This Chapter

Related Information in the Resource Kit

- For more information about testing the deployment process before the final rollout, see "Setting Up and Administering a Pilot Program."

- For more information about preparing to use the Microsoft Internet Explorer Administration Kit (IEAK), see "Preparing for the IEAK."

- For more information about using the sample Internet sign-up files, see "Setting Up Servers."

- For more information about creating custom browser packages, see "Running the Microsoft Internet Explorer Customization Wizard."

- For more information about rolling out Internet Explorer 6 to your users, see "Deploying Microsoft Internet Explorer 6."

Overview: Customizing Microsoft Internet Explorer for Multiple User Groups

By using some customization features of the IEAK and Internet Explorer, you can accommodate the diverse needs of multiple user groups in your organization. You can customize the browser and setup program for different user groups without repeating all the customization steps for each group or rebuilding your custom browser packages.

Determine whether one or more of the following scenarios apply to your organization:

- **Using automatic configuration in a corporate setting.** If you are a corporate administrator, after deploying Internet Explorer, you can use the automatic configuration feature to change browser settings on users' computers. This feature uses IEAK profiles to maintain browser settings for different user groups, so you can update and redeploy the profiles to change browser settings without rebuilding your custom browser packages.

- **Creating multiple .isp files for Internet services.** If you are an Internet service provider (ISP), when you run the Internet Explorer Customization Wizard to create your custom browser packages, you can create multiple Internet sign-up (.isp) files. These files automate the registration and setup tasks for your users. The files provide a variety of sign-up options for your users without requiring you to create multiple packages.

- **Efficiently creating custom browser packages.** When you create multiple custom browser packages, you can use certain strategies to reduce the number of customization steps and make this process faster and easier. For example, you can use the **Feature Selection** page, you can enable Automatic Version Synchronization (AVS), and you can import preexisting .ins files.

- **Using batch files to customize setup options.** You can use batch files to customize Microsoft Windows Update Setup for Internet Explorer 6 and Internet Tools without creating custom browser packages. If you have already specified setup options in custom browser packages, you can also use batch files to change those options without rebuilding the packages.

- **Starting Internet Explorer by using command-line switches.** If you need to customize the way Internet Explorer installs, starts, or appears during the browsing session, but you do not want to customize the browser program, you can start Internet Explorer by using command-line switches. These switches eliminate the need to customize the setup process by running the Internet Explorer Customization Wizard.

Using Automatic Configuration in a Corporate Setting

As a corporate administrator, you can create your custom browser packages and turn on the automatic configuration feature, which enables you to change browser settings globally after you deploy Internet Explorer. Automatic configuration uses a pointer to an IEAK profile on a server to update the browser settings automatically on users' computers.

You can use the IEAK Profile Manager to create and maintain IEAK profiles, which consist of auto-configuration .ins files and any custom cabinet (.cab) files associated with your custom browser packages. If you want to specify different browser settings for different user groups, you can create a separate IEAK profile for each of your custom browser packages. Then, whenever you want to update the browser settings for a user group, you can use the IEAK Profile Manager to update the appropriate IEAK profile and redeploy the profile on your server.

Changing Automatic-Configuration Paths

If you want to create multiple IEAK profiles for different user groups, you can rebuild your custom browser packages, each with a different automatic-configuration path.

▶ **To change the automatic-configuration path for different user groups**

1. In Stage 1 of the Customization Wizard, on the **Feature Selection** page, select the **Connections Customization** check box.

2. In Stage 4, on the **Automatic Configuration** page, select the **Enable Automatic Configuration** check box, and then in the **Auto-config URL (.INS file)** text box, type the location of the IEAK profile.

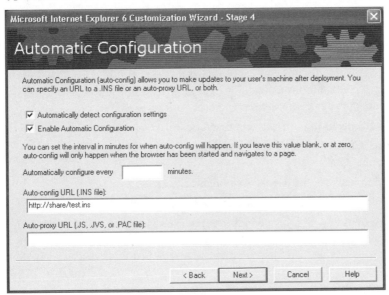

You can also change the automatic-configuration path for a group of users after you deploy your custom browser packages, either by changing the path manually or by using a script. For more information about changing the automatic-configuration path after deployment, see "Using Automatic Configuration, Automatic Proxy, and Automatic Detection" in this Resource Kit.

Automating Server Solutions

If you want to use multiple IEAK profiles but do not want to rebuild your custom browser package for each profile, you can use an automated server solution. The IEAK includes a sample automated server solution in the \IEAK6\Toolkit\Corp folder of your IEAK installation directory. If you use a Web server that supports Active Server Pages (.asp) files, you can modify this sample file to fit your organization's needs. The file Asphelp.htm, which accompanies this sample, provides procedures for working with an automated server solution.

To customize the sample for your organization

1. Assign users to groups based on their needs.
2. Create an IEAK profile for each group.
3. On your Web server, create global groups that correspond to your auto-configuration .ins file name (without the extension). For example, you might name the .ins file for the finance department Finance.ins, and the group name on your automatic-configuration server IE_finance.
4. Add the user names to the global groups in your domain.
5. Post your .asp files to the Web server.

Creating Multiple .isp Files for Internet Services

As an ISP, you can create a single custom browser package that includes multiple .isp files for the different Internet sign-up server solutions that you want to offer to your users. These .isp files contain registration, connection, gateway, server, and other information.

You can create multiple .isp files by using the following methods:

*   Run the Internet Explorer Customization Wizard to produce the .isp files as part of your custom browser package.
*   Use the ISP File Wizard to generate the .isp files automatically.
*   Edit the .isp files manually with a text editor, such as Microsoft® Notepad.

The following procedure describes how to produce multiple .isp files as part of your custom browser package when you run the Internet Explorer Customization Wizard. For more information about using the ISP File Wizard to generate the .isp files automatically, see "Setting Up Servers" in this Resource Kit.

To produce multiple .isp files as part of your custom browser package

1. In Stage 1 of the Customization Wizard, on the **Feature Selection** page, select the **Sign-up Settings** check box.
2. In Stage 2, on the **Automatic Version Synchronization** page, verify that you have downloaded the Dynamic HTML Data Binding component, which is required for multiple .isp files.

3. In Stage 4, on the **Sign-up Server Information** page, type values for the sign-up server fields, and then click **Add** to add each of your Internet sign-up solutions.

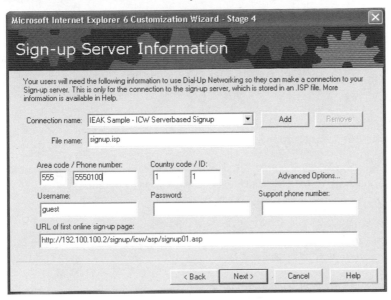

The IEAK includes an Internet sign-up server sample in the \IEAK6\Toolkit\Isp\Server\ICW folder of your IEAK installation directory. For more information about using the sample files, see "Setting Up Servers" in this Resource Kit.

Efficiently Creating Custom Browser Packages

If you do not want to use multiple .ins or .isp files but you need to create more than one custom browser package, you can use the following methods to create multiple packages more efficiently:

- If you want to create a new custom browser package that will contain many of the same settings as those found in an existing package, import these settings from the existing package's .ins file rather than resetting all the options with the Customization Wizard.

- When you run the Customization Wizard, use the **Feature Selection** page to select and view only those settings that you want to change. You do not need to view and reset options on every wizard page.

- Use AVS to keep track of downloaded components so that you do not need to download all the program files for each custom browser package that you create. You need to download only new and updated components that you want to deploy to your users.

Importing a Preexisting .ins File

If you have already created a custom browser package and want to create a second package with many of the same settings, you can import the existing package's .ins file when you run the Customization Wizard. You can locate the .ins file for an existing custom browser package in that package's *\build location*Ins folder. The settings from this .ins file can serve as a starting point for your new custom browser package. You do not need to reset the options that you want to retain—you need to set only the options that you want to change, as well as any new options in the version of the Customization Wizard that you are using.

▶ **To import settings from an existing .ins file**

1. In Stage 1 of the Customization Wizard, on the **File Locations** page, type a new build location for your custom browser package in the **Destination Folder** text box. You must type a new build location so that you do not overwrite a previously created package.

2. Click **Advanced Options**.

3. In the **Path of .INS file to import settings from** box, type the path of your .ins file, or to locate the .ins file that you want to import, click **Browse**.

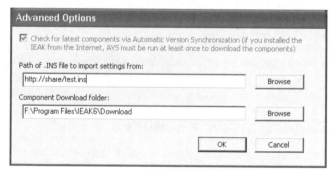

Note When you import an .ins file, verify that it applies to the package type that you want to create. For example, if you create a custom browser package using the corporate version of the IEAK, you do not want to import an .ins file from a package created using the ISP version.

Using the Feature Selection Page

When you create a custom browser package, you can use the **Feature Selection** page in Stage 1 of the Customization Wizard to select the features that you want to customize. The wizard displays the pages for the selected features and a few pages that are required to create the package. Using the **Feature Selection** page can help you save time, because you can view only the pages that you need to use rather than all the pages in the wizard.

▷ **To use the Feature Selection page**

1. In Stage 1 of the Customization Wizard, on the **File Locations** page, type a new build location for your custom browser package in the **Destination Folder** text box. You must type a new build location so that you do not overwrite a previously created package.

2. On the **Feature Selection** page, select the check boxes for the features that you want to customize.

    If you do not want to change any settings associated with a feature, you can clear its check box. The wizard will not display the pages associated with that feature.

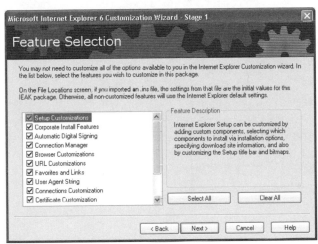

For more information about the **Feature Selection** page, see "Running the Microsoft Internet Explorer Customization Wizard" in this Resource Kit.

Using Automatic Version Synchronization

When you run the Customization Wizard to create your custom browser packages, AVS can check the Internet for new or updated components. If you have already downloaded components for an existing custom browser package, AVS identifies those components so that you do not need to download them a second time. AVS also detects whether new versions have become available since the last time you ran the wizard.

You do not need to download the latest versions of all the components, although this is recommended for most scenarios. To retain a consistent version across your organization, you might not want to deploy a newer version of a component if some members of your organization already use an earlier one.

▷ **To use AVS**

1. In Stage 1 of the Customization Wizard, on the **File Locations** page, type a new build location for your custom browser package in the **Destination Folder** text box. You must type a new build location so that you do not overwrite a previously created package.

2. Click **Advanced Options**.

3. In the **Component Download Folder** text box, type the folder location for your existing Internet Explorer components, or to locate the folder, click **Browse**.

   To use AVS, specify the same component download folder that you used for a previous package and keep the previously downloaded components on your computer.

4. In Stage 2, on the **Automatic Version Synchronization** page, review the list of components.

   The icon next to the component is one of three possible colors:

   o If your component download folder contains the latest version, the icon is green.

   o If a newer version is available, the icon is yellow.

   o If the component does not exist in your component download folder, the icon is red.

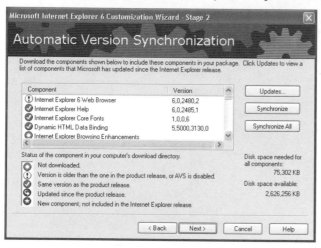

5. Choose from the following options:

   o To download an updated version of a component, select that component from the list, and then click **Synchronize**.

   o To download the latest versions of all the components in your component download folder, click **Synchronize All**.

   Note When you download a newer version of a component using **Synchronize** or **Synchronize All**, the wizard prompts you if the files associated with the component already exist in your component download folder. You can then choose whether you want to download the files again.

o   To check for new components that do not exist in your component download folder, click **Updates**, and then select any new components that you want to deploy with your custom browser package.

For more information about using AVS, see "Keeping Programs Updated" in this Resource Kit.

Using Batch Files to Customize Setup Options

If you want to customize setup options for your Internet Explorer installation without creating or rebuilding a custom browser package, you can use a batch file to control the setup process. You can create the Internet Explorer batch file, IEBatch.txt, by using a simple text editor, such as Notepad. You can then place this file in the same installation location as Windows Desktop Update (IE6Setup.exe), such as in the same download server folder or in the same folder on the installation CD-ROM, and deploy it with the Internet Explorer installation files.

☑   **Note** If you plan to use a batch file in combination with command-line switches, you do not need to name the file IEBatch.txt, providing the name you specify in the command line matches the name of the batch file.

The following scenarios describe some of the ways that you can use batch files:

• You can create a single custom browser package and then create several batch files to address the setup needs of different user groups. You can also use these batch files to customize the setup program without creating a custom browser package.

• If you create a custom browser package and later need to change a setup option, you can use a batch file to make this change without rebuilding the package.

• If you need to change a setup option temporarily—for example, if a network server does not work and you want to use an alternate download location for a short time—you can use a batch file to change the option without affecting the settings in your custom browser package.

• You can integrate browser functionality into your custom program—for example, by using the WebBrowser control—and use a batch file to suppress user feedback and prompts. If you use a batch file to suppress restarting, though, your custom program must restart Internet Explorer after the installation to complete the setup process. For more information about developing custom programs with Internet Explorer, see the MSDN® Web site at http://msdn.microsoft.com/.

For more information about working with batch files or for a sample batch file, see the appendix "Batch-Mode File Syntax and Command-Line Switches" in this Resource Kit.

Starting Microsoft Internet Explorer by Using

Command-Line Switches

When you run Setup, you can use command-line switches to customize the way Internet Explorer installs, starts, or appears during the browsing session. You might want to use command-line switches if you need to customize the Internet Explorer installation for a specific browsing session. If you use command-line switches, you do not need to use the Internet Explorer Customization Wizard to customize the browser program before you install it.

You can either type the command-line syntax that runs the Internet Explorer executable program at the command-line prompt or use a script to perform this task automatically. To package your setup files and command-line switches for installation, you can use the IExpress Wizard, which is part of the IEAK, or your own setup program. For more information about using the IExpress Wizard, see "Preparing for the IEAK" in this Resource Kit.

The following scenarios describe some of the ways that you can use command-line switches:

- Command-line switches take precedence over the settings specified in batch files and custom browser packages. Therefore, you can use command-line switches to change settings temporarily and deploy your Internet Explorer installation without rebuilding your custom browser package. For example, you might want to change the download site temporarily to do troubleshooting. You can use command-line switches to override the download sites that you specified for your custom browser package and install Internet Explorer from a different location.

- You can use command-line switches to control how the setup program runs during the installation. For example, you can choose the installation mode, specify quiet mode (which removes or reduces the prompts that the user receives), or control whether the computer restarts automatically after the installation.

- As part of your command-line syntax, you can include the name and location of a batch file, and the batch file will run and customize the setup options that you specify. For more information about batch files, see "Using Batch Files to Customize Setup Options" earlier in this chapter.

- If you want to redistribute Internet Explorer as part of a custom program, you can use command-line switches to suppress user feedback and prompts from Internet Explorer. If you use command-line switches to suppress restarting, though, your custom program must restart Internet Explorer after the installation to complete the setup process.

For a list of command-line switches and some examples of how to use them, see the appendix "Batch-Mode File Syntax and Command-Line Switches" in this Resource Kit.

CHAPTER 23

Deploying Microsoft Internet Explorer 6

After extensive research, planning, testing, and analysis, the final step in the deployment process is rolling out the installation of Microsoft® Internet Explorer 6 and Internet Tools to your users. This chapter describes the steps to follow when you are ready to deploy Internet Explorer.

> ⚠ **Important** Although the processes described in this chapter assume deployment within a corporate business setting, Internet service providers and Internet content providers can follow similar procedures when they deploy Internet Explorer.

In This Chapter

Related Information in the Resource Kit

- For more information about preparing the teams, tools, resources, and plans for deploying Internet Explorer, see "Planning the Deployment."
- For more information about testing the deployment process before the final rollout, see "Setting Up and Administering a Pilot Program."
- For more information about building custom browser packages for installation, see "Running the Microsoft Internet Explorer Customization Wizard."

Announcing the Installation

Before users begin installing Internet Explorer, inform them about the installation process. You might want to announce the installation through an e-mail memo or in face-to-face meetings. Either way, communicate the benefits of using Internet Explorer 6, the details of the overall deployment plan, and the specific installation process that each group or department must follow.

Next, distribute preliminary instructions, including any preparatory steps that users need to complete. Users who are not familiar with Internet Explorer might require training sessions before the installation begins. For more information about user training, see "Providing User Training and Support" later in this chapter.

Preparing the Users' Computers

To prepare for the installation, make sure that each user's computer is working properly. If necessary, upgrade the computer hardware. Also, make a backup copy of critical data and configuration files, and defragment the hard disks.

Technicians can perform these tasks on each computer, or your users can complete the tasks by using instructions that you provide. If your organization uses system management software, such as Microsoft® Systems Management Server, you can also perform these tasks remotely from a central location.

 Note To install Internet Explorer and Internet Tools on computers with the Microsoft® Windows® XP, Microsoft® Windows® 2000, or Microsoft® Windows NT® 4.0 operating system, you must enable administrative privileges. For more information about installing Internet Explorer and Internet Tools on supported versions of Windows platforms, see "Working with Different Platforms" in this Resource Kit.

Providing User Training and Support

User training and support are critical to the success of your Internet Explorer deployment. Time and resources spent on training can help decrease the demand for user support.

As the final rollout of Internet Explorer approaches, the training and support teams can promote the benefits of using the browser. It is important to set expectations and build users' mastery of browser skills. Users need to understand the advantages of participating in the training program and the benefits of learning how to use the browser software. You can promote Internet Explorer by giving presentations and demonstrations and by providing users with tips and answers to frequently asked questions.

Typically, users receive training before they install Internet Explorer and Internet Tools. You can then provide support to your users during the final rollout. Training and support teams should carry out the user training and support according to the training and support plans, which were revised and improved following the pilot program. For more information about training and support during the pilot program, which precedes the final rollout of Internet Explorer, see "Setting Up and Administering a Pilot Program" in this Resource Kit.

Building Custom Browser Package Files

You can use the Internet Explorer Customization Wizard to build custom browser packages and tailor them to meet the needs of your user groups. By specifying the user setup options and controlling most browser and Microsoft® Outlook® Express features, you can ensure that users install Internet Explorer and Internet Tools with the most appropriate settings for their needs.

After you build your custom browser packages, the Internet Explorer Customization Wizard places the package files, including the Internet Explorer setup file, IE6Setup.exe, in the directory location you entered during Stage 1. Within this build directory, the Customization Wizard uses separate folders to distinguish the files for different language versions and distribution media types. For example, the Customization Wizard creates the English language version for the Flat media type in the following folder: \build_directory\Flat\Win32\En.

For more information about using the Internet Explorer Customization Wizard to build your custom browser packages, see "Running the Microsoft Internet Explorer Customization Wizard" in this Resource Kit.

Signing Custom Browser Package Files

Digital signatures identify the source of programs and guarantee that the code has not changed since it was signed. Depending on the operating systems that users are running and how their security levels are set, Internet Explorer might prevent users from or warn them against downloading programs that are not digitally signed.

Therefore, digitally sign the cabinet (.cab) files created by the Internet Explorer Customization Wizard—unless you specify a Low security setting for the Local intranet zone, which allows users to download unsigned files from sites in this zone. Also digitally sign any custom components that you want to distribute with Internet Explorer. If you have a digital certificate, the Customization Wizard can sign these files automatically.

▶ To digitally sign .cab files and custom components

1. Obtain a digital certificate.
2. When you run the Customization Wizard, specify your digital certificate information.

For more information about signing your files, see "Preparing for the IEAK" in this Resource Kit.

Preparing the Distribution Media

After you build your custom browser packages, prepare the media that you will use to distribute Internet Explorer to your users. Depending on the media types that you selected in Stage 1 of the Internet Explorer Customization Wizard, you might need to prepare one or more of the following distribution media:

- Download Web or FTP sites on the Internet or your intranet
- Flat network share (all files in one directory)
- CD-ROMs
- Single-disk branding

Using Download Web or FTP Sites

If you selected the **Download** media type during Stage 1 of the Internet Explorer Customization Wizard, the wizard creates a custom browser package that you can distribute to your users from download sites on the Internet or your corporate intranet. You can provide IE6Setup.exe directly to your users as an e-mail attachment if your network can support sending multiple copies of the setup file. Or you can direct users to an Internet or intranet site from which they can choose to run IE6Setup.exe directly or download the file to their hard disk.

If you created your custom browser package on an Internet or intranet server, set up your download sites so that users can access the package files. The location or locations where you post files for download should correspond to the URLs that you specified on the **Component Download Sites** page in Stage 2 of the Internet Explorer Customization Wizard.

If you created the browser package on your hard disk or on a network drive, move the following items to your Internet or intranet server:

- The folder that contains the language version you are posting and the folder contents. This folder is located within the build directory that you specified when you ran the Customization Wizard. For example, the Customization Wizard creates the English language version for the Download media type in the following folder: \build_directory\Download\Win32\En.

- The IE6Sites.dat file. This file points to the download site (or sites) you specified when you ran the Customization Wizard.

Using a Flat Network Share

If you selected the **Flat** media type during Stage 1 of the Internet Explorer Customization Wizard, the wizard places all of the installation files in the \build_directory\Flat folder. Use this media type when you build custom browser packages on a local area network (LAN) or when you plan to distribute your packages from a LAN. You can then direct users to the designated directory on your LAN, and they can run the setup program directly from this location.

Using CD-ROMs

If you selected **CD-ROM** as the media type during Stage 1 of the Internet Explorer Customization Wizard, the wizard creates a custom browser package that you can distribute to your users on CD-ROMs. You can copy or move the files from the \build_directory\CD folder to a CD-ROM imaging program. If the media imaging program supports drag-and-drop operations, you can simply drag the CD folder to the CD-ROM imaging software interface. For more information about whether your program provides this option, see your imaging software documentation.

Users can then install Internet Explorer and Internet Tools by running IE6Setup.exe from the AutoRun splash screen that appears when users open the CD-ROMs. Windows Update Setup for Internet Explorer 6 and Internet Tools offers users the choice of installing the custom browser package or viewing more information. If users already have the current version of Internet Explorer and Internet Tools installed, the AutoRun program automatically detects it.

Using Single-Disk Branding

If you selected **Single disk branding** as the media type during Stage 1 of the Internet Explorer Customization Wizard, the wizard creates a custom browser package that customizes an existing installation of Internet Explorer, including Internet sign-up settings. It does not install Internet Explorer and Internet Tools, and you cannot include any custom components with this media type. The single-disk branding files are located in the *build_directory*\\BrndOnly folder. You can distribute these files on any media or server.

Using a Combination of Distribution Media

If you want to create a single custom browser package and distribute it using several types of media, you need to run the Internet Explorer Customization Wizard only once. The Customization Wizard creates separate folders for each of the media types that you choose. For example, you can build a downloadable package and a CD-ROM package at the same time. Because the packages are built in separate folders within your build directory, you can simply copy the files to the different distribution or imaging locations.

Installing Microsoft Internet Explorer and Internet Tools

Users can install Internet Explorer and Internet Tools by running the setup file, IE6Setup.exe. When users run IE6Setup.exe, Setup carries out the following steps to install the browser and any custom components that you included as part of your custom browser package:

- IE6Setup.exe extracts the setup files into a temporary directory.
- IESetup.inf checks the **[String]** section for the URL location of the file IE6Sites.dat.
- Setup finds IE6Sites.dat, which points to the location of the download .cab files, and then displays the download options to the user.
- Setup downloads the .cab files, which are placed in the specified directory—for example, C:\Program Files\Internet Explorer.
- Setup extracts the .cab files.
- Setup installs the browser and any custom components.

After installing the browser, Setup prompts the user to restart the computer. After the computer restarts, Setup configures the user's desktop and opens the Welcome splash screen to introduce the user to Internet Explorer 6.

Troubleshooting the Setup Process

To troubleshoot Setup:

- Review the Internet Explorer Active Setup Log.txt file in the Windows folder. Each installation creates a log file, which collects information about that particular installation. If an Internet Explorer Active Setup Log.txt file already exists, Setup renames the existing log as a .bak file and creates a new log file.

- Make sure the download URLs that you specify during setup are the same as the URLs for the download server.

- See the appendix "Troubleshooting," which includes information about commonly reported problems and useful tools, such as Internet Explorer Repair, which can help you identify and resolve problems caused by out-of-date, deleted, or corrupted files.

Assisting Users During Installation

The support team should monitor the progress of the browser installation and assist users as necessary. It is recommended that you create an online support Web site that provides users with resources to help them solve common problems. You can integrate the support Web site with your help desk and provide ways to refer unusual or difficult problems to user-support specialists. Then as solutions are developed to solve users' problems, you can update the support Web site to provide that information.

Using SMS to Install Microsoft Internet Explorer 6

This chapter describes the steps required to deploy Microsoft® Internet Explorer 6 and Internet Tools by using Microsoft® Systems Management Server (SMS). This systems management software can help you automate a large-scale deployment by automatically distributing and installing your custom browser packages on users' computers. This automated installation requires no intervention from you or your users.

In This Chapter

Related Information in the Resource Kit

- For more information about planning the deployment process, see "Planning the Deployment."

- For more information about building custom browser packages, see "Running the Microsoft Internet Explorer Customization Wizard."

- For more information about installing Internet Explorer and Internet Tools, see "Deploying Microsoft Internet Explorer 6."

Overview: Automating the Deployment of

Microsoft Internet Explorer 6

Using SMS to automate your deployment can help eliminate desktop visits and human error by electronically distributing your custom browser package from a central location to client computers on the network. You can choose the group of client computers on which you want to automatically install the package and the dates and times when you want the installation to occur. This flexibility can help you avoid network congestion and ensure that the deployment occurs after users have had sufficient time to prepare and receive training.

SMS installs the browser software without requiring any user interaction and can install the software with administrator rights even if a user without administrative rights is logged on. Servers and desktops based on Microsoft® Windows NT® never need to log on, making SMS ideal for off-hours distribution or distribution to physically secured servers. SMS also provides status reports so that you know when the software has been successfully installed.

 Note Before beginning deployment tasks, it is recommended that you install the most current version of SMS and service pack, which is SMS 2.0 with Service Pack 3 at the time of this Resource Kit's publication.

Step 1: Building a Custom Browser Package for

SMS Deployment

First, use the Internet Explorer Customization Wizard to build the custom browser package that you want to deploy to your users. You can use the wizard to customize the appearance and functionality of the browser, its components, and Windows Update Setup for Internet Explorer 6 and Internet Tools. You can also preset browsing options and set system policies and restrictions for your users.

When you build a custom browser package for SMS deployment, you must select the following options:

- **The Corporate version of the Internet Explorer Customization Wizard.** This option is selected when you install the IEAK and requires that you accept the Corporate Administrator License Agreement. The IEAK does not support switching to a different version of the Customization Wizard.

- **The Flat media type.** The required **User Rights** deployment option is available only with this media type.

- **The User Rights deployment option.** The account used to log on to the client computers is then granted the administrative rights necessary to perform the installation. This change in user rights is temporary—administrative rights are granted only for the Internet Explorer installation and expire when the installation is completed.

Important If you deploy your package with the User Rights deployment option on computers running Microsoft® Windows® 2000, after the computers are restarted, all members of the user group to which you deployed the package receive a prompt indicating that Internet Explorer is not the default browser. Attempts to set Internet Explorer as the default browser do not succeed. To resolve the issue, you must add two registry keys for Internet Explorer during the processing of the RunOnceTemp key. For more information, see "User Rights Deployment on Microsoft Windows 2000" later in this chapter.

▶ **To build a custom browser package for SMS deployment**

1. When you install the IEAK, click **Site License and Intranet (internal use) Distribution License (e.g. Corporate Administrators)** so that you are running the Internet Explorer Customization Wizard—Corporate Version. This option requires you to confirm that you signed a license agreement permitting the functionality included with this version of the IEAK.

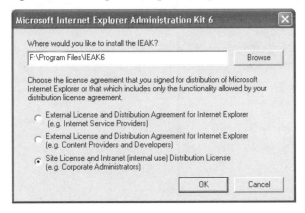

2. To start the Customization Wizard, click **Start**, point to **All Programs**, point to **Microsoft IEAK 6**, and then click **Internet Explorer Customization Wizard**.

3. Follow the steps in the wizard, selecting the following required options:

    o   In Stage 1, on the **Media Selection** page, select the **Flat** check box.

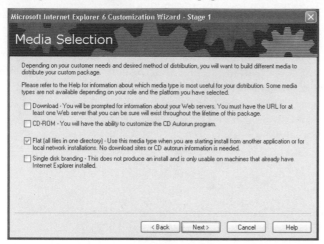

    o   In Stage 3, on the **User Experience** page, select the **Enable logon after restart with user-level access** check box.

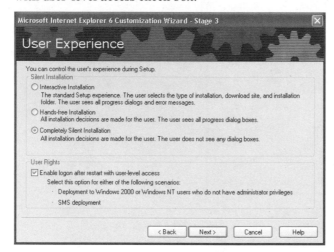

When you click **Finish**, the Customization Wizard builds the custom browser package in the *build_directory*\Flat\Win32*language* folder. The file IE55Urd.exe, which is included with the package, grants the administrative rights necessary for the Internet Explorer installation.

Step 2: Creating an SMS Package for Microsoft Internet Explorer 6

On Microsoft® Windows® 2000 Server or Microsoft® Windows NT® 4.0 Server, you can use the SMS Administrator Console to import the Internet Explorer .sms file, IE6-Sms.sms, and create a package for the Internet Explorer installation. A package consists of a package source folder, which contains all the Internet Explorer installation files, and the package definition (.sms) file. The file IE6-Sms.sms is located in the \SMS Resource Kit folder. Manually copy this file to the local computer where you are creating the SMS package.

IE6-Sms.sms describes the setup commands that define how Internet Explorer is installed on users' computers. It contains command-line definitions for the installation types and for the uninstall options. Each of these command-line definitions contains a command line that directs Setup to run in batch mode with the specific installation type (except for Custom installations, which always run interactively). To view the contents of this file, see "Contents of the IE6-Sms.sms File" later in this chapter.

Complete the following steps to create the SMS package, which is the actual package that SMS uses for distribution. Do not confuse this package with the custom browser package that you created with the Internet Explorer Customization Wizard in "Step 1: Building a Custom Browser Package for SMS Deployment" earlier in this chapter.

▶ **To create an SMS package for Internet Explorer**

1. Copy the file IE6-Sms.sms to your local computer, and update this file as necessary. For example, you might want to change the command-line switches that determine how Internet Explorer is installed. For a description of the available command-line switches, see the appendix "Batch-Mode File Syntax and Command-Line Switches" in this Resource Kit.

   Note When creating an SMS package by using IE6-Sms.sms, you might not get the correct package status because the status .mif file is generated with a wrong version number. The version number in the status .mif file is set to 55 and the version in IE6-Sms.sms is set to 6. If you want to correct this issue, change all Version parameters in IE6-Sms.sms to 55.

2. To open the SMS Administrator Console, click **Start**, point to **All Programs**, point to **Systems Management Server**, and then click **SMS Administrator Console**.

3. In the left pane, expand **Site Database**.

4. Right-click **Packages**, click **New**, and then click **Package from Definition**.

5. On the Create Package from Definition Wizard welcome page, click **Next**.

6. On the **Package Definition** page, click **Browse**, and then locate the file IE6-Sms.sms on your local computer.

    The wizard adds Internet Explorer to the **Package definition** list.

7. On the **Package definition** list, click **Internet Explorer**, and then click **Next**.

8. On the **Source Files** page, click **Always obtain files from a source directory**, and then click **Next**.

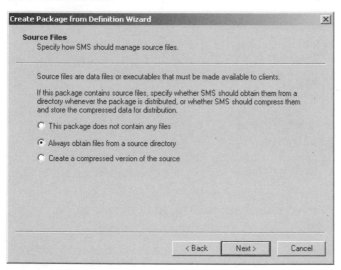

9. On the **Source Directory** page, click either **Network path (UNC name)** or **Local drive on site server**, depending on the location of the custom browser package that you built in "Step 1: Building a Custom Browser Package for SMS Deployment."

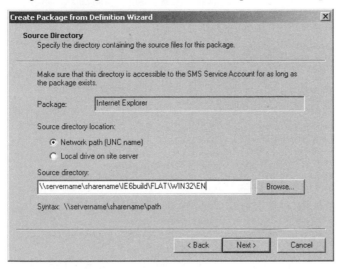

10. For the **Source directory**, type the path for your custom browser package, or click **Browse** to locate the package.

11. Click **Next**, and then click **Finish**.

    On the SMS Administrator Console, in the left pane under **Packages**, the SMS package for Internet Explorer appears.

Step 3: Selecting the SMS Distribution Servers

Select your SMS distribution servers, which are the distribution points for your SMS package. SMS copies all the files from the package source folder to a folder on your SMS distribution servers. Setup runs from these SMS distribution servers, which support the users on your network.

▶ **To select the SMS distribution servers**

1. On the SMS Administrator Console, in the left pane under **Packages**, right-click the SMS package for Internet Explorer, and then click **Distribution Points**.

2. On the New Distribution Points Wizard welcome page, click **Next**.

3. On the **Copy Package** page, select your distribution servers from the **Distribution points** list, and then click **Finish**.

Step 4: Creating and Running a Job to Distribute the SMS Package

After you create the SMS package for Internet Explorer, you must create a job to distribute it. This job includes the list of client computers on which you want to install the SMS package for Internet Explorer and the schedule on which you want the package to run. Also, this job advertises the package to client computers.

▶ **To create and run a job to distribute the SMS package**

1. On the SMS Administrator Console, in the left pane, expand **Site Database**.
2. Right click **Advertisements**, point to **New**, and then click **Advertisement**.
3. In the **Advertisement Properties** dialog box, select values for the following fields:
   - **Name.** The name for the job.
   - **Comment.** A description of the package. This field is optional.
   - **Package.** The SMS package for Internet Explorer that you created in "Step 2: Creating an SMS Package for Microsoft Internet Explorer 6" earlier in this chapter.
   - **Program.** The Internet Explorer executable file, which is part of the custom browser package that you built in "Step 1: Building a Custom Browser Package for SMS Deployment" earlier in this chapter.
   - **Collection.** The collection of client computers that are targeted to receive the SMS package for Internet Explorer.

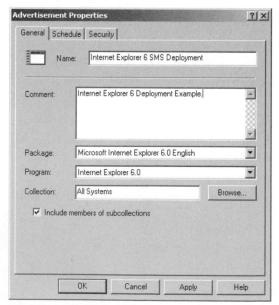

4. Click the **Schedule** tab, and then select the dates and times that you want the package to run.

When the job runs, you can view it by clicking **Advertised Programs** in the Windows Control Panel. The job also creates an error log file, Iesmswrap.mif, which is located in the \Windows\Temp folder. You can perform a search for ***.mif** to quickly locate the file.

The Installation Process

At the scheduled date and time, SMS offers the package to the specified client computers. After these computers recognize that the package is available, the installation process begins. This process occurs in three phases.

Phase 1. IE6Setup.exe performs the following tasks:

*   Modifies the registry to enable automatic logon.
*   Disables the functionality of the keyboard and mouse.
*   Records the path to the SMS distribution server from which the package is executed.
*   Executes the shutdown function to restart the client computer.

Phase 2. The client restarts with automatic logon enabled, and the keyboard and mouse are disabled. At this point, all tasks are running with administrative rights. The following activities occur:

*   IE6Setup.exe runs from the registry. It starts Setup in Quiet mode.
*   Setup finishes the initial phase of its installation.
*   IE6Setup.exe calls the shutdown function to restart the client computer again.

Phase 3. Setup continues with the final phase of the installation. IE6Setup.exe makes one last call to the shutdown function with a 30-second timer. You might need to adjust the timer to allow sufficient time for Internet Explorer to finish its configuration.

> **Note** Depending on the processor speed, the amount of RAM, the size of the hard disk, and other factors, the 30-second timer might not be sufficient. Take these factors into account during your lab testing, and resolve any issues prior to deploying the package to your users.

At this point, the Internet Explorer installation is complete. After the installation, the following activities occur:

*   Automatic logon is disabled, administrative rights are removed, and the keyboard and mouse services are enabled.
*   The client computer is restarted and is ready for the user to log on.
*   When the user logs on, Internet Explorer configures itself for the user's computer.

Contents of the IE6-Sms.sms File

The following code shows the contents of the file IE6-Sms.sms.

```
[PDF]
Version=2.0

[Package Definition]
Publisher=Microsoft
Name=Internet Explorer
Version=6.0
Language=English
MIFNAME=IE
MIFPUBLISHER=MS
MIFVERSION=6
MIFFILENAME=iesmswrap.mif
Programs=IE6

[IE6]
Name=Internet Explorer 6.0
CommandLine=ie6setup.exe /Q /R:S
AdminRightsRequired=True
UserInputRequired=True
DriveLetterConnection=False
AfterRunning=ProgramRestart
CanRunWhen=UserLoggedOn
SupportedClients=Win NT (I386), Win 9x
Win NT (I386) MinVersion1=4.00.0000.0
Win NT (I386) MaxVersion1=4.00.9999.9999
Win NT (I386) MinVersion2=5.00.0000.0
Win NT (I386) MaxVersion2=5.01.9999.9999
Win 9x MinVersion1=0.00.0000.0
Win 9x MaxVersion1=99.99.9999.9999
```

User Rights Deployment on Microsoft Windows 2000

If you deploy your package with the User Rights deployment option on computers running Microsoft Windows 2000, after the computers are restarted, all members of the user group to which you deployed the package receive a prompt indicating that Internet Explorer is not the default browser. This prompt appears even if you select the option in the Customization Wizard to make Internet Explorer the default browser. Also, attempts to set Internet Explorer as the default browser on the computers do not succeed. This behavior continues to occur until users with administrative rights log on to the computers.

During the implementation of the User Rights deployment option, the **RunOnceEx** registry key is moved to the **RunOnceTemp** registry key, and this key is registered in the Windows Installer with the **Execute with Elevated Permissions** option enabled. During the registration, Shdocvw.dll is registered through its DLLRegister and DLLInstall internal functions. One of the functions of these registry keys is to set up the file associations in **HKEY_CLASSES_ROOT** for HTMLFILE and MTHTMLFILE associations. Because of this registration design, if these keys existed, Internet Explorer will not be selected as the default browser. This design prevents Internet Explorer from replacing a competitor's browser as the default browser when users install a program that required the installation of Internet Explorer.

The option in the Customization Wizard to set Internet Explorer as the default browser is accomplished during client branding, which occurs on the first execution of the browser. Because the first execution is not performed with elevated permissions, the registry keys for setting Internet Explorer as the default browser will not be successfully added on Windows 2000. This processing occurs when Internet Explorer calls into Shell32.dll with the RegSetValue() function. Windows 2000 Shell32.dll will first attempt to create the key in question. If the call to RegCreateKey() does not succeed, users do not have permissions to this key, and the operating system returns an "Access Denied" message to the requesting application that called RegSetValue().

To resolve the issue, the following registry keys must be written during the processing of the **RunOnceTemp** key where C:\Program Files\Internet Explorer is the folder in which Internet Explorer is currently installed:

- **HKey_Classes_Root\htmlfile\shell\opennew\command\"",,"C:\Program Files\Internet Explorer\iexplore.exe"**
- **HKey_Classes_Root\mhtmlfile\shell\opennew\command\"",,"C:\Program Files\Internet Explorer\iexplore.exe"**

To add these registry keys, use one of the following methods:

- **Windows 2000 Group Policy.** Group Policy adds the registry keys with the System context, so the logged-on user context does not matter.

- **SMS.** You can add the registry keys by using SMS or another maintenance utility. For more information, see your SMS documentation.

- **An IExpress package.** You can include the keys as part of an IExpress package, and then add the package as a custom component when you run the Customization Wizard. Set the package to execute after restarting the computer, and only if the installation of Internet Explorer is successful. For more information about using the IExpress Wizard to create a package, see "Preparing for the IEAK" in this Resource Kit.

For example, you could create an IExpress package that include the following sample .inf file to add the registry keys:

```
[Version]
Signature=$Chicago$
AdvancedINF=2.5


[DefaultInstall]
AddReg=DefaultKeys


[DefaultKeys]
HKCR,"htmlfile\shell\opennew\command","",0,"""C:\Program Files\
Internet Explorer\iexplore.exe"""
HKCR,"mhtmlfile\shell\opennew\command","",0, """C:\Program Files\
Internet Explorer\iexplore.exe"""
```

Additional Resources

These resources contain additional information and tools related to this chapter.

Related Information Outside the Resource Kit

- *Microsoft® Systems Management Server 2.0 Administrator's Companion*

- Microsoft® BackOffice® Server Web site at http://www.microsoft.com/backofficeserver/

- Microsoft Windows Technologies Internet Explorer Web site at http://www.microsoft.com/windows/ie/

Implementing the Sign-up Process

Internet service providers (ISPs) can use the Microsoft® Internet Explorer Customization Wizard to create custom browser packages that specify how new users sign up with their service and connect to the Internet. You can select a server-based or a serverless sign-up process, or disable the sign-up feature altogether. This chapter describes how to implement a sign-up process, with or without a server, for your custom browser installation.

In This Chapter

Related Information in the Resource Kit

- For more information about preparing custom sign-up files, see "Preparing for the IEAK."
- For more information about setting up an Internet sign-up server, see "Setting Up Servers."
- For more information about using the Internet Explorer Customization Wizard to create custom browser packages, see "Running the Microsoft Internet Explorer Customization Wizard."

Implementing a Server-Based Sign-up Process

The server-based sign-up process automates the registration and set-up tasks for new and existing users. This process uses an Internet sign-up server (ISS) to collect information from each user. The sign-up server adds the data to your customer database and then sends a configuration package back to the user's computer. This package configures the browser for subsequent connections to your Internet services.

The following server-based sign-up methods are available to ISPs:

- **Internet Connection Wizard.** Using the Internet Explorer Customization Wizard, you can specify the Internet Connection Wizard (ICW) as the tool that customers will use to sign up and configure their computers for Internet services. This is the recommended method, because it uses a standard wizard interface that you can customize to fit the needs of your organization and its users. The ICW automatic-configuration feature also enables you to configure settings for users who already have Internet accounts.

  For more detailed information about how to develop an ICW sign-up process, including the files that you need to generate and install on your server for ICW sign-up, see "Setting Up Servers" in this Resource Kit.

- **Full-screen kiosk mode.** Using the Internet Explorer Customization Wizard, you can specify that the sign-up process screens you create be displayed in full-screen kiosk mode.

> **Note** If you are using single-disk branding and members of your user community have Internet Explorer 4.01 Service Pack 1 installed, it is recommended that you use the kiosk-mode sign-up method. The ICW is not available through single-disk branding unless users are running version 5 of the ICW (the ICW version that accompanies Microsoft® Windows® 98 is not enabled for the Internet Explorer ICW sign-up method).

Creating a Custom Browser Package with a Server-Based Sign-up Method

To create a custom browser package that includes a server-based sign-up method, specify the following information in Stage 4 of the Internet Explorer Customization Wizard:

- Either **Server-based sign-up using the Internet Connection Wizard** or **Server-based sign-up using full-screen Kiosk mode** as your sign-up method.
- The path of the working folder that contains your custom sign-up files. These files enable users to configure their computers to connect to your sign-up server.
- The sign-up server information, including dial-up networking parameters that enable users to establish a connection to your sign-up server and the URL of the first online sign-up page.
- The ICW customization information, including your title bar and custom images (if you selected **Server-based sign-up using the Internet Connection Wizard**).

To ensure that your package installs correctly, the folder that contains your custom sign-up files must include the following files:

- **Signup.htm.** This HTML page provides information about your Internet services and must include a link to an appropriate HTML page on the sign-up server. You can customize the sample Signup.htm file, which is located in the Program Files\IEAK6\Toolkit\Isp\Server\ICW folder in your IEAK installation directory. For example, you can add technical support data or include links to Internet sign-up (.isp) files.

- **Signup.isp.** This Internet sign-up file is used to dial your sign-up server and is referenced in Signup.htm. This file should also contain a link to the URL of the server script that generates your Internet settings (.ins) files. Using the Internet Explorer Customization Wizard, you can edit the parameters contained in this sign-up file. The Internet Explorer Customization Wizard also generates other .isp files used in the sign-up process.

  The IEAK also includes a tool, the ISP File Wizard, that you can use to generate the Signup.isp file automatically. For more information about the ISP File Wizard, see "Setting Up Servers" in this Resource Kit.

- **All other sign-up files.** All related files, including .gif and .jpg graphics files, must be saved in the same folder as your custom sign-up files. For example, you might want to include your own customized versions of the Install.gif file.

For more information about building a browser package with custom sign-up files, see "Preparing for the IEAK" and "Running the Microsoft Internet Explorer Customization Wizard" in this Resource Kit.

Distributing a Custom Browser Package with a Server-based Sign-up Method

If you use a server-based sign-up method, the sign-up process for your custom browser package occurs in three steps:

1. The user's computer establishes a connection with the sign-up server.
2. The sign-up server collects information from the user and adds the data to your customer database.
3. The sign-up server passes a configuration package back to the user's computer, which is then configured with the appropriate browser settings.

Establishing a Connection with the Sign-up Server

After the user installs Internet Explorer and restarts the computer, the ICW automatically appears. The ICW dials the sign-up server, and posts an initial connection request. Then the sign-up server performs the following activities:

- Accepts the request from the user's computer (the HTTP client) and establishes an HTTP connection.
- Creates a local data store for accumulating the information that the user enters.
- Assigns a unique session handle that is embedded in all subsequent HTTP transactions with the client.

HTTP is a sessionless protocol; however, the sign-up server operates in a session-oriented mode and uses the session handle to identify all transactions associated with the sign-up process for a particular user. For example, the session handle could be an automatically generated number sequence assigned to the transaction by your database. For more information about sign-up server processing, see "Setting Up Servers" in this Resource Kit.

Collecting the User's Sign-up Information

The sign-up server collects user information from a sequence of HTML pages that walk the user through the sign-up process, much like a wizard in a program based on Microsoft® Windows®. The sign-up server uploads the pages, on demand, to the user's computer. The sign-up process concludes when the user clicks the appropriate button on the final HTML page to either accept or decline the sign-up agreement.

You can choose your own content and format for the HTML pages. Typically, each HTML page includes the following:

- A form for the user to fill out.

- Navigation buttons that the user can click to move forward or backward between pages.

- A button that the user can click to cancel the sign-up session.

Each HTML form includes controls for collecting input text, navigating between pages, and identifying the session. The form gathers information from the user and passes it to the sign-up server when the user clicks a navigation button. Also, the sign-up server can validate the data and post an error page to the user's computer if the data is not acceptable. For more information about setting up HTML forms on your sign-up server, see "Setting Up Servers" in this Resource Kit.

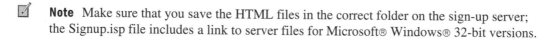

   Note Make sure that you save the HTML files in the correct folder on the sign-up server; the Signup.isp file includes a link to server files for Microsoft® Windows® 32-bit versions.

Passing a Configuration Package Back to the User's Computer

If the user accepts the sign-up agreement, the sign-up server builds a configuration package with an .ins file (generated by the Internet Explorer Customization Wizard) that includes information about the user and your Internet services. The .ins file can contain only connection settings, or it can contain connection, browser, and mail settings that include graphics.

The sign-up server passes the configuration package back to the user's computer by using the .ins file, which can be generated during the sign-up process using the client's information, or simply redirected to the client computer. Then the user's computer can continue the process of installing the custom browser package. If the user declines or quits the sign-up agreement, the sign-up server redirects the client computer to a file that cancels the sign-up process.

The configuration package includes the following information:

- Data for configuring Internet connections

- Capabilities of the user's account (including e-mail and newsreaders)

- Branding information, which customizes the appearance of the sign-up pages for your organization
- The local phone number, so the user can access your Internet services

The first two types of data are created as part of the sign-up server. The Internet Explorer Customization Wizard prepares the .ins file for branding. Some settings, such as Entry, User, Phone, Device, Server, and TCP/IP, can be specified in the wizard.

If you want to provide a variety of custom "private-branded" versions of Internet Explorer for different user groups, you can maintain multiple sets of branding information that the sign-up server downloads in the .ins file. For example, you might want to customize versions with different logos, title bars, favorites, search pages, start pages, special links, or locations for online assistance. All of the compact discs that you distribute to users will be the same, but versions of Internet Explorer will be branded differently when the users sign up for Internet services.

Implementing a Serverless Sign-up Process

The serverless sign-up process enables ISPs that do not want to use a sign-up server to provide customized installations to their users. A serverless sign-up process avoids the creation of a sign-up server by manually giving account information to the users.

Creating a Custom Browser Package with a Serverless Sign-up Method

To create a custom browser package that includes a serverless sign-up method, specify the following information in Stage 4 of the Internet Explorer Customization Wizard:

- **Serverless sign-up** as your sign-up method.
- The path of the folder that contains your custom sign-up files. These files enable users to configure their computers for Internet services.
- The dial-up networking parameters that enable users to establish a connection for Internet services.

To ensure that your package installs correctly, the folder that contains your custom sign-up files must include the following:

- **Signup.htm.** This HTML page provides information about your Internet service and must include a link to the .ins file, which contains the configuration settings for your custom browser package. You can customize the sample Signup.htm file, which is located in the Advanced or Basic subfolder within the Program Files\IEAK6\Toolkit\Isp\Serverless folder in your IEAK installation directory. For example, you can add technical support data.
- **All other sign-up files.** You must save all related files, including .gif and .jpg graphic files, in the same folder as your custom sign-up files. For example, you might want to include your own customized versions of the Install.gif and Logohere.gif files.

For more information about building a browser package with custom sign-up files, see "Preparing for the IEAK" and "Running the Microsoft Internet Explorer Customization Wizard" in this Resource Kit.

Distributing a Custom Browser Package with a Serverless Sign-up Method

Your custom browser package includes a configuration file, named Install.ins, that contains the settings you specified for your custom browser. Unlike the Internet sign-up server method, this .ins file contains no user-specific configuration information. When the user starts the sign-up program, a link from the local HTML page starts the .ins file. The user provides the user name, password, and connection information. Then the .ins file configures the user's account to connect to the Internet using the custom browser.

 Note The serverless sign-up process also includes an advanced option, which uses a Microsoft® ActiveX® control to generate an .ins file that incorporates the user's information.

Maintenance and Support

Chapter 26: Using Automatic Configuration, Automatic Proxy, and Automatic Detection

This chapter describes the automatic configuration, automatic proxy, and automatic detection features that make it possible, after Microsoft® Internet Explorer has been installed, to change settings globally without having to change each user's computer. The information in this chapter is particularly useful if you expect the needs of your organization or users to change, and you, therefore, anticipate frequent changes to browser settings.

Chapter 27: Keeping Programs Updated

After you install Microsoft® Internet Explorer 6 and Internet Tools, you can use the following tools to keep browser components and settings updated:

- **Automatic version synchronization (AVS).** Use AVS to obtain new and updated Internet Explorer components, including security patches and new product releases that you can deploy as part of your updated browser packages.

- **IEAK Profile Manager.** Use the IEAK Profile Manager to create and modify IEAK profiles, which use auto-configuration .ins files to update the browser settings on users' computers.

- **Update notification page.** Set the update notification page to notify users automatically bout new versions of Internet Explorer. You can customize or disable this update capability.

- **Group Policy.** On client computers that are running Microsoft® Windows® XP and Microsoft® Windows® 2000 operating systems (particularly client computers that are part of a Windows XP or Windows 2000 domain), you must customize the browser and administer system policies and restrictions by using the Microsoft Management Console (MMC) with Microsoft® Active Directory™ and the Internet Explorer Maintenance (IEM) snap-in extension for Group Policy.

Chapter 28: Implementing an Ongoing Training and Support Program

After your users install Microsoft Internet Explorer 6 and Internet Tools, you can begin implementing an ongoing training and support program. Because learning how to use Internet Explorer is an ongoing process, basic training and support during deployment, followed by an ongoing program customized for your organization's needs, is the best means for getting the most out of your investment in Internet Explorer. This chapter describes ongoing training and support options.

Using Automatic Configuration, Automatic Proxy, and Automatic Detection

This chapter describes the automatic configuration, automatic proxy, and automatic detection features that make it possible, after Microsoft® Internet Explorer has been installed, to change settings globally without having to change each user's computer. The information in this chapter is particularly useful if you expect the needs of your organization or users to change, and you, therefore, anticipate frequent changes to browser settings.

In This Chapter

Related Information In the Resource Kit

- For more information about the administration of your Internet Explorer installations, see "Understanding Customization and Administration."

- For more information about building custom browser packages, see "Running the Microsoft Internet Explorer Customization Wizard"

- For more information about tools and programs that can help you maintain Internet Explorer after deployment, see "Keeping Programs Updated."

Using Automatic Configuration

With automatic configuration, you can control browser settings on your users' computers from one central location. To use automatic configuration, you must create an IEAK Profile by using the IEAK Profile Manager. This profile consists of an auto-configuration .ins file and associated cabinet (.cab) files that contain information for configuring your users' browsers. You must then copy the .ins and .cab files to a server location that is accessible from your users' computers. For information about how to create an IEAK Profile by using the IEAK Profile Manager, see "Keeping Programs Updated" in this Resource Kit.

When you run the Internet Explorer Customization Wizard, you can set up automatic configuration for your custom browser packages.

▶ **To set up automatic configuration**

1. In Stage 4 on the **Automatic Configuration** page, select the Enable Automatic Configuration check box.

2. Specify the interval for how often automatic configuration will occur.

3. Type the location of the .ins file on your server.

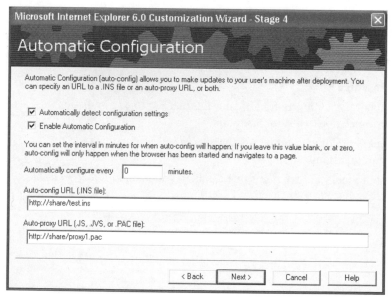

For more information about setting up automatic configuration when you run the Customization Wizard, see "Running the Microsoft Internet Explorer Customization Wizard" in this Resource Kit.

If you need to change browser settings later, you can simply use the IEAK Profile Manager to edit the .ins file, and then replace the existing .ins file on the server with your updated version. The next time your users start their browsers, or on a schedule that you specify, the configuration changes are reflected on each user's computer.

Using Automatic Proxy

Automatic proxy (auto-proxy) makes system administration easier, because you can automatically configure proxy settings such as server addresses and bypass lists. When you use the IEAK Profile Manager to create your IEAK Profile for automatic configuration, you can specify standard proxy settings. These settings are then included in the .ins file that is used to automatically configure browser settings on your users' computers. For more information about how to create an IEAK Profile by using the IEAK Profile Manager, see "Keeping Programs Updated" in this Resource Kit.

To configure more advanced settings for auto-proxy, you can create a separate .js, .jvs, or .pac script file and then copy the file to a server location. Then, when you run the Internet Explorer Customization Wizard, you can specify the server location for the script file on the Automatic Configuration page. If you specify server locations for both automatic configuration and auto-proxy, the location of the auto-proxy script file is incorporated into the .ins file. For more information about setting up automatic proxy when you run the Customization Wizard, see "Running the Microsoft Internet Explorer Customization Wizard" in this Resource Kit.

The auto-proxy script file is executed whenever a network request is made. Within the script, you can configure multiple proxy servers for each protocol type; then, if a proxy server connection fails, Internet Explorer automatically attempts to connect to another proxy server that you have specified.

Proxy Selection and Proxy Bypass Lists

As an administrator, you can use a proxy server with a firewall to create a barrier between your organization and the Internet, to cache frequently used content, and to balance server load. You can specify the proxy server in the Internet Explorer Customization Wizard, in the IEAK Profile Manager, or through the browser. You can also restrict users' ability to change the proxy settings by using the Restrictions page in the Customization Wizard or in the IEAK Profile Manager.

The following procedure describes how to specify your proxy server and proxy bypass lists through the browser. For more information about performing these tasks by using the Customization Wizard or the IEAK Profile Manager, see "Running the Microsoft Internet Explorer Customization Wizard" or "Keeping Programs Updated" in this Resource Kit.

▶ **To specify your proxy server and proxy bypass settings through the browser**

1. In Internet Explorer, click the **Tools** menu, and then click **Internet Options**.
2. Click the **Connections** tab, and then click **LAN Settings**.

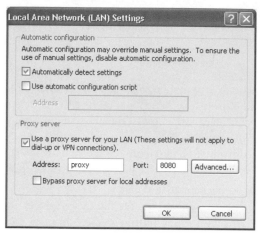

3. In the **Proxy server** area, select the **Use a proxy server** check box.
4. Type the **Address** and **Port** number for your proxy server.
5. If you want to assign different proxy server information for HTTP, Secure, FTP, Gopher, and Socks protocols, click **Advanced**, and then in the Proxy Settings page, fill in the proxy location and port number for each protocol.

JavaScript or JScript Auto-proxy Examples

The following 10 scripts provide JavaScript or Microsoft® JScript® examples of how an auto-proxy configuration (.pac) file could be used to specify an auto-proxy URL. To use these examples, you must change the proxy server names, port numbers, and IP addresses.

📝 **Note** The **isInNet()**, **isResolvable()**, and **dnsResolve()** functions query a DNS server. References to Object Model objects, properties, or methods cause the .pac file to fail silently. For example, the references window.open(...) and password(...) cause the .pac file to fail on Internet Explorer.

Example 1: Local hosts connect directly; all others connect through a proxy server.

The following function checks whether the host name is a local host, and if it is, whether the connection is direct. If the host name is not a local host, the connection is made through a proxy server.

```
function FindProxyForURL(url, host)
  {
    if (isPlainHostName(host))
      return "DIRECT";
    else
      return "PROXY proxy:80";
  }
```

The **isPlainHostName()** function checks whether there are any dots in the host name. If there are, it returns FALSE; otherwise, it returns TRUE.

Example 2: Hosts inside the firewall connect directly; outside local servers connect through a proxy server.

The following function checks whether the host name is a "plain" host name (meaning it does not contain the domain name) or part of a particular domain (*.domain.com*), and does not contain "www" or "home."

```
function FindProxyForURL(url, host)
  {
    if ((isPlainHostName(host) ||
      dnsDomainIs(host, ".microsoft.com")) &&
      !localHostOrDomainIs(host, "www.microsoft.com") &&
      !localHostOrDomainIs(host, "home.microsoft.com"))
      return "DIRECT";
    else
      return "PROXY proxy:80";
  }
```

Note The **localHostOrDomainIs()** function is executed only for URLs in the local domain. The **dnsDomainIs()** function returns TRUE if the domain of the host name matches the domain given.

Example 3: If host is resolvable, connect directly; otherwise, connect through a proxy server.

The following function asks the DNS server to resolve the host name passed to it. If it can resolve the host name, a direct connection is made. If it cannot resolve the host name, the connection is made through a proxy server. This function is useful if you use an internal DNS server to resolve all internal host names.

```
function FindProxyForURL(url, host)
  {
    if (isResolvable(host))
      return "DIRECT";
    else
      return "PROXY proxy:80";
  }
```

Example 4: If the host is in the specified subnet, connect directly; otherwise, connect through a proxy server.

The following function compares a given IP address pattern and mask with the host name. This is useful if certain hosts in a subnet should be connected directly and others should be connected through a proxy server.

```
function FindProxyForURL(url, host)
  {
    if (isInNet(host, "999.99.9.9", "255.0.255.0"))
      return "DIRECT";
    else
      return "PROXY proxy:80";
  }
```

The **isInNet(host, pattern, mask)** function returns TRUE if the host IP address matches the specified pattern. The mask indicates which part of the IP address to match (255=match, 0=ignore).

Example 5: Determine connection type based on host domain.

The following function specifies a direct connection if the host is local. If the host is not local, this function determines which proxy server to use based on the host domain. This is useful if the host domain name is one of the criteria for proxy server selection.

```
function FindProxyForURL(url, host)
  {
    if (isPlainHostName(host))
      return "DIRECT";
    else if (shExpMatch(host, "*.com"))
      return "PROXY comproxy:80";
    else if (shExpMatch(host, "*.edu"))
      return "PROXY eduproxy:80";
    else
      return "PROXY proxy";
  }
```

The **shExpMatch(str, shexp)** function returns TRUE if str matches the shexp using shell expression patterns.

Example 6: Determine connection type based on protocol being used.

The following function extracts the protocol being used and makes a proxy server selection accordingly. If no match is made for the protocol, a direct connection is made. This function is useful if the protocol being used is one of the criteria for proxy server selection.

```
function FindProxyForURL(url, host)
  {
  if (url.substring(0, 5) == "http:") {
return "PROXY proxy:80";
  }
  else if (url.substring(0, 4) == "ftp:") {
return "PROXY fproxy:80";
  }
  else if (url.substring(0, 7) == "gopher:") {
return "PROXY gproxy";
  }
  else if (url.substring(0, 6) == "https:") {
return "PROXY secproxy:8080";
  }
  else {
return "DIRECT";
  }
  }
```

The **substring()** function extracts the specified number of characters from a string.

Example 7: Determine proxy setting by checking whether the host name matches the IP address.

The following function makes a proxy server selection by translating the host name into an IP address and comparing it to a specified string.

```
function FindProxyForURL(url, host)
  {
  if (dnsResolve(host) == "999.99.99.999") { // = http://secproxy
return "PROXY secproxy:8080";
  }
  else {
return "PROXY proxy:80";
  }
  }
```

The **dnsResolve()** function translates the host name into the numeric IP address.

Example 8: If the host IP matches the specified IP, connect through a proxy server; otherwise, connect directly.

The following function is another way to make a proxy server selection based on a specific IP address. Unlike Example 7, this one uses the function call to explicitly get the numeric IP address.

```
function FindProxyForURL(url, host)
  {
  if (myIpAddress() == "999.99.999.99") {
return "PROXY proxy:80";
  }
  else {
return "DIRECT";
  }
  }
```

The **myIpAddress()** function returns the IP address (in integer-dot format) of the host that the browser is running on.

Example 9: If there are any dots in the host name, connect through a proxy server; otherwise, connect directly.

The following function checks how many dots are in the host name. If there are any dots, the connection is made through a proxy server. If there are no dots, a direct connection is made. This is another way to determine connection types based on characteristics of the host name.

```
function FindProxyForURL(url, host)
  {
  if (dnsDomainLevels(host) > 0) { // if number of dots in host > 0
return "PROXY proxy:80";
  }
return "DIRECT";
  }
```

The **dnsDomainLevels()** function returns an integer equal to the number of dots in the host name.

Example 10: Specify days of the week to connect through a proxy server; other days connect directly.

The following function determines the connection type by specifying the days of the week that are appropriate for a proxy server. Days that do not fall within these parameters use a direct connection. This function could be useful in situations where you might want to use a proxy server when traffic is heavy and allow a direct connection when traffic is light.

```
function FindProxyForURL(url, host)
  {
if(weekdayRange("WED", "SAT", "GMT"))
 return "PROXY proxy:80";
else
 return "DIRECT";
  }
```

The **weekdayRange**(<day1> [,<day2>] [,<GMT>]) function returns whether the current system time falls within the range specified by the parameters <day1>, <day2>, and <GMT>. Only the first parameter is necessary. The GMT parameter sets the times to be taken in GMT rather than in the local time zone.

Note Where the function is called with <day1> == <day2>, previous versions of Internet Explorer would yield results different from results with Netscape Navigator. Specifically, previous versions of Internet Explorer would interpret this day range as an entire week, while Internet Explorer 6 and Netscape Navigator interpret the range as a single day. For example, if the current day is Monday, the call **weekdayRange**("TUE", "TUE") returns TRUE on previous versions of Internet Explorer and FALSE on Internet Explorer 6 and Netscape Navigator.

Using Automatic Detection

The automatic detection feature enables automatic configuration and automatic proxy to work when a user connects to a network the first time. With automatic detection turned on, the browser is automatically configured when it is started, even if you did not customize the browser. For example, if a user downloads a non-customized browser from the Internet instead of installing a customized version from the corporate servers, automatic detection can automatically configure and customize the user's browser. This feature can help reduce administrative overhead and potentially reduce help desk calls about browser settings.

When you run the Internet Explorer Customization Wizard, you can turn on automatic detection of browser settings by selecting **Automatically detect configuration settings** on the Automatic Configuration screen. Automatic detection can also be set in the **Internet Options** dialog box of the Internet Explorer browser. For more information about turning on automatic detection for your custom browser packages, see "Running the Microsoft Internet Explorer Customization Wizard" in this Resource Kit.

Automatic detection of browser settings is based on Web Proxy AutoDiscovery (WPAD) and is supported by both Dynamic Host Configuration Protocol (DHCP) and Domain Name System (DNS). With the appropriate settings, DHCP and DNS servers can automatically detect and configure a browser's settings. Your DHCP server must support the DHCPINFORM message; otherwise, use DNS. For details about setting up a DHCP or DNS server for automatic detection of browser settings, see "Setting Up Servers" in this Resource Kit.

C H A P T E R   2 7

Keeping Programs Updated

After you install Microsoft® Internet Explorer 6 and Internet Tools, you can use the following tools to keep browser components and settings updated:

- **Automatic version synchronization (AVS).** Use AVS to obtain new and updated Internet Explorer components, including security patches and new product releases that you can deploy as part of your updated browser packages.

- **IEAK Profile Manager.** Use the IEAK Profile Manager to create and modify IEAK profiles, which use auto-configuration .ins files to update the browser settings on users' computers.

- **Update notification page.** Set the update notification page to notify users automatically about new versions of Internet Explorer. You can customize or disable this update capability.

- **Group Policy.** On client computers that are running Microsoft® Windows® XP and Microsoft® Windows® 2000 operating systems (particularly client computers that are part of a Windows XP or Windows 2000 domain), you must customize the browser and administer system policies and restrictions by using the Microsoft Management Console (MMC) with Microsoft® Active Directory™ and the Internet Explorer Maintenance (IEM) snap-in extension for Group Policy.

> **Note** This chapter provides a brief overview of Group Policy. For complete information about the Microsoft Management Console (MMC), Active Directory, and the Internet Explorer Maintenance (IEM) snap-in extension for Group Policy, see the online Help and Resource Kits for Windows XP and Windows 2000.

In This Chapter

Related Information in the Resource Kit

- For more information about Internet Explorer Customization Wizard settings, see "Running the Microsoft Internet Explorer Customization Wizard."

- For more information about system policies and restrictions, see the appendix "Setting System Policies and Restrictions."

Automatic Version Synchronization

After you install Internet Explorer and Internet Tools, you can run the Internet Explorer Customization Wizard and use the wizard's AVS feature to obtain any updated or new components released by Microsoft that have become available since your deployment of Internet Explorer. You can then download and install these components as part of your updated browser packages.

To use the AVS feature when you run the Customization Wizard, do the following:

- In Stage 1, on the **File Locations** page, use the **Advanced Options** dialog box to specify a component download folder where the current versions of the Internet Explorer components that you deployed to your users' computers are located. AVS determines which components need to be updated by comparing the latest versions of Internet Explorer components that are available on the Internet to the versions in the component download folder that you specify.

   The **Check for latest components via Automatic Version Synchronization** check box, which turns on the AVS feature, is selected by default. If you clear this check box, the Customization Wizard cannot verify whether you have the latest versions of Internet Explorer components.

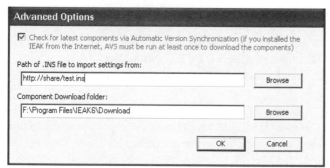

   In Stage 2 on the **Automatic Version Synchronization** page, use the **Updates** dialog box to identify any new or updated component versions that are not in the download folder you specified in Stage 1. You can then select the new or updated components that you want to download and include in your updated browser packages, and these items appear in the components list.

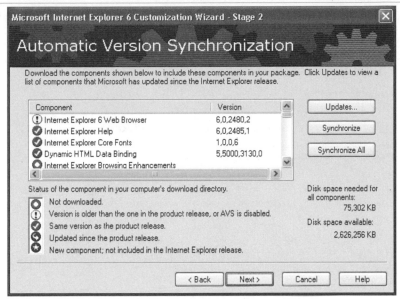

For more information about using the AVS feature when you run the Customization Wizard, see "Running the Microsoft Internet Explorer Customization Wizard" in this Resource Kit.

IEAK Profile Manager

When you run the Internet Explorer Customization Wizard to create your custom browser packages, you can turn on automatic configuration and automatic detection. These features enable browser settings to be automatically configured on your users' computers based on the settings you specify in IEAK profiles.

You can use the IEAK Profile Manager to create the IEAK profiles for automatic configuration as well as to update the profiles after the browser is installed. Each profile consists of an autoconfiguration .ins file and associated cabinet (.cab) files that contain information for configuring your users' browsers. For more information about automatic configuration and automatic detection, see "Using Automatic Configuration, Automatic Proxy, and Automatic Detection" in this Resource Kit.

Creating and Updating IEAK Profiles

When you use the IEAK Profile Manager to create and update IEAK profiles, you can specify two types of browser settings:

- **Wizard settings.** These settings correspond to browser and component options that you initially configured in Stages 2 through 5 of the Internet Explorer Customization Wizard.
- **Policies and restrictions.** These settings correspond to options that you initially configured on the System Policies and Restrictions page in Stage 5 of the Internet Explorer Customization Wizard.

▶ **To create and update IEAK Profiles**

1. On the **Start** menu, point to **Programs** (in Windows XP, click **All Programs**), point to **Microsoft IEAK 6**, and then click **IEAK Profile Manager**.

2. On the **File** menu, click **New** to create a new IEAK profile, or click **Open**, and then open the .ins file for an existing IEAK profile that you want to update.

3. On the left side of the window, click **Wizard Settings** or **Policies and Restrictions**.

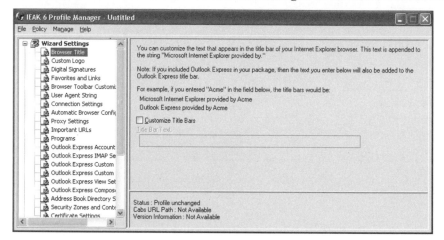

4. On the left side of the window, click each category, and then on the right side, specify the options you want.

5. On the **File** menu, click **Save as**. Type a name for the file, keeping its .ins extension. The default location for saving the .ins file is the *build directory*\Ins*operating system**language* folder. For example, an English version of the .ins file that was created for the Microsoft® Windows® 32-bit platform might be saved in the \Build1\Ins\Win32\En folder.

Files Generated by the IEAK Profile Manager

When you save an IEAK profile, the IEAK Profile Manager generates the following files:

- **Auto-configuration .ins file.** This file contains the browser and component settings that Internet Explorer uses to update the browser configuration on users' computers. You can specify these settings in the Wizard Settings section of the IEAK Profile Manager.

- **Cabinet (.cab) files.** These files are used to organize the installation files that are downloaded to users' computers. Every time you save an .ins file, the associated .cab files are automatically saved as well.

  You should digitally sign the .cab files created by the IEAK Profile Manager. For more information about signing your .cab files, see "Preparing for the IEAK" in this Resource Kit.

- **Information (.inf) files.** Included within the .cab files, the .inf files contain the system policies and restrictions that the operating system uses to update the system configuration on users' computers. You can specify these settings in the Policies and Restrictions section of the IEAK Profile Manager.

Each .inf file also contains version information. The version information consists of the date the .ins file was modified and the number of times the file has been revised. When you change browser settings, the IEAK Profile Manager updates the affected .inf files and their version information and repackages the associated .cab files.

Before updating the browser settings on your users' computers, you should copy the .ins file and the associated .cab files generated by the IEAK Profile Manager to a working directory and test the configuration. After you validate your settings, copy the new .ins file to your production server.

If you turned on automatic configuration and automatic detection, Internet Explorer downloads and processes the contents of the .ins file and makes the necessary configuration changes on users' computers. Internet Explorer also downloads and unpacks the associated .cab files for the operating system to process. If the version number of the .ins file did not change, new .cab files are not downloaded.

Creating Unique Configurations for Different Groups of Users

If you have users with different needs or if you want to change some users' configuration settings independently of others', you can create multiple IEAK profiles. You can use the IEAK Profile Manager to specify different configuration settings for each group and save them as individual *usergroup*.ins files, where *usergroup* is a unique name for each user group. The IEAK Profile Manager automatically generates the companion .cab files. For example, you could specify a unique configuration for the Finance Department and save the configuration as Finance.ins. The IEAK Profile Manager would then generate the necessary companion .cab files.

Note If you create multiple .ins files, make sure that your custom browser packages are configured to use the correct file. You can also use an automated server solution, which enables you to use multiple .ins files without rebuilding your custom packages. For more information about using an automated server solution, see "Time-saving Strategies That Address Diverse User Needs" in the Resource Kit.

Using Custom Policy Templates

The IEAK Profile Manager uses a default set of Windows policy templates, or administration (.adm) files, to define the rules for system policies and restrictions. The .adm files and system policies and restrictions are standard features of the Windows 32-bit platform. If you are familiar with .adm files, you can create your own templates to define additional restrictions. Then you can use the IEAK Profile Manager to import your own custom .adm files and include them with your updated browser settings.

The IEAK Profile Manager generates an associated .inf file, using the file prefix for the custom .adm file that you import. For example, if you import a file named Custom.adm, a Custom.inf file is generated and added to the companion .cab files. For more information about using custom .adm files, see the appendix "Setting System Policies and Restrictions" in this Resource Kit.

Note The System Policies and Restrictions settings for Windows XP and Windows 2000 are not available through the IEAK Profile Manager. To manage restrictions and policies for these operating systems, use Group Policy.

Changing the Location of an .ins File

If you need to move an .ins file to a different production server, you can use the IEAK Profile Manager to update the automatic configuration URL. This process involves updating the IEAK profile with the new automatic configuration URL, saving the profile to its existing location, and then saving the profile to its new location. When you save the package to its new location, you can specify the path for both the new .ins file and the associated .cab files. If you set an .ins file to update at a specified interval, you must allow two intervals after you update the automatic configuration URL before the change takes effect.

Note You should not remove the IEAK profile from its existing location until all client computers are using the profile at the new location.

▶ **To update the automatic configuration URL**

1. On the **Start** menu, point to **Programs** (in Windows XP, click **All Programs**), point to **Microsoft IEAK 6**, and then click **IEAK Profile Manager**.

2. On the **File** menu, click **Open**, and then open the .ins file from your custom browser package.

3. On the left side of the window under Wizard Settings, click **Automatic Browser Configuration**.

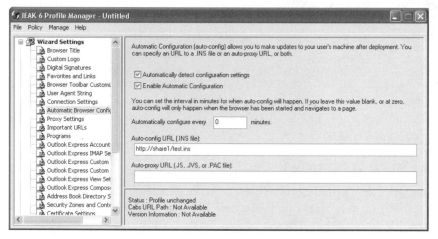

4. On the right side of the window, type the new server path in the **Auto-config URL (.INS file)** box.

5. To save your updated profile to its existing location, on the **File** menu, click **Save**.

6. To save your updated profile to its new location, on the **File** menu, click **Save as**. Type a name for the file, keeping its .ins extension.

7. Type the new server location for your .ins file and associated .cab files to match the URL you entered.

When the user starts the browser and the browser settings are scheduled to be updated, the pointer to the automatic configuration URL is then updated on the user's computer. At this point, the browser is still using the settings from the original .ins file (for example, http://*existing path*/Default.ins).

When the user starts the browser a second time and the browser settings are scheduled to be updated again, the browser reads the new .ins file (for example, http://*new path*/Default.ins). When you are sure that the settings on all users' computers have been updated, you can remove the copy of the .ins file from its original location.

Specifying Browser Settings for Windows XP and Windows 2000 Unattended Setup

To install Windows XP or Windows 2000 automatically, you can run Setup with an *answer file*, which automates the setup process. An answer file contains settings that customize Setup without user or administrator intervention. This type of Setup is often referred to as *unattended Setup*.

If you plan to use unattended Setup, in the branding section of the answer file, you can specify an .ins file, which contains your custom settings for Internet Explorer. Then the browser settings that you specify are automatically configured on users' computers during unattended Setup. For more details about unattended Setup, see the Resource Kits for Windows XP and Windows 2000. For more information about creating an .ins file, see "Creating and Updating IEAK Profiles" earlier in this chapter.

Update Notification Page

Internet Explorer automatically notifies your users when a new version of the browser is available. At a specified interval, the version of the browser installed on the users' computers is compared against the most current browser version that is available on the Internet. If the current browser version on the Internet is newer than the version on users' computers, the Internet Explorer home, or start, page is temporarily replaced by an update notification page when the user starts the browser.

The default update notification page is the Microsoft Windows Update page. From this page, users can download the newer version of the browser, add the update notification page to their Favorites list, or cancel the browser update. The update notification page does not force the user to install the browser update. If the user closes the browser without selecting the update or the update is not completed, the user does not see the page again until the next update interval.

If you want to force the installation of a new or updated program on your users' computers, you can use other system management tools, such as Microsoft System Management Server (SMS). For more information about using SMS, see "Using SMS to Install Microsoft Internet Explorer 6" in this Resource Kit.

Specifying a Different Update Notification Page and Update Interval

You can use either the Internet Explorer Customization Wizard or the IEAK Profile Manager to replace the URL of the default update notification page with a URL of your own custom Web page or another Web site. You can also change the update interval, which specifies how often the update notification page is displayed.

You might want to customize the update notification page for the following reasons:

- If your users' computers do not have Internet access (which is needed to access Internet Explorer updates from Microsoft distribution sites), you must change the URL to a location on your intranet.

  For example, you can re-create the Microsoft Windows Update page on your intranet and then redirect users to this location. The IEAK includes the necessary .asp pages and Microsoft® ActiveX® control so that you can use this Windows Update technology. For more information, see the IEAK Help.

- You might want to redirect users to your custom Addon.htm file rather than to the Windows Update page. For more information about Addon.htm, see "Preparing for the IEAK" in this Resource Kit.

- You might want to provide other information, news, or software updates at a regular interval. For software updates of programs other than Internet Explorer, the browser prompts users to install the update without comparing the update version with the version on their computers.

- You might want to redirect the update notification page temporarily to an executable (.exe) file for a program that you want to install on your users' computers. When the users start the browser, the .exe file begins to install the program automatically, and the update notification page does not appear.

For more information about specifying a different URL and update interval for the update notification page when you build your custom browser packages, see "Running the Microsoft Internet Explorer Customization Wizard" in this Resource Kit.

After you deploy Internet Explorer, you can use the IEAK Profile Manager to change the settings for the update notification page.

▶ **To change the settings for the update notification page by using the IEAK Profile Manager**

1. On the **Start** menu, point to **Programs** (in Windows XP, click **All Programs**), point to **Microsoft IEAK 6**, and then click **IEAK Profile Manager**.

2. On the **File** menu, click **Open**, and then open the .ins file for your custom browser package.

3. On the left side of the window under Policies and Restrictions, click **Internet Settings**, and then click **Component Updates**.

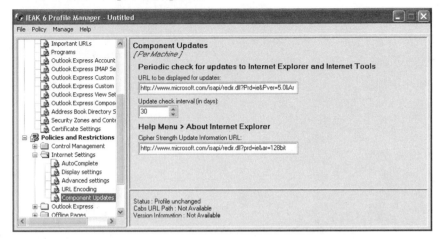

4. On the right side of the window, in the **URL to be displayed for updates** box, type the URL for your custom update notification page.

5. In the **Update check interval (in days)** box, type the number of days for the update interval.

6. On the **File** menu, click **Save as**. Type a name for the file, keeping its .ins extension.

Disabling the Update Notification Page

When you use the Internet Explorer Customization Wizard to build your custom browser packages of Internet Explorer, you can disable the update notification page. For more information, see "Running the Microsoft Internet Explorer Customization Wizard" in this Resource Kit.

You can also disable the update notification page after you deploy Internet Explorer by using the IEAK Profile Manager.

▶ **To disable the update notification page by using the IEAK Profile Manager**

1. On the **Start** menu, point to **Programs** (in Windows XP, click **All Programs**), point to **Microsoft IEAK 6**, and then click **IEAK Profile Manager**.

2. On the **File** menu, click **Open**, and then open the .ins file from your custom browser package.

3. On the left side of the window, under Policies and Restrictions, click **Internet Settings**, and then click **Advanced settings**.

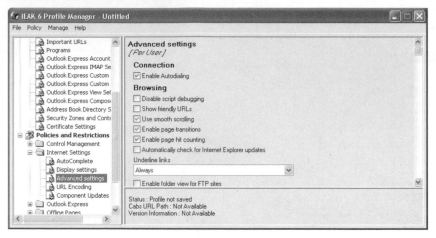

4. On the right side of the window, clear the **Automatically check for Internet Explorer updates** check box.

5. On the **File** menu, click **Save as**. Type a name for the file, keeping its .ins extension.

Note   After you disable the update notification page, users can still turn on the page in the browser. To disable the page completely so that users cannot enable it in the browser, set the **Update check interval** to a value of 0. For more information about setting the update check interval, see "Specifying a Different Update Notification Page and Update Interval" earlier in this chapter.

Group Policy

If you installed Internet Explorer and Internet Tools on users' computers that are running Windows XP and Windows 2000, you must use the MMC with Active Directory and the IEM snap-in extension for Group Policy to customize and maintain Internet Explorer installations. This snap-in extension for Group Policy enables you to customize most of the same features that you can configure by using the IEAK. It includes Internet Explorer maintenance features to customize the browser and administrative template settings to prevent users from changing settings that you want to control.

Group Policy is a collection of settings used to define configurations for groups of users and computers. Group Policy is flexible and includes options for registry-based policy settings, security settings, software installation, scripts (during computer startup and shutdown, and to log on and log off), and folder redirection. Administrators use Group Policy to specify options for managed desktop configurations.

Administrators can apply settings to various hierarchical groups of users, known as *organizational units*. This structure enables an administrator to set broad standards or restrictions for a company or division while specifying exceptions for smaller departments or groups. Also you can use the Software Installation snap-in for Group Policy to manage software distribution from a centralized source in your organization. You can assign and publish software for groups of users and groups of computers.

When you use the IEM snap-in extension for Group Policy, you can also export your settings to an .ins file, which allows you to maintain the settings for other supported operating systems, such as Microsoft® Windows® 98 and Microsoft® Windows NT® 4.0 with Service Pack 6 (SP6), by using the IEAK Profile Manager. For more information about exporting Group Policy settings, see "Exporting Group Policy Settings for Internet Explorer" later in this chapter.

For information about the MMC, Active Directory, and the IEM snap-in extension for Group Policy, see Help and the Resource Kits for Windows XP and Windows 2000.

Customizing Internet Explorer with Group Policy

You can customize the following areas by using the IEM snap-in extension for Group Policy:

- The user interface and the appearance of the browser
- Connection settings, such as dial-up and local area network (LAN) connections and user agent string
- Custom URLs, such as favorites, the search page, and the home page
- Security settings, such as security zones and content ratings
- Default programs for common Internet tasks, such as reading e-mail and viewing newsgroups

Before you open the MMC and begin configuring Group Policy settings for your users, you can view the Internet Explorer features that are available for customization by running Gpedit.msc on your local computer. This opens the IEM snap-in extension for Group Policy and allows you to review the configuration pages and available settings.

▶ **To run Gpedit.msc on your local computer**

1. On the **Start** menu, click **Run**.
2. In the **Open** text box, type **GPEDIT.MSC**, and then click **OK**.

For information about running the IEM snap-in extension for Group Policy and configuring Group Policy setting for your users, see Help and Resource Kits for Windows XP and Windows 2000.

Exporting Group Policy Settings for Internet Explorer

You can use Group Policy in Windows XP and Windows 2000 to export all of the Internet Explorer settings to an .ins file and, if necessary, to .cab files. These settings can then be used for automatic configuration on computers that run other operating systems.

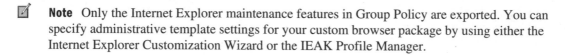

Note Only the Internet Explorer maintenance features in Group Policy are exported. You can specify administrative template settings for your custom browser package by using either the Internet Explorer Customization Wizard or the IEAK Profile Manager.

▶ **To export all of the Internet Explorer settings to an .ins file**

1. In Group Policy, right-click the Internet Explorer screen that contains the settings you want to export.

2. Click **Export Browser Settings**.

3. Type the names of the .ins file and, if applicable, the .cab files where you want to export the settings.

4. Type the URL where the files are located on the Web server.

For more information about the automatic configuration feature, see "Using Automatic Configuration, Automatic Proxy, and Automatic Detection" in this Resource Kit.

Implementing an Ongoing Training and Support Program

After your users install Microsoft® Internet Explorer 6 and Internet Tools, you can begin implementing an ongoing training and support program. Because learning how to use Internet Explorer is an ongoing process, basic training and support during deployment, followed by an ongoing program customized for your organization's needs, is the best means for getting the most out of your investment in Internet Explorer. This chapter describes ongoing training and support options.

In This Chapter

Related Information in the Resource Kit

- For more information about developing your training and support plans, see "Planning the Deployment."

- For more information about testing your training and support plans before deploying Internet Explorer, see "Setting Up and Administering a Pilot Program."

- For more information about implementing training and support plans during your Internet Explorer rollout, see "Deploying Microsoft Internet Explorer 6."

Overview of Training and Support

An ongoing training and support program can increase productivity by promoting, expanding, and enhancing your users' Internet Explorer knowledge and skills. If your organization employs an internal training and support staff, they can effectively implement the program by using their experience from the pilot program and Internet Explorer deployment.

Ongoing Training Options

Consider the following options for ongoing user training:

- **Offer follow-up training sessions for continuing education.** Building on the content of your deployment training and feedback from your users, you might want to offer additional formal or informal training sessions. These sessions can cover some skills in more detail or provide training for different features and functionality, based on the changing needs of your organization and its users. You might also want to repeat training sessions as new users join your organization.

- **Provide a Web page on the Internet or intranet for ongoing training.** You can develop a training Web page on the Internet or corporate intranet and then use an e-mail message or memo to tell your users about the page and point them to the URL. To make the Web page most useful, you should update it frequently with new tips, hints, and answers to frequently asked questions. For ongoing education about features, benefits, and enhancements, users can also review Internet Explorer information on the Microsoft Windows Technologies Internet Explorer Web page at http://www.microsoft.com/windows/ie/.

- **Periodically distribute a newsletter or other written communication about the features and functionality of Internet Explorer.** You can produce and distribute an Internet Explorer memo, e-mail message, newsletter, or other written communication on a regular basis to all of your users. The communication can announce news that is relevant to your ongoing training efforts, including tips about new browser features and dates for additional training sessions. You also can ask users to contribute articles that contain helpful advice and convey information that they have learned.

- **Supply users with additional publications and training materials about Internet Explorer.** As part of your ongoing training and support program, you can supply users with additional publications and training materials, such as Microsoft Press books, for more detailed information about browser features and functions. For more information about Internet Explorer publications that are available from Microsoft Press, visit the Microsoft Press Online Web site at http://mspress.microsoft.com/. Microsoft Press books are available in stores that sell computer books.

- **Employ Microsoft training services.** Microsoft offers a variety of training services for educating computer professionals about Microsoft products. As part of your ongoing training program, you may want to offer these training services to your users. The following section describes Microsoft training services in greater detail.

Microsoft Training Services

Microsoft offers different training services to help users become experts in Microsoft product solutions. These services include the Microsoft Certified Professional Program and Microsoft technical training courses.

Microsoft Certified Professional Program

The Microsoft Certified Professional Program offers an excellent way to gain the knowledge and skills necessary to build, implement, and support effective solutions with Microsoft products. To become a Microsoft Certified Professional, users must pass a series of rigorous, standardized certification exams.

Users who become Microsoft Certified Professionals receive many benefits, including access to technical information, use of the Microsoft Certified Professional logo, and special invitations to Microsoft conferences and technical events. For more information about the Microsoft Certified Professional Program, visit the Microsoft Training & Certification Web site at http://www.microsoft.com/trainingandservices/.

Microsoft Technical Training Courses

Microsoft technical training courses provide computer professionals with the knowledge to expertly install and support Microsoft solutions. Courses have been developed in close cooperation with the Microsoft product-support groups. They include in-depth, accurate information and hands-on lab exercises based on real-world experience. Microsoft technical training courses are designed to help users prepare effectively for Microsoft Certified Professional exams.

The Microsoft technical training curriculum is available in three forms:

- **Classroom instruction.** Instructor-led classes are given by Microsoft Certified Professional trainers at Microsoft Authorized Certified Education Centers (CTECs). As members of the Certified Solution Provider Program, the CTECs are independent businesses qualified to teach the official Microsoft curriculum.

- **Online training.** For a more flexible alternative to instructor-led classes, users can turn to online training. They can learn at their own pace and on their own schedule in a virtual classroom, often with easy access to an online instructor. Without ever leaving their desks, users can gain the expertise they need. Because this is training on demand, users can access learning resources 24 hours a day.

- **Self-paced training.** Microsoft's self-paced curriculum enables users to learn at their own convenience. For motivated learners who are ready for the challenge, self-paced training is the most flexible, cost-effective way to increase knowledge and skills. This self-paced curriculum includes a wide variety of comprehensive training kits, books, online resources, and CD-ROM-based multimedia—all developed or approved by Microsoft.

For more information about Microsoft technical training courses, visit the Microsoft Training & Services Web site at http://www.microsoft.com/trainingandservices/.

Ongoing Support Options

Consider the following options for ongoing user support:

- **Use the built-in product support.** Help files included with Internet Explorer provide users with a comprehensive set of topics, which they can view from within the browser. To view Help topics, click the **Help** menu, and then click **Contents and Index**. Also, users can find updates and technical information in the readme (.txt) files that come with Internet Explorer.

- **Provide help desk services for ongoing user support.** Depending on resources, an organization can staff a help desk or use existing help desk services to support Internet Explorer users on an ongoing basis. Your organization should encourage users to call the help desk with their questions. The staff at the help desk should monitor the types of questions that users ask and assess how well the staff provides accurate, timely answers. To help the staff respond to users' questions, this book also includes a series of chapters in the part "Multimedia, Accessibility, and Other Features," that provide information and procedures for using new Internet Explorer features.

- **Provide a page on the Internet or intranet for ongoing support.** Internet Explorer provides an **Online Support** command on the **Help** menu. By default, when users click **Online Support**, the Microsoft Product Support Services home page appears in the browser window. On this Web site, users can gain access to the Microsoft Product Support problem-solving tools and technical information, including the Knowledge Base, the "Ask Maxwell" service, and troubleshooting wizards, and download sites. Users can get up-to-date answers 24 hours a day, 7 days a week.

  An organization can also create its own customized Web site to provide online technical support that is tailored to the needs of its users. When the organization creates custom browser packages, the URL for this customized Web site can replace the default link used by the **Online Support** command. For additional information about using a customized Web site to provide online technical support, see "Preparing for the IEAK" and "Running the Microsoft Internet Explorer Customization Wizard" in this Resource Kit.

- **Employ Microsoft support services.** In addition to the extensive online Help and support services that users can use within the browser, Microsoft offers a variety of other support services for Internet Explorer. The following section describes these Microsoft support services in greater detail.

Microsoft Product Support Services

Customers can choose from a variety of Microsoft personal and business support services that are available by telephone and through various online services.

> **Note** For a complete listing of support services, including telephone numbers, pricing, terms, and conditions, visit the Microsoft Product Support Services Web site at http://support.microsoft.com/directory/.

No-Charge Assisted Support

If Internet Explorer users cannot find the answers they need by using the built-in product and online help resources, they can use one of the following options for no-charge assisted support:

- If Internet Explorer and Internet Tools was part of the preinstalled software on a purchased computer, the computer manufacturer can provide support for Internet Explorer. For more information about manufacturer support, see the Support for Preinstalled Microsoft Products Web page. You can access this page by selecting your location at http://support.microsoft.com/directory/getitem.asp?ITEM=OP and then clicking **Assisted Support Directory**.

- If users install Internet Explorer and Internet Tools from a CD-ROM or the Internet, they can contact Microsoft Product Support Services for support. Although Internet Explorer and Internet Tools does not include no-charge, assisted support, users can obtain personal assistance from Microsoft Product Support Services by using the no-charge assisted support that is included with their Microsoft Windows operating system.

When users call for support or use the Web Response service, they can use their available support incidents that are included with retail versions of Windows. If users have an OEM version of Windows or if they have already used all of their support incidents included with their retail versions of Windows, they can use the paid support options described in the following sections.

Internet Explorer users can submit issues instantly on the Personal or Professional Support Incident Submission Web page at http://support.microsoft.com/support/webresponse.asp. Or if they prefer, they can call Microsoft support engineers by using the telephone numbers listed on the Call Microsoft *country/region* Support Web page at http://support.microsoft.com/directory/phone.asp.

In the United States, no-charge assisted support is available between 5:00 A.M. and 9:00 P.M. Pacific time, Monday through Friday, and between 9:00 A.M. and 3:00 P.M. Pacific time on Saturday, excluding holidays (toll charges may apply). In Canada, no-charge assisted support is available between 8:00 A.M. and 11:00 P.M. Eastern time, Monday through Friday, and between 10:00 A.M. and 6:00 P.M. on Saturday, excluding holidays (toll charges may apply).

Outside the United States and Canada, users can contact Microsoft Product Support Services at the Microsoft subsidiary office that serves their area. For a list of these subsidiaries, see the Worldwide Support Web page at http://support.microsoft.com/directory/ww.asp. If no Microsoft subsidiary office is located in your country or region, you can contact the business from which you obtained the Microsoft product.

Users who call Microsoft Product Support Services should be at their computers and have the appropriate product documentation in hand. Microsoft support engineers request the following information:

- The version number of the Microsoft product in use
- The type of hardware in use
- The exact wording of any messages that appear on the screen
- A description of what happened and what was being done when the problem occurred
- A description of the methods used in any attempts to resolve the problem

Pay-per-Incident Support

By using pay-per-incident support, Internet Explorer users can pay to speak directly to the experts who can answer their questions. They can submit issues instantly on the Personal or Professional Support Incident Submission Web page at http://support.microsoft.com/support/webresponse.asp. Or if they prefer, in the United States they can call Microsoft support engineers at (800) 936-5700; in Canada they can call Microsoft support engineers at (800) 668-7975. Microsoft charges a fixed rate per incident, which appears on the user's telephone bill (not available in Canada) or is billed to the user's VISA, MasterCard, or American Express card.

In the United States, pay-per-incident support on the Web and by telephone is available 24 hours a day, 7 days a week, including holidays. In Canada, pay-per-incident support is available between 8:00 A.M. and 11:00 P.M. Eastern time, Monday through Friday, and between 10:00 A.M. and 6:00 P. M. on Saturday, excluding holidays.

Business Support

Microsoft Product Support Services offers annual fee-based support plans. These plans are designed for expert users and businesses that require priority access to support engineers for business-critical needs 24 hours a day, 7 days a week. These expert users and businesses anticipate a high volume of calls or require access to specialized information.

The following support plans are available:

- **Professional.** The Professional support plan provides advanced support services for expert users and small to medium-size businesses that are developing, deploying, and maintaining business systems based on Microsoft operating systems, products, and tools. This support plan includes advance-purchase support at a per-incident rate for online and telephone assistance. Professional support customers can gain access to custom support sites, online information, technical resources, and responsive incident support from engineers trained to address their specific needs.

- **Premier.** The Premier support plan provides large enterprises with proactive access to the professional services and technical expertise that they need to help maximize the use of their business systems and minimize their total costs. This support plan provides the well-planned, managed systems support necessary to maintain large, enterprisewide systems that are running integrated applications. Premier support customers can gain access to a wide range of product and application expertise through priority technical support and custom support sites.

- **Alliance.** The Alliance support plan is designed to help very large enterprises successfully develop, deploy, and manage mission-critical business systems that are built around a broad range of Microsoft technologies and solutions for the server and the desktop. These enterprises need the maximum level of support to ensure the smoothest, most finely tuned operation of their enterprisewide business applications and solutions. Alliance support provides a fully personalized service with the highest level of attention available from Microsoft, including personnel dedicated to the enterprise, the creation and management of exclusive information resources, and executive-level contact between the enterprise and Microsoft.

For more information about these priority business support options, contact your Microsoft account representative, or call Microsoft Professional Support Sales at (800) 936-3500 or Microsoft Enterprise Support Sales at (800) 936-3200.

Other Custom Support Resources

Microsoft offers a variety of other custom support resources to meet the unique needs of organizations and their users.

Microsoft Gold Certified Partners for Support Services

Microsoft Gold Certified Partners for Support Services (formerly Microsoft Certified Support Centers—MCSCs) are a select group of strategic support partners who offer high-quality, customized support services for each phase of system development, including planning, implementing, and maintaining multi-vendor environments. These partners are trained and certified to support the latest Microsoft technologies.

Services available from Microsoft Gold Certified Partners include:

- On-site support
- Integration and implementation services
- Help desk services
- Hardware support
- Development resources

A Microsoft Gold Certified Partner can provide comprehensive technical support and services to supplement an in-house help desk or a Microsoft support option. For more information about Microsoft Gold Certified Partners, visit the Microsoft Gold Certified Partner Web site at http://www.microsoft.com/support/partner/.

Microsoft Certified Partners

Microsoft Certified Partners are independent organizations that provide consulting, integration, development, training, technical support, and other services related to Microsoft products. The Microsoft Certified Partner program supplies partners with information, business development assistance, and tools that help create additional value for Microsoft-based software technologies. For more information about the program, visit the Microsoft Certified Partner Web site at http://www.microsoft.com/certpartner/.

MSDN

The Microsoft Developer Network (MSDN®) is the official source for comprehensive programming information, development toolkits, and testing platforms. A subscription to MSDN includes quarterly updates of information and technology. For more information about subscribing to this development resource, visit the MSDN Web site at http://msdn.microsoft.com/.

Microsoft Multimedia Central

Microsoft Multimedia Central (formerly Microsoft Seminar Online) delivers valuable media content over the Internet, including the latest information about Microsoft solutions, technologies, and products. Business professionals and developers can instantly gain access to technical topics, which are tailored to their interests and available at a time that fits their schedules. To view this media content, visit the Microsoft Multimedia Central Web site at http://www.microsoft.com/seminar/.

Microsoft TechNet

Microsoft TechNet is the comprehensive CD-ROM information resource for evaluating, implementing, and supporting Microsoft business products. A one-year subscription to Microsoft TechNet includes two CD-ROMs every month with over 150,000 pages of up-to-date technical information. The first CD-ROM includes current technical notes, reviewers' guides, background papers, Microsoft product resource kits, and the entire Microsoft Knowledge Base. The second CD-ROM contains the Microsoft Software Library with the latest drivers and service packs for Microsoft products. For more information about subscribing to Microsoft TechNet, visit the Microsoft TechNet Web site at http://www.microsoft.com/technet/.

International Support

Microsoft provides support outside the United States through its subsidiary offices. To locate a subsidiary office near you, go to the Worldwide Support Web page at http://support.microsoft.com/directory/ww.asp. If no Microsoft subsidiary office is located in your country or region, you can contact the business from which you obtained the Microsoft product.

PART 7

Appendices

Appendix A: What's Included with This Resource Kit?

The Microsoft® Internet Explorer 6 Resource Kit contains comprehensive technical information, software tools, and sample files for deploying and supporting Microsoft® Internet Explorer 6. This appendix provides a list of the Resource Kit contents, including applications, tools, and documentation.

Appendix B: Troubleshooting

This appendix provides detailed information for troubleshooting Microsoft Internet Explorer 6, including an effective troubleshooting strategy and a description of the most commonly reported problems. For easy troubleshooting, problems are categorized into several broad areas.

Appendix C: Batch-Mode File Syntax and Command-Line Switches

This appendix describes how you use batch files and command-line switches to customize Microsoft® Windows® Update Setup, as well as command-line parameters for starting Microsoft Internet Explorer 6.

Appendix D: Checklist for Preparing to Use the IEAK

When preparing to use the Microsoft® Internet Explorer Administration Kit (IEAK) 6, you may find a checklist helpful. This appendix contains a checklist for the files you will need to prepare and information you will need to gather before using the IEAK.

Appendix E: Setting System Policies and Restrictions

This appendix describes how you can use system policies and restrictions to control user and computer access to Microsoft Internet Explorer 6 features and functions. Using the Microsoft® Internet Explorer Customization Wizard or Internet Explorer Administration Kit (IEAK) Profile Manager, you can predefine Internet Explorer options and customize the Internet Explorer environment for different groups of users.

Appendix F: Country/Region and Language Codes

As an Internet service provider, you might find helpful the lists of country/region and language codes provided in this appendix.

Appendix G: Microsoft Internet Explorer 6 File Types

This appendix provides an overview of the common types of files that are used as part of Microsoft® Windows® Update Setup for Microsoft® Internet Explorer 6 and Internet Tools. Learning about the purposes of these files and how they work together can make it easier to troubleshoot setup issues.

Appendix H: Structural Definition of .inf Files

Although the Microsoft Internet Explorer Customization Wizard, Internet Explorer batch files, and third-party applications can customize Setup, you can also use setup information (.inf) files to develop a customized setup solution. This appendix describes the sections of an .inf file and provides a sample.

Appendix I: Microsoft Internet Explorer 6 Resource Directory

This appendix contains lists of books, compact discs, and Web sites. These lists provide sources of additional information about Microsoft Internet Explorer 6 and Internet Tools and about related Microsoft products.

APPENDIX A

What's Included with This Resource Kit?

The *Microsoft® Internet Explorer 6 Resource Kit* contains comprehensive technical information, software tools, and sample files for deploying and supporting Microsoft® Internet Explorer 6. This appendix provides a list of the Resource Kit contents, including applications, tools, and documentation.

In This Appendix

Related Information in the Resource Kit

- For general information about this Resource Kit and its contents, see the "Welcome" at the beginning of the Resource Kit.

- For a list of additional resources that provide information about the browser and its components and about related Microsoft products, see the appendix "Microsoft Internet Explorer 6 Resource Directory."

Microsoft Internet Explorer 6

Internet Explorer 6 includes a comprehensive set of components that help you meet your Internet-based and intranet-based communication needs. Using the Internet Explorer Setup program or the Internet Explorer Customization Wizard, you can select the components that you want to install with the Web browser. Internet Explorer 6 includes the following components for communication and collaboration across the Internet or local intranet:

- Microsoft® Outlook® Express for e-mail and newsgroups
- Additional Microsoft and third-party components that enhance Web browser features and functionality, such as Microsoft® Visual Basic® Scripting Support

Internet Explorer components work together seamlessly, because the applications are tightly integrated and have a common menu and toolbar. Internet Explorer gives you the flexibility to implement these applications as a stand-alone communication solution or to integrate them with your existing software applications. An organization that uses Internet Explorer does not need to discard its existing applications. For example, a corporation can use its existing messaging solution together with Internet Explorer components.

If you need advanced applications, Internet Explorer offers a scalable solution. For example, Microsoft Outlook can replace Outlook Express for those users who need a more full-featured messaging client.

System policies and restrictions enable you to configure and manage Internet Explorer components easily. You can control user and computer access to components as well as restrict the types of component features and functionality that are available to users. For more information about system policies and restrictions, see the appendix "Setting System Policies and Restrictions" in this Resource Kit.

Microsoft Outlook Express

Outlook Express provides online communication tools that you can access instantly from your desktop. Whether you want to exchange e-mail with colleagues and friends or join newsgroups to trade ideas and information, Outlook Express provides the tools you need. This messaging client includes powerful mail management features, efficient messaging and newsgroup use, enhanced security, and full support for Internet standards and technologies.

You can take advantage of the following messaging services:

- Manage multiple e-mail and newsgroup accounts within a single window. To separate work-related and personal messages, create multiple identities for the same computer, each with unique e-mail folders and an individual Address Book.
- Use the message list and preview pane to view a list of messages and read individual messages at the same time. To stay organized, create folders to sort your messages, set up rules to control incoming messages, and create your own views to customize the Outlook Express window.
- Keep your messages on a server, and view them from any computer that can connect to the server. If your Internet service provider (ISP) uses an Internet message access protocol (IMAP) e-mail server, Outlook Express allows you to read, store, and organize your incoming messages in folders on the server without downloading the messages to your computer.

- Save names and addresses in the Address Book automatically by simply replying to a message. Also, import names and addresses from other applications, type them into the Address Book, add them from messages you receive, or add them from a search of popular Internet directory services.

- Add a personal signature or stationery to your outgoing messages. Include essential data, such as your business contact information, as part of your personal signature, or create multiple signatures to use for different purposes. In addition, add stationery patterns and backgrounds, and change the color and style of the text.

- Send and receive secure messages by using digital IDs to digitally sign and encrypt messages. Digitally signing your message assures recipients that the message really is from you. Encryption ensures that only intended recipients can read the message.

- Find newsgroups and view newsgroup conversations efficiently. Keyword searches can help you locate newsgroups quickly. Or browse through all the newsgroups available from your Usenet provider, and then add them to your Subscribed list to view them again. For each newsgroup, expand and collapse conversations to quickly find what interests you.

For additional information about Outlook Express, see the Microsoft Windows Technologies Internet Explorer Web site at http://www.microsoft.com/windows/ie/.

Additional Microsoft and Third-Party Components

In addition to the primary components described in the previous sections, Internet Explorer contains other Microsoft and third-party components that you can install. Select from the following additional components when you run the Internet Explorer Customization Wizard:

- **Microsoft Internet Explorer Help.** Internet Explorer provides a comprehensive set of Help topics that you can access to find answers to questions, troubleshoot potential problems, or get additional product information.

- **Microsoft Internet Explorer Core Fonts.** This core set of TrueType fonts are optimized to provide maximum on-screen legibility.

- **Dynamic HTML Data Binding.** Data-binding components allow Internet Explorer to access information from a database and display it in Web pages.

- **Microsoft Internet Explorer Browsing Enhancements.** Browsing enhancements include a graphical File Transfer Protocol (FTP) helper.

- **Microsoft® Windows Media® Player.** The Windows Media Player control allows you to play media within the browser.

- **Microsoft Windows Media Player Codecs.** These codecs support audio and video playback for Windows Media Player.

- **Microsoft DirectAnimation.** The Microsoft® DirectAnimation® component provides animation and multimedia services for your computer, making available both Web content and stand-alone products.

- **Vector Graphics Rendering (VML).** This rendering tool enables you to view vector graphics images with Internet Explorer.

- **AOL Art Image Format Support.** This component enables you to view in Internet Explorer images that were created in AOL Art format.

- **Microsoft Visual Basic Scripting Support.** This component provides support for viewing Web pages that use the VBScript scripting language.

- **Additional Web Fonts.** This set of additional TrueType fonts enables you to read Web-page text designed for viewing with Arial, Comic, Courier, Impact, and Times New Roman fonts.

- **Language Auto-Selection.** This feature enables Internet Explorer to automatically detect the language encoding of Web pages.

- **Arabic Text Support.** The Arabic language pack includes TrueType fonts and other support files that enable Internet Explorer to display Arabic text.

- **Chinese (Simplified) Text Display Support.** The simplified Chinese language pack includes TrueType fonts and other support files that enable Internet Explorer to display simplified Chinese text.

- **Chinese (Simplified) Text Input Support.** The simplified Chinese IME allows simplified Chinese characters to be entered as text in other language versions of Windows.

- **Chinese (Traditional) Text Display Support.** The traditional Chinese language pack includes TrueType fonts and other support files that enable Internet Explorer to display traditional Chinese text.

- **Chinese (Traditional) Text Input Support.** The traditional Chinese IME allows traditional Chinese characters to be entered as text in other language versions of Windows.

- **Hebrew Text Support.** The Hebrew language pack includes TrueType fonts and other support files that enable Internet Explorer to display Hebrew text.

- **Japanese Text Display Support.** The Japanese language pack includes TrueType fonts and other support files that enable Internet Explorer to display Japanese text.

- **Japanese Text Input Support.** The Japanese Input Method Editor (IME) allows Japanese characters to be entered as text in other language versions of Windows.

- **Korean Text Display Support.** The Korean language pack includes TrueType fonts and other support files that enable Internet Explorer to display Korean text.

- **Korean Text Input Support.** The Korean IME allows Korean characters to be entered as text in other language versions of Windows.

- **Pan-European Text Display Support.** The Pan-European language pack includes TrueType fonts and other support files that enable Internet Explorer to display Central European, Cyrillic, Greek, Turkish, and Baltic text.

- **Thai Text Support.** The Thai language pack includes TrueType fonts and other support files that enable Internet Explorer to display Thai text.

- **Vietnamese Text Support.** The Vietnamese language pack includes TrueType fonts and other support files that enable Internet Explorer to display Vietnamese text.

Microsoft Windows Service Pack

The Resource Kit includes the Microsoft® Windows NT® 4.0 Service Pack (SP) 6a, which include advanced management and security features. You can update your Windows installations with this service pack, which is required for Internet Explorer 6.

Microsoft Internet Explorer 6 Resource Kit Book

This comprehensive guide for deploying, administering, and maintaining Internet Explorer is a technical supplement to browser product documentation. The Resource Kit book is presented in Help format with Contents, Search, and Index features to help you locate topics quickly and easily.

Microsoft Internet Explorer 6 Administration Kit

IEAK applications and tools make it easy for you to create and deploy custom browser packages and to manage the browser after the installation. The Resource Kit contains the following IEAK applications and tools:

- **Internet Explorer Customization Wizard.** The Internet Explorer Customization Wizard divides the browser customization into five stages. Step-by-step screens for each stage guide you through the process of creating custom browser packages. When these packages are installed on users' desktops, your users receive customized versions of Internet Explorer with the settings and options you selected.

- **IEAK Profile Manager.** After you deploy Internet Explorer, you can use the IEAK Profile Manager to change browser settings and restrictions automatically on users' computers from a central location.

- **IEAK Toolkit.** The IEAK Toolkit contains helpful tools, applications, and sample files, such as the animated bitmap tools and sample signup and add-on files, which you can use to extend the IEAK functionality for your organization. The toolkit also includes the IExpress Wizard. You can use this wizard to control setup options and to integrate command-line switches, which control how your custom browser packages are installed. The Toolkit contents are located in the Toolkit folder in your IEAK installation directory.

- **IEAK Help.** IEAK Help includes many conceptual and procedural topics about customizing the browser components and setup process. You can view these topics by using the Index, Contents, and Search tabs.

Other Resources in the Resource Kit

This Resource Kit includes additional tools, files, and documentation that corporate administrators, Internet service providers, and Internet content providers might find useful. For example, install Microsoft Web Accessories, or copy the file necessary for Systems Management Server (SMS) deployment of Internet Explorer.

Troubleshooting

This appendix provides detailed information for troubleshooting Microsoft® Internet Explorer 6, including an effective troubleshooting strategy and a description of the most commonly reported problems. For easy troubleshooting, problems are categorized into several broad areas.

In This Appendix

Related Information in the Resource Kit

- For more information about setting up a pilot program, which enables you to troubleshoot potential Internet Explorer issues before deployment, see "Setting Up and Administering a Pilot Program."

- For more information about installing Microsoft® Internet Explorer 6 and Internet Tools and assisting users with setup issues, see "Deploying Microsoft Internet Explorer 6."

Overview: Troubleshooting Strategy

You can follow four basic steps when you troubleshoot any problem with Internet Explorer.

▷ **To troubleshoot problems with Internet Explorer**

1. Identify and analyze the problem.
2. Check to see whether the problem is a common one by reviewing this appendix, Internet Explorer Help, the Microsoft Knowledge Base (http://support.microsoft.com/directory/), and the Readme file included with this product.
3. Isolate and test the error conditions.
4. If you still cannot resolve the problem, consult online troubleshooting and support options.

Identifying and Analyzing the Problem

Start the troubleshooting process by analyzing symptoms to determine a strategy for resolving the problem. Consider the following questions:

- Are there any error messages?
- When does the problem occur?
- Is the problem reproducible or random?
- Is the problem specific to an Internet Explorer feature, such as privacy settings?
- Does the problem occur in any or all other applications?
- Have you changed any applications, programs, or settings on your computer, for example, by adding or removing programs or adding new hardware?
- Has Internet Explorer worked previously? If so, what behavior has changed?
- Does the problem occur on only one computer, on only one operating system, or on only one Web site, or does it occur on many?
- Does your computer meet the necessary hardware and software requirements for running Internet Explorer 6? (For a list of requirements, see "Planning the Deployment" in this Resource Kit.)

Checking for Common Problems

Check whether the problem is a commonly reported one described in this appendix, the Internet Explorer Help, the Microsoft Knowledge Base (http://support.microsoft.com/directory/), or the Internet Explorer Readme file. Internet Explorer Help includes topics that can help you solve problems related to Internet Explorer features and components.

▶ **To use Internet Explorer Help**

1. In Internet Explorer, click **Help**, and then click **Contents and Index**.
2. Click the **Contents**, **Index**, or **Search** tab, and then select the topic you want.

Isolating and Testing Error Conditions

You can resolve a problem more quickly by systematically isolating and testing error conditions. To isolate your error conditions, use the following methods:

- Eliminating variables helps to determine a problem's cause. For example, consider closing all other programs except Internet Explorer to eliminate the other programs as the potential cause of your problem.

- You can isolate the cause by changing a specific value and then testing to see whether the problem is corrected or altered. For example, if you are unable to play videos or animations, changing the Multimedia options in the **Internet Options** dialog box might resolve the issue.

- If a component does not work properly after you upgrade to new hardware or software, replace the new version with the original item and then retest it. For example, if you install a new sound card driver and lose audio capability, you can replace the new driver with the original version and retest it to see whether the problem still occurs.

Test each modification individually to see whether the change resolves your problem. Make note of all modifications and their effect on symptoms. If you contact product support personnel, this information helps them troubleshoot your problem. Also, the information provides an excellent reference for future troubleshooting.

Consulting Online Troubleshooting and Support Options

Whenever possible, check the appropriate online forum. Other users might have discovered and reported your problem and found workarounds for it. Suggestions from others could save you time when you attempt to track the source of the problem, and they might give you ideas that can help with troubleshooting.

▶ **To get online support**

- On the Internet Explorer **Help** menu, click **Online Support**.

  Internet Explorer displays the Microsoft Product Support Services Web page. From this page, you can choose from several topics, including Knowledge Base articles, Frequently Asked Questions, Troubleshooting wizards, newsgroups, and other support options.

Installation and Uninstallation

This section describes some of the problems you might encounter during and after installation and uninstallation of Internet Explorer and Internet Tools. Troubleshooting topics include:

- Problems occur because of out-of-date, deleted, or corrupted files.
- The Internet Explorer setup process fails.
- The download server connection times out.
- You cannot install Internet Explorer and Internet Tools after download.
- The Internet Explorer uninstall process fails.

Problems occur because of out-of-date, deleted, or corrupted files

Internet Explorer 6 includes a Repair tool, which you can use to diagnose and possibly fix problems that you might have with Internet Explorer. You can use this tool to do the following:

- Identify problems with Internet Explorer caused by files that are out-of-date.
- Fix problems caused by the incorrect or incomplete registration of Internet Explorer files.
- Restore or repair the desktop or **Start** menu shortcuts for Internet Explorer that have been deleted or do not function properly.

The results of the repair process are logged in the Fix IE Log.txt file in the Microsoft® Windows® folder. The error checking done by the Repair tool varies slightly from one operating system to another. The following procedure describes how to start the Internet Explorer Repair tool.

▶ **To use the Internet Explorer Repair tool on Microsoft Windows 2000 and earlier versions of Windows**

1. Click **Start**, point to **Settings**, and then click **Control Panel**.
2. Double-click the **Add/Remove Programs** icon.
3. Click **Microsoft Internet Explorer 6 and Internet Tools**.
4. Click **Change/Remove** (Microsoft® Windows® 2000).

   -Or-

   Click **Add/Remove** (Microsoft® Windows® 95, Microsoft® Windows® 98, and Microsoft® Windows NT® 4.0).
5. Click **Repair Internet Explorer**.

If the Repair tool detects an error, it might generate the following error message or one similar to it:

Internet Explorer 6 cannot be repaired. Please reinstall Internet Explorer 6.

If you receive this error message, it is recommended that you reinstall Internet Explorer 6. To read a description of the problem, click **Details**. For example, you might receive the following types of explanations:

- **Internet Explorer 6 cannot be repaired due to the following errors: File** *file name* **is missing.**
- **Internet Explorer 6 cannot be repaired due to the following errors: Version 4.72.3110.0 of file** *file name* **exists but needs to be greater than 6.0.20x.xxxx.**

The version number listed for a file is the minimum version required by Internet Explorer 6. If no version number is associated with a file, the Repair tool verifies the existence of the file but not its version.

The Internet Explorer setup process fails

If the Internet Explorer setup process fails, you can troubleshoot setup errors by using the appropriate log files for your operating systems—Active Setup Log.txt, SetupAPI.log, IE Setup Log.txt, or RunOnceEx Log.txt.

Active Setup Log.txt

The file Active Setup Log.txt contains a log of the setup process from the moment IE6Setup.exe is executed until the last .cab file is downloaded. When IE6Setup.exe is executed, Active Setup Log.txt is created in the folder where Windows is installed (typically, C:\Windows or C:\Winnt). If a file Active Setup Log.txt from a previous Internet Explorer setup session exists, it is renamed to Active Setup Log.bak.

The file Active Setup Log.txt begins with the date and time Windows Update Setup for Internet Explorer 6 and Internet Tools is started and ends with the date and time it successfully downloads the last .cab file. As you go through the Setup Wizard, logging entries are continually written to this file. It is the most informative log file for determining the cause of a download failure and when the failure occurred. Most entries logged in this file are also written to the registry; this data is recorded to assist with safe recovery.

The following HResult error codes identify the download phases when errors occur. This information can help you determine what Setup was doing when it failed and also help you determine the cause of the failure.

HResult error code	Download phase
0	Initializing (making a Temp folder, checking disk space)
1	Dependency (checking for all dependencies)
2	Downloading (server to download folder)
3	Copying (download folder to the Temp installation folder)
4	Retrying (restarting download because of timeout or some other download error)
5	Checking trust
6	Extracting
7	Running (.inf or .exe)
8	Finished (installation complete)
9	Download finished (downloading complete)

The following table identifies other common error codes.

Error code	Description
80100003	During the installation, one or more files are missing from the download folder.
800b*xxx*	Any error starting with 800b indicates a trust failure.
800C*xxx*	Any error starting with 800C indicates a Urlmon failure (for example, 800C005—file or server not found, or 800C00B—connection timeout).
8004004	The user canceled setup.

SetupAPI.log and IE Setup Log.txt

After Active Setup is completed, Acme Setup starts for all installations except Windows XP and Windows 2000, which have .inf file-based installations. These operating systems use SetupAPI and log installation information in the file SetupAPI.log. On other Windows 32-bit platforms, Acme Setup unpacks the individual .cab files and copies the files to their appropriate locations. The file IE Setup Log.txt provides a log of the Acme Setup steps.

RunOnceEx Log.txt

In Windows 95, Windows 98, and Windows NT 4.0, the file RunOnceEx Log.txt records the files that Setup registers during the final restart of your computer. You can use the file RunOnceEx Log.txt to identify whether or not a file is successfully registered when your computer is restarted the first time during Internet Explorer 6 Setup. Setup can also use RunOnceEx Log.txt to register the files again without reinstalling Internet Explorer.

RunOnceEx Log.txt contains two sections. The first section contains a copy of the registry section that Setup is modifying with Internet Explorer 6 registration information. Specifically, it logs information about the settings of the current browser prior to the installation of Internet Explorer. The second section contains the file registration information that Setup will add when it processes the RunOnceEx section of the registry during the first restart of your computer.

The file RunOnceEx Log.txt uses the same HResult error codes as the file Active Setup Log.txt.

The download server connection times out

Setup can switch servers during an installation to maintain maximum throughput or recover from a download site that is not responding. Switching of servers occurs when Setup detects no throughput or the throughput of less than one byte in two minutes.

If a connection times out, Setup attempts to connect to the next download site in the list and continue the setup process at the beginning of the partially downloaded .cab file.

If a connection times out and Setup does not switch servers, Setup attempts to reconnect to the download site and continue the setup process where it left off. If Setup cannot establish a connection to the download site, it prompts you about whether you want to cancel the installation or try again.

You cannot install Microsoft Internet Explorer and Internet Tools after download

When you download Internet Explorer and Internet Tools, Setup determines the version of the operating system that is currently running on your computer and automatically downloads the appropriate files. Because these files are unique to the operating system, you typically cannot download the Internet Explorer installation files by using one operating system and then install Internet Explorer and Internet Tools on a different operating system.

If you try to install Internet Explorer and Internet Tools from files that were downloaded by using a different operating system than the one you are currently running, the following error message might appear:

The Internet Explorer files on your computer are not the correct files for your operating system. To continue, you must download the correct files from the Internet. Do you want to continue?

To quit Setup, click **No**. Or, to resolve this installation issue, you can do one of the following:

- To continue Setup and try to download the appropriate files from the Internet, click **Yes**. You must be connected to the Internet for the download to continue.

- To download the installation files for both operating systems in one session on Windows 95, Windows 98, and Windows NT 4.0, select **Install Minimal, or customize your browser**, click the **Advanced** button, and then select the appropriate operating systems in the **Download Options** dialog box.

- To download the installation files for both operating systems in one session on Windows 2000, you do not have the **Install Minimal, or customize your browser** option available during Setup. To access the **Download Options** dialog box in Windows XP and Windows 2000, use the following command line:

  Ie6setup.exe /c:"ie6wzd.exe /d /s:""""#e"""""

- To create an installation package that includes files for all versions of the Windows 32-bit platform, use the Internet Explorer Customization Wizard to create a custom browser package for your Internet Explorer installation.

The Internet Explorer uninstall process fails

When you uninstall Internet Explorer 6 on Windows 2000 or an earlier version of Windows, your computer is restored to the previous version of Internet Explorer that is named in the uninstall information. On Windows XP, you cannot restore a previous version of Internet Explorer because Internet Explorer 6 is the browser version installed with Windows XP.

If you are using an operating system other than Windows 2000, when the uninstall process fails, your most important troubleshooting tool is the uninstall log, IE6 Uninstall Log.txt, which is located in the Windows folder. This log covers the entire uninstall process, including every file addition or removal; every registry addition, change, or removal; and any dialog boxes shown to the user.

The log is divided into Passes, which denote the different phases of the uninstall process. Entries in the log also include an Object number that corresponds to the line entry in Setup.stf. Lines without an Object number result from custom actions specific to Internet Explorer 6 and are contained in the IE6.inf file or in an .inf file from an uninstall process for an external component.

Note   Setup does not create the file IE6 Uninstall Log.txt in Windows 2000.

Browser Features and Functions

This section describes some of the problems you might encounter when you use the features and functions of the browser. Troubleshooting topics include:

- Temporary Internet Files use more disk space than specified.

- The Media bar is unavailable on Internet Explorer 6 for Windows NT 4.0.

- The **Don't display online media content in the media bar** option does not take effect.

- You are unable to move Internet Explorer toolbars.
- You want to disable third-party browser features.
- You do not want to disconnect from the Internet when closing Internet programs.
- You are unable to remove a Microsoft® ActiveX® control.
- You cannot enable or disable style sheets in Internet Explorer.
- An ActiveX control does not run properly.
- You cannot connect to the Internet because the proxy server configuration is not working.

Temporary Internet Files use more disk space than specified

You might experience the following problems with the Temporary Internet Files folder:

- Your Temporary Internet Files folder might use more disk space than you specified in **Amount of disk space to use** (in the **Internet Options** dialog box, click the **General** tab, and then click **Settings**).
- After you click **Delete Files** on the **General** tab in the **Internet Options** dialog box and then select the **Delete all offline content** check box, files that are downloaded from Web sites might remain in your Temporary Internet Files folder.

These problems can occur when the content of a Web page is only partially downloaded (for example, if you click **Stop** while the browser is opening a page, or if you navigate to another page before the browser completely downloads a page).

To work around these problems, move your Temporary Internet Files folder to another location, delete the old folder, and then (if you want to) move your Temporary Internet Files folder back to the original location.

▶ **To relocate the Temporary Internet Files folder**

1. In either My Computer or Windows Explorer, create a new folder.
2. In Internet Explorer, on the **Tools** menu, click **Internet Options**.
3. On the **General** tab, under **Temporary Internet Files**, click **Settings**.
4. Click **Move Folder**.
5. Select the folder that you created in step 1, and then click **OK**.
6. If you are prompted to log off, click **Yes**, and then log on to Windows again. If you are not prompted to log off, click **OK** to close all of the dialog boxes.
7. In either My Computer or Windows Explorer, delete the old Temporary Internet Files folder, and then create a new folder in the same location with the same name.
8. Repeat steps 2 through 6, but in step 5, select the new folder that you created in step 7.

The Media bar is unavailable on Internet Explorer 6 for Windows NT 4.0

The Media bar depends on the Microsoft® Windows Media™ Player, which is not available for the Windows NT 4.0 operating system. Therefore, in Internet Explorer 6 for Windows NT 4.0, the Media bar is not available to users. Also, on the **Advanced** tab in the **Internet Options** dialog box, the **Don't display online media content in the media bar** check box in the **Multimedia** area does not work.

The "Don't display online media content in the media bar" option does not take effect

If you select or clear the **Don't display online media content in the media bar** check box, this option might not take effect. Also, the Help topic that is associated with the **Don't display online media content in the media bar** check box might be missing.

When you select the **Don't display online media content in the media bar** check box, you must restart your computer for this option to take effect.

You are unable to move Internet Explorer toolbars

You might be unable to rearrange or move the toolbars in Internet Explorer 6. This behavior occurs because the toolbars are locked by default.

To resolve this issue, unlock the toolbars.

▶ **To unlock the Internet Explorer toolbars**

1. In Internet Explorer 6, right-click any toolbar.
2. Clear the **Lock the Toolbars** check box.
3. Move the toolbars to the desired locations.

You want to disable third-party browser features

When you troubleshoot Internet Explorer problems, you might need to disable the third-party Tool Bands and Browser Helper Objects features that you installed for use with Internet Explorer.

Tool Bands support the Radio Toolbar in Internet Explorer. This feature can place a window on a band contained by the Rebar control that holds the toolbars in Internet Explorer. Browser Helper objects are Component Object Model (COM) components that Internet Explorer loads whenever it starts. These objects run in the same memory context as the browser, and they can perform any action on the available windows and modules.

▷ **To disable the Tool Bands and Browser Helper Objects features on Windows XP**

1. Close all instances of Internet Explorer.
2. Click **Start**, and then click **Control Panel**.
3. Click **Network and Internet Connections**.
4. Click **Internet Options**.
5. Click the **Advanced** tab.
6. Under **Browsing**, clear the **Enable third-party browser extensions (requires restart)** check box, and then click **OK**.
7. Restart Internet Explorer.

▷ **To disable the Tool Bands and Browser Helper Objects features on Windows 2000**

1. Close all instances of Internet Explorer.
2. Click **Start**, point to **Settings**, and then click **Control Panel**.
3. Double-click **Internet Options**.
4. Click the **Advanced** tab.
5. Under **Browsing**, clear the **Enable third-party browser extensions (requires restart)** check box, and then click **OK**.
6. Restart Internet Explorer.

You do not want to disconnect from the Internet when closing Internet programs

For dial-up connections, you might be prompted to disconnect from the Internet when you close all Internet programs, such as Microsoft® Outlook® Express and Internet Explorer. You can change this setting on a per-connection basis. For example, you can specify that a dial-up connection to your corporate network does not disconnect when an ISP connection prompts you to disconnect from the Internet.

▷ **To change whether you are prompted to disconnect from the Internet when closing Internet programs**

1. On the Internet Explorer **Tools** menu, click **Internet Options**, and then click the **Connections** tab.
2. Under **Dial-up and Virtual Private Network Settings**, select the connection that you want to change.
3. Click **Settings**, and then under **Dial-up Settings**, click **Advanced**.
4. Select or clear the Disconnect when connection may no longer be needed check box, as appropriate.

You are unable to remove an ActiveX control

Internet Explorer includes the Occache.dll file, which is used to enumerate, update, and safely uninstall ActiveX controls by using a shell folder. Internet Explorer supports multiple Occache folders. The list of Occache folders is located in the following registry key:

HKEY_LOCAL_MACHINE\SOFTWARE\Microsoft\Windows\ CurrentVersion\Internet Settings\ActiveX Cache

By default, Internet Explorer stores ActiveX controls in the Windows\Downloaded Program Files or Winnt\Downloaded Program Files folder. If you upgraded from Internet Explorer 3.*x*, both an Occache and Downloaded Program Files folder might exist. In this case, all new ActiveX controls are installed in the Downloaded Program Files folder. Previously installed ActiveX controls in the Occache folder appear in the Downloaded Program Files folder but still run from the Occache folder.

Restoring the ability to easily uninstall ActiveX controls

The Downloaded Program Files folder contains functionality that enables you to easily uninstall ActiveX controls. When this folder is deleted, a new Downloaded Program Files folder is created the next time Internet Explorer downloads new program files. However, the newly created folder does not contain the functionality to easily uninstall ActiveX controls. You can restore this ability to the Downloaded Program Files folder by using the Internet Explorer Repair tool. For more information about the Repair tool, see the topic "Problems occur because of out-of-date, deleted, or corrupted files" under "Installation and Uninstallation" earlier in this appendix.

You receive an error message when removing an ActiveX control

When you attempt to remove an ActiveX control by using **Add/Remove Programs** in Control Panel (in Windows 2000 and earlier versions of Windows), you might receive an error message because of share violations. In this case, the following message appears:

These program files are currently being used by one or more programs. Please close some programs, and try again. You may need to restart Windows.

This message occurs if the ActiveX control you are trying to remove is currently loaded in memory by Internet Explorer or an Internet Explorer desktop component.

▶ **To resolve this share violation**

1. Close all open Internet Explorer windows.
2. To disable the Internet Explorer desktop, right-click an empty area on the desktop, point to **Active Desktop**, and then click **Show Web Content** (Windows 2000) or **View as Web Page** (Windows 9.*x* and Windows NT 4.0) to clear the check mark.
3. Restart Windows.
4. To remove the ActiveX control, click the **Add/Remove Programs** icon in Control Panel.

You cannot enable or disable style sheets in Internet Explorer

When you use Internet Explorer, you might experience the following symptoms:

- You disabled the use of style sheets in Internet Explorer 3.*x*, but you cannot re-enable them in Internet Explorer 6.
- You cannot disable the use of style sheets in Internet Explorer 6.

These symptoms can occur when the ability to disable style sheets has been removed from Internet properties. You can resolve this problem by setting registry values to disable or re-enable the use of style sheets.

⚠️ **WARNING** This section contains information about editing the registry. Before you edit the registry, make sure that you understand how to restore it if a problem occurs. Before you edit the registry, always make a backup copy. If you are running Windows 2000 or Windows NT 4.0, also update your Emergency Repair Disk (ERD).

For more information about how to restore the registry, see the "Restoring the Registry" Help topic in the Registry Editor (Regedit.exe) or the "Restoring a Registry Key" Help topic in Regedt32.exe. For more information about how to edit the registry, see the "Change Keys and Values" Help topic in Regedit.exe or the "Add and Delete Information in the Registry" and the "Edit Registry Information" Help topics in Regedt32.exe.

▶ **To disable or re-enable the use of style sheets**

1. Open Windows Registry Editor and locate the following registry key:

   HKEY_CURRENT_USER\Software\Microsoft\Internet Explorer\Main

2. To disable the use of style sheets, set the string value of **Use StyleSheets** to **no**.

   To enable the use of style sheets, set the string value of **Use StyleSheets** to **yes**.

📝 **Note** When you disable the use of style sheets, it can affect the appearance of Web sites or the Internet Explorer desktop.

An ActiveX control doesn't run properly

If a Web page is not displayed properly, an ActiveX control might not have loaded or might be out-of-date. The following procedure helps you determine whether an ActiveX control is the cause of the problem.

▷ **To determine whether an ActiveX control may not have loaded or may be out-of-date**

1. On the Internet Explorer **View** menu, click **Source**.

2. Look for source code similar to the following code:

```
<OBJECT ID=NewsBrowser WIDTH=92 HEIGHT=244 BORDER=0
STANDBY="Click here for help installing MSNBC News Menu"
CLASSID=CLSID:2FF18E10-DE11-11d1-8161-00A0C90DD90C
CODEBASE=/download/nm0713.cab#Version=3,0,0713,0>
```

This source code indicates that the MSNBC NewsBrowser is an ActiveX control by listing the CLASSID (CLSID) where it is stored in the registry under HKCR\CLSID. It also lists the CODEBASE, which indicates where to retrieve the .cab file for installing the control and the version that it currently needs.

The control is loaded from the Downloaded Program Items folder. This process is not visible to the user. If the control cannot be loaded from this folder, Internet Explorer tries to download the control from the CODEBASE. If the control is corrupted, it might not load and will not display the proper control needed to view the Web page properly.

After you check the source code to determine whether an ActiveX control might not have loaded or might be out-of-date, update the control, if necessary.

▷ **To update the ActiveX control**

1. On the **Tools** menu, click **Internet Options**.

2. In the **Temporary Internet Files** area, click Settings.

3. To view the ActiveX control installed on the computer, click **View Objects**.

4. Right-click the ActiveX control, and then click **Update**.

   If you are not sure which control in the Downloaded Program Files folder is associated with the control identified in the source code, you can check the registry under HKCR\CLSID\<*clsid number that is listed in the source*>. Click the number, and it will list the name of the control at that registry key.

5. Try to view the Web page.

6. If the Web page is still not being displayed correctly, repeat steps 1 through 3, right-click the ActiveX control, and then click **Remove**.

7. Try to view the Web page again. Internet Explorer should automatically reinstall the control based on the CODEBASE information.

You cannot connect to the Internet because the proxy server configuration is not working

Your organization might use a proxy server on a local area network (LAN) to connect to the Internet. A proxy server acts as a gateway for the computers on the network to access the Internet. A proxy server does not prevent other people on the Internet from accessing your network—a firewall can serve this purpose.

To successfully connect to the Internet, you must correctly configure Internet Explorer to use your proxy server. If Internet Explorer is configured for your proxy server but you cannot connect to the Internet, complete the troubleshooting steps described in the following sections.

Step 1: Verify the proxy server address.

If you configured the settings for the proxy server manually within the browser, verify the proxy server address.

▶ To verify your proxy server address

1. On the **Tools** menu, click **Internet Options**, and then click the **Connections** tab.
2. Click **Settings** or **LAN Settings**.
3. In the **Proxy server** area, verify the address.

Step 2: Verify that automatic detection and automatic configuration are enabled within the browser.

If you are using automatic detection and automatic configuration, the Dynamic Host Configuration Protocol (DHCP) and Domain Name System (DNS) servers should automatically detect and configure the browser's proxy settings on a per-connection basis. Verify that automatic detection and automatic configuration are enabled within the browser. Your DHCP server must support the DHCPINFORM message; otherwise, use DNS.

▶ To verify that automatic detection and automatic configuration are enabled

1. On the **Tools** menu, click **Internet Options**, and then click the **Connections** tab.
2. Click **Settings** or **LAN Settings**.
3. In the **Automatic configuration** area, verify that the **Automatically detect settings** check box is selected.

   Note that automatic detection is enabled by default for LAN connections and disabled by default for RAS connections. For more information about automatic detection and automatic configuration, see "Using Automatic Configuration, Automatic Proxy, and Automatic Detection" in this Resource Kit. For more information about setting up DHCP and DNS servers for automatic detection and automatic configuration, see "Setting Up Servers" in this Resource Kit.

If you determine that automatic detection and automatic configuration are configured correctly and the proxy server detection still fails, click **Detect my network settings** on the error dialog box to attempt the proxy server detection again.

Step 3: Verify that the browser is configured with the correct URL address.

If you are using an auto-proxy URL, verify that the browser is configured with the correct URL address.

▶ **To verify that the browser is configured with the correct auto-proxy URL address**

1. On the **Tools** menu, click **Internet Options**, and then click the **Connections** tab.
2. Click **Settings** or **LAN Settings**.
3. In the **Automatic Configuration** area, verify that the **Use automatic configuration script** check box is selected and that the address is correct for your auto-proxy URL.

Privacy and Security

This section describes some of the problems you might encounter when you use privacy and security settings in Internet Explorer 6. Troubleshooting topics include:

- Cookie settings are not retained after upgrading to Internet Explorer 6.
- A Web site reports that you must enable cookies.
- Privacy tab settings affect only the Internet zone.
- Cookie Pal from Kookaburra Software requires advanced privacy settings.
- Existing cookies can still be read by Web sites after you select the **Block** option.
- The Privacy icon displays in the status bar even though privacy settings allow cookies.
- Per-site privacy actions do not work as expected.
- You are unable to remove per-site privacy actions for Web sites in the Local intranet zone.
- Cookies are unexpectedly blocked or saved on the computer.
- The Privacy report changes after you cancel a file download.
- You cannot export custom privacy settings.
- You want to restore default settings after importing custom privacy settings.
- All security zones are set to Custom after upgrading to Internet Explorer 6.
- You cannot negotiate Kerberos authentication after upgrading to Internet Explorer 6.

Cookie settings are not retained after upgrading to Internet Explorer 6

After you upgrade from an earlier version of Microsoft Internet Explorer to Microsoft Internet Explorer 6, your cookies settings are not retained as expected. This behavior occurs because cookie settings are configured differently in Internet Explorer 6. In Internet Explorer 4 and Internet Explorer 5.*x*, security levels for cookie settings are configured on a per-zone basis on the **Security** tab in the **Internet Options** dialog box. These settings are removed when you upgrade to Internet Explorer 6.

In Internet Explorer 6, a new **Privacy** tab in the **Internet Options** dialog box enables you to configure the cookie settings for the Internet zone. For more information about using the new Privacy tab, see "Users' Privacy" in this Resource Kit.

A Web site reports that you must enable cookies

When you attempt to use services on a secondary Web site that you access through a frameset (or portal) on a primary Web site, Internet Explorer might block cookies that the secondary Web site attempts to set depending on the privacy settings.

Internet Explorer determines that the secondary Web site is in the third-party context. The Medium privacy level blocks third-party cookies that do not have a compact policy or third-party cookies that have a compact policy specifying that personally identifiable information is used without your implicit consent.

This behavior is by design. To work around it, connect to the secondary Web site directly, add the site on the **Per-Site Privacy Actions** dialog box with a setting of **Always Allow**, or set your privacy level to Low or to accept all cookies.

▶ **To add the site on the Per-Site Privacy Actions dialog box**

1. On the **Tools** menu, click **Internet Options**, and then click the **Privacy** tab.
2. Click **Edit**.
3. In the **Address of Web site** box, type the URL for the Web site, and then click **Allow**.

   Internet Explorer adds the site to the **Managed Web sites** list with a setting of **Always Allow**.

▶ **To set your privacy level to low or to accept all cookies**

1. In Internet Explorer, on the **Tools** menu, click **Internet Options**.
2. Click the **Privacy** tab, and then move the slider to **Low** or to **Accept All Cookies**.

Privacy tab settings affect only the Internet zone

Privacy preferences that you specify on the **Privacy** tab in the Internet Options dialog box, including the privacy level, settings in the **Advanced Privacy Settings** dialog box, and settings in the **Per Site Privacy Actions** dialog box affect only the Internet zone.

This behavior is by design. Privacy settings are designed to work only in the Internet zone. Internet Explorer automatically accepts all cookies from Web sites in both the Local intranet and the Trusted sites zones, and blocks all cookies from Web sites in the Restricted sites zone.

If you browse to a Web site in the Local intranet, Trusted sites, or Restricted sites zone using the IP address of the Web site or the Fully Qualified Domain Name (FQDN) rather than the NetBIOS name, Internet Explorer treats the Web site as if it were located in your Internet zone.

Cookie Pal from Kookaburra Software requires advanced privacy settings

When you install Cookie Pal version 1.6c from Kookaburra Software, you might experience either of the following symptoms:

- The Setup program for Cookie Pal states that it has enabled cookie warnings (or prompts) for Internet Explorer, but Internet Explorer might not be configured to prompt for cookies after you install Cookie Pal.
- After you install Internet Explorer 6, Cookie Pal might not prompt you when an unknown Web site attempts to create a cookie on your computer.

This problem can occur because cookie settings, which are configured on the **Security** tab in the **Internet Options** dialog box in Internet Explorer 4.*x* and 5.*x* (or on the **Advanced** tab in Internet Explorer 3.*x*), are removed when you upgrade to Internet Explorer 6. In Internet Explorer 6, a new **Privacy** tab on the **Internet Options** dialog box enables you to configure cookie settings for the Internet zone.

To resolve this problem, configure Internet Explorer to prompt for cookies.

▶ **To configure Internet Explorer to prompt for cookies**

1. In Internet Explorer, on the **Tools** menu, click **Internet Options**.
2. Click the **Privacy** tab, and then click **Advanced**.
3. Select the **Override automatic cookie handling** check box.
4. Click **Prompt** for both **First-party Cookies** and **Third-Party Cookies**.

Existing cookies can still be read by Web sites after you select the Block option

Any cookies that are currently stored on your computer can still be read by the Web site that created them (without a prompt). This behavior occurs even if you have selected to block or prompt for cookies by using either the **Block** or **Prompt** options for either first-party or third-party cookies on the **Advanced Privacy Settings** dialog box.

This occurs by design. In Internet Explorer 6, the **Block** and **Prompt** options on the **Advanced Privacy Settings** dialog box apply only to new cookies that Web sites attempt to create on your computer. Web sites that created existing cookies on your computer can still read them.

To work around this behavior, use one of the following methods:

- Delete any existing cookies that are stored on your computer for the Web site.
- Add the Web site to the **Per Site Privacy Actions** dialog box with a setting of **Block**. This method deletes any existing cookies that are stored on your computer for that Web site.
- On the **Privacy** tab in the **Internet Options** dialog box, move the slider to select **Block All Cookies**. This setting prevents all Web sites from saving or reading any of its cookies on your computer. The **Edit** button on the **Privacy** tab becomes unavailable, because Internet Explorer ignores per-site privacy actions if you block all cookies.

▷ **To delete any existing cookies that are stored on your computer**

1. In Internet Explorer, on the **Tools** menu, click **Internet Options**.
2. On the **General** tab, under **Temporary Internet files**, click **Delete Cookies**.

▷ **To add the Web site to the Per Site Privacy Actions dialog box with a setting of Block**

1. In Internet Explorer, on the **Tools** menu, click **Internet Options**.
2. Click the **Privacy** tab, and then click **Edit**.
3. In the **Address of Web site** box, type the address of the Web site, and then click **Block**.

The Privacy icon displays in the status bar even though privacy settings allow cookies

When you visit a Web site, the Privacy icon might display in the Microsoft Internet Explorer status bar even though your privacy settings allow cookies from this Web site and all cookies are already set or read.

By design, the Privacy icon appears in the status bar each time Internet Explorer restricts a cookie based on your privacy settings or when Internet Explorer retrieves a cached file that has a history of privacy violations from the Temporary Internet Files folder. The Privacy icon might still appear if you change your privacy settings during the current browser session so that the cookie is no longer restricted.

To work around this behavior, press F5 to refresh the Web page, or delete the contents of your Temporary Internet Files folder.

▶ **To delete the contents of your Temporary Internet Files folder**

1. In Internet Explorer, on the **Tools** menu, click **Internet Options**.
2. On the **General** tab, under **Temporary Internet Files**, click **Delete Files**, and then click **OK**.
3. To close the **Internet Options** dialog box, click **OK**.
4. Click the **Refresh** button on the browser toolbar to ensure that you are viewing the latest version of the Web page.

Per-site privacy actions do not work as expected

When you override cookie handling for an individual Web site and then visit that site on the Web, one of the following behaviors can occur:

*   The privacy icon might not be displayed on the status bar, and cookies might be saved to your computer, even though you configured Internet Explorer to block the Web site from saving cookies on your computer.
*   Cookies might not be saved to your computer, even though you configured Internet Explorer to allow the Web site to save cookies on your computer.

This problem can occur when you incorrectly type the Uniform Resource Locator (URL)—or Web address—of the site in the **Address of Web site** box on the **Per Site Privacy Actions** dialog box. When you override cookie handling for individual Web sites, Internet Explorer does not warn you if you add an incorrect or invalid URL to the Managed Web sites list, provided that it contains at least one period (.). For example, if you type **1.2** or **www.microsoft.comm** in the **Address of Web site** box, and then click either **Block** or **Allow**, Internet Explorer adds the invalid address to the Managed Web sites list.

To resolve this issue, remove the invalid address from the list, and then add the correct address for the Web site that you want to manage. You must type the exact address of the Web site (for example, type **www.microsoft.com**).

▶ **To remove the invalid address from the list, and then add the correct address for the Web site that you want to manage**

1. In Internet Explorer, on the **Tools** menu, click **Internet Options**.
2. Click the **Privacy** tab, and then click **Edit**.
3. In the **Managed Web sites** list, click the incorrect address, click **Remove**, and then click **OK**.
4. In the **Address of Web site** box, type the correct Web address, and then if you do not want to allow the Web site to save cookies on your computer, click **Block**. Or, if you want to allow the Web site to save cookies on your computer, click **Allow**.

You are unable to remove per-site privacy actions for Web sites in the Local intranet zone

After you import a custom privacy settings file that specifies an action of "Prompt for cookies in the Local intranet zone," you might experience the following symptoms:

- Internet Explorer might automatically accept or reject cookies from a local intranet Web site without a prompt, but the local intranet Web site might not appear in the **Per Site Privacy Actions** dialog box.
- Re-importing the custom privacy settings file that specifies an action of "Prompt for cookies in the Local intranet zone" might not cause Internet Explorer to prompt you for cookies from a local intranet Web site.

This problem can occur after you select the **Apply my decision to all cookies from this Web site** check box when you were previously prompted for cookies from the local intranet site.

> **WARNING** This section contains information about editing the registry. Before you edit the registry, make sure that you understand how to restore it if a problem occurs. Before you edit the registry, always make a backup copy. If you are running Windows 2000 or Windows NT 4.0, also update your Emergency Repair Disk (ERD).
>
> For more information about how to restore the registry, see the "Restoring the Registry" Help topic in the Registry Editor (Regedit.exe) or the "Restoring a Registry Key" Help topic in Regedt32.exe. For more information about how to edit the registry, see the "Changing Keys and Values" Help topic in Regedit.exe or the "Add and Delete Information in the Registry" and the "Edit Registry Data" Help topics in Regedt32.exe.

To work around this problem, use one of the following methods:

- **Method 1.** Import a custom privacy settings file that specifies the **flushSiteList** element (<flushSiteList/>).

  When Internet Explorer imports the customized privacy settings, this element deletes all per-site privacy actions.

- **Method 2.** Delete the registry key for the local intranet site at the following location:

  HKEY_CURRENT_USER\Software\Microsoft\Windows\ CurrentVersion\Internet Settings\P3P\History

Cookies are unexpectedly blocked or saved on the computer

On Windows 98, Windows 98 Second Edition, and Microsoft® Windows® Millennium Edition, when you visit a Web site, cookies might be unexpectedly blocked or saved on your computer, and your privacy settings might be set at a level other than one you specified. This behavior can occur if the privacy settings are configured by another user on your computer and all users of your computer use the same privacy and desktop settings.

To work around this behavior, enable all users of your computer to customize their privacy settings, and then configure the cookie settings to the desired security level for each user after they log on to Windows.

▶ **To enable all users to customize their privacy settings**

1. Click **Start**, point to **Settings**, and then click **Control Panel**.
2. Double-click **Passwords**.
3. In the **Passwords Properties** dialog box, click the **User Profiles** tab.
4. Click **Users can customize their preferences and desktop settings. Windows switches to your personal settings when you log on.**
5. Under **User profile settings**, select the check boxes that correspond to the settings you want Windows to save in the user profiles, and then click **OK**.

▶ **To reconfigure the privacy settings for each user**

1. Log on to Windows separately for each user.
2. In Internet Explorer, on the **Tools** menu, click **Internet Options**.
3. Click the **Privacy** tab, and then configure each user's cookie settings.

The Privacy report changes after you cancel a file download

After you cancel a file download request, the privacy report for a Web site might change. To work around this problem, press F5 to update the Web site, and then view the privacy report again.

▶ **To view a privacy report for a Web site**

- In Internet Explorer, on the **View** menu, click **Privacy Report**.

You cannot export custom privacy settings

On the **Privacy** tab in the **Internet Options** dialog box, you can use the available option to import custom privacy settings from a file, but you cannot export these settings to a file.

This behavior is by design. In Internet Explorer 6, no option is available to export custom privacy settings.

You want to restore default settings after importing custom privacy settings

You can import custom privacy settings in Internet Explorer by clicking **Import** on the **Privacy** tab in the **Internet Options** dialog box and then opening a custom privacy settings (.xml) file. After you import custom privacy settings, at some point, you might want to remove these settings and restore the default privacy settings for the Internet, Local intranet, or Trusted sites zones.

⚠ **WARNING** This section contains information about editing the registry. Before you edit the registry, make sure that you understand how to restore it if a problem occurs. Before you edit the registry, always make a backup copy. If you are running Windows 2000 or Windows NT 4.0, also update your Emergency Repair Disk (ERD).

For more information about how to restore the registry, see the "Restoring the Registry" Help topic in the Registry Editor (Regedit.exe) or the "Restoring a Registry Key" Help topic in Regedt32.exe. For more information about how to edit the registry, see the "Change Keys and Values" Help topic in Regedit.exe or the "Add and Delete Information in the Registry" and the "Edit Registry Information" Help topics in Regedt32.exe.

▶ **To remove imported custom privacy settings and restore the default privacy settings**

1. In Internet Explorer, on the **Tools** menu, click **Internet Options**.
2. Click the **Privacy** tab.
3. Click **Default** (if available), and then click **Edit**.

   The Default button will not be available if the imported custom privacy settings file does not contain a **p3pCookiePolicy** element that specifies zone="internet" or contains only an **alwaysReplayLegacy** element and your privacy level was set to Medium (the default privacy level) prior to importing the file.
4. In the **Per Site Privacy Actions** dialog box, under **Managed Web sites**, click each Web site for which you imported per-site privacy actions, and then click **Remove**.

   This step might be necessary if per-site privacy actions were imported by using the **MSIESiteRules** element.
5. Click **OK** twice, and then run Regedit.exe.
6. Delete any keys for Local intranet sites that exist in the following registry key:

   HKEY_CURRENT_USER\Software\Microsoft\Windows\ CurrentVersion\Internet Settings\P3P\History

   This step is necessary if the imported custom privacy settings file specifies an action of **Prompt** for Local intranet sites, and you changed this setting to **Accept** or **Reject** by using the prompt for cookies on specific Web sites.

7. If the following DWORD value exists in the registry, delete it:

    **HKEY_CURRENT_USER\Software\Microsoft\Windows\
    CurrentVersion\Internet Settings\LeashLegacyCookies**

    The LeashLegacyCookies DWORD value will exist only if the imported custom privacy settings file contains the **alwaysReplayLegacy** element. This setting allows all existing cookies (cookies that existed when Internet Explorer 6 was installed) to be sent in the Internet zone. If this element is not specified, legacy cookies are sent only in the first-party context for the Internet zone.

8. If the privacy GUIDs for the Local intranet and Trusted sites zones exist under the following registry key, delete them:

    **HKEY_CURRENT_USER\Software\Microsoft\Windows\
    CurrentVersion\Internet Settings\Zones**

    The Local intranet zone key is named 1, and the Trusted sites zone key is named 2. For first-party cookie settings, the GUID is a binary value that is named {AEBA21FA-782A-4A90-978D-B72164C80120}. For third-party cookie settings, the GUID is a binary value that is named {A8A88C49-5EB2-4990-A1A2-0876022C854F}.

    For the Local intranet (1) and Trusted sites (2) zones, no GUIDs exist for cookie settings by default, so they will exist only if you imported a custom privacy settings file with a **p3pCookiePolicy** element that specified zone="intranet" or zone="trustedSites." Internet Explorer does not allow you to customize settings for the Restricted sites (4) zone by using an imported custom privacy settings file. Also, custom settings for the Internet (3) zone are removed, except for the LeashLegacyCookies DWORD value (Step 7).

The previous procedure does not restore cookies that are deleted or per-site privacy actions that are removed when you import a custom privacy settings file that contains **flushCookies** or **flushSiteList** elements. The **flushCookies** element deletes all cookies when you import custom privacy settings. The **flushSiteList** element deletes all per-site privacy actions when you import custom privacy settings.

All security zones are set to Custom after upgrading to Internet Explorer 6

After you upgrade to Internet Explorer 6, all security zones are set to **Custom** on the **Security** tab in the **Internet Options** dialog box. As a result, the slider that you use to change your security settings might be missing.

This behavior can occur because the default security settings have changed in Internet Explorer 6. All security zones are set to **Custom** to indicate that your existing security settings do not match the new default security settings for Internet Explorer 6.

To work around this behavior, reset your security settings for each zone.

▶ **To reset your security settings for each zone**

1. In Internet Explorer, on the **Tools** menu, click **Internet Options**.
2. Click the **Security** tab.
3. Select each zone, and then click **Default Level**.
4. If necessary, reconfigure any custom settings that you defined for a security zone.

You cannot negotiate Kerberos authentication after upgrading to Internet Explorer 6

After you upgrade to Internet Explorer 6, the browser might not be able to negotiate Kerberos authentication with a server that supports Kerberos (for example, Microsoft Internet Information Services version 5.0).

This problem can occur because Internet Explorer 6 for Windows 2000 does not respond to a negotiate challenge and defaults to NTLM, or Windows NT Challenge/Response, authentication by default.

To resolve this problem, enable Internet Explorer 6 to respond to a negotiate challenge and to perform Kerberos authentication.

▶ **To enable Internet Explorer 6 to respond to a negotiate challenge and perform Kerberos authentication**

1. In Internet Explorer, on the **Tools** menu, click **Internet Options**.
2. Click the **Advanced** tab.
3. In the **Security** area, select the **Enable Integrated Windows Authentication (requires restart)** check box, and then click **OK**.
4. Restart Internet Explorer.

Microsoft Outlook Express

This section describes some of the problems you might encounter when you use Microsoft Outlook Express. Troubleshooting topics include:

*   You cannot import an address book in Outlook Express.
*   The preview pane does not display news messages.
*   You receive the following error message:

    The command failed to execute.

*   Windows Address Book files are changed.

You cannot import an address book in Outlook Express

When you attempt to import an address book in Outlook Express, the address book might not be imported, so that you do not see an error message. This problem occurs when the Wabmig.exe file is missing or damaged.

If the Wabmig.exe file is damaged, rename the file, and then reinstall Outlook Express.

▷ **To rename the Wabmig.exe file on Windows XP**

1. On the **Start** menu, point to **Search**, and then click **All Files and Folders**.
2. In the **All or part of the file name** box, type Wabmig.exe, and then click Search.
3. Right-click the file, and then click **Rename**.
4. Rename the file to **Wabmig.xxx**.
5. Reinstall Outlook Express.

▷ **To rename the Wabmig.exe file on other versions of Windows**

1. On the **Start** menu, point to **Find**, and then click **Files or Folders**.
2. In the **Named** box, type **Wabmig.exe**, and then click **Find Now**.
3. Right-click the file, and then click **Rename**.
4. Rename the file to **Wabmig.xxx**.
5. Reinstall Outlook Express.

The preview pane does not display news messages

While you are reading news messages in Outlook Express, you might receive the following message in the preview pane:

Press <Space> to display the selected message. You can also choose to automatically show messages in the preview pane from the Options command.

To redisplay the message, press the SPACEBAR. If you double-click the news message to open it, you might receive the following error message:

There was an error opening the message.

This problem occurs when there is not enough free space on your hard disk to open the news message. To resolve this problem, increase the amount of free space on your hard disk by using one or more of the following methods, and then attempt to open the news message again:

- Remove any unnecessary files from the hard disk.
- Empty the Recycle Bin.
- Delete unnecessary files from the Internet Explorer 6 Setup folder. Deleting this entire folder is not recommended. Although it does not affect the performance of Internet Explorer, you will not be able to reinstall or uninstall Internet Explorer and Internet Tools from the hard disk. In this case, you must download another copy from the Microsoft Windows Technologies Internet Explorer Web site at http://www.microsoft.com/windows/ie/.

⚠ **WARNING** The Setup folder contains important backup files that are necessary for reinstalling and uninstalling Internet Explorer and Internet Tools. The following files are critical: IE6bak.dat, IE6bak.ini, and, if Windows Desktop Update is installed, Integrated Browser.dat and Integrated Browser.ini. It is recommended that you not delete these files. If you need to free up more disk space, it is recommended that you delete other files in the folder.

You receive the following error message:
The command failed to execute

When you attempt to save a mail attachment to your hard disk in Outlook Express, you might receive the following error message:

The command failed to execute.

This problem occurs when there is not enough free disk space on your hard disk to save the ttachment. To resolve this problem, increase the amount of free space on your hard disk by using one or more of the following methods, and then attempt to save the attachment again:

- Remove any unnecessary files from the hard disk.
- Empty the Recycle Bin.
- Delete unnecessary files from the Internet Explorer 6 Setup folder. Deleting this entire folder is not recommended. Although it does not affect the performance of Internet Explorer, you will not be able to reinstall or uninstall Internet Explorer and Internet Tools from the hard disk. In this case, you must download another copy from the Microsoft Windows Technologies Internet Explorer Web site at http://www.microsoft.com/windows/ie/.

 WARNING The Setup folder contains important backup files that are necessary for reinstalling and uninstalling Internet Explorer and Internet Tools. The following files are critical: IE6bak.dat, IE6bak.ini, and, if Windows Desktop Update is installed, Integrated Browser.dat and Integrated Browser.ini. It is recommended that you not delete these files. If you need to free up more disk space, it is recommended that you delete other files in the folder.

Windows Address Book files are changed

When you install the Windows Address Book, files used by earlier versions are backed up and removed, and new versions of the files are installed. Note that Windows Address Book files are shared with other applications in addition to Outlook Express.

The following table identifies the files, previously located in the Windows\System or Winnt\System32 folder, and their new directory locations.

File name	New location
Wab32.dll	Program Files\Common Files\System
Wabfind.dll	Program Files\Outlook Express
Wabimp.dll	Program Files\Outlook Express

The following table identifies the files, previously in the Windows folder, and their new directory locations.

File name	New location
Wab.exe	Program Files\Outlook Express
Wabmig.exe	Program Files\Outlook Express

HTML Authoring

This section describes some of the problems related to Hypertext Markup Language (HTML) authoring in Microsoft Internet Explorer. Troubleshooting topics include:

- Text does not wrap in text boxes.
- Background images are not displayed.
- Internet Explorer is not automatically redirected.
- Frames are not displayed in Web pages.
- Permission is denied when scripting across frames.

Text does not wrap in text boxes

When you type text in a text box created by using the <TEXTAREA> tag on an HTML page, the text might not wrap correctly. In this case, the text continues to flow to the right side of the text box without breaking or wrapping. This problem occurs because the HTML page does not contain the parameters that activate text wrapping in a text box.

To wrap text in a text box, use one of the following methods:

- Use the WRAP attribute of the <TEXTAREA> tag with either the Physical or Virtual value to enable word wrapping.

  For example, you might type the following <TEXTAREA> tag:

  ```
  <TEXTAREA NAME="Name" ROW99S=6 COL99S=40>
  </TEXTAREA>
  ```

- Insert WRAP=Physical as part of the <TEXTAREA> tag.

  For example, you might type the following <TEXTAREA> tag:

  ```
  <TEXTAREA NAME="Name" ROW99S=6 COL99S=40 WRAP=Physical>
  </TEXTAREA>
  ```

Note When you are typing in the text box, press ENTER to manually insert line breaks, which force the text to wrap.

Background images are not displayed

Pages created by using the Data Form Wizard in Microsoft® Visual InterDev® might not display background images in Internet Explorer. This problem occurs because cascading style sheet (CSS) tags take precedence over HTML tags. Pages created by using the Data Form Wizard reference a CSS. The CSS has a tag for the background image of Transparent, which overrides any value in the body tag of the Active Server Page (.asp) file. The following procedure describes how to display the background images.

▶ **To display background images**

- In the BODY property of the CSS, delete the **background: transparent** line.

Internet Explorer is not automatically redirected

When you load a Web page that contains the <meta http-equiv="refresh"...> HTML tag, the browser might not automatically be redirected to another Web page. This problem might occur for one of the following reasons:

- On the **Security** tab in the **Internet Options** dialog box, you have turned off the new **Allow META REFRESH** option for the security zone that includes the Web page. By default, this option is turned off only in the Restricted sites zone.

- The author of the page did not place the <meta http-equiv="refresh"...> tag in the <HEAD> section of the HTML source code.

- The syntax of the <meta http-equiv="refresh"...> HTML tag is incorrect.

To resolve this problem, update the Web page by using the appropriate method:

- If the <META> tag is not located in the <HEAD> section, modify the HTML source code to place the <META> tag in the <HEAD> section of the Web page. This change might require that you add the <HEAD> and </HEAD> tags to the Web page.

- If the syntax of the <META> tag is incorrect, Modify the HTML source code to correct the syntax of the <META> tag. For example, a <META> tag might include the following code:

```
<meta http-equiv="refresh" content="n;url=http://www.domain.com/
pagename.htm">
```

The n is the number of seconds the browser program pauses before loading the new Web page.

Frames are not displayed in Web pages

When you are using Internet Explorer to view a Web page, a blank page might appear instead of a defined set of frames. If you right-click an empty area of the Web page and then click **View Source**, the following message might appear:

This document might not display properly because there is a <FRAMESET> within the <BODY> of the document.

This behavior is by design and occurs when the Web author puts the <FRAMESET> tag after the <BODY> tag in the main (or "framing") HTML document. All <FRAMESET> tags and underlying instructions should precede any <BODY> tags. The following procedure describes how to display the frames on the blank Web page.

▶ **To display frames on the blank Web page**

1. Remove the <BODY> tag.
2. Remove any additional HTML code between the <HEAD> of the document and the <FRAMESET>.

The framing HTML document defines the frame regions that appear in the browser and the documents or objects that initially appear in the frames.

Permission is denied when scripting across frames

If your script code tries to access a script or an object in a different frame, you might see the following script error message:

Permission denied: 'Parent.RemoteFrame.RemoteObject'

Internet Explorer implements cross-frame security. A script or an object in one frame is not allowed to access scripts or objects in another frame when the documents referenced by the frames' SRC attribute specify Web servers in different second-level domains. This corresponds to the *domain-name.xxx* portion of the full server-name syntax *server.domain-name.xxx*.

The Internet Explorer Dynamic HTML object model allows a certain subset of safe actions to be scripted. For example, the window.location property of a remote server's frame can be set to allow navigation, but it cannot be scripted to prevent one frame from accessing the contents of another frame. For example, it is valid for a document retrieved from http://test.microsoft.com to manipulate another document retrieved from http://test.microsoft.com. It is not valid for a document retrieved from http://server1.*domain-name*.org to manipulate a document retrieved from http://server2 or http://server3.microsoft.com.

The intention of cross-frame security is to prevent the author of a Web page from accessing or misusing the trusted objects authored by the author of another Web page. Only pages hosted in the same domain can be trusted to safely script the contents of a particular page. Cross-frame security should also prevent unwanted communication between documents on opposite sides of a corporate firewall. For more information, visit the MSDN Web site at http://msdn.microsoft.com/.

In order for two documents hosted on the same second-level domain to interact, both documents must set the document.domain property to their shared second-level domain. For example, one document on http://example.microsoft.com could script and access another document on http://test.microsoft.com if both documents used the following line of script code:

```
<SCRIPT LANGUAGE="VBScript">
document.domain = "microsoft.com"
</SCRIPT>
```

In the following FRAMESET example, script in the "Server1Frame" frame is not permitted to access script or objects in the "Server2Frame" frame, and vice versa:

```
<FRAMESET COLS="50%, *" FRAMEBORDER=1>
<FRAME SRC="http://server1/server1.html" ID="Server1Frame">
<FRAME SRC="http://server2/server2.html" ID="Server2Frame">
</FRAMESET>
```

In the following sample script code, server1.html causes the "Permission Denied" error assuming that **RemoteTextBox** is an object created on the server2.html document:

```
<!-- From server1.html -->
<SCRIPT LANGUAGE="VBScript">
Sub CommandButtonLocal_Click()
Parent.Server2Frame.RemoteTextBox.Text = "Changed Text"
'Server2Frame has SRC on different server'
end sub
</SCRIPT>
```

Additional Resources

These resources contain additional information and tools related to this chapter.

Related Information Outside the Resource Kit

- The Microsoft Knowledge Base, which is part of the Microsoft Product Support Services Web site at http://support.microsoft.com/directory/.
- Internet Explorer Help.

Batch-Mode File Syntax and Command-Line Switches

This appendix describes how you use batch files and command-line switches to customize Microsoft® Windows® Update Setup, as well as command-line parameters for starting Microsoft® Internet Explorer 6.

In This Appendix

Related Information in the Resource Kit

- For more information about using batch files and command-line switches to customize the setup program, see "Time-saving Strategies That Address Diverse User Needs."

Using Internet Explorer Batch-Mode Setup

In addition to using the Internet Explorer Customization Wizard to control the functionality and user experience during Windows Update Setup for Internet Explorer 6 and Internet Tools, you can further control the setup process by using a batch file. For example, you can create a batch file that specifies a silent, hands-free installation of Internet Explorer 6 and Internet Tools, determines all of the users' setup choices, and does not show any error messages to users. You can use a batch file when you install only Internet Explorer and Internet Tools or when you install the browser with other applications.

You can also use a combination of a batch file and command-line switches. In most cases, the batch file gives you more control over the installation of individual components and involves fewer steps. The command-line switches are provided for backward compatibility and to support custom solutions. For more information about command-line switches, see "Using Command-Line Switches" later in this chapter.

Using a Batch File to Modify the Setup Program

To create a batch file, use a text editor such as Microsoft® Notepad, and name the file IEBatch.txt. Then use one of the following methods to modify the setup program by using your IEBatch.txt file:

- **Include the batch file with the setup program.** You can use the batch file with or without creating a custom browser package. If you distribute Internet Explorer over the Internet or an intranet, copy the batch file to the site where users will download Internet Explorer. If you distribute Internet Explorer on other media, such as a compact disc, copy the batch file to the same folder as the file IE6Setup.exe on the disc.

- **Include the batch file as part of your custom browser package.** Place the batch file in the \Iebin\<*Language*>\Optional folder. <*Language*> represents the language of the version you create. For example, English-language versions are created in the En folder.

Batch-File Syntax

The following table identifies the sections and entries for the IEBatch.txt file.

Batch file entry	Description
[Options]	
SaveUninstallInfo=[0,1]	Determines whether the setup program will store uninstall information for Internet Explorer and Internet Tools on users' computers.
	0 The setup program will not store uninstall information. If you use this entry, users will not be able to uninstall Internet Explorer and Internet Tools from Windows Control Panel.
	1 (default) The setup program will store uninstall information.

Batch file entry	Description
[Options]	
ExtraSection=<*section,section*>	Identifies the sections, specified in the file IESetup.inf, that the setup program will run. Separate sections with commas (for example, *section1,section2,section3*).
Quiet=[A,C,U]	Specifies that the installation will run silently with little or no input from users.
	A The installation will run in administrative mode. Users will not see the setup program, and the setup program will not perform error checking.
	C The **Cancel** button will not appear on the installation progress page. Users will not be able to cancel the installation.
	U Users will not see the setup program unless required input, such as the download location, is not available.
ShowErrors=[0,1]	Determines whether the setup program will display error messages to users.
	0 The setup program will not display error messages. It will automatically perform the default action for each error message without requesting input from users.
	1 (default) The setup program will display error messages.
[Welcome]	
Display=[0,1]	Determines whether the setup program will display the initial setup page to users.
	0 The setup program will not display the initial setup page.
	1 (default) The setup program will display the initial setup page.
[SetupChoice]	
Display=[0,1]	Determines whether the setup program will display the setup-type page. This page allows users to choose whether to customize the setup program.
	0 The setup program will not display the setup-type page.
	1 (default) The setup program will display the setup-type page.
SetupChoice=[0,1]	Determines which setup option the setup program will select.
	0 (default) The setup program will select **Install now—Typical Setup of Components**.
	1 The setup program will select **Custom Setup**.

Batch file entry	Description
[Custom]	
Display=[0,1]	Determines whether the setup program will display the Component Options page. This page allows users to select components and click **Advanced** to specify more options. **0** The setup program will not display the Component Options page. **1** (default) The setup program will display the Component Options page.
InstallDir=foldername	Specifies the folder where the setup program will copy the installation files. If you do not include this setting, the setup program will use the current settings in the file IESetup.inf. If users have installed an earlier version of Internet Explorer, the setup program will copy the installation files to the same folder as the earlier version.
InstallDirRO=[0,1]	Specifies whether users will be able to change the installation folder. **0** (default) Users will not be able to change the installation folder. **1** Users will be able to change the installation folder.
UseInfInstallDir=[0,1]	Specifies the folder where the setup program will install Internet Explorer and Internet Tools. **0** (default) The setup program will use the default installation folder or the same folder in which an earlier version of Internet Explorer is already installed. **1** The setup program will use the installation folder specified in the file IESetup.inf.
SetupMode=[0,1,2]	Specifies the type of installation that the setup program will perform. **0** The setup program will perform a Minimal installation. **1** (default) The setup program will perform a Typical installation. **2** The setup program will perform a Full installation.
SetupModeRO=[0,1]	Determines whether users will be able to change the type of installation that occurs. **0** Users will be able to change the type of installation. **1** (default) Users will not be able to change the type of installation.

Batch file entry	Description
[Custom]	
Component= [*ComponentID,ComponentID*]	Specifies that the setup program will install only the listed components, which are identified by their *ComponentID*. The *ComponentID* is a string that uniquely identifies the component; you can find the corresponding string in the component sections of the file IESetup.cif.
ComponentListRO=[0,1]	Determines whether users will be able to specify which components are installed (in addition to the standard components for the selected type of installation). **0** (default) Users will be able to specify which components are installed. **1** Users will not be able to specify which components are installed.
DownloadOnly=[0,1]	Determines whether the setup program will only download Internet Explorer and Internet Tools or both download and install it. **0** (default) The setup program will download and install the files. **1** The setup program will download the files but not install them.
DownloadOnlyRO=[0,1]	Determines whether users will be able to specify if the setup program will only download Internet Explorer and Internet Tools or both download and install it. **0** (default) Users will be able to specify the download and installation activities. **1** Users will not be able to specify the download and installation activities.
ShowAdvanced=[0,1]	Determines whether the setup program will display the **Advanced** button on the Component Options page. When users click the **Advanced** button, the setup program displays the **Download only**, **Compatibility**, and **Don't associate file types** options. **0** The setup program will not display the **Advanced** button. **1** (default) The setup program will display the **Advanced** button.

Batch file entry	Description
[Custom]	
IEDefault=[0,1]	Determines whether Internet Explorer will be set as the default browser. **0** Internet Explorer will not be set as the default browser. **1** (default) Internet Explorer will be set as the default browser.
IEDefaultRO=[0,1]	Specifies whether users will be able to determine if Internet Explorer is set as the default browser. **0** Users will not be able to choose their default browser. **1** (default) Users will be able to choose their default browser.
[Download]	
Display=[0,1]	Determines whether the setup program will display the option to download or install files on users' computers. **0** The setup program will not display the option to download or install files. **1** (default) The setup program will display the option to download or install files.
DownloadDir=foldername	Specifies the folder that the setup program will use for downloading files. If you do not include this setting, the setup program will create a folder named Windows Update Setup Files on the drive that has the most disk space.
DownloadDirRO=[0,1]	Specifies whether users will be able to change the folder that the setup program uses for downloading files. **0** (default) Users will be able to change the folder. **1** Users will not be able to change the folder.
DownloadOS=[0,1]	Specifies whether the setup program will download installation files for a specific operating system. This setting is valid only if users download but do not install files (**DownloadOnly=1**). **0** (default) The setup program will download installation files for the current operating system. **1** The setup program will download installation files for all operating systems.

Batch file entry	Description
[Download]	
DownloadOSRO=[0,1]	Determines whether users will be able to specify the operating system for the installation files that the setup program downloads to their computers. **0** (default) Users will be able to specify the operating system for the installation files. **1** Users will not be able to specify the operating system for the installation files.
[DownloadSite]	
Display=[0,1]	Determines whether the setup program will display the download sites to users. **0** The setup program will not display the download sites. **1** (default) The setup program will display the download sites.
DownloadLocation=URL	Specifies the address of the Web site that users will download cabinet (.cab) files from, if you plan to distribute Internet Explorer from the Web. If you set **Display=0** for this section, or create any entry that would result in the download sites page not being displayed, specify a download site for this entry.
DownloadSiteList=URL	Specifies the location where the setup program will retrieve the list of download sites. By default, this list is the file IE6Sites.dat. If you do not include this setting, the setup program uses the current settings in the file IESetup.inf.
[PrepareSetup]	
Display=[0,1]	Determines whether the setup program will display the Preparing Setup page on users' computers. **0** The setup program will not display the Preparing Setup page. **1** (default) The setup program will display the Preparing Setup page.
[Diskspace]	
Display=[0,1]	Specifies whether the setup program will display the amount of disk space needed on users' computers. **0** The setup program will not display the amount of disk space needed on users' computers. If computers do not have enough disk space, the setup program will close. **1** (default) The setup program will display the amount of disk space needed on users' computers.

Batch file entry	Description
[Progress]	
Display=[0,1]	Specifies whether the setup program will display the installation progress to users. **0** The setup program will not display the installation progress. **1** (default) The setup program will display the installation progress.
[RebootPartial]	
Display=[0,1]	Determines whether the setup program will display the Installation Incomplete page if a component fails to install. **0** The setup program will not display the Installation Incomplete page. **1** (default) The setup program will display the Installation Incomplete page.
[Finish]	
Display=[0,1]	Specifies whether the setup program will display the message about the computer restarting after setup is completed. **0** The setup program will not display the message about the computer restarting. Use this option if you plan to turn off restarting after installation (**Reboot=0**). **1** (default) The setup program will display the message about the computer restarting.
[Reboot]	
Reboot=[0,1]	Specifies whether the setup program will restart users' computers when the installation is completed. **0** The setup program will not restart users' computers when the installation is completed. If you turn off restarting, your program must take care of restarting the computers. Internet Explorer will not be configured correctly until the computers are restarted. **1** (default) The setup program will restart users' computers when the installation is completed.
[Upgrade]	
ReinstallAll=[0,1]	Specifies whether the setup program will reinstall all components if it is run a second time. **0** (default) The setup program will not run a second time if all components are already installed. **1** The setup program will reinstall all components if it is run a second time.

Sample Batch File

The following sample batch file shows installation directory choices, performs the first listed installation option, and automatically restarts the computer.

```
[Welcome]
Display=0

[SetupChoice]
Display=0

[Custom]
Display=0
Mode=0
InstallDir=c:\ie\en\

[Download]
Display=0
DownloadDir=c:\iedown\
[Finish]
Display=0
[Reboot]
Reboot=1
```

Using Command-Line Switches

You might want to control the way that the installation program (IE6wzd.exe) is run. You can use command-line switches to choose the type of installation, specify a quiet mode (which removes or reduces the prompts the user receives), or control whether the computer is restarted after installation.

You can have users include these switches when they run Setup, but a more typical scenario is to package Internet Explorer with another program for a batch installation. You can use the IExpress Wizard or another program to package your setup files.

The following table identifies Internet Explorer switches.

Internet Explorer switch	Description
/B:*iebatch.txt*	Specifies the batch file that the setup program will use.
/D	Specifies that the setup program will download only the files for the current operating system.
/D:1	Specifies that the setup program will download files for Windows and Microsoft® Windows NT® operating systems.
/E:*ComponentID, ComponentID*	Specifies additional components that the setup program will install, regardless of the type of installation. Use this switch to install components that are not a part of the installation type you specified in the Customization Wizard. This switch also overrides settings in the batch file, if used. The *ComponentID* is a string that uniquely identifies a component; you can find the corresponding string in the component sections of the file IESetup.cif.
/F -(Fix)	Specifies that the setup program will reinstall all items on users' computers that are the same version or newer than the Internet Explorer files being installed.
/G: *section,section*	Identifies the sections, specified in the file IESetup.inf, that the setup program will run. Separate sections with commas (for example, *section1,section2,section3*).
/M:[0|1|2|3...]	Specifies the type of installation that the setup program will perform. For custom browser packages, **0** refers to the first installation choice, **1** refers to the second choice, and so on (for example, 0=minimal, 1=typical (default), 2=full).
/P	Specifies that the setup program will display the amount of disk space needed for the installation based on the options selected.
/Q	Specifies that the installation will run in a quiet "hands-free" mode. The setup program will prompt users only for information that is not already specified.
/Q:A	Specifies that the installation will run in a quiet mode with no user prompts.
/Q:C	Specifies that the installation will run in a quiet mode, and the setup program will not display the **Cancel** button. Users will not be able to cancel the installation. The Corporate version of the Internet Explorer Customization Wizard uses this switch if you select the **Install package silently** option.

Internet Explorer switch	Description
/R:N	Specifies that the setup program will not restart users' computers when the installation is completed. If you turn off restarting, your program must take care of restarting the computers. Internet Explorer will not be configured correctly until the computers are restarted.
/S:""\"#e\"""	Designates the source path where Setup will locate IE6Setup.exe. The ""#e"" refers to the full path and name of the executable (.exe) file. You must enclose the path with two pairs of double quotation marks.
/X	Specifies that the setup program will install Internet Explorer and Internet Tools without the shell, icons, or links. This option is useful for hosting browser controls in your own application.
/X:1	Specifies that the setup program will install Internet Explorer and Internet Tools with the shell, icons, or links, but will not take over default browser or HTTP protocol associations.

IExpress Switches

The following table identifies frequently used IExpress switches that control the extraction process during the setup. These switches are not specific to Internet Explorer.

IExpress switch	Description
/Q	Specifies that the installation will run in quiet mode.
/QU	Specifies that the installation will run in user-quiet mode, which presents some dialog boxes to users.
/QA	Specifies that the installation will run in administrator-quiet mode, which does not present any dialog boxes to users.
/C:<>	Specifies the path and name of the Setup.inf or .exe file that the setup program will use.
/R:N	Specifies that the setup program will never restart the computers after installation.
/R:A	Specifies that the setup program will always restart the computers after installation.
/R:S	Specifies that the setup program will restart the computers after installation without prompting users.
/T:<*directory path*>	Specifies the target folder that the setup program will use for extracting files.

Examples of Command-Line Switches

The following scenarios provide examples of how to use command-line switches:

- The following command line runs the third installation option:

  ```
  IE6Setup.exe /C:"ie6wzd /S:""#e""" /M:2"
  ```

- The following command line performs an installation in quiet mode. It does not prompt users, and their computers are not restarted after the installation:

  ```
  IE6Setup.exe /C:"ie6wzd /S:""#e""" /Q /R:N"
  ```

Command-Line Parameters for Starting Internet Explorer

In addition to using command-line switches to customize Setup, you can use command-line parameters to customize how Internet Explorer is started. For example, you can start Internet Explorer in Kiosk (full-screen) mode by adding a parameter to the Internet Explorer executable file name, as shown in the following syntax:

```
/path/Iexplore.exe -k
```

The following table identifies the parameters that you can use for starting Internet Explorer.

Parameter	Description
-new	Specifies that the browser window will start a new browsing process.
-k	Specifies that the browser will start in Kiosk (full-screen) mode.
-nohome	Specifies that the browser will start without its home page.
-embedding	Specifies that the Web browser control will start if no home page is displayed.
-channelband	Specifies that the browser will display the Channels folder.

APPENDIX D

Checklist for Preparing to Use the IEAK

When preparing to use the Microsoft® Internet Explorer Administration Kit (IEAK) 6, you may find a checklist helpful. This appendix contains a checklist for the files you will need to prepare and information you will need to gather before using the IEAK.

In This Appendix

Related Information in the Resource Kit

- For more information about preparing for the IEAK, see "Preparing for the IEAK."
- For more information about using the Internet Explorer Customization Wizard, see "Running the Microsoft Internet Explorer Customization Wizard."

Files and Information to Gather Before Running the IEAK

Before you use the IEAK to create and deploy your custom browser package, you should have on hand the kinds of information shown in the following checklist. This checklist is organized according to the stages of the Internet Explorer Customization Wizard. Within each stage, the checklist identifies the data required for each wizard page.

You can photocopy this checklist and then enter your data in the blanks provided.

Stage 1—Gathering Information

File Locations

Specify the folder where you want to build the package.

❑ Destination folder

Advanced Options

Decide whether you want to select the following option.

❑ Check for latest components via Automatic Version Synchronization.

Specify other advanced options.

❑ Path of .ins file to import settings from

❑ Component download folder

Language Selection

Specify the language for the package.

❑ Target language

Media Selection

Select one or more types of distribution media.

❑ Download

❑ CD-ROM

❑ Flat (all files in one directory)

❑ Single-disk branding

Feature Selection

Select the features that you want to customize.

❑ Setup Customizations

❑ Corporate Install Features (Corporate version only)

❑ Automatic Digital Signing

❑ Connection Manager (Corporate and ISP versions only)

❑ Browser Customizations

❑ URL Customizations

❑ Favorites and Links

❑ User Agent String

❑ Connections Customization (Corporate and ISP versions only)

❑ Sign-up Settings (ISP version only)

❑ Certificate Customization (Corporate and ISP versions only)

❑ Security Zones and Content Ratings (Corporate version only)

❑ Programs Customization

❑ Outlook Express Customization (Corporate and ISP versions only)

❑ Policies and Restrictions

Stage 2—Specifying Setup Parameters

Automatic Version Synchronization

Select the components for which you want to download the latest version as part of your custom browser package. The Microsoft® Internet Explorer 6 Web Browser is required.

❑ Internet Explorer 6 Web Browser

❑ Internet Explorer Help

❑ Internet Explorer Core Fonts

❑ Dynamic HTML Data Binding

❑ Internet Explorer Browsing Enhancements

❑ Outlook Express

❑ Windows Media Player

❑ Windows Media Player Codecs

❑ DirectAnimation

- ❑ Vector Graphics Rendering (VML)
- ❑ AOL ART Image Format Support
- ❑ Visual Basic Scripting Support
- ❑ Additional Web Fonts
- ❑ Language Auto-Selection
- ❑ Japanese Text Display Support
- ❑ Japanese Text Input Support
- ❑ Korean Text Display Support
- ❑ Korean Text Input Support
- ❑ Pan-European Text Display Support
- ❑ Chinese (Traditional) Text Display Support
- ❑ Chinese (Traditional) Text Input Support
- ❑ Chinese (Simplified) Text Display Support
- ❑ Chinese (Simplified) Text Input Support
- ❑ Vietnamese Text Support
- ❑ Hebrew Text Support
- ❑ Arabic Text Support
- ❑ Thai Text Support

Add Custom Components

Add up to 16 custom components.

Component #1

- ❑ Name
- ❑ Location
- ❑ Command
- ❑ Globally unique identifier (GUID)
- ❑ Description
- ❑ Parameter
- ❑ Uninstall key
- ❑ Version

Component #2

- ☐ Name
- ☐ Location
- ☐ Command
- ☐ Globally unique identifier (GUID)
- ☐ Description
- ☐ Parameter
- ☐ Uninstall key
- ☐ Version

Component #3

- ☐ Name
- ☐ Location
- ☐ Command
- ☐ Globally unique identifier (GUID)
- ☐ Description
- ☐ Parameter
- ☐ Uninstall key
- ☐ Version

Install Conditions

Select one of the installation timing options.

- ☐ Install before Internet Explorer.
- ☐ Install after Internet Explorer.
- ☐ Install after system restarts.

Decide whether you want to select the following option.

- ☐ Only install if Internet Explorer is installed successfully.

Stage 3—Customizing Setup

CD Autorun Customizations

If you plan to distribute the custom browser package on CD-ROM, specify information to customize the CD-ROM Autorun screen.

- ❏ Title bar text
- ❏ Custom background bitmap location
- ❏ Standard text color
- ❏ Highlight text color

Button Style

Select one of the button styles.

- ❏ Standard beveled buttons
- ❏ 3D bitmap buttons
- ❏ Custom button bitmap (specify location)

More CD Options

If you plan to distribute the custom browser package on CD-ROM, specify information to customize the CD-ROM Autorun links.

- ❏ More information text file
- ❏ Use kiosk mode start page.

HTML file:

Customize Setup

Customize the title bar and bitmaps for the Internet Explorer Setup Wizard.

- ❏ Setup Wizard title bar text
- ❏ Left Setup Wizard bitmap path (first page)
- ❏ Top banner Setup Wizard bitmap path (all pages except first)
- ❏ Custom components installation title

User Experience (Corporate Version Only)

Select options to control the user experience during Setup.

Silent Installation

Select one of the silent installation options.

- ❑ Interactive installation
- ❑ Hands-free installation
- ❑ Completely silent installation

User Rights

Decide whether you want to select the following option (available only if you select Flat media).

- ❑ Enable logon after restart with user-level access.

Installation Options

Select one or more of the installation options, and identify any additional components that you want to install with each option. You can specify up to ten unique installation options.

❑ Minimal	Additional components:
❑ Typical	Additional components:
❑ Full	Additional components:
❑ Custom Option #1	Additional components:
❑ Custom Option #2	Additional components:
❑ Custom Option #3	Additional components:

Component Download Sites

If you plan to distribute a downloadable custom browser package, specify information for one or more download sites.

Download Site #1

❏ Site name

❏ Site URL

❏ Site region

Download Site #2

❏ Site name

❏ Site URL

❏ Site region

Download Site #3

❏ Site name

❏ Site URL

❏ Site region

Component Download

Select one of the Windows Update options.

❏ Remove the Windows Update option from the Tools menu. (Corporate version only)

❏ Use the default URL for the Windows Update.

❏ Use a custom add-on URL and menu text.

If you select **Use a custom add-on URL and menu text**, specify the menu text and URL.

❏ Menu text for add-on component URL

❏ URL of add-on component page

Decide whether you want to select the following option.

❏ Download components from Microsoft after install.

Installation Directory (Corporate Version Only)

Decide whether you want to select the following option.

❑ Allow the user to choose the installation directory.

Select one of the folder options.

❑ Install in the specified folder within the Program Files folder.

❑ Specify the full path of a custom folder.

Corporate Install Options (Corporate Version Only)

Select any custom installation options that apply.

❑ Prohibit users from selecting the Custom installation option.

❑ Disable saving uninstall information.

❑ Prohibit users from installing Internet Explorer Compatibility Mode.

❑ Integrate the Windows Desktop Update into the package.

Default Browser

Select one of the default browser options.

❑ Set Internet Explorer as the default browser.

❑ Do not set Internet Explorer as the default browser.

❑ Allow user to choose.

Advanced Installation Options

Decide whether you want to select the following option.

❑ Optimize for Web Download (if a compatible version exists, do not download it)

Select the components that you want to appear on the Customize Component Options page during Setup.

❑ Offline Browsing Pack

❑ Internet Explorer Help

❑ Internet Explorer Core Fonts

❑ Dynamic HTML Data Binding

❑ Internet Explorer Browsing Enhancements

❑ Outlook Express

- ❏ Windows Media Player
- ❏ Windows Media Player Codecs
- ❏ Vector Graphics Rendering (VML)
- ❏ AOL ART Image Format Support
- ❏ Visual Basic Scripting Support
- ❏ Additional Web Fonts
- ❏ Language Auto-Selection
- ❏ Japanese Text Display Support
- ❏ Japanese Text Input Support
- ❏ Korean Text Display Support
- ❏ Korean Text Input Support
- ❏ Pan-European Text Display Support
- ❏ Chinese (Traditional) Text Display Support
- ❏ Chinese (Traditional) Text Input Support
- ❏ Chinese (Simplified) Text Display Support
- ❏ Chinese (Simplified) Text Input Support
- ❏ Vietnamese Text Support
- ❏ Hebrew Text Support
- ❏ Arabic Text Support
- ❏ Thai Text Support

Components on Media

Select the components that will be available to your users through Install on Demand.

- ❏ Japanese Text Display Support
- ❏ Japanese Text Input Support
- ❏ Korean Text Display Support
- ❏ Korean Text Input Support
- ❏ Pan-European Text Display Support
- ❏ Chinese (Traditional) Text Display Support
- ❏ Chinese (Traditional) Text Input Support
- ❏ Chinese (Simplified) Text Display Support

- ❏ Chinese (Simplified) Text Input Support
- ❏ Vietnamese Text Support
- ❏ Hebrew Text Support
- ❏ Arabic Text Support
- ❏ Thai Text Support

Connection Manager Customization (Corporate and ISP Versions Only)

Decide whether you want to import a custom profile created using the Connection Manager Administration Kit (CMAK).

- ❏ Use specified custom profile.

Digital Signatures

Specify information about the digital certificate that will be used to automatically sign your custom browser package.

- ❏ Company name on certificate
- ❏ Software Publishing Certificates (.spc) file
- ❏ Private Key (.pvk) file
- ❏ Description text
- ❏ More information URL
- ❏ Timestamp URL

Stage 4—Customizing the Browser

Browser Title

Specify the text that appears in the browser's title bar.

- ❏ Customize title bars.   Text:

Toolbar Customizations

Customize the appearance of the Internet Explorer bitmap.

Background

Select one of the background bitmap options.

- ❏ Use Windows default toolbar background bitmap.
- ❏ Customize toolbar background bitmap.

Buttons

Decide whether you want to delete the existing toolbar buttons and add your own.

❑ Delete existing toolbar button, if present. (Corporate version only)

Specify information for one or more buttons that you want to add.

Button #1

❑ Toolbar caption (required)

❑ Toolbar action, as script file or executable (required)

❑ Toolbar color icon (required)

❑ Toolbar grayscale icon (required)

Decide whether you want to select the following option.

❑ This button should be shown on the toolbar by default.

Button #2

❑ Toolbar caption (required)

❑ Toolbar action, as script file or executable (required)

❑ Toolbar color icon (required)

❑ Toolbar grayscale icon (required)

Decide whether you want to select the following option.

❑ This button should be shown on the toolbar by default.

Button #3

❑ Toolbar caption (required)

❑ Toolbar action, as script file or executable (required)

❑ Toolbar color icon (required)

❑ Toolbar grayscale icon (required)

Decide whether you want to select the following option.

❑ This button should be shown on the toolbar by default.

Custom Logo and Animated Bitmaps

Decide whether you want to replace the Internet Explorer logos with your own.

❑ Customize the static logo bitmaps.

❑ Small (22 x 22) bitmap

❑ Large (38 x 38) bitmap

❑ Customize the animated bitmaps.

❑ Small (22 x 22) bitmap

❑ Large (38 x 38) bitmap

Important URLs

Specify custom URLs for the Home page, Search bar, and Online Support page.

❑ Customize Home page URL.

❑ Customize Search bar URL.

❑ Customize Online Support page URL.

Favorites and Links

Select the options for Favorites and Links that apply.

❑ Place Favorites and Links (default) at the top of the list.

❑ Delete existing Favorites and Links, if present. (Corporate version only)

❑ Only delete the Favorites created by the administrator. (Corporate version only)

❑ Delete existing channels, if present. (Corporate version only)

Decide whether you want to import existing Favorites and Links.

❑ Import   Folder to import from:

Add URLs

Specify the following information for one or more additional URLs.

URL #1

❑ Name

❑ URL

❑ Icon

Decide whether you want to select the following option.

❑ Make available offline.

URL #2

❑ Name

❑ URL

❑ Icon

Decide whether you want to select the following option.

❑ Make available offline.

URL #3

❑ Name

❑ URL

❑ Icon

Decide whether you want to select the following option.

❑ Make available offline.

Add Folders

Specify the following information for one or more additional folders.

Folder #1

❑ Name

❑ URL

❑ Icon

Decide whether you want to select the following option.

❑ Make available offline.

Folder #2

❑ Name

❑ URL

❑ Icon

Decide whether you want to select the following option.

❑ Make available offline.

Folder #3

❑ Name

❑ URL

❑ Icon

Decide whether you want to select the following option.

❑ Make available offline.

Welcome Page

Select one of the welcome page options.

❑ Display default Microsoft Internet Explorer 6 welcome page.

❑ Do not display a welcome page.

❑ Use a custom welcome page (specify URL).

User Agent String

Specify custom text for the user agent string.

❑ Customize string to be appended to user
    agent string.

Connection Settings (Corporate and ISP Versions Only)

Select one option for connection settings.

❑ Do not customize connection settings.

❑ Import the current connection settings from this machine.

Decide whether you want to select the following option.

❑ Delete existing dial-up connection settings. (Corporate version only)

Automatic Configuration (Corporate Version Only)

Select options for automatic configuration.

❑ Automatically detect configuration settings.

❑ Enable automatic configuration.

If you select **Enable automatic configuration**, specify automatic configuration options.

❑ Automatic configuration interval
    (in minutes)

❑ Auto-configuration URL (.ins file)

❑ Auto-proxy URL (.js, .jvs, or .pac file)

Proxy Settings (Corporate and ISP Versions Only)

Decide whether you want to select the following option.

❑   Enable proxy settings.

Proxy Servers

If you selected **Enable proxy settings**, specify proxy server information.

❑ HTTP	Address:	Port:
❑ Secure	Address:	Port:
❑ FTP	Address:	Port:
❑ Gopher	Address:	Port:
❑ Socks	Address:	Port:

Decide whether you want to select the following option.

❑   Use the same proxy server for all addresses.

Exceptions

If you selected **Enable proxy settings**, specify exception information.

❑   Do not use proxy server for
    addresses beginning with:

Decide whether you want to select the following option.

❑   Do not use proxy server for local (intranet) addresses.

Add a Root Certificate (ISP Version Only)

The customization option on this wizard page does not work properly. If you add any root certificate information, it will not be applied.

Sign-up Method (ISP Version Only)

Select one sign-up method.

❑   Server-based sign-up using the Internet Connection Wizard (recommended)

❑   Server-based sign-up using full-screen kiosk mode

❑   Serverless sign-up

❑   No sign-up

Sign-up Files (ISP Version Only)

Specify the working directory for your sign-up files.

❑   Working directory

Sign-up Server Information (ISP Version Only)

Specify the information for the connection to your sign-up server.

❑   Connection name

❑   File name

❑   Area code/Phone number

❑   Country code/ID

❑   Username

❑   Password

❑   Supported phone number

❑   URL of first online sign-up page

Advanced Options

Specify advanced sign-up options.

❑   Use static DNS address.

Primary:	Alternate:

Select the connection options that apply.

❑   Requires logon

❑   Negotiate TCP/IP

❑   Disable LCP

❑   Dial number as shown

❑   Encrypt passwords

❑   Use software compression

❑   Use IP header compression

❑   Use default remote gateway

Internet Connection Wizard (ISP Version Only)

Specify the text and images for the sign-up wizard that users see.

❑   Customize title bar.

❑   Top image

❑   Left image

Text:

Security (Corporate Version Only)

Decide whether you want to customize security settings.

Certification Authorities

Select one option for certification authorities.

❑   Do not customize certification authorities.

❑   Import current certification authorities.

Authenticode Security

Select one option for Microsoft® Authenticode® security.

❑   Do not customize Authenticode security.

❑   Import current Authenticode security information.

Security and Privacy Settings (Corporate Version Only)

Decide whether you want to customize security and privacy settings.

Security Zones and Privacy

Select one option for security zones and privacy.

❑   Do not customize security zones and privacy.

❑   Import the current security zones and privacy settings.

Content ratings

Select one option for content ratings.

❑   Do not customize content ratings.

❑   Import the current content ratings settings.

Stage 5—Customizing Components

Programs

Select one option for the default programs that Microsoft® Windows® automatically uses for Internet services.

❑ Do not customize program settings.

❑ Import the current program settings.

Outlook Express Accounts (Corporate and ISP Versions Only)

Specify information to preconfigure mail and news accounts for Outlook Express.

❑ Incoming mail server (POP3 or IMAP)		❑ Logon using SPA
❑ Outgoing (SMTP) server		❑ Logon using SPA
❑ Internet news (NNTP) server		❑ Logon using SPA

Select the options that apply.

❑ Make server names read-only.

❑ Disable access to accounts (accounts cannot be added, removed, or modified).

Outlook Express IMAP Settings (Corporate and ISP Versions Only)

Specify information for IMAP accounts.

❑ Root folder path		
❑ Store special folders on IMAP server	Sent Items path:	Drafts folder path:

Decide whether you want to select the following option.

❑ Check for new messages in all folders.

Outlook Express Custom Content (Corporate and ISP Versions Only)

Specify information for a custom HTML welcome message in users' Inbox.

❑ HTML path	
❑ Sender	
❑ Reply-to	

The InfoPane feature is not available in Outlook Express 6. If you add any InfoPane customization information on this wizard page, it will not be applied.

Outlook Express Custom Settings (Corporate and ISP Versions Only)

Select the options that apply.

❑ Make Outlook Express the default program for mail.

❑ Make Outlook Express the default program for news.

Specify one or more newsgroups to be automatically subscribed.

❑ Newsgroup #1

❑ Newsgroup #2

❑ Newsgroup #3

Specify information for obtaining additional mail accounts after installation.

❑ Service name

❑ Service URL

Decide whether you want to select the following option.

❑ Delete all Outlook Express links.

Outlook Express View Settings (Corporate and ISP Versions Only)

Select settings for viewing items in Outlook Express.

Basic

Select the basic items that you want to view in Outlook Express.

❑ Folder bar

❑ Outlook Bar

❑ Folder list

❑ Status bar

❑ Contacts

❑ Tip of the day

Toolbar

Select the settings for viewing the toolbar in Outlook Express.

❑ Show toolbar.

❑ Show text on toolbar buttons.

Preview Pane

Select the settings for viewing the preview pane in Outlook Express.

❑ Show preview pane.

❑ Below messages	❑ Beside messages

❑ Show preview pane header.

Outlook Express Compose Settings (Corporate Version Only)

Specify information for the message signature and format.

❑ Append a signature to each message.

❑ Use a different signature for news messages.

Decide whether you want to select these options.

❑ For mail messages, make HTML message composition the default.

❑ For news messages, make HTML message composition the default.

Address Book Directory Service (Corporate and ISP Versions Only)

Specify information for the Internet Directory Service (LDAP server).

❑ Service name

❑ Server name   ❑ Logon using SPA

❑ Service Web site

❑ Search base

❑ Service bitmap

❑ Search timeout (30 seconds to 5 minutes)

❑ Maximum number of matches to return (1 to 9999)

Decide whether you want to select the following option.

❑ Check names against this server when sending mail.

Targeting Policies and Restrictions (Corporate Version Only)

Select one option for displaying policies and restrictions.

❑ Display all IEAK policies.

❑ Display the subset of IEAK policies for non-administrator users.

Policies and Restrictions

Select the categories for which you want to specify policies and restrictions.

❑ Control Management (Corporate version only)

❑ Corporate Settings (Corporate version only)

❑ Corporate Restrictions (Corporate version only)

❑ Internet Settings

❑ Outlook Express (Corporate and ISP versions only)

❑ Web Desktop (Corporate version only)

❑ Offline Pages (Corporate version only)

❑ Microsoft Windows Media Player

Decide whether you want to import existing settings for policies and restrictions.

❑ Import

File name:

Setting System Policies and Restrictions

This appendix describes how you can use system policies and restrictions to control user and computer access to Microsoft® Internet Explorer 6 features and functions. Using the Internet Explorer Customization Wizard or Internet Explorer Administration Kit (IEAK) Profile Manager, you can predefine Internet Explorer options and customize the Internet Explorer environment for different groups of users.

 Note You can also use Group Policy in Microsoft® Windows® XP and Microsoft® Windows® 2000 and the System Policy Editor in Microsoft® Windows® 98 and Microsoft® Windows NT® 4.0 to set system policies and restrictions. For more information about Group Policy, see "Keeping Programs Updated" in this Resource Kit. For specific instructions about how to install and use the System Policy Editor, see the *Microsoft Windows 98 Resource Kit* or the *Microsoft® Windows NT® Workstation 4.0 Resource Kit.*

In This Appendix

Related Information in the Resource Kit

- For more information about planning your system policy choices, see "Planning the Deployment."
- For more information about implementing system policies and restrictions as part of your custom browser packages, see "Running the Microsoft Internet Explorer Customization Wizard."

Overview

System policies and restrictions for Internet Explorer are a powerful mechanism for improving the control and manageability of computers. System policies and restrictions, which are defined in a policy file, control user and computer access privileges by overriding default registry values when the user logs on.

You can use the Internet Explorer Customization Wizard to predefine system policies and restrictions and to create a standard Internet Explorer configuration as part of your custom browser package. After the browser has been installed, you can use the IEAK Profile Manager to centrally manage and update system policies and restrictions on your users' desktops. Also, if different groups of users have unique needs, you can use the IEAK Profile Manager to create separate policy files for each group.

Important For Windows XP and Windows 2000 clients, you should use Group Policy, instead of the system policies and restrictions in the Internet Explorer Customization Wizard, to set user restrictions. For information about Internet Explorer settings in Group Policy, see "Keeping Programs Updated" in this Resource Kit.

If you are using Microsoft® Windows® 2000 Server to administer other operating systems, however, you can set restrictions by using the system policies and restrictions feature in the Internet Explorer Customization Wizard.

For example, you might want to implement system policies and restrictions to do the following:

- Determine the features that users can change, such as the Microsoft® Active Desktop® and Internet Explorer toolbars.
- Manage bandwidth and control the behavior and appearance of Internet Explorer.
- Specify server lists for components.
- Determine which applications users access to send and receive electronic mail and to place Internet calls.
- Specify users' connection settings.

Benefits of Using System Policies and Restrictions

Organizations can realize the following benefits from implementing system policies and restrictions:

- System policies and restrictions enable you to implement a standard Internet Explorer configuration. You can create a custom browser package for your users that includes common settings for browser features and functions.
- You can restrict the features that users can access within Internet Explorer by using system policies and restrictions. Also, you have the option to lock down features and functions so that they either do not appear or appear dimmed on users' desktops.
- Setting system policies and restrictions enables you to change default registry values. You can use the settings in a policy file to change registry values on multiple computers, eliminating the need to specify settings individually on each user's computer.

Issues to Consider Before Setting System Policies and Restrictions

Before implementing system policies and restrictions, you should consider the following issues:

- What types of system policies and restrictions do you want to define and manage centrally? For example, do you want to limit access to a particular feature or specify settings in advance for a program?

- Do you want to use one set of standard system policies and restrictions for all users and computers, or do you want to create multiple policy files for groups of users? Different groups of users can have unique needs.

- What types of security settings do you want to implement? You can choose to lock down all the settings, to control the settings but make them available for roaming users to download, or to customize the settings while allowing users to modify them.

  You should consider the impact of these settings, especially if you have roaming users who share computers with other people. For example, what are the implications of removing icons from the desktop or not allowing users to change their security settings? Make sure that your users understand which features they can access.

- Do you want to store the policy files in a central location or on users' computers? You might want to store the file on a server so that roaming users can access the settings from computer to computer. This capability could be useful, for example, for a user who needs low security settings but who uses a computer that is operated by another person whose security settings are higher.

Setting System Policies and Restrictions

On the Policies and Restrictions page, you can select a category and change the corresponding system policies and restrictions. A default set of policy templates, or administration (.adm) files, define the rules for the wide range of settings that appear on the Policies and Restrictions page. These same settings appear in both the Internet Explorer Customization Wizard (Stage 5) and the IEAK Profile Manager. The first time that the wizard is run, it creates the .adm files in the C:\Program Files\IEAK6\Policies folder.

▶ **To set system policies and restrictions with the IEAK**

1. To display the system policies and restrictions that you can define for a category, double-click the category name that appears in bold type.

    The following Internet Explorer Customization Wizard page shows the Policies and Restrictions categories.

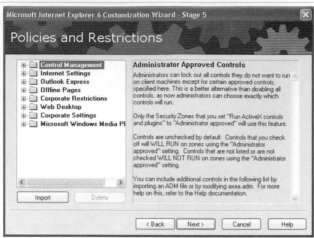

> **Note** The system policies and restrictions that you can set depend on the title that you select as your role in Stage 1 of the Internet Explorer Customization Wizard—Content Provider/Developer, Service Provider, or Corporate Administrator.

2. Select or clear the check boxes. For example, you can expand the **Web Desktop** category and click **Desktop** to specify Desktop options, such as **Disable Active Desktop**.

The following table briefly describes each of the categories for which you can specify system policies and restrictions.

Area	Description
Control Management	Selects the approved set of controls for data binding, Internet Explorer, MSN®, and third-party components. All other controls will be locked down and will not run on users' computers.
Internet Settings	Specifies a variety of Internet settings for users, including options for printing, searching, multimedia, and security. Most of these settings apply to default values in the Internet Control Panel.
Outlook Express	Prevents users from creating and managing multiple identities within a Windows logon profile by using the Identity Manager in Microsoft® Outlook® Express. Also restricts users from saving or opening attachments that could potentially contain harmful viruses.
Offline Pages	Controls the amount of information downloaded by disabling or limiting access to offline functions, such as the number of offline pages that users can download and the maximum number of minutes between scheduled updates. These settings improve server load by restricting bandwidth usage.

Area	Description
Corporate Restrictions	Specifies and locks down Internet Options settings and other browser options, such as search customization and software updates. These settings can lock out features of Internet Explorer that might be unnecessary or undesirable for users, and prevent modifications to settings made during setup or automatic configuration.
Web Desktop	Restricts users' ability to add, access, modify, or delete various portions of the desktop. These settings control how users manage files, use printers, and accomplish other everyday tasks.
Corporate Settings	Specifies and locks down settings for Temporary Internet files, code download, and browsing errors. For example, you can choose the amount of disk space to allocate for Temporary Internet files.
Microsoft Windows Media Player	Customizes the Microsoft® Windows® Media Player and Microsoft® Internet Explorer Radio. Also prevents the installation of Windows Media Player Favorites in the Media folder.

Using Custom Policy Templates

If you are familiar with .adm files, you can create your own policy templates with custom settings that you can distribute to users.

Important   Be sure that you thoroughly test your templates before using them to make changes to users' systems.

▶ **To import your custom .adm file**

- In the Internet Explorer Customization Wizard, on the Policies and Restrictions page, click **Import**.
  -Or-
  In the IEAK Profile Manager, on the **Policy** menu, click **Import**.

Note   On the IEAK Profile Manager **Policy** menu, you can click **Check Duplicate Keys** to check for duplicate registry keys in the templates.

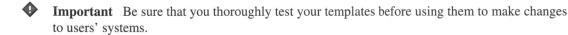

When you use custom policy templates, an information (.inf) file is generated using the file name of the imported custom template. For example, if you import custom.adm, a custom.inf file is generated and added to the companion cabinet (.cab) files. When unpacked, the .inf files are used to change policies and restrictions on users' systems.

Updating System Policies and Restrictions After Installation

After you have set the system policies and restrictions and distributed the browser, you can use the IEAK Profile Manager to manage these settings. The IEAK Profile Manager enables you to open an auto-configuration .ins file and make changes to system policies and restrictions. By storing an .ins file on the server and downloading it every time users log on, you can adjust system policies and restrictions on an ongoing basis. Tying into existing logon scripts enables you to manage and regularly update these settings from a centralized server.

Note   You must reboot the computer in order for some system policies and restrictions to take effect.

For more information about using the IEAK Profile Manager to update system policies and restrictions, see "Keeping Programs Updated" in this Resource Kit.

Country/Region and Language Codes

As an Internet service provider, you might find helpful the lists of country/region and language codes provided in this appendix.

 Note Because this information is subject to change, periodically consult the most recent telephone reference materials for updates to these codes.

In This Appendix

Related Information in the Resource Kit

- For general information about creating sign-up solutions, see "Implementing the Sign-up Process."

Country/Region Codes

Use the country/region names and Telephony API (TAPI) telephone codes where required in your Internet sign-up files. On users' computers, the codes for each of the countries and regions supported by TAPI are stored in the **HKEY_LOCAL_MACHINE\SOFTWARE\Microsoft\Windows \CurrentVersion\Telephony\Country List** registry key.

Country/Region	TAPI telephone code
Afghanistan	93
Albania	355
Algeria	213
American Samoa	684
Andorra	376
Angola	244
Anguilla	101
Antarctica	—
Antigua and Barbuda	102, 120
Argentina	54
Armenia	374
Aruba	297
Ascension Island	247
Ashmore and Cartier Islands	—
Australia	61
Austria	43
Azerbaijan	994
Bahamas, The	103
Bahrain	973
Baker Island	—
Bangladesh	880
Barbados	104
Belarus	375
Belgium	32

Country/Region	TAPI telephone code
Belize	501
Benin	229
Bermuda	105
Bhutan	975
Bolivia	591
Bosnia and Herzegovina	387
Botswana	267
Bouvet Island	—
Brazil	55
British Indian Ocean Territory	—
Brunei	673
Bulgaria	359
Burkina Faso	226
Burundi	257
Cambodia	855
Cameroon	237
Canada	107
Cape Verde	238
Cayman Islands	108
Central African Republic	236
Chad	235
Channel Islands	—
Chile	56
China	86
Christmas Island	—
Clipperton Island	—
Cocos (Keeling) Islands	6101
Colombia	57
Comoros	2691

Country/Region	TAPI telephone code
Congo	242
Congo (DRC)	243
Cook Islands	682
Coral Sea Islands	—
Costa Rica	506
Côte d'Ivoire	225
Croatia	385
Cuba	53
Cyprus	357
Czech Republic	420
Denmark	45
Diego Garcia	246
Djibouti	253
Dominica	109
Dominican Republic	110
East Timor	670
Ecuador	593
Egypt	20
El Salvador	503
Equatorial Guinea	240
Eritrea	291
Estonia	372
Ethiopia	251
Falkland Islands (Islas Malvinas)	500
Faroe Islands	298
Fiji Islands	679
Finland	358
France	33
France, Metropolitan	—

Country/Region	TAPI telephone code
French Guiana	594
French Polynesia	689
French Southern and Antarctic Lands	—
Gabon	241
Gambia, The	220
Georgia	995
Germany	49
Ghana	233
Gibraltar	350
Greece	30
Greenland	299
Grenada	111
Guadeloupe	590
Guam	124
Guantanamo Bay	5399
Guatemala	502
Guernsey	—
Guinea	224
Guinea-Bissau	245
Guyana	592
Haiti	509
Heard Island and McDonald Islands	—
Honduras	504
Hong Kong SAR	852
Howland Island	—
Hungary	36
Iceland	354
India	91
Indonesia	62

Country/Region	TAPI telephone code
Iran	98
Iraq	964
Ireland	353
Israel	972
Italy	39
Jamaica	112
Japan	81
Jarvis Island	—
Jersey	—
Johnston Atoll	—
Jordan	962
Kazakhstan	705
Kenya	254
Kingman Reef	—
Kiribati	686
Korea	82
Kuwait	965
Kyrgyzstan	996
Laos	856
Latvia	371
Lebanon	961
Lesotho	266
Liberia	231
Libya	218
Liechtenstein	423
Lithuania	370
Luxembourg	352
Macau SAR	853
Macedonia, Former Yugoslav Republic of	389

Country/Region	TAPI telephone code
Madagascar	261
Malawi	265
Malaysia	60
Maldives	960
Mali	223
Malta	356
Man, Isle of	—
Marshall Islands	692
Martinique	596
Mauritania	222
Mauritius	230
Mayotte	269
Mexico	52
Micronesia	691
Midway Islands	—
Moldova	373
Monaco	377
Mongolia	976
Montserrat	113
Morocco	212
Mozambique	258
Myanmar	95
Namibia	264
Nauru	674
Nepal	977
Netherlands Antilles	599
Netherlands, The	31
New Caledonia	687
New Zealand	64

Country/Region	TAPI telephone code
Nicaragua	505
Niger	227
Nigeria	234
Niue	683
Norfolk Island	672
North Korea	850
Northern Mariana Islands	—
Norway	47
Oman	968
Pakistan	92
Palau	680
Palestinian Authority	—
Palmyra Atoll	—
Panama	507
Papua New Guinea	675
Paraguay	595
Peru	51
Philippines	63
Pitcairn Islands	—
Poland	48
Portugal	351
Puerto Rico	121
Qatar	974
Reunion	262
Romania	40
Rota Island	
Russia	7
Rwanda	250
Saipan	—

Country/Region	TAPI telephone code
Samoa	685
San Marino	378
São Tomé and Príncipe	239
Saudi Arabia	966
Senegal	221
Seychelles	248
Sierra Leone	232
Singapore	65
Slovakia	421
Slovenia	386
Solomon Islands	677
Somalia	252
South Africa	27
South Georgia and the South Sandwich Islands	—
Spain	34
Sri Lanka	94
St. Helena	290
St. Kitts and Nevis	115
St. Lucia	122
St. Pierre and Miquelon	508
St. Vincent and the Grenadines	116
Sudan	249
Suriname	597
Svalbard and Jan Mayen	—
Swaziland	268
Sweden	46
Switzerland	41
Syria	963
Taiwan	886

Country/Region	TAPI telephone code
Tajikistan	992
Tanzania	255
Thailand	66
Tinian Island	—
Togo	228
Tokelau	690
Tonga	676
Trinidad and Tobago	117
Tristan da Cunha	—
Tunisia	216
Turkey	90
Turkmenistan	993
Turks and Caicos Islands	118
Tuvalu	688
Uganda	256
Ukraine	380
United Arab Emirates	971
United Kingdom	44
United States	1
Uruguay	598
U.S. Minor Outlying Islands	—
Uzbekistan	998
Vanuatu	678
Vatican City	379
Venezuela	58
Viet Nam	84
Virgin Islands	123
Virgin Islands, British	106
Wake Island	—

Country/Region	TAPI telephone code
Wallis and Futuna	681
Yemen	967
Yugoslavia	381
Zambia	260
Zimbabwe	263

Language Codes

Use the appropriate languages and their associated decimal values where required in your Internet sign-up files.

Language	Decimal Value
Afrikaans	1078
Albanian	1052
Arabic (Algeria)	5121
Arabic (Bahrain)	15361
Arabic (Egypt)	3073
Arabic (Iraq)	2049
Arabic (Jordan)	11265
Arabic (Kuwait)	13313
Arabic (Lebanon)	12289
Arabic (Libya)	4097
Arabic (Morocco)	6145
Arabic (Oman)	8193
Arabic (Qatar)	16385
Arabic (Saudi Arabia)	1025
Arabic (Syria)	10241
Arabic (Tunisia)	7169
Arabic (U.A.E.)	14337
Arabic (Yemen)	9217
Basque	1069

Language	Decimal Value
Belarusian	1059
Bulgarian	1026
Catalan	1027
Chinese (Hong Kong SAR)	3076
Chinese (PRC)	2052
Chinese (Singapore)	4100
Chinese (Taiwan)	1028
Croatian	1050
Czech	1029
Danish	1030
Dutch	1043
Dutch (Belgium)	2067
English (Australia)	3081
English (Belize)	10249
English (Canada)	4105
English (Ireland)	6153
English (Jamaica)	8201
English (New Zealand)	5129
English (South Africa)	7177
English (Trinidad)	11273
English (United Kingdom)	2057
English (United States)	1033
Estonian	1061
Faeroese	1080
Farsi	1065
Finnish	1035
French (Standard)	1036
French (Belgium)	2060
French (Canada)	3084

Language	Decimal Value
French (Luxembourg)	5132
French (Switzerland)	4108
Gaelic (Scotland)	1084
German (Standard)	1031
German (Austrian)	3079
German (Liechtenstein)	5127
German (Luxembourg)	4103
German (Switzerland)	2055
Greek	1032
Hebrew	1037
Hindi	1081
Hungarian	1038
Icelandic	1039
Indonesian	1057
Italian (Standard)	1040
Italian (Switzerland)	2064
Japanese	1041
Korean	1042
Latvian	1062
Lithuanian	1063
Macedonian (FYROM)	1071
Malay (Malaysia)	1086
Maltese	1082
Norwegian (Bokmål)	1044
Polish	1045
Portuguese (Brazil)	1046
Portuguese (Portugal)	2070
Raeto (Romance)	1047
Romanian	1048

Language	Decimal Value
Romanian (Moldova)	2072
Russian	1049
Russian (Moldova)	2073
Serbian (Cyrillic)	3098
Setsuana	1074
Slovak	1051
Slovenian	1060
Sorbian	1070
Spanish (Argentina)	11274
Spanish (Bolivia)	16394
Spanish (Chile)	13322
Spanish (Columbia)	9226
Spanish (Costa Rica)	5130
Spanish (Dominican Republic)	7178
Spanish (Ecuador)	12298
Spanish (El Salvador)	17418
Spanish (Guatemala)	4106
Spanish (Honduras)	18442
Spanish (Mexico)	2058
Spanish (Nicaragua)	19466
Spanish (Panama)	6154
Spanish (Paraguay)	15370
Spanish (Peru)	10250
Spanish (Puerto Rico)	20490
Spanish (Spain)	1034
Spanish (Uruguay)	14346
Spanish (Venezuela)	8202
Sutu	1072
Swedish	1053

Language	Decimal Value
Swedish (Finland)	2077
Thai	1054
Turkish	1055
Tsonga	1073
Ukranian	1058
Urdu (Pakistan)	1056
Vietnamese	1066
Xhosa	1076
Yiddish	1085
Zulu	1077

Microsoft Internet Explorer 6 File Types

This appendix provides an overview of the common types of files that are used as part of Microsoft® Windows® Update Setup for Microsoft® Internet Explorer 6 and Internet Tools. Learning about the purposes of these files and how they work together can make it easier to troubleshoot setup issues.

In This Appendix

Related Information in the Resource Kit

- For more information about the setup process, see "Deploying Microsoft Internet Explorer 6."
- For more information about Internet Explorer system policy files, see the appendix "Setting System Policies and Restrictions."

Common Setup Files

The following table describes the common file types that are used as part of Setup. For a complete list of files that are downloaded to your computer during the setup process, see the Internet Explorer Knowledge Base, which is available on the Microsoft Windows Technologies Internet Explorer Support Web site at http://www.microsoft.com/windows/Ie/Support/default.asp.

File type	Description
.adm	An administration (.adm) file defines the system policies and restrictions for the desktop, shell, and security. You can customize and restrict the settings in an .adm file by using the Internet Explorer Administration Kit (IEAK) or the Windows System Policy Editor. For a list of system policies and restrictions that you can set in the .adm file, see the appendix "Setting System Policies and Restrictions" in this Resource Kit. You can maintain .adm files on your users' computers or from a central location. After Internet Explorer 6 and Internet Tools is installed, you can use the IEAK Profile Manager to update the .adm file settings on your users' computers. For more information about using the IEAK Profile Manager, see "Keeping Programs Updated" in this Resource Kit.
.asp	If you distribute Internet Explorer from a Web server, you can include Active Server Page (.asp) files in your custom browser package. By using .asp files, you can embed script within your HTML pages to create dynamic, interactive Web content. For example, you can create sign-up pages that enable users to download the browser and register for Internet services. You can point to .asp files in the Internet Explorer Customization Wizard or the IEAK Profile Manager. The IEAK6\Toolkit\Isp\Server\ICW\Signup folder in your IEAK installation directory includes sample .asp files.
.bat	A batch (.bat) file is an ASCII text file that contains a sequence of operating system commands, such as parameters and operators supported by the batch command language. When the user types the name of the .bat file at the command prompt, the computer processes the commands sequentially.
.bmp, .gif, .jpeg, .jpg	Internet Explorer can include static and animated graphics that have .bmp, .gif, .jpeg, or .jpg file formats. In addition to using graphics files supplied with the IEAK, you can create your own graphics and include them with your custom browser package. For example, you can replace the Internet Explorer logo or the AutoRun splash screen with your own static or animated graphic files. The IEAK includes two tools to help you create customized, animated graphics. For more information about the requirements for graphics that you customize, see "Preparing for the IEAK" in this Resource Kit.

File type	Description
.cab	Cabinet (.cab) files organize and store compressed installation files. Setup (IE6Setup.exe) downloads the .cab files necessary for Internet Explorer installation to users' computers. These .cab files can contain both browser and custom components. After the files are downloaded successfully, Setup is complete. The IEAK contains a set of tools that can help you build .cab files for custom components.
.cif	A component information (.cif) file named IESetup.cif identifies the components that you can install with Internet Explorer 6 and Internet Tools, including any new components or component updates. In the .cif file, each component has an associated *ComponentID*. Setup reads the .cif file to determine whether a component with a specific *ComponentID* has already been installed and whether a newer version is available for installation.
.exe	An executable (.exe) file named IE6Setup.exe is the installation program that controls the setup process for Internet Explorer and Internet Tools. This .exe file downloads the .cab files that install your custom browser package on users' computers. Those .cab files can, in turn, include additional self-extracting .exe files for browser and custom components.
.htt	The HTML template (.htt) files provide customizable templates for My Computer (Mycomp.htt), Control Panel (Controlp.htt), Printers (Printers.htt), and the default Web view for folders (Folder.htt). Using a text or HTML editor, you can customize these files with special instructions, logos, or links to Web sites. You can include Mycomp.htt and Controlp.htt in your custom browser package. You need to customize the Printers.htt and Folder.htt templates directly on your users' computers.
.inf	Typically, each Internet Explorer .cab file contains an associated information (.inf) file, which provides further installation information. The .inf file can reference files in the .cab file, as well as files at other locations.
.ins	Setup contains an Internet settings (.ins) file, which configures the browser and its components. You can create multiple versions of your browser package by customizing copies of this .ins file. For more information about this process, see "Time-saving Strategies That Address Diverse User Needs" in this Resource Kit. The IEAK Profile Manager also enables you to create, save, and load .ins files for updating Internet Explorer configuration settings.
.isp	If you implement a sign-up process with your custom browser package, an Internet sign-up (.isp) file named Signup.isp provides dial-up information for your Internet services. Using the Internet Explorer Customization Wizard, you can edit the parameters contained in the Internet sign-up file. For a server-based sign-up method, this sign-up file also contains a link to the URL of the server script that generates your .ins configuration file.

File type	Description
.pac, .js, .jvs	You can use a text editor to create an auto-proxy script file for your custom browser package. An auto-proxy script file can be a proxy auto-configuration (.pac), JScript (.js), or JavaScript (.jvs) file. When an auto-proxy script file is specified, Internet Explorer uses the script to determine dynamically whether it should connect directly to a host or use a proxy server. In Stage 4 of the Internet Explorer Customization Wizard, you can specify an auto-proxy URL for configuring and maintaining advanced proxy settings.
.pvk	The private key (.pvk) file contains the private key associated with the digital signature that you use to sign your custom browser package. For more information about digital certificates, see "Digital Certificates," in this Resource Kit.
.pwl	The password (.pwl) file contains the Windows password for the user of the computer.
.sms	If you use Microsoft® Systems Management Server to distribute Internet Explorer, your custom browser package consists of a folder that contains the Internet Explorer installation files and a package definition (.sms) file. This file, named IE6-Sms.sms, contains a setup program, installation options, and command-line syntax for automatically installing Internet Explorer 6 and Internet Tools on your server or users' computers. This .sms file enables the installation to occur without administrative or user intervention.
.spc	The software publishing certificate (.spc) file contains the name and other identity information for the owner of the certificate, the public key associated with the certificate, a serial number, a validity period for the certificate, and the digital signature of the certification authority that issued the certificate.

Structural Definition of .inf Files

Although the Microsoft® Internet Explorer Customization Wizard, Internet Explorer batch files, and third-party applications can customize Setup, you can also use setup information (.inf) files to develop a customized setup solution. This appendix describes the sections of an .inf file and provides a sample.

In This Appendix

Related Information in the Resource Kit

- For more information about how to use .inf files, see "Working with .inf Files."

Sections of an .inf File

The following table describes the sections of a basic information (.inf) file. More complex .inf files can include additional sections. Section names in bold are reserved keywords. Section names in italic are arbitrary names created by the author of the .inf file.

Section	Description
[Version]	Provides basic version information for validating the .inf file.
[DefaultInstall]	Contains pointers to other sections specifying files to copy and delete, registry updates, .ini file updates, and so on. This section is executed by default.
[OtherInstall]	Uses the same format as the **[DefaultInstall]** section, but must explicitly be called. This section is useful for defining how you want a component to be uninstalled.
[CopyFiles] *[RenFiles]* *[DelFiles]*	Lists the files that you want to copy, rename, and delete.
[UpdateInis] *[UpdateIniFields]*	Specifies updates to .ini files. Links are created in these sections.
[AddReg] *[DelReg]* *[Ini2Reg]*	Specifies registry additions and deletions.
[UpdateCfgSys]	Adds, updates, and renames commands in the Config.sys file.
[UpdateAutoBat]	Specifies commands that manipulate lines in the Autoexec.bat file.
[DestinationDirs]	Specifies the location on the hard disk where a section's files will be copied, deleted, or renamed (for example, Windows or Windows\System).
[SourceDisksNames]	Lists the source disks that contain the source files.
[SourceDisksFiles]	Lists the source files and the source disk for each listed source file.
[Strings]	Lists localizable strings.
[Optional Components]	Lists Install selections that are displayed when the user clicks the **Add or Remove Programs** icon in Control Panel, clicks the **Windows Setup** tab, and then clicks the **Have Disk** button. For situations in which this section is ignored, see the description for this section later in the appendix.

[Version] Section

[Version]

Signature="$Chicago$"

LayoutFile=*filename.inf*

This section defines the standard header for all Microsoft® Windows® .inf files. If you do not use a signature of **$Chicago$**, Windows does not accept the .inf file as belonging to any of the classes of devices recognized by Windows.

The signature string recognition is not case-sensitive. For example, you can type either **$Chicago$** or **$CHICAGO$**.

filename.inf

> The .inf file containing the layout information (source disks and files) required to install the component. This line is optional. If this information is not provided elsewhere, you must list the **[SourceDisksNames]** and **[SourceDisksFiles]** sections in this .inf file.

The following example shows a typical **[Version]** section:

```
[Version]
Signature="$CHICAGO$"
```

[DefaultInstall] and *[OtherInstall]* Sections

[install-section-name]

CopyFiles=*file-list-section[,file-list-section]...*

RenFiles=*file-list-section[,file-list-section]...*

DelFiles=*file-list-section[,file-list-section]...*

UpdateInis=*updateinis-section-name[,updateinis-section-name]...*

UpdateIniFields=*updateinifields-section-name[,updateinifields-section-name]...*

AddReg=*addreg-section-name[,addreg-section-name]...*

DelReg=*delreg-section-name[,delreg-section-name]...*

Ini2Reg=*ini2reg-section-name[,ini2reg-section-name]...*

UpdateCfgSys=*updatecfgsys-section-name*

UpdateAutoBat=*updateautobat-section-name*

The Install sections, **[DefaultInstall]** and *[OtherInstall]*, identify the additional sections in the .inf file that contain installation information for the component. These sections use the same format.

Not all the entries shown in the preceding syntax are needed or required in the Install sections. If you use an entry, it must specify the name of a section in the .inf file. (The **CopyFiles** entry is an exception because you can use the @ symbol along with a file name to copy a single file without specifying a section name.) The section name must consist of printable characters.

You can use only one of each type of entry in an Install section. You can list more than one section name in an entry, but you must precede each additional name with a comma.

install-section-name

> The name of the Install section, which can be **[DefaultInstall]** or *[OtherInstall]* (a name that you specify).
>
> If you name the Install section **[DefaultInstall]**, it will execute when you right-click the .inf file and then click **Install**. This section will also execute when you select an .inf file as the setup option by using the Cabpack Wizard.

The following example shows a typical Install section. It contains **Copyfiles** and **AddReg** entries that identify the sections containing information about which files to install.

```
[MyApplication]
Copyfiles=MyAppWinFiles, MyAppSysFiles, @SRSutil.exe
AddReg=MyAppRegEntries
```

Note that if you rename the **[MyApplication]** section in this example to **[DefaultInstall]**, the section is executed when you right-click the .inf file and then click **Install**.

The **CopyFiles** entry provides a special notation that allows a single file to be copied directly from the command line. You can copy an individual file by adding an @ symbol as a prefix to the file name. The destination for any file that you copy using this notation is the **DefaultDestDir** entry, as defined in *"[DestinationDirs] Section"* later in this appendix.

The following example shows how to copy individual files:

```
CopyFiles=FileSection1,@myfile.txt,@anotherfile.txt,LastSectionName
```

[CopyFiles] Section

[file-list-section]

destination-file-name[, source-file-name][,temporary-file-name][,flag]

[destination-file-name[,source-file-name][, temporary-file-name]][,flag]

This section lists the names of files that you want to copy from a source disk to a destination directory. You must specify the source disk and destination directory associated with each file in other sections of the .inf file.

You can specify the copying of a single file in the **CopyFiles** entry of the Install section without creating a *[CopyFiles]* section. To do this, specify the *file-list-section* name in the **CopyFiles** entry of the Install section and use the @ symbol to force a single-file copy. For an example of the @ symbol in a **CopyFiles** entry, see the previous section. Copying a single file in this way imposes limitations, because you must use the same name for the source and destination file names, and you cannot use a temporary file.

file-list-section

> The section name, which must appear in the **CopyFiles** entry in an Install section of the .inf file.

destination-file-name

> The name of the destination file. If you do not provide a source file name, this name also specifies the source file.

source-file-name

> The name of the source file. If you use the same name for the source and destination files for the file-copy operation, you do not need to include *source-file-name*.

temporary-file-name

> The name of a temporary file for the file-copy operation. The installer copies the source file but gives it the temporary file name. The next time the operating system starts, it renames the temporary file to the destination file name. You might find this useful for copying files to a destination that is currently open or in use by Windows.

flag

> An optional flag used to perform special actions during the installation process. You can use multiple flags by adding the values together to create the combined flag. The following table identifies valid flags.

Value	Meaning
1	Warn if the user attempts to skip the file.
2	Setup-critical: Do not allow the user to skip the file.
4	Ignore version checking and always copy the file. This action will overwrite a newer file.
8	Force a rename operation. The setup program treats a file as if it were in use. This operation occurs only if the file already exists on the user's computer.
16	If the file already exists on the target computer, do not copy it.
32	Suppress the **Version Conflict** dialog box, and do not overwrite newer files.

The following example copies three files:

```
[CopyTheseFilesSec]
file11; copies file11
file21, file22, file23 ; copies file22, temporarily naming it file23
file31, file32 ; copies file32 to file31
```

In this example, you must define all of the source file names in a **[SourceDisksFiles]** section of the .inf file, and you must define the logical disk numbers that appear in that section in a **[SourceDisksNames]** section of the .inf file. For an alternate solution, you can use a Layout.inf file to supply this information.

[RenFiles] Section

[file-list-section]

new-file-name, old-file-name

This section lists the names of files that you want to rename.

file-list-section
> The section name, which must appear in the **RenFiles** entry in an Install section of the .inf file.

new-file-name
> The new name of the file.

old-file-name
> The old name of the file.

The following example renames file42 to file41, file52 to file51, and file62 to file61:

```
[RenameOldFilesSec]
file41, file42
file51, file52
file61, file62
```

In the previous example, you must define all the old file names (file42, file52, and file62) in a **[SourceDisksFiles]** section of the .inf file, and you must define the logical disk numbers that appear in that section in a **[SourceDisksNames]** section of the .inf file.

[DelFiles] Section

[file-list-section]

file-name[,,,flag]

.

.

This section lists the names of files that you want to delete.

file-list-section
> The section name, which must appear in the **Delfiles** entry in an Install section of the .inf file.

file-name
> The file that you want to delete.

flag
> An optional flag used to force Windows to delete the named file if it is in use during the installation process. To instruct Windows to initialize the file-deletion operation in Wininit.ini after the computer has restarted, set the flag value to 1. If a file marked with the flag=1 setting cannot be deleted because it is in use, the computer will restart after the device installation is completed.

> If you do not use the flag=1 setting together with *file-name* and the file is in use when the *[DelFiles]* section executes, it will not be deleted from the computer.

The following example deletes three files:

```
[DeleteOldFilesSec]
file1
file2
file3
```

[UpdateInis] Section

[updateinis-section-name]

ini-file, ini-section, [old-ini-entry], [new-ini-entry], [flags]

.

.

This section replaces, deletes, or adds complete entries in the specified .ini file.

updateinis-section-name
> The section name, which must appear in the **UpdateInis** entry in an Install section of the .inf file.

ini-file
> The name of the .ini file containing the entry to change. This name can be a string or a strings key. A strings key has the form *%strkey%*, where *strkey* is defined in the **[Strings]** section in the .inf file. In either case, you must use a valid file name.

> The .ini file name should include the name of the directory containing the file, but you should specify the directory name as a logical directory identifier (LDID) rather than an actual name. The installer replaces an LDID with the actual name during installation.

> An LDID has the form *%ldid%*, where *ldid* is one of the predefined identifiers or an identifier defined in the **[DestinationDirs]** section. Note that when the constants LDID_BOOT and LDID_BOOTHOST are replaced, the backslash is included in the path. For example, LDID_BOOT can be replaced with C:\. However, in your .inf file, you can either use the backslash character or not. For example, you can use either "%30%boot.ini" or "%30%\boot.ini" to reference Boot.ini in the root directory of the boot drive.

ini-section
> The name of the section containing the entry to change.

old-ini-entry
> An optional entry that usually has the form *Key=Value*.

new-ini-entry
> An optional entry that usually has the form *Key=Value*. Either the key or the value can specify replaceable strings. For example, you could use %String1% as either the key or the value specified in *new-ini-entry*, and define the string that replaces %String1% in the **[Strings]** section of the .inf file. You can use the asterisk (*) wildcard character when specifying the key and value, and it will be interpreted correctly.

flags

Optional action flags that specify the conditions under which *old-ini-entry* is replaced with *new-ini-entry*. The following table identifies valid flags.

Value	Meaning
0	Default. If *old-ini-entry* is present in an .ini file entry, that entry is replaced with *new-ini-entry*. Note that only the keys of *old-ini-entry* and the .inf file entry must match; the value of each entry is ignored. To add *new-ini-entry* to the .ini file unconditionally, set *old-ini-entry* to NULL. To delete *old-ini-entry* from the .ini file unconditionally, set *new-ini-entry* to NULL.
1	If both the key and the value of *old-ini-entry* exist in an .ini file entry, that entry is replaced with *new-ini-entry*. Note that both the key and the value for *old-ini-entry* and the .inf file entry must match so that the replacement can be made. This requirement is in contrast to using an action flag value of 0, where only the keys must match for the replacement to be made.
2	If the key in *old-ini-entry* does not exist in the .ini file, no operation is performed on the .ini file. If the key in *old-ini-entry* exists in an .ini file entry and the key in *new-ini-entry* exists in an .ini file entry, the .ini file entry that matches the key in *new-ini-entry* is deleted. Also, the key of the .ini file entry that matches *old-ini-entry* is replaced with the key in *new-ini-entry*. If the key in *old-ini-entry* exists in an .ini file entry and the key in *new-ini-entry* does not exist in an .ini file entry, an entry is added to the .ini file made up of the key in *new-ini-entry* and the old value. Note that the match of *old-ini-entry* and an .ini file entry is based on the key alone, not the key and the value.
3	Same as a flag value of 2, except matching of *old-ini-entry* and an entry in the .inf file is based on both the key and the value, not just the key.

The following examples illustrate individual entries in an *[UpdateInis]* section of an .inf file:

```
%11%\sample.ini, Section1,, Value1=2 ; adds new entry
%11%\sample.ini, Section2, Value3=*, ; deletes old entry
%11%\sample.ini, Section4, Value5=1, Value5=4 ; replaces old entry
```

The following set of entries in an *[UpdateInis]* section of an .inf file work together to perform operations on the **[Boot]** section of System.ini.

```
system.ini, boot, "comm.drv=*vcoscomm.drv","~CommDrvTemp~=*", 3
system.ini, boot, "comm.drv=*r0dmdcom.drv","~CommDrvTemp~=*", 3
system.ini, boot,,"comm.drv=comm.drv"
system.ini, boot, "~CommDrvTemp~=*","comm.drv=*", 3
```

In the previous set of .inf file entries, the conditionality built into the flags is used to add the entry "comm.drv=comm.drv" to the **[Boot]** section, unless the entries "comm.drv=*vcoscomm.drv" or "comm.drv=*r0dmdcom.drv" exist in the **[Boot]** section. In that case, the existing entry is preserved, and the entry "comm.drv=comm.drv" is not added to the .ini file. In other words, after the four .inf file entries are executed, one "comm.drv=" entry will exist in the **[Boot]** section of the .ini file: "comm.drv=*vcoscomm.drv", "comm.drv=*r0dmdcom.drv", or "comm.drv=comm.drv."

[UpdateIniFields] Section

[updateinifields-section-name]

ini-file, ini-section, profile-name, [old-field], [new-field],[flags]

.

.

This section replaces, adds, and deletes fields in a value of a specified .ini file entry. Unlike the *[UpdateIniFile]* section, the *[UpdateIniFields]* section replaces, adds, or deletes portions of a value in an .ini file entry rather than the whole value.

Any comments in the .ini file entry are removed, because they might no longer apply. When fields in this entry are processed, spaces, tabs, and commas are used as field delimiters. However, a space is used as the separator when the new field is appended to the entry.

updateinifields-section-name

The section name, which must appear in the **UpdateIniFields** entry in an Install section of the .inf file.

ini-file

The name of the .ini file containing the entry to change. For more information about specifying the .ini file name, see the previous section.

ini-section

The name of the .ini file section containing the entry to change.

profile-name

The name of the entry to change.

old-field

The field value to delete.

new-field

The field value to add, if it is not already there.

flags

Optional flags that specify whether to treat *old-field* and *new-field* as if they had a wildcard character and to indicate what separator character to use when appending a new field to an .ini file entry. The following table identifies valid flags.

Value	Meaning
0	Default. When matching fields, treat the * character literally and not as a wildcard character. When adding a new field to an entry, use a blank space as a separator.
1	When matching fields, treat the * character as a wildcard character. When adding a new field to an entry, use a blank space as a separator.
2	When matching fields, treat the * character literally and not as a wildcard character. When adding a new field to an entry, use a comma as a separator.
3	When matching fields, treat the * character as a wildcard character. When adding a new field to an entry, use a comma as a separator.

[AddReg] Section

[addreg-section-name]

reg-root-string, [subkey], [value-name], [flag], [value]

[reg-root-string, [subkey], [value-name], [flag], [value]]

.

.

This section adds subkeys or value names to the registry, optionally setting the value.

addreg-section-name

   The section name, which must appear in the **AddReg** entry in an Install section of the .inf file.

reg-root-string

   The registry root name, which can be one of the following values:

   o   HKCR—Same as HKEY_CLASSES_ROOT

   o   HKCU—Same as HKEY_CURRENT_USER

   o   HKLM—Same as HKEY_LOCAL_MACHINE

   o   HKU—Same as HKEY_USERS

   o   HKR—Uses the value of the *RelativeKeyRoot* entry in the **SetupInstallFromInfSection** function (called by the setup program) as the registry root

subkey

   An optional subkey to set. You can express this subkey, which uses the form *key1\key2\key3...*, as a replaceable string. For example, you could use %Subkey1% and define the string that replaces %Subkey1% in the **[Strings]** section of the .inf file.

value-name

   The optional value name for *subkey*. For a string type, if *value-name* is left empty, the value of the subkey specified in *subkey* is set to a NULL string. Note that you can express *value-name* as a replaceable string. For example, you could use %Valname1% and define the string that replaces %Valname1% in the **[Strings]** section of the .inf file.

flag

    The optional flag that specifies the type of value and whether the registry key is replaced if it already exists. The following table identifies valid flags.

Value	Meaning
0	Default. The value is an ANSI string. Replace the key if it exists.
1	The value is a hexadecimal number. Replace the key if it exists.
2	The value is an ANSI string. Do not replace the key if it exists.
3	The value is a hexadecimal number. Do not replace the key if it exists.

value

    An optional value to set. This value can be either an ANSI string or a number in hexadecimal notation and Intel format. You can use a backslash (\) character to extend any item containing a binary value beyond the 128-byte line maximum. You can also include a string key by using the form *%strkey%* and define *strkey* in the **[Strings]** section of the .inf file. To use a % character in the line, use %%.

    At least two fields are required; however, one can be null (empty). Therefore, when you use this form, you must include at least one comma.

In the following example, the two entries add two value names to the registry. Note that %25% will be expanded to the computer's Windows directory.

```
[MyAppRegEntries]
HKLM,Software\MyApp,ProgramName,,"My Application"
HKLM,Software\MyApp,"Program Location",,"%25%\MyApp.exe"
```

[DelReg] Section

[delreg-section-name]

reg-root-string, subkey, [value-name]

[reg-root-string, subkey, [value-name]]

.

.

This section deletes a subkey or value name from the registry. This section can contain any number of entries. Each entry deletes one subkey or value name from the registry.

delreg-section-name

    The section name, which must appear in the **DelReg** entry in an Install section of this .inf file.

reg-root-string

    The registry root name, which can be one of the following values:

    o   HKCR—Same as HKEY_CLASSES_ROOT

    o   HKCU—Same as HKEY_CURRENT_USER

- o   HKLM—Same as HKEY_LOCAL_MACHINE
- o   HKU—Same as HKEY_USERS
- o   HKR—Uses the value of the *RelativeKeyRoot* entry in the **SetupInstallFromInfSection** function (called by the setup program) as the registry root

subkey
A subkey to delete. You can express the subkey, which uses the form *key1\key2\key3...*, as a replaceable string. For example, you could use %Subkey1% and define the string that replaces %Subkey1% in the **[Strings]** section of the .inf file.

value-name
The optional value name for *subkey*. You can express *value-name* as a replaceable string. For example, you could use %Valname1% and define the string that replaces %Valname1% in the **[Strings]** section of the .inf file.

[Ini2Reg] Section

[ini2reg-section-name]

ini-file, ini-section, [ini-key], reg-root-string, subkey[,flags]

.

.

This section moves lines or sections from an .ini file to the registry, creating or replacing a registry entry under the specified key in the registry.

ini2reg-section-name
The section name, which must appear in the **Ini2Reg** entry in an Install section of the .inf file.

ini-file
The name of the .ini file containing the key to copy. For more information about specifying the .ini file name, see *"[UpdateInis] Section"* earlier in this appendix.

ini-section
The name of the section in the .ini file containing the key to copy.

ini-key
The name of the key in the .ini file to copy to the registry. If *ini-key* is empty, the entire section is transferred to the specified registry key.

reg-root-string
The registry root name, which can be one of the following values:

- o   HKCR—Same as HKEY_CLASSES_ROOT
- o   HKCU—Same as HKEY_CURRENT_USER
- o   HKLM—Same as HKEY_LOCAL_MACHINE
- o   HKU—Same as HKEY_USERS
- o   HKR—Uses the value of the *RelativeKeyRoot* entry in the **SetupInstallFromInfSection** function (called by the setup program) as the registry root

subkey
The subkey that receives the value. This subkey uses the form *key1\key2\key3...*

flags

Flags that indicate whether to delete the key in the .ini file after transfer to the registry and whether to overwrite the value in the registry if the registry key already exists. The following table identifies the valid flags.

Value	Meaning
0	Default. After moving the information in the entry to the registry, do not delete the entry from the .ini file. If the registry subkey already exists, do not replace its current value.
1	After moving the information in the entry to the registry, delete the entry from the .ini file. If the registry subkey already exists, do not replace its current value.
2	After moving the information in the entry to the registry, do not delete the entry from the .ini file. If the registry subkey already exists, replace its current value with the value from the entry in the .ini file.
3	After moving the information in the entry to the registry, delete the .ini entry from the .ini file. If the registry subkey already exists, replace its current value with the value from the entry in the .ini file.

For example, the following code shows the **[Windows]** section in the Win.ini file:

```
[Windows]
CursorBlinkRate=15
```

If a **CursorBlinkRate** subkey does not exist under Control Panel\Desktop, the following entry in an *[Ini2Reg]* section creates the subkey, sets the value of the subkey to 15, and leaves the original line in Win.ini unchanged:

```
win.ini,Windows,CursorBlinkRate,HKCU,"Control Panel\Desktop"
```

If the subkey already exists, the .inf file entry sets the value of the subkey to 15 and leaves the original line in Win.ini unchanged.

[UpdateCfgSys] Section

[updatecfgsys-section-name]

Buffers=*legal-dos-buffer-value*

DelKey=*key*

DevAddDev=*driver-name,configkeyword[,flag][,param-string]*

DevDelete=*device-driver-name*

DevRename=*current-dev-name,new-dev-name*

Files=*legal-dos-files-value*

PrefixPath=*ldid[,ldid]*

RemKey=*key*

Stacks=*dos-stacks-values*

This section contains entries that add, delete, or rename commands in the Config.sys file.

Not all entries shown in the preceding syntax are needed or required. An update configuration section can contain as many **DelKey**, **DevAddDev**, **DevDelete**, **DevRename**, and **RemKey** entries as needed, but you can use the **Buffers**, **Files**, and **Stacks** entries only once in a section. When processing this section, the installer processes all **DevRename** entries first, all **DevDelete** entries second, and all **DevAddDev** entries last.

updatecfgsys-section-name

> The section name, which must appear in the **UpdateConfigSys** entry in an Install section of the .inf file.

Buffers Entry

Buffers=*legal-dos-buffer-value*

This entry sets the number of file buffers. As it does with the **Stacks** entry, the installer compares the existing value with the proposed value and sets the file buffers to the larger of the two values.

legal-dos-buffer-value

> A legal MS-DOS buffer value.

DelKey Entry

DelKey=*key*

This entry causes the command with the specified key to be remarked-out in the Config.sys file. For example, the following .inf file entry causes a Break=on command to be remarked-out in the Config.sys file:

```
DelKey=Break
```

The **DelKey** entry has the same effect as the **RemKey** entry. You can use multiple **DelKey** and/or **RemKey** entries in a section of the .inf file.

key

> The key of the command to be remarked-out in the Config.sys file.

DevAddDev Entry

DevAddDev=*driver-name,configkeyword[,flag][,param-string]*

This entry adds a **device** or **install** command to the Config.sys file.

driver-name

> The name of the driver or executable file to add. The installer validates the file name extension, ensuring that it is .sys or .exe.

configkeyword

> The command name, which can be **device** or **install**.

flag

> An optional placement flag that specifies the location of the **device** or **install** command. The following table identifies valid flags.

Value	Meaning
0	Default. The command is placed at the bottom of the file.
1	The command is placed at the top of the file.

param-string
> Optional command strings, which must be valid for the specified device driver or executable file.

DevDelete Entry

DevDelete=*device-driver-name*

This entry deletes any line containing the specified file name from the Config.sys file.

device-driver-name
> The name of a file or device driver. The installer searches the Config.sys file for the name and deletes any line containing it. Because Microsoft® MS-DOS® does not permit implicit file name extensions in Config.sys, each *device-driver-name* must explicitly specify the file name extension.

In the following example, the **DevDelete** entry in an *[UpdateCfgSys]* section deletes lines 1 and 3 of the Config.sys file, but not line 2:

```
DevDelete=Filename.sys
;; lines in Config.sys
Device=Filename.sys;; line #1
Install=Filename.exe;; line #2
Device=Filename.sys /d:b800 /I:3 ;; line #3
```

DevRename Entry

DevRename=*current-dev-name,new-dev-name*

This entry renames a device driver in the Config.sys file.

current-dev-name
> The name of the device driver or executable file to rename. The installer looks for the name on the right side of a **device** or **install** command in the Config.sys file.

new-dev-name
> The new name for a device driver or executable file.

Files Entry

Files=*legal-dos-files-value*

This entry sets the maximum number of open files in the Config.sys file. As it does with the **Stacks** entry, the installer compares the existing value with the proposed value and sets the maximum number of open files to the larger of the two values.

legal-dos-files-value
> A legal MS-DOS files value.

PrefixPath Entry

PrefixPath=*ldid[,ldid]...*

This entry appends the path associated with the given LDID to the **path** command.

ldid
> An identifier that can be any of the predefined LDID values or a new value defined in the .inf file. For definitions of all the predefined LDID values, see *"[DestinationDirs] Section"* later in this appendix.

RemKey Entry

RemKey=*key*

This entry causes the command with the specified key to be remarked-out in the Config.sys file. For example, the following .inf file entry causes a Break=on command to be remarked-out in the Config.sys file:

```
RemKey=Break
```

The **RemKey** entry has the same effect as the **DelKey** entry. You can use multiple **RemKey** and/or **DelKey** entries in a section of the .inf file.

key

> The key of the command to be remarked-out in the Config.sys file.

Stacks Entry

Stacks=*dos-stacks-values*

This entry sets the number and size of stacks in the Config.sys file. The installer compares the existing value with the proposed value and always sets **Stacks** to the larger of the two values. For example, if the Config.sys file contains **Stacks=9,218** and the .inf file contains **Stacks = 5,256**, the installer sets the new value to **Stacks=9,218**.

dos-stacks-values

> Legal MS-DOS stacks values.

[UpdateAutoBat] Section

[updateautobat-section-name]

CmdAdd=*command-name[,command-parameters]*

CmdDelete=*command-name*

PrefixPath=*ldid[,ldid]*

RemOldPath=*ldid[,ldid]*

TmpDir=*ldid[,subdir]*

UnSet=e*nv-var-name*

This section contains commands that manipulate lines in the Autoexec.bat file.

Not all entry types shown in the preceding syntax are needed or required. The section can contain as many **CmdAdd**, **CmdDelete**, and **UnSet** entries as needed, but you can use the **PrefixPath**, **RemOldPath**, and **TmpDir** entries only once in an .inf file.

The installer processes all **CmdDelete** entries before any **CmdAdd** entries.

updateautobat-section-name

> The section name, which must appear in the **UpdateAutoBat** entry in an Install section of the .inf file.

CmdAdd Entry

CmdAdd=*command-name[,"command-parameters"]*

This entry adds the specified command and optional command parameters to the end of the Autoexec.bat file.

command-name

> The name of an executable file with or without an extension. If the file name is also defined in the **[DestinationDirs]** and **[SourceDisksFiles]** sections of the .inf file, the installer adds the appropriate path to the file name before writing it to the Autoexec.bat file.

command-parameters

> A string enclosed in double-quotation marks or a replaceable string. For example, you could use %String1% or %Myparam%, and define the string that replaces %String1% or %Myparam% in the **[Strings]** section of the .inf file. The installer appends the string to *command-name* before appending the line to the end of the Autoexec.bat file. The format of this line depends on the command-line requirements of the specified executable file.

CmdDelete Entry

CmdDelete=*command-name*

This entry deletes any lines from the Autoexec.bat file that include the specified *command-name*. The installer searches for and deletes any occurrence of the given name that has an extension of .exe, .com, or .bat.

command-name

> The name of an executable file without an extension.

PreflxPath Entry

PrefixPath=*ldid[,ldid]...*

This entry appends the path associated with the specified LDID to the **path** command.

ldid

> An identifier that can be any of the predefined LDID values or a new value defined in the .inf file. For definitions of all the predefined LDID values, see *"[DestinationDirs] Section"* later in this appendix.

RemOldPath Entry

RemOldPath=*ldid[,ldid]*

This entry removes the path associated with the given LDID from the **path** command. For example, if the user installs the new version of Windows into C:\Newwin and has an old copy of Windows in C:\Windows, the following .inf file entry removes C:\Windows from the **path** environmental variable:

```
RemOldPath=10
```

ldid

> An identifier that can be any of the predefined LDID values or a new value defined in the .inf file. For definitions of all the predefined LDID values, see *"[DestinationDirs] Section"* later in this appendix.

TmpDir Entry

TmpDir=*ldid[,subdir]*

This entry creates a temporary directory within the directory identified by the LDID, if it does not already exist.

ldid

An identifier that can be any of the predefined LDID values or a new value defined in the .inf file. For definitions of all the predefined LDID values, see *"[DestinationDirs] Section"* later in this appendix.

subdir

The path name. If the Ldid\Subdir directory does not already exist, it is created.

UnSet Entry

UnSet=*env-var-name*

This entry removes any **set** command that includes the specified environment variable name from the Autoexec.bat file.

env-var-name

The name of an environment variable.

[DestinationDirs] Section

[DestinationDirs]

file-list-section=ldid[, subdir]

.

.

[DefaultDestDir=*ldid[, subdir]]*

The **[DestinationDirs]** section defines the destination directories for the operations specified in *file-list-section* of **CopyFiles**, **RenFiles**, or **DelFiles** entries. Optionally, you can specify a default destination directory for any **CopyFiles**, **RenFiles**, or **DelFiles** entries in the .inf file that are not explicitly named in the **[DestinationDirs]** section.

file-list-section

The name of a **CopyFiles**, **RenFiles**, or **DelFiles** entry. You must also include the **Copyfiles**, **RenFiles**, or **DelFiles** entry in an Install section of the .inf file.

Ldid

The logical disk identifier. The following table identifies valid LDID values.

Value	Meaning
00	Null LDID—can be used to create a new LDID
01	*Source Drive:\pathname*
10	Computer directory (maps to the Windows directory for server-based setup)
11	System directory
12	IOSubsys directory
13	Command directory
17	Inf directory

Value	Meaning
18	Help directory
20	Fonts
21	Viewers
22	VMM32
23	Color directory
24	Root directory of the drive containing the Windows directory
25	Windows directory
26	Guaranteed boot device for Windows (Winboot)
28	Host Winboot
30	Root directory of the boot drive
31	Root directory for host drive of a virtual boot drive

subdir
>The name of the directory within the directory named by LDID as the destination directory.

The optional **DefaultDestDir** entry provides a default destination for any **CopyFiles** entries that use the direct copy (@file name) notation or any **CopyFiles**, **RenFiles**, or **DelFiles** entries not specified in the **[DestinationDirs]** section. If you do not include the optional **DefaultDestDir** entry in a **[DestinationDirs]** section, the default directory is set to LDID_WIN.

The following example sets the destination directory for the **MoveMiniPort** entry to Windows\Iosybsys and sets the default directory for other sections to the Bin folder on the boot drive:

```
[DestinationDirs]
MoveMiniPort=12 ; Destination for MoveMiniPort section is ;
windows\iosubsys
DefaultDestDirs=30,bin ; Direct copies go to boot:\bin
```

[SourceDisksNames] Section

[SourceDisksNames]

disk-ordinal="disk-description",disk-label,disk-serial-number

.

.

This section identifies the source disk(s) that contain the source files for file copy and rename operations.

disk-ordinal
>The unique number that identifies a source disk. If more than one source disk exists, each disk must have a unique ordinal.

disk-description

The string or strings key describing the contents or purpose of the source disk. The installer displays this string to the user to identify the disk. The description is enclosed in double quotation marks.

disk-label

The volume label of the source disk that is set when the source disk is formatted.

disk-serial-number

This unused value must be 0.

The following example identifies one source disk with the disk description specified as a strings key:

```
[SourceDisksNames]
55 = %ID1%, Instd1, 0

[Strings]
ID1="My Application Installation Disk 1"
```

[SourceDisksFiles] Section

[SourceDisksFiles]

file-name=disk-number[,subdir] [,file-size]

```
.

.
```

This section specifies the source files used during installation and the source disks that contain the source files.

file-name

The name of the file on the source disk.

disk-number

The ordinal of the source disk that contains the file. You must define this ordinal in the **[SourceDisksNames]** section, and it must have a value greater than or equal to 1 (zero is not a valid value for *disk-number*).

subdir

An optional subdirectory on the source disk where the file resides. If *subdir* is not specified, the root directory of the source disk is the default.

file-size

An optional entry that specifies the size of the file, in bytes.

The following example shows a **[SourceDisksFiles]** section that identifies a single source file, SRS01.386, on the disk having ordinal 1:

```
[SourceDisksFiles]
SRS01.386 = 1
```

[Strings] Section

[Strings]

strings-key=value

.

.

This section defines one or more strings keys. A *strings key* is a name that represents a string of printable characters. Although the **[Strings]** section is generally the last section in the .inf file, a strings key defined in this section can be used anywhere in the .inf file that the corresponding string would be used. The installer expands the strings key to the specified string and uses it for further processing. You must enclose a strings key in percent signs (%).

The **[Strings]** section makes translation of strings for international markets easier by placing all strings that can be displayed in the user interface in a single section of the .inf file. Strings keys should be used whenever possible.

strings-key
> A unique name consisting of letters and digits.

value
> A string consisting of letters, digits, or other printable characters. If you use the corresponding strings key in an entry that requires double-quotation marks, you must also enclose *value* in double quotation marks.

The following example shows the **[Strings]** section for a sample .inf file:

```
[Strings]
String0="My Application"
String1="My Application Readme File"
String2="CX2590 SCSI Adapter"
```

[Optional Components] Section

[Optional Components]

install-section-name
[install-section-name]

.

.

This section lists Install sections that are displayed when the user clicks **Add or Remove Programs** in Control Panel, clicks the **Windows Setup** tab, and then clicks the **Have Disk** button. The Install sections appear as check boxes in the list.

Note that the **[Optional Components]** section is ignored when you right-click an .inf file and then click **Install** to execute the file. When you use an .inf file in this way, the **[DefaultInstall]** section executes. The **[Optional Components]** section is also ignored if the .inf file is being executed through the **InstallHinfSection** entry-point function in Setupx.dll. When executing an .inf file by using this entry-point function, the Install section specified in the parameter of the entry point is executed.

The Install sections follow the same format as described in *"[DefaultInstall] and [OtherInstall] Sections"* earlier in this appendix. To create the interface in the **Have Disk** dialog box, you can include the following additional keys in an Install section:

OptionDesc=*option-description*

Tip=*tip-description*

InstallDefault=0 | 1

IconIndex=*icon-index*

Parent=*install-section-name*

Needs=*install-section-name, [install-section-name]*

Include=*inf-file, [inf-file]*

option-description
> The string value that displays as the component name in the list box. For example, you could use %String1% and define the string that replaces %String1% in the **[Strings]** section of the .inf file.

tip-description
> The string value that displays in the description box when the user selects the component in the list box. The value has a 255-character limit. For example, you could use %String1% and define the string that replaces %String1% in the **[Strings]** section of the .inf file.

icon-index
> The numeric value that determines the mini-icon that displays next to the component name. The following table identifies valid values for *icon-index*.

0 | 1 (**InstallDefault**)
> A numerical value that identifies whether to install this component by default. A value of 0 equals **No**, and a value of 1 equals **Yes**.

Value	Icon
0	Machine (base and display)
1	Integrated circuit chip
2	Display
3	Network wires
4	Windows flag
5	Mouse
6	Keyboard (3 keys)
7	Phone

Value	Icon
8	Speaker
9	Hard disks
10	Comm connector
11	Diamond (default value)
12	Checked box
13	Unchecked box
14	Printer
15	Net card
16	Same as 0
17	Same as 0 with a sharing hand underneath
18	Unknown (question mark)
19	At work
20	Dimmed check box
21	Dial-up networking
22	Direct cable connection
23	Briefcase
24	Exchange
25	Partial check
26	Accessories group
27	Multimedia group
28	QuickView
29	MSN®
30	Calculator
31	Defrag
32	Generic document
33	DriveSpace®
34	Solitaire
35	HyperTerminal
36	Object Packager

Value	Icon
37	Paint
38	Screen saver
39	WordPad
40	Clipboard Viewer
41	Accessibility
42	Backup
43	Bitmap document
44	Character map
45	Mouse pointers
46	Net Watcher
47	Phone Dialer
48	System Monitor
49	Help book
50	Globe (international settings)
51	Audio compression
52	CD player
53	Windows Media™ Player
54	Sound scheme
55	Video clip
56	Video compression
57	Volume control
58	Musica sound scheme
59	Jungle sound scheme
60	Robotz sound scheme
61	Utopia sound scheme

install-section-name (**Parent**)

The list box displayed in the optional components interface can contain sublevels. If the optional component is a child, *install-section-name* for the **Parent** key defines the Install section that is the parent.

install-section-name (**Needs**)

If this component has dependencies on other components, *install-section-name* defines Install sections that this component requires. If the component is selected, the user will be warned that the component requires the component(s) described in the Install section(s) listed for the **Needs** key.

Note that the Install sections listed for the **Needs** key must be in the same .inf file. However, if dependent components from other .inf files are listed for the **Needs** key, the .inf files must be specified for the **Include** key.

inf-file (**Include**)

Additional .inf files that the setup program must also load into memory when it loads your .inf file. These .inf files contain sections that must be run in addition to the Install sections in your .inf file. The **Needs** key specifies the names of the sections you intend to run in the additional .inf file(s).

The following example shows two **[Optional Components]** sections, with each section specifying additional entries for interface elements and dependencies:

```
[Optional Components]
InstallMyToys
InstallOtherApps


[InstallMyToys]
OptionDesc=%Toys_DESC%
Tip=%Tomytoysys_TIP%
IconIndex=35 ;Phone mini-icon for dialogs
Parent=MailApps
Needs=MSMAIL, MAPI, MicrosoftNetwork
Include=mos.inf, msmail.inf
CopyFiles=MyToysFiles
UpdateInis=MyToysLinks
AddReg=MyToysRegItems


[InstallOtherApps]
OptionDesc=%Other_DESC%
Tip=%Other_TIP%
IconIndex=4 ;Windows mini-icon for dialogs
CopyFiles=OtherFiles
UpdateInis=OtherLinks
AddReg=OtherRegItems
```

```
[Strings]
Toys_DESC="Mail Utilities"
Toys_TIP="Additional utilities for sending and organizing mail"
Other_DESC="Other Helpful Utilities"
Other_TIP="Calculator, disk checker, and performance monitor"
```

Sample .inf File

The following example shows an .inf file that performs a number of different actions:

```
; - Copies files to the Windows, System, Inf, and Help folders.
; - Makes a number of registry entries (including entries that
;   will rename the copied files to long file names).
; - Creates a link on the Help menu.
; - Has an uninstall section that registers the uninstall
;   action in the Add or Remove Programs dialog box in Control Panel.
; - Uses replaceable strings to make localization easy.
[Version]
Signature=$CHICAGO$

[DestinationDirs]
SampleCopy = 24,%PROGRAMF%\Sample
SampleDel = 24,%PROGRAMF%\Sample
SampleWinCopy = 25
SampleSysCopy = 11
SampleINFCopy = 17
sampleHLPCopy = 18

[DefaultInstall]
CopyFiles = SampleCopy, SampleWinCopy, SampleSysCopy, SampleINFCopy,
SampleHLPCopy
AddReg = SampleRegisterApp, SampleRegUninstall, SampleRenameFiles
UpdateInis = SampleAddLinks

[RemoveSample]
DelFiles = SampleWinCopy, SampleSysCopy, SampleINFCopy, SampleHLPCopy
DelReg = SampleUnRegisterApp, SampleRegUninstall
AddReg = SampleRemoveLFNs
UpdateInis = SampleRemoveLinks

[SampleCopy]
sample.bmp

[SampleWinCopy]
sample.exe
```

```
[SampleSysCopy]
sample.dll

[SampleINFCopy]
sample.inf

[SampleHLPCopy]
sample.hlp

[SampleRegisterApp]
;Makes an arbitrary registry entry (for private use of Sample.exe):
HKLM,Software\Sample,Installed,,"1"

[SampleUnRegisterApp]
;Deletes the registry entry (note that this deletes the entire key):
HKLM,Software\Sample

[SampleRegUninstall]
;Adds entry to the Add or Remove Programs dialog box in Control Panel
;to uninstall the program:
HKLM,SOFTWARE\Microsoft\Windows\CurrentVersion\Uninstall\Sample,
"DisplayName",,"Sample Application"
HKLM,SOFTWARE\Microsoft\Windows\CurrentVersion\Uninstall\Sample,
"UninstallString",,"RunDll setupx.dll,InstallHinfSection RemoveSample
4 sample.inf"

[SampleRenameFiles]
;Renames 8.3 file names to long file names:
HKLM,Software\Microsoft\Windows\CurrentVersion\RenameFiles\Sample,,,"%24%\
%PROGRAMF%\Sample"
HKLM,Software\Microsoft\Windows\CurrentVersion\RenameFiles\Sample,
sample.bmp,,"Sample Bitmap.bmp"

[SampleRemoveLFNs]

;Deletes files with long file names during uninstall:
HKLM,Software\Microsoft\Windows\CurrentVersion\DeleteFiles\Sample,,,"%24%\
%PROGRAMF%\Sample"
HKLM,Software\Microsoft\Windows\CurrentVersion\DeleteFiles\Sample,
sample.bmp,,"Sample Bitmap.bmp"

[SampleAddLinks]
;Adds shortcut to Sample.exe on the Start menu:
setup.ini, progman.groups,, "Sample=%SampleFolder%" ;creates folder
setup.ini, Sample,, """%SampleDesc%""", %25%\SAMPLE.EXE" ;creates link

[SampleRemoveLinks]
;Removes shortcut to Sample.exe on the Start menu during uninstall:
setup.ini, progman.groups,, "Sample=%SampleFolder%" ;creates folder
setup.ini, Sample,, """%SampleDesc%""" ;deletes link

[SourceDisksNames]
99 = %DiskName%,Sample,0
```

```
[SourceDisksFiles]
sample.exe = 1,,13456
sample.dll = 1,,20987
sample.bmp = 1,,64098
sample.hlp = 1,,55441
sample.inf = 1,,5687

[Strings]
PROGRAMF = "PROGRA~1"
SampleFolder = "Samples"
SampleDesc = "Sample Application"
DiskName = "Sample Application Installation Disk"
```

Additional Resources

These resources contain additional information and tools related to this chapter.

Related Information Outside the Resource Kit

- *Microsoft® Windows® 98 Resource Kit*
- *Microsoft® Windows® 2000 Server Resource Kit*
- *Microsoft® Windows®XP Professional Resource Kit*

Microsoft Internet Explorer 6 Resource Directory

This appendix contains lists of books, compact discs, and Web sites. These lists provide sources of additional information about Microsoft® Internet Explorer 6 and Internet Tools and about related Microsoft products.

In This Appendix

Books and Compact Discs

Many resources are available to help you administer Internet Explorer and related products. These resources are available from Microsoft Corporation.

Microsoft Internet Explorer 6 Administration Kit

The *Microsoft® Internet Explorer 6 Administration Kit* (IEAK 6) is an indispensable tool for Internet service providers, corporate administrators, and Internet content providers. Find out how to customize, distribute, and maintain Internet Explorer on 32-bit versions of the Microsoft® Windows® platform.

Microsoft Windows XP Professional Resource Kit

The *Microsoft® Windows® XP Professional Resource Kit* provides important information for organizations that plan to deploy this latest version of Windows. Topics include customizing and automating Windows XP Professional installations, managing Windows XP Professional desktops, configuring multimedia components, ensuring interoperability with other operating systems, and developing troubleshooting strategies.

Microsoft Windows 2000 Server Resource Kit

The *Microsoft® Windows® 2000 Server Resource Kit* delivers in-depth operating system information and tools to help you deploy, manage, and support the Windows 2000 Server operating system. This Resource Kit includes an easy-to-navigate book in both online and print formats, as well as important tools and references.

Microsoft Windows NT 4.0 Server Resource Kit

The *Microsoft® Windows NT® 4.0 Server Resource Kit* provides valuable information and tools for deploying and supporting Windows NT 4.0 Server in an organization. This Resource Kit includes many special utilities that add features, enhance functionality, and streamline support for Windows NT 4.0 Server.

Microsoft BackOffice Resource Kit

The *Microsoft® BackOffice® Resource Kit* provides dozens of tools for BackOffice products. It also contains comprehensive resource information about deploying and administering Microsoft Windows NT Server, Microsoft Systems Management Server, Microsoft SQL Server, Microsoft Exchange Server, and Microsoft SNA Server.

Microsoft Office XP Resource Kit

The *Microsoft® Office® XP Resource Kit* brings together the tools, information, and examples that you need to customize and deploy Microsoft Office XP throughout an organization. This Resource Kit provides comprehensive information about deployment strategies, international support, and messaging services. In addition, the Resource Kit tools have been updated to help you configure, secure, and manage your installations more quickly and efficiently.

Microsoft Office 2000 Resource Kit

The *Microsoft® Office 2000 Resource Kit* provides detailed instructions for rolling out, supporting, and optimizing the Office 2000 suite. Topics in this technical reference include deploying Office 2000, supporting and managing Office 2000, and using Office 2000 in a multinational organization. The Resource Kit also includes exclusive tools and utilities designed to help you save time, reduce support costs, and lower the total cost of ownership.

Web Application Development Using Microsoft Visual Interdev 6

Web Application Development Using Microsoft® Visual Interdev® 6 provides detailed instructions and information for developing dynamic Web sites and Web-based applications by using the Microsoft Visual InterDev 6.0 Web development system. Learn about Microsoft's Web application development framework and the tools and technologies that can help you plan and implement your solutions.

Web Sites

Visit the following Web sites for up-to-date information about Internet Explorer and related products.

Microsoft Internet Explorer

The Microsoft Windows Technologies Internet Explorer Web site contains a wealth of information about the product, including access to the Internet Explorer Knowledge Base, product support information, and answers to frequently asked questions. Also, access additional information and tools for Internet Explorer components, including Microsoft® Outlook® Express and Microsoft® Windows Media™ Player. Visit the Microsoft Windows Technologies Internet Explorer Web site at http://www.microsoft.com/windows/ie/.

Microsoft Internet Explorer Administration Kit

The Microsoft Windows Technologies Internet Explorer Administration Kit Web site allows you to download the IEAK 6, Microsoft's latest version of the toolkit for customizing, deploying, and maintaining Internet Explorer. The IEAK has an integrated license agreement, which eliminates the need to sign up and use a customization code to run it. Visit the Microsoft Windows Technologies Internet Explorer Administration Kit Web site at http://www.microsoft.com/windows/ieak/.

Microsoft Windows

The Microsoft Windows Web site provides the latest news and information about the Windows family of products, including the Windows 64-bit and Windows 32-bit versions. Download product add-ons, updates, service packs, and accessories. Also, learn more about these versions of the Windows platform through product demonstrations and partners' resources. Visit the Microsoft Windows Web site at http://www.microsoft.com/windows/.

Microsoft Windows Media Player

The Microsoft Windows Technologies Windows Media Web site provides information about product features and benefits and supplies answers to frequently asked questions. Read the Windows Media Guide and Windows Media Showcase to learn more about Windows Media Player. Visit the Windows Media Technologies Web site at http://www.microsoft.com/windows/windowsmedia/.

Microsoft Office

The Microsoft Office Web site is the definitive source for information about Office programs, enhancements, and product support. From this site, view tours and demos that can help you evaluate the product, and access product documentation, including the *Microsoft® Office® XP Resource Kit*. Visit the Microsoft Office Web site at http://www.microsoft.com/office/.

Microsoft Visual InterDev

The Microsoft Visual InterDev Web site provides the latest product information and tools for the Visual InterDev development environment. Find out how to build database-driven Web applications for Web platform products, Internet Explorer, and IIS. Visit the Microsoft Visual InterDev Web site at http://msdn.microsoft.com/vinterdev/.

Microsoft BackOffice Server

The Microsoft® BackOffice® Server Web site showcases the BackOffice family of servers, including Microsoft Internet Information Server, Index Server, and Windows Terminal Server. From this Web site, review product information about a specific BackOffice server, or visit the site's Solutions Base for comprehensive information about intranet, collaboration, and commerce solutions. Visit the Microsoft BackOffice Server Web site http://www.microsoft.com/backofficeserver/.

Microsoft Windows Update Corporate

The Microsoft Windows Update Corporate Web site provides a comprehensive catalog of program and driver updates, including Windows Update content and Microsoft Windows Hardware Quality Lab (WHQL) logo device drivers, that you can distribute over a corporate network. From this Web site, search the Program Updates catalog and download product fixes, updates, and enhancements, including critical and security updates and management and deployment tools. Also, this Web site provides a history of the program updates that you have downloaded and the location of each update. Visit the Microsoft Windows Update Corporate Web site at http://corporate.windowsupdate.microsoft.com/.

Microsoft Product Support Services

You can use the Microsoft Product Support Services Web site to search the entire Microsoft Knowledge Base, troubleshooting wizards, and downloadable files to find answers to your questions. From this site, review popular Knowledge Base topics, access product newsgroups, or contact Microsoft Product Support Services. Visit the Microsoft Product Support Services Web site at http://support.microsoft.com/directory/.

MSDN

The MSDN® Web site features product and technology information to help you use Microsoft tools and applications. Find out how to bring state-of-the-art Web technology to Internet and intranet sites, and learn how to author for different versions and platforms. Visit the MSDN Web site at http://msdn.microsoft.com/.

Microsoft Internet Services Network

The Microsoft Internet Services Network Web site contains the latest news and information about Microsoft Internet technologies. This Web site is a valuable resource for companies that provide Internet access, Web-hosting, and network services. Visit the Microsoft Internet Services Network Web site at http://www.microsoft.com/isn/.

Microsoft TechNet

The Microsoft TechNet Web site provides comprehensive information for evaluating, implementing, and supporting Microsoft business products. Review up-to-date technical information, including current technical notes, reviewers' guides, background papers, Microsoft product Resource Kits, and the entire Microsoft Knowledge Base. Also, download the latest drivers and service packs for Microsoft products. Visit the Microsoft TechNet Web site at http://www.microsoft.com/technet/.

The Microsoft TechNet Web site also includes a special Security page that provides security bulletins with vital security information for Microsoft products. This page also includes a Hot Topics section that describes security issues that are important to organizations and users. Visit the Security page on the Microsoft TechNet Web site at http://www.microsoft.com/technet/itsolutions/security/.

Microsoft Download Center

The Microsoft Download Center Web site is a portal to the many Microsoft sites that offer you free downloads. This site makes it easy to locate and download software. Search for any Microsoft product by keyword, product name, or category. If the download you are looking for is not in English, choose another language, and the Download Center directs you to the appropriate download page for the selected language. Visit the Microsoft Download Center Web site at http://www.microsoft.com/downloads/.

Microsoft Training & Certification

The Microsoft Training & Certification Web site provides resources to help you get trained and certified on Microsoft products. Read about Microsoft Official Curriculum and choose the courseware format that best suits your training needs. Also, find out about recent exam updates for Microsoft Certified Professional (MCP) credentials and learn about new and upcoming courses for Microsoft products. Visit the Microsoft Training & Certification Web site at http://www.microsoft.com/trainingandservices/.

Microsoft Small Business Services

The Microsoft bCentral Web site provides the tools, resources, and information that your small business needs. You can learn how to create and manage a Web site, and you can access marketing tools that help you advertise on well-known sites, submit to top search engines, target customer audiences, and more. This Web site also includes tools that help you manage and increase your business on the Web, from managing your business finances through a secure online accounting service to tracking sales leads and managing customer information. Visit the Microsoft bCentral Web site at http://www.bcentral.com/.

Microsoft Press

The Microsoft® Press® Web site is the official online bookstore for Microsoft publications. Select from a comprehensive list of titles for Microsoft hardware and software. Visit the Microsoft Press Web site at http://mspress.microsoft.com/.

Glossary

.adm file

A system policy template file that defines the system policies and restrictions that you can set for the desktop, shell, and/or system security. *See also* System Policy.

.cab file

See cabinet (.cab) file.

.inf file

See information (.inf) file.

.ins file

See Internet settings (.ins) file.

Active Desktop

One of the two components installed with Windows Desktop Update. Active Desktop allows users to add active content, such as a stock ticker, to their desktop, taskbar, or folders. Users can also single-click files to run and open them. Active Desktop can be disabled in the Internet Explorer Administration Kit, even if Windows Desktop Update is installed.

ActiveX control

A reusable software component based on Microsoft's ActiveX technology that is used to add interactivity and more functionality, such as animation or a popup menu, to a Web page, applications, and software development tools.

add-on component

A component that is not included in your package, but is one that your users can install after they complete Windows Update Setup for Internet Explorer 6 and Internet Tools.

address

In reference to the Internet, the name of a site that users can connect to, such as www.microsoft.com, or the address of an e-mail recipient, such as name@example.microsoft.com. A typical address starts with a protocol name (such as ftp:// or http://) followed by the name of the organization that maintains the site. The suffix identifies the kind of organization. For example, commercial site addresses often end with .com.

answer file

A text file that scripts the answers for a series of graphical user interface (GUI) dialog boxes. The answer file for Setup, for example, automates the setup process. You can create or modify an answer file in a text editor or through Setup Manager. *See also* unattended Setup.

attached behavior

>A behavior that binds asynchronously to a standard HTML element either through a CSS declaration of the behavior property or procedurally through the **addBehavior** and **removeBehavior** methods. Attached behaviors overwrite the default behavior of the element to which they are attached. *See also* element behavior.

Authenticode

>A technology that makes it possible to identify who has published a piece of software and verify that it has not changed since publication.

automatic configuration

>A process that lets corporate administrators manage and update user settings, system policies, and restrictions for Microsoft Internet Explorer from a central location. A pointer to an automatic-configuration file can be manually set within the browser or by configuring the browser installation using the IEAK.

automatic detection

>A feature in the IEAK, based on Web Proxy AutoDiscovery (WPAD), that enables automatic configuration and automatic proxy to work when a user connects to a network the first time. With automatic detection turned on, the browser is automatically configured when it is started, even if the corporate administrator did not customize the browser. *See also* automatic configuration; automatic proxy; Web Proxy AutoDiscovery (WPAD).

automatic image resizing

>The automatic resizing of larger pictures so that they fit within the dimensions of the browser window.

automatic proxy

>A feature that allows an administrator to configure Internet Explorer so that the browser determines dynamically whether to connect directly to a host or to use a proxy server.

automatic search

>A feature of Internet Explorer that enables users to type a word into the Address bar to search for frequently used pages. Users do not need to remember the exact URLs for these pages.

Automatic Version Synchronization (AVS)

>A technology that automatically checks for updated versions of each Internet Explorer component every time the Internet Explorer Administration Kit (IEAK) is run. Updated components can be downloaded from Microsoft and included in subsequent IEAK packages.

AVS

>*See* Automatic Version Synchronization (AVS).

cabinet (.cab) file

>A single file that stores multiple compressed files. These files are commonly used in software installation and to reduce the file size and the associated download time for Web content.

cache

>An area on the hard disk reserved for storing images, text, and other files that the user previously viewed on the Internet.

certificate

>*See* digital certificate.

certification authority (CA)

An entity responsible for establishing and vouching for the authenticity of public keys belonging to users (end entities) or other certification authorities. Activities of a certification authority can include binding public keys to distinguished names through signed certificates, managing certificate serial numbers, and certificate revocation. *See also* public key.

CMAK

See Connection Manager Administration Kit (CMAK).

code signing

The process of signing a completed Internet Explorer package with a digital certificate. Signing the package requires two steps: obtaining a digital certificate and signing the code. *See also* digital certificate.

Connection Manager

A client dialer used to obtain Internet access. It can be customized with the Connection Manager Administration Kit (CMAK).

Connection Manager Administration Kit (CMAK)

A tool for customizing the appearance and functionality of the Connection Manager.

cookie

A small file that an individual Web site stores on your computer. Web sites can use cookies to maintain information and settings, such as your customization preferences.

corporate administrator

An individual who is responsible for setting up and maintaining computers and applications across a corporation. Administrators also manage user and group accounts, assign passwords and permissions, and help users with networking issues.

custom element

In an HTML document, a user-defined element that has explicit namespaces.

Customization Wizard

See Internet Explorer Customization Wizard.

data binding

The process of associating the objects or controls of an application to a data source, such as a database field. The contents of a control associated with a data source are associated with values from a database.

DHCP

See Dynamic Host Configuration Protocol (DHCP).

DHTML

See Dynamic HTML (DHTML).

Dial-Up Networking (DUN)

A connection to a data communications network using a public-switch telecommunications network rather than a dedicated circuit or other private network.

digital certificate

An electronic certification issued by certification authorities that shows where a program comes from and proves that the installation package has not been altered. Administrators should sign their code with a digital certificate if planning to distribute an Internet Explorer package over the Internet.

digital signature

A means for originators of a message, file, or other digitally encoded information to bind their identity to the information. The process of digitally signing information entails transforming the information, as well as some secret information held by the sender, into a tag called a signature.

DNS

See Domain Name System (DNS).

DNS server

A computer maintained by an ISP that matches IP addresses to host names. Some ISPs provide a specific DNS address.

Document Object Model

A World Wide Web Consortium specification that describes the structure of Dynamic HTML and XML documents in a way that allows them to be manipulated through a Web browser.

domain name

Name of the network connection used by DNS that defines the owner of that organization in a hierarchical format: server.organization.type. For example, www.whitehouse.gov identifies the Web server at the White House, which is part of the U.S. government. In an e-mail address, the domain name is located after the "@" sign.

Domain Name System (DNS)

A set of guidelines and rules developed by the Internet community at large, which allows the use of both domain name addresses (such as bluestem.prairienet.org) and IP addresses (such as 192.12.3.4) to navigate the Internet. The domain name address is used by human users and is automatically translated into the numerical IP address, which is used by packet-routing software.

DUN

See Dial-Up Networking (DUN).

Dynamic Host Configuration Protocol (DHCP)

A TCP/IP protocol that enables a network connected to the Internet to assign a temporary IP address to a host automatically when the host connects to the network. *See also* Transmission Control Protocol/Internet Protocol (TCP/IP); IP address.

Dynamic HTML (DHTML)

A collection of features that extends the capabilities of traditional HTML, giving Web authors more flexibility, design options, and creative control over the appearance and behavior of Web pages. *See also* Hypertext Markup Language (HTML).

element behavior

A behavior that binds to a standard HTML element such that it can never be detached; it is considered an intrinsic part of the element being defined. Element behaviors are used to define new elements. *See also* attached behavior.

encryption

A method for making data indecipherable to protect it from unauthorized viewing or use.

Explorer bar

The left side of the browser where the Search, History, and Favorites lists appear when the user clicks the corresponding buttons on the toolbar. The user can also create a custom Explorer bar, as well as a custom toolbar button to open it.

Favorites

Predefined links to Web sites. Favorites are also known as "bookmarks." Favorites in Internet Explorer can be configured to automatically notify the user when content changes.

gateway

A connection or interchange point that connects two networks that otherwise would be incompatible.

Group Policy

A collection of settings used to define configurations for groups of users and computers. Group Policy is flexible and includes options for registry-based policy settings, security settings, software installation, scripts (during computer startup and shutdown, and to log on and log off), and folder redirection. Administrators use Group Policy to specify options for managed desktop configurations.

hands-free installation

A configuration of Windows Update Setup for Internet Explorer and Internet Tools in which users are not prompted to make decisions but are informed of the installation progress and errors. This option is available only to corporate administrators. *See also* silent installation.

home page

The first page that users see when they start Internet Explorer. Also, the main page of a Web site, which usually contains a main menu or table of contents with links to other pages within the site.

HTML

See Hypertext Markup Language (HTML).

HTML+TIME

See HTML+Timed Interactive Multimedia Extensions (TIME).

HTML+Timed Interactive Multimedia Extensions (TIME)

An Internet Explorer feature that adds timing, media synchronization, and animation support to Web pages.

Hypertext Markup Language (HTML)

A simple markup language used to create and design Web pages. HTML files are simple ASCII text files with codes embedded (indicated by markup tags) to denote formatting and hypertext links.

ICP

See Internet Content Provider (ICP).

IEAK

See Internet Explorer Administration Kit (IEAK).

IIS

See Internet Information Services (IIS).

IMAP

See Internet Message Access Protocol (IMAP).

IMAP server

A server that uses IMAP to provide access to multiple server-side folders. *See also* Internet Message Access Protocol (IMAP); POP3 server.

independent software vendor (ISV)

A third-party software developer; an individual or an organization that independently creates computer software.

information (.inf) file

A file that provides Windows Update Setup for Internet Explorer and Internet Tools with the information required to set up a device or program. The file includes a list of valid configurations, the name of driver files associated with the device or program, and so on.

Input Method Editor (IME)

Programs used to enter the thousands of different characters in written Asian languages with a standard 101-key keyboard. An IME consists of both an engine that converts keystrokes into phonetic and ideographic characters and a dictionary of commonly used ideographic words.

Integrated Windows Authentication

A secure authentication method that uses a cryptographic exchange between a client and a server rather than transmitting a user name and a password to determine the client's authentication.

Internet Content Provider (ICP)

An organization that prepares content for posting to the Web.

Internet Explorer Administration Kit (IEAK)

A set of tools that enables corporate administrators, ISPs, and ICPs to create, distribute, and manage customized Internet Explorer packages across an organization. The IEAK contains the Internet Explorer Customization Wizard, the IEAK Profile Manager, and the IEAK Toolkit.

Internet Explorer Customization Wizard

The primary component of the Internet Explorer Administration Kit (IEAK), used to generate a customized version of Internet Explorer for installation in a specific organization.

Internet Information Services (IIS)

Software services that support Web site creation, configuration, and management, along with other Internet functions. Internet Information Services include Network News Transfer Protocol (NNTP), File Transfer Protocol (FTP), and Simple Mail Transfer Protocol (SMTP). *See also* Network News Transfer Protocol (NNTP).

Internet Message Access Protocol (IMAP)

A popular protocol for receiving e-mail messages. It allows an e-mail client to access and manipulate a remote e-mail file without downloading it to the local computer. It is used mainly by corporate users who want to read their e-mail from a remote location. *See also* POP3 (Post Office Protocol 3).

Internet Protocol (IP)

A routable protocol in the TCP/IP protocol suite that is responsible for IP addressing, routing, and the fragmentation and reassembly of IP packets. *See also* Transmission Control Protocol/Internet Protocol (TCP/IP).

Internet Protocol address (IP address)

A 32-bit binary number used to identify a node on an IP internetwork. Each node must be assigned a unique IP address, which is made up of the network ID, plus a unique host ID. This address consists of the decimal values of its 4 bytes, separated with periods (for example, 192.168.7.27).

Internet service provider (ISP)

An organization that maintains a server directly connected to the Internet. Users who are not directly connected to the Internet typically connect through a service provider. To acquire these connections, users call the provider and set up an account.

Internet settings (.ins) file

A file that provides Windows Update Setup for Internet Explorer and Internet Tools with Internet settings that configure the browser and associated components. You can create multiple versions of your browser package by changing the .ins file used by each package. Use the Profile Manager to create, save, and load .ins files.

IP address

See Internet Protocol address (IP address).

ISP

See Internet service provider (ISP).

ISV

See independent software vendor (ISV).

Kerberos authentication

A protocol that provides a mechanism for mutual authentication between a client and a server before a network connection is opened between them. The protocol assumes that initial transactions between clients and servers take place on an open network.

kiosk mode

A browser mode in which the browser toolbar and menu bar are not displayed.

lab

A collection of non-production machines used to test an Internet Explorer package. The lab is not the same as a pilot group.

LDAP

See Lightweight Directory Access Protocol (LDAP).

Lightweight Directory Access Protocol (LDAP)

An open standard for storing and retrieving people's names, e-mail addresses, phone numbers, and other information.

lightweight HTML component

An HTML component in which the lightweight attribute is signified for the PUBLIC:COMPONENT element. Because the .htc files for this component contain no HTML content or contain static HTML content that is ignored, the HTML document is less complex.

Media bar

In Internet Explorer, an Explorer bar that provides a simple user interface for locating and playing media within the browser window.

MIME

See Multipurpose Internet Mail Extensions (MIME).

MSDN

Microsoft Developer Network.

Multipurpose Internet Mail Extensions (MIME)

A standard that extends SMTP to allow the transmission of such data as video, sound, and binary files across the Internet without translating the data into ASCII format. *See also* SMTP (Simple Mail Transfer Protocol).

namespace

A collection of names that are used to uniquely qualify elements.

Network News Transfer Protocol (NNTP)

A member of the TCP/IP suite of protocols used to distribute network news messages to NNTP servers and clients (newsreaders) on the Internet. NNTP is designed so that news articles are stored on a server in a central database, thus enabling a user to select specific items to read. *See also* Transmission Control Protocol/Internet Protocol (TCP/IP).

NNTP

See Network News Transfer Protocol (NNTP).

Parental Internet Content Selection (PICS)

Rules that enable Web content providers to use meta tags to voluntarily rate their content according to agreed-upon PICS criteria. A browser can then block user access to Web sites based on the values of the tags.

PICS

See Parental Internet Content Selection (PICS).

platform

A type of client, such as Windows 2000, Windows NT 4.0, Windows Millennium Edition, Windows 98, Windows 3.*x*, Macintosh, or UNIX.

policy file

A file that defines system policies and restrictions. *See also* system policies and restrictions.

POP3 (Post Office Protocol 3)

A popular protocol used for receiving e-mail messages. This protocol is often used by ISPs. POP3 servers allow access to a single Inbox in contrast to IMAP servers, which provide access to multiple server-side folders. *See also* SMTP (Simple Mail Transfer Protocol); Internet Message Access Protocol (IMAP).

POP3 server

A server that provides access to a single Inbox. *See also* IMAP server.

private key

The secret half of a cryptographic key pair that is used with a public key algorithm. Private keys are typically used to decrypt a symmetric session key, digitally sign data, or decrypt data that has been encrypted with the corresponding public key. *See also* public key.

Profile Manager

A tool in the Internet Explorer Administration Kit (IEAK) used by corporate administrators to create and dynamically manage browser and desktop automatic configuration settings.

proxy

A firewall and content cache server that provides Internet security and improves network performance.

proxy server

A server that works as a barrier between an internal network (intranet) and the Internet. Proxy servers can work with firewalls, which help keep other people on the Internet from gaining access to confidential information on the intranet. A proxy server also allows the caching of Web pages for quicker retrieval.

public key

The nonsecret half of a cryptographic key pair that is used with a public key algorithm. Public keys are typically used when encrypting a session key, verifying a digital signature, or encrypting data that can be decrypted with the corresponding private key. *See also* private key.

quiet mode

The state in which a command-line application runs with little or no input from the user.

registry

A database repository for information about a computer's configuration. The registry contains information that Windows continually references during operation, such as:

o   Profiles for each user.

o   The programs installed on the computer and the types of documents each can create.

o   Property settings for folders and program icons.

o   What hardware exists on the system.

o   Which ports are being used.

The registry is organized hierarchically as a tree and is made up of keys and their subkeys, hives, and value entries.

registry key

An identifier for a record or group of records in the registry.

Resultant Set of Policy (RSoP)

An IEAK snap-in that helps you plan browser policies before you deploy your custom browser packages.

root certificate

A self-signed certification authority certificate. *See also* certification authority (CA); digital certificate.

RSoP

See Resultant Set of Policy (RSoP).

RunOnce application

An application that is configured to run the next time the computer is restarted. The application does not run after any subsequent reboots of the system.

sandbox

In Java, an area in memory outside of which the program cannot make calls.

scratch space

The storage area on the client computer that an applet can safely access without needing full access to the client file system.

Secure Password Authentication (SPA)

A protocol where the server uses an encrypted password to confirm the identity of the user.

Secure Sockets Layer (SSL)

A protocol that supplies secure data communication through data encryption and decryption. This protocol enables communications privacy over networks through a combination of public-key cryptography and bulk data encryption.

security zone

In Internet Explorer, a segment of the Internet or intranet assigned a particular level of security, depending on how much the administrator trusts the content of the Web site. Security zones allow an administrator to restrict user access to certain Web sites.

Seek bar

A control on the Media bar that allows the user to view and change the progress of a media file while it is playing.

Server Gated Cryptography (SGC)

An extension of Secure Sockets Layer (SSL) that makes possible the use of 128-bit encryption. *See also* Secure Sockets Layer (SSL).

SGC

See Server Gated Cryptography (SGC).

signature

See digital signature.

silent installation

A configuration of Windows Update Setup for Internet Explorer and Internet Tools in which users are not prompted to make decisions about installation options and are not informed of the installation progress or errors. This option is available only to corporate administrators. *See also* hands-free installation.

single-disk branding

Customizing an existing installation of Internet Explorer, including Internet sign-up for ISPs, without reinstalling Internet Explorer. This option does not enable you to package and install custom components.

SMTP (Simple Mail Transfer Protocol)

A protocol used for transferring or sending e-mail messages between servers. Another protocol (such as POP3) is used to retrieve the messages.

SSL

See Secure Sockets Layer (SSL).

subkey

An element of the registry that contains entries or other subkeys. A tier of the registry that is immediately below a key or a subtree (if the subtree has no keys).

System Management Server (SMS)

Systems management software that can help you automate a large-scale deployment by automatically distributing and installing your custom browser packages on users' computers.

system policies and restrictions

Settings, defined in a policy file, that control user and computer access privileges by overriding default registry values when the user logs on.

System Policy

A Windows NT 4.0-style policy based on registry settings made using Poledit.exe, the System Policy Editor. *See also* registry.

System Policy Editor

The utility Poledit.exe, used by administrators to set system policy on Windows NT 4.0-based and Windows 95-based computers.

TCP/IP

See Transmission Control Protocol/Internet Protocol (TCP/IP).

Transmission Control Protocol/Internet Protocol (TCP/IP)

A set of networking protocols widely used on the Internet that provides communications across interconnected networks of computers with diverse hardware architectures and various operating systems. TCP/IP includes standards for how computers communicate and conventions for connecting networks and routing traffic. *See also* Internet Protocol (IP).

unattended Setup

An automated, hands-free method of installing Windows. During installation, unattended Setup uses an answer file to supply data to Setup instead of requiring that an administrator interactively provide the answers.

user-agent string

Text that identifies the specific version and origin of the browser.

Viewlink

A feature of the DHTML behavior component model that enables you to write fully encapsulated element behaviors and then import them as custom elements in Web pages.

virtual machine (VM)

A program that provides an independent operating system environment within another operating system. A virtual machine permits the user to run programs that are native to a different operating system.

VM

See virtual machine (VM).

watermark

A bitmap that is displayed behind the Internet Explorer toolbar. Color the watermark so that it does not obscure the text or graphics of toolbar buttons.

Web Proxy AutoDiscovery (WPAD)

A standard networking protocol used to help Internet client software automatically locate and interface with cache services within a network.

Welcome page

The page displayed the first time the user runs Internet Explorer. Subsequently, Internet Explorer displays the user's home page each time the user starts the browser.

Windows Desktop Update

A feature included in Windows 98, Windows 98 Second Edition, Windows Millennium Edition, Windows 2000, and Windows XP that can be used to make users' desktop and folders look and work more like the Web.

Windows Update Setup for Internet Explorer 6 and Internet Tools

The setup program that installs Internet Explorer and other Internet components. The IEAK allows you to customize Windows Update Setup for Internet Explorer and Internet Tools to provide a better experience for your users.

Index

B

C

D

M

proxy servers

    accessing FTP sites 231

    bypassing 230

    importing from Netscape Navigator 183

    network performance issues 191

    overview 228

    security issues 191

    setting up using the Customization Wizard 229

    setting with Customization Wizard 274

    specifying the URL for the auto-proxy script 274

    troubleshooting, connecting to the Internet 379

    using with firewalls 329

    using with security zones 37

    verifying the address in the browser 379

    viewing settings in the browser 229

    See also Proxy settings

proxy settings

    configuring automatically 329, 335

    configuring in the browser 330

    configuring in the Customization Wizard 229

    exceptions for complex addresses 231

    limiting access to the Internet 329

    local domain, bypassing the proxy 231

    protocol values in proxy bypass entries 231

    registry settings 230

    secure setting for HTTPS requests 229

    syntax for specifying proxy locations 229

    using the proxy bypass list 230

    using wildcards 231

    verifying the proxy server address 379

    viewing in the browser 229

public key cryptography

    illustration of encryption and decryption 60

    overview of digital certificates 60

publications for training and support, providing 350

Publications Web site (Microsoft Press) 490

publishers of software

    adding trusted publishers and certification authorities 69

    certificate revocation 66

    certificates, described 62

.pwl files

    in setup files 461

Q

/Q switch 406, 407

/QA switch 407

/QU switch 407

Quick Launch toolbar, keyboard navigation 136

Quick Links toolbar, keyboard navigation 137

Quiet mode *See* Silent installation

R

/R switch 407

Radio, Internet Explorer 435

RAM requirements 179

RAS connections *See* remote-access connections, remote dialing

rating systems, importing 56

ratings *See* content ratings

ratings bureau, specifying 57

readability

    creating a style sheet for high visibility 144

    high-contrast color scheme 147

    See also accessibility

Readme file for users on CD Autorun screen 201

readme.txt files for Internet Explorer 352

RealAudio 151

reasons to customize Internet Explorer 165

reboot modes 217

Reboot section, batch file entries 404

reboot suppression

    using a batch file 404

    using command-line switches 407

    using IExpress switches 407

rebooting the computer after setup

    using a batch file 404

    using command-line switches 407

    using IExpress switches 407

RebootPartial section, batch file entries 404

rebuilding custom packages

    building multiple packages efficiently 295

    using multiple .ins files 293

X

Z

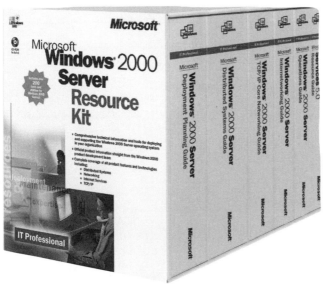

Ready solutions for the
IT administrator

Keep your IT systems up and running with the ADMINISTRATOR'S COMPANION series from Microsoft. These expert guides serve as both tutorials and references for critical deployment and maintenance of Microsoft products and technologies. Packed with real-world expertise, hands-on numbered procedures, and handy workarounds, ADMINISTRATOR'S COMPANIONS deliver ready answers for on-the-job results.

In-depth. Focused. *And* ready for work.

Get the technical drilldown you need to deploy and support Microsoft products more effectively with the MICROSOFT TECHNICAL REFERENCE series. Each guide focuses on a specific aspect of the technology—weaving in-depth detail with on-the-job scenarios and practical how-to information for the IT professional. Get focused—and take technology to its limits—with MICROSOFT TECHNICAL REFERENCES.

Data Warehousing with Microsoft® SQL Server™ 7.0 Technical Reference
U.S.A. $49.99
Canada $76.99
ISBN 0-7356-0859-8

Microsoft SQL Server 7.0 Performance Tuning Technical Reference
U.S.A. $49.99
Canada $76.99
ISBN 0-7356-0909-8

Building Applications with Microsoft Outlook® 2000 Technical Reference
U.S.A. $49.99
Canada $72.99
ISBN 0-7356-0581-5

Microsoft Windows NT® Server 4.0 Terminal Server Edition Technical Reference
U.S.A. $49.99
Canada $72.99
ISBN 0-7356-0645-5

Microsoft Windows® 2000 TCP/IP Protocols and Services Technical Reference
U.S.A. $49.99
Canada $76.99
ISBN 0-7356-0556-4

Active Directory™ Services for Microsoft Windows 2000 Technical Reference
U.S.A. $49.99
Canada $76.99
ISBN 0-7356-0624-2

Microsoft Windows 2000 Security Technical Reference
U.S.A. $49.99
Canada $72.99
ISBN 0-7356-0858-X

Microsoft Windows 2000 Performance Tuning Technical Reference
U.S.A. $49.99
Canada $72.99
ISBN 0-7356-0633-1

Microsoft®
mspress.microsoft.com

For the skills you need on the job. And on the MCP exam.

Learn by doing—learn for the job—with official MCSE TRAINING KITS. Whether you choose a book-and-CD Training Kit or the all-multimedia learning experience of an Online Training Kit, you'll gain hands-on experience building essential systems support skills—as you prepare for the corresponding MCP exam. It's official Microsoft self-paced training—how, when, and where you study best.

Windows 2000 Track

MCSE Training Kit, Microsoft® Windows® 2000 Core Requirements
ISBN 0-7356-1130-0

MCSE Training Kit, Microsoft Windows 2000 Server
ISBN 1-57231-903-8

MCSE Online Training Kit, Microsoft Windows 2000 Server
ISBN 0-7356-0954-3
COMING SOON

MCSE Training Kit, Microsoft Windows 2000 Professional
ISBN 1-57231-901-1

MCSE Online Training Kit, Microsoft Windows 2000 Professional
ISBN 0-7356-0953-5
COMING SOON

MCSE Training Kit, Microsoft Windows 2000 Active Directory™ Services
ISBN 0-7356-0999-3

MCSE Training Kit, Microsoft Windows 2000 Network Infrastructure Administration
ISBN 1-57231-904-6

Upgrading to Microsoft Windows 2000 Training Kit
ISBN 0-7356-0940-3

Microsoft SQL Server™ 7.0 System Administration Online Training Kit
ISBN 0-7356-0678-1

Windows NT® 4.0 Track

Microsoft Certified Systems Engineer Core Requirements Training Kit
ISBN 1-57231-905-4

MCSE Training Kit, Networking Essentials Plus, Third Edition
ISBN 1-57231-902-X

MCSE Online Training Kit, Networking Essentials Plus
ISBN 0-7356-0880-6

Electives

Microsoft SQL Server 7.0 Database Implementation Training Kit
ISBN 1-57231-826-0

Microsoft SQL Server 7.0 Database Implementation Online Training Kit
ISBN 0-7356-0679-X

Microsoft SQL Server 7.0 System Administration Training Kit
ISBN 1-57231-827-9

Microsoft®
mspress.microsoft.com

MICROSOFT LICENSE AGREEMENT
Microsoft Internet Explorer 6 Resource Kit CD

IMPORTANT—READ CAREFULLY: This Microsoft End-User License Agreement ("EULA") is a legal agreement between you (either an individual or an entity) and Microsoft Corporation for the Microsoft product identified above, which includes computer software and may include associated media, printed materials, and "on-line" or electronic documentation ("SOFTWARE PRODUCT"). Any component included within the SOFTWARE PRODUCT that is accompanied by a separate End-User License Agreement shall be governed by such agreement and not the terms set forth below. By installing, copying, or otherwise using the SOFTWARE PRODUCT, you agree to be bound by the terms of this EULA. If you do not agree to the terms of this EULA, you are not authorized to install, copy, or otherwise use the SOFTWARE PRODUCT; you may, however, return the SOFTWARE PRODUCT, along with all printed materials and other items that form a part of the Microsoft product that includes the SOFTWARE PRODUCT, to the place you obtained them for a full refund.

THIS SOFTWARE PRODUCT MAY INCLUDE, WITHOUT LIMITATION, INTERNET EXPLORER 6, OUTLOOK EXPRESS, WINDOWS MEDIA PLAYER, WINDOWS NT 4.0 SERVICE PACK 6A AND THE INTERNET EXPLORER ADMINISTRATION KIT ("COMPONENTS"). AS INDICTED ABOVE, IF ANY COMPONENT IS ACCOMPANIED BY A SEPARATE END USER LICENSE AGREEMENT, THEN THE COMPONENT SHALL BE GOVERNED BY THE TERMS OF SUCH AGREEMENT.

SOFTWARE PRODUCT LICENSE

The SOFTWARE PRODUCT is protected by United States copyright laws and international copyright treaties, as well as other intellectual property laws and treaties. The SOFTWARE PRODUCT is licensed, not sold.

1. GRANT OF LICENSE. This EULA grants you the following rights:

a. **Software Product.** You may install and use one copy of the SOFTWARE PRODUCT on a single computer. The primary user of the computer on which the SOFTWARE PRODUCT is installed may make a second copy for his or her exclusive use on a portable computer.

b. **Storage/Network Use.** You may also store or install a copy of the SOFTWARE PRODUCT on a storage device, such as a network server, used only to install or run the SOFTWARE PRODUCT on your other computers over an internal network; however, you must acquire and dedicate a license for each separate computer on which the SOFTWARE PRODUCT is installed or run from the storage device. A license for the SOFTWARE PRODUCT may not be shared or used concurrently on different computers.

c. **Sample Code.** Solely with respect to portions, if any, of the SOFTWARE PRODUCT that are identified within the SOFTWARE PRODUCT as sample code (the "SAMPLE CODE"):

  i. **Use and Modification.** Microsoft grants you the right to use and modify the source code version of the SAMPLE CODE, provided you comply with subsection (d)(iii) below. You may not distribute the SAMPLE CODE, or any modified version of the SAMPLE CODE, in source code form.

  ii. **Redistributable Files.** Provided you comply with subsection (d)(iii) below, Microsoft grants you a nonexclusive, royalty-free right to reproduce and distribute the object code version of the SAMPLE CODE and of any modified SAMPLE CODE, other than SAMPLE CODE (or any modified version thereof) designated as not redistributable in the Readme file that forms a part of the SOFTWARE PRODUCT (the "Non-Redistributable Sample Code"). All SAMPLE CODE other than the Non-Redistributable Sample Code is collectively referred to as the "REDISTRIBUTABLES."

  iii. **Redistribution Requirements.** If you redistribute the REDISTRIBUTABLES, you agree to: (i) distribute the REDISTRIBUTABLES in object code form only in conjunction with and as a part of your software application product; (ii) not use Microsoft's name, logo, or trademarks to market your software application product; (iii) include a valid copyright notice on your software application product; (iv) indemnify, hold harmless, and defend Microsoft from and against any claims or lawsuits, including attorney's fees, that arise or result from the use or distribution of your software application product; and (v) not permit further distribution of the REDISTRIBUTABLES by your end user. Contact Microsoft for the applicable royalties due and other licensing terms for all other uses and/or distribution of the REDISTRIBUTABLES.

2. DESCRIPTION OF OTHER RIGHTS AND LIMITATIONS.

  • **Limitations on Reverse Engineering, Decompilation, and Disassembly.** You may not reverse engineer, decompile, or disassemble the SOFTWARE PRODUCT, except and only to the extent that such activity is expressly permitted by applicable law notwithstanding this limitation.

  • **Separation of Components.** The SOFTWARE PRODUCT is licensed as a single product. Its component parts may not be separated for use on more than one computer.

- **Rental.** You may not rent, lease, or lend the SOFTWARE PRODUCT.

- **Support Services.** Microsoft may, but is not obligated to, provide you with support services related to the SOFTWARE PRODUCT ("Support Services"). Use of Support Services is governed by the Microsoft policies and programs described in the user manual, in "on-line" documentation, and/or in other Microsoft-provided materials. Any supplemental software code provided to you as part of the Support Services shall be considered part of the SOFTWARE PRODUCT and subject to the terms and conditions of this EULA. With respect to technical information you provide to Microsoft as part of the Support Services, Microsoft may use such information for its business purposes, including for product support and development. Microsoft will not utilize such technical information in a form that personally identifies you.

- **Software Transfer.** You may permanently transfer all of your rights under this EULA, provided you retain no copies, you transfer all of the SOFTWARE PRODUCT (including all component parts, the media and printed materials, any upgrades, this EULA, and, if applicable, the Certificate of Authenticity), and the recipient agrees to the terms of this EULA.

- **Termination.** Without prejudice to any other rights, Microsoft may terminate this EULA if you fail to comply with the terms and conditions of this EULA. In such event, you must destroy all copies of the SOFTWARE PRODUCT and all of its component parts.

- **Reservation of Rights.** Microsoft reserves all rights not expressly granted to you in this EULA.

3. **COPYRIGHT.** All title and copyrights in and to the SOFTWARE PRODUCT (including but not limited to any images, photographs, animations, video, audio, music, text, SAMPLE CODE, REDISTRIBUTABLES, and "applets" incorporated into the SOFTWARE PRODUCT) and any copies of the SOFTWARE PRODUCT are owned by Microsoft or its suppliers. The SOFT-WARE PRODUCT is protected by copyright laws and international treaty provisions. Therefore, you must treat the SOFTWARE PRODUCT like any other copyrighted material except that you may install the SOFTWARE PRODUCT on a single computer provided you keep the original solely for backup or archival purposes. You may not copy the printed materials accompanying the SOFTWARE PRODUCT.

4. **U.S. GOVERNMENT RESTRICTED RIGHTS.** All Product provided to the U.S. Government pursuant to solicitations issued on or after December 1, 1995 is provided with the commercial license rights and restrictions described elsewhere herein. All Product provided to the U.S. Government pursuant to solicitations issued prior to December 1, 1995 is provided with "Restricted Rights" as provided for in FAR, 48 CFR 52.227-14 (JUNE 1987) or DFAR, 48 CFR 252.227-7013 (OCT 1988), as applicable.

5. **EXPORT RESTRICTIONS.** You acknowledge that the Software Product is subject to U.S. export jurisdiction. You agree to comply with all applicable international and national laws that apply to the Software Product, including the U.S. Export Administration Regulations, as well as end-user, end-use and destination restrictions issued by U.S. and other governments. For additional information, see http://www.microsoft.com/exporting/.

6. **APPLICABLE LAW.** If you acquired this Product in the United States, this EULA is governed by the laws of the State of Washington. If you acquired this Product in Canada, unless expressly prohibited by local law, this EULA is governed by the laws in force in the Province of Ontario, Canada; and, in respect of any dispute which may arise hereunder, you consent to the jurisdiction of the federal and provincial courts sitting in Toronto, Ontario. If this Product was acquired outside the United States, then local law may apply.

DISCLAIMER OF WARRANTY

DISCLAIMER OF WARRANTIES. TO THE MAXIMUM EXTENT PERMITTED BY APPLICABLE LAW, MICROSOFT AND ITS SUPPLIERS PROVIDE TO YOU THE PRODUCT, AND ANY (IF ANY) SUPPORT SERVICES RELATED TO THE SOFTWARE PRODUCT ("SUPPORT SERVICES") *AS IS AND WITH ALL FAULTS;* AND MICROSOFT AND ITS SUPPLIERS HEREBY DISCLAIM WITH RESPECT TO THE SOFTWARE PRODUCT AND SUPPORT SERVICES ALL WARRANTIES AND CONDI-TIONS, WHETHER EXPRESS, IMPLIED OR STATUTORY, INCLUDING, BUT NOT LIMITED TO, ANY (IF ANY) WARRAN-TIES, DUTIES OR CONDITIONS OF OR RELATED TO: MERCHANTABILITY, FITNESS FOR A PARTICULAR PURPOSE, LACK OF VIRUSES, ACCURACY OR COMPLETENESS OF RESPONSES, RESULTS, WORKMANLIKE EFFORT AND LACK OF NEGLIGENCE. ALSO THERE IS NO WARRANTY, DUTY OR CONDITION OF TITLE, QUIET ENJOYMENT, QUIET POSSESSION, CORRESPONDENCE TO DESCRIPTION OR NON-INFRINGEMENT. THE ENTIRE RISK ARISING OUT OF USE OR PERFORMANCE OF THE SOFTWARE PRODUCT AND ANY SUPPORT SERVICES REMAINS WITH YOU.

LIMITATION OF LIABILITY. NOTWITHSTANDING ANY DAMAGES THAT YOU MIGHT INCUR FOR ANY REASON WHATSOEVER (INCLUDING, WITHOUT LIMITATION, ALL DAMAGES REFERENCED ABOVE AND ALL DIRECT OR GENERAL DAMAGES), THE ENTIRE LIABILITY OF MICROSOFT AND ANY OF ITS SUPPLIERS UNDER ANY PROVISION OF THIS EULA AND YOUR EXCLUSIVE REMEDY FOR ALL OF THE FOREGOING SHALL BE LIMITED TO ACTUAL DAMAGES INCURRED BY YOU BASED ON REASONABLE RELIANCE UP TO THE GREATER OF THE AMOUNT ACTU-ALLY PAID BY YOU FOR THE PRODUCT OR U.S.$5.00. THE FOREGOING LIMITATIONS, EXCLUSIONS AND DISCLAIM-ERS SHALL APPLY TO THE MAXIMUM EXTENT PERMITTED BY APPLICABLE LAW, EVEN IF ANY REMEDY FAILS ITS ESSENTIAL PURPOSE.

Should you have any questions concerning this EULA, or if you desire to contact Microsoft for any reason, please contact the Microsoft subsidiary serving your country, or write: Microsoft Sales Information Center/One Microsoft Way/Redmond, WA 98052-6399.

Get a **Free**
e-mail newsletter, updates,
special offers, links to related books,
and more when you
register on line!

Register your Microsoft Press® title on our Web site and you'll get a FREE subscription to our e-mail newsletter, *Microsoft Press Book Connections.* You'll find out about newly released and upcoming books and learning tools, online events, software downloads, special offers and coupons for Microsoft Press customers, and information about major Microsoft® product releases. You can also read useful additional information about all the titles we publish, such as detailed book descriptions, tables of contents and indexes, sample chapters, links to related books and book series, author biographies, and reviews by other customers.

Registration is easy. Just visit this Web page and fill in your information:

http://www.microsoft.com/mspress/register

Microsoft®

- -

Proof of Purchase

Use this page as proof of purchase if participating in a promotion or rebate offer on this title. Proof of purchase must be used in conjunction with other proof(s) of payment such as your dated sales receipt—see offer details.

Microsoft® Internet Explorer 6 Resource Kit
0-7356-1401-6

CUSTOMER NAME

Microsoft Press, PO Box 97017, Redmond, WA 98073-9830

System Requirements

To use the Microsoft Internet Explorer 6 Resource Kit CD-ROM, you need a computer equipped with the following minimum configuration:

- PC with Pentium-compatible 486/66-MHz or higher processor

- Microsoft Windows 98, Microsoft Windows NT 4.0 Service Pack6a, or later operating system

- CD-ROM drive

- Microsoft Mouse or compatible pointing device

Requirements for Internet Explorer 6, minimal installation on Windows 32-bit operating systems

Operating system	Processor	Minimum memory (RAM)	Size of full installation
Microsoft® Windows® XP	486/66 (Intel Pentium recommended)	(automatically installed)	(automatically installed)
Microsoft® Windows® 2000	486/66 (Intel Pentium recommended)	32 MB	12 MB
Microsoft® Windows® Millennium Edition	486/66 (Intel Pentium recommended)	32 MB	8.7 MB
Microsoft® Windows® 98 Second Edition (SE)	486/66 (Intel Pentium recommended)	16 MB	12.4 MB
Microsoft® Windows® 98	486/66 (Intel Pentium recommended)	16 MB	11.5 MB
Microsoft® Windows NT® 4.0 Service Pack 6a and later	486/66 (Intel Pentium recommended)	32 MB	12.7 MB

For information about requirements for other operating systems, including the Windows 64-bit version, see the Microsoft Windows Technologies Internet Explorer Web site at http://www.microsoft.com/windows/ie/.

Requirements for the Customization Wizard of the IEAK

Item	Requirements
Processor	486/66
Operating system	Windows 32-bit versions
Minimum memory (RAM)	Same as the requirements for installing Internet Explorer 6 and Internet Tools
Disk space	80 MB to install the IEAK and download all components Add an additional 100 MB for each media type